Oregon
Brew Tour™

Oregon Brew Tour_{TM}
Craft Beers...Microbrews, Nanobrews, Festivals, & Homebrew Info

First Edition

Copyright 2011

Bob & Debra Ledford

Ledford Publishing

ISBN: 978-0-9840777-1-7

To order additional books, for comments, or corrections, please contact:

www.brewtourbooks.com

info@brewtourbooks.com

OR

Ledford Publishing
P.O. Box 6756
Brookings, OR 97415

Oregon Brew Tour

Craft Beers...
Microbrews, Nanobrews,
Festivals,
& Homebrew Info

Bob & Debra Ledford

Bob's Dedication

To my wife, Debra, for running with the idea.
To all the people who generously gave time for interviews.
To my brother, Casey Ledford and brother-in-law, Jim Adams
for sharing my enthusiasm for craft beer.
To my brother, Tracy, in hopes that this book will open his eyes to the
"real" taste of beer.
To my parents, Bob & Dovy Ledford.

Debra's Dedication

To the beer lovers in my life:
My husband, partner, best friend, and soul mate, Bob Ledford
My late father, Paul Rard
My late brother, Gary Rard
My brother-in-law and encourager, Jim Adams

And to my mom, Deretha Rard, who smiles anyway when Bob has her
try his hoppy beers.

Special thanks to:
Linda Adams
Casey Ledford
Judy May-Lopez
Garrick Rard
Nick Talley
Guy Rheurk
For their editorial assistance

And to:
Victoria Haskins
Laura Ledford
Jason Kappel
Adam VanCleave
For their graphics assistance

Table of Contents

"Do what you love to do, and do it so well that those who come to see you do it will bring others to watch you do it again and again."

-- Mark Victor Hansen

Oregon Craft Beer

While walking through the beer isle in the grocery store you may have noticed some odd additions to the usual beers. Or you may be one of the great many who have already embraced these beers. These interesting shaped bottles of many sizes, often with bizarre names and catchy labels, have become a central feature in most grocery beer coolers, especially in Oregon. Are they a special release? Are they a tactic by the beer manufacturers to increase sales? Or are they one of a multitude of products produced almost solely for the collecting consumer? Actually, they are craft beers, also known as microbrews.

By definition, a microbrew is a beer which is brewed in small quantities, specifically, less than 15,000 barrels per year. Craft brewing uses traditional methods and superior ingredients, showing attention to detail and quality.

By taste, according to connoisseurs, it is "real" beer. Its taste and flavors seem to be limited only by the number of brewers and varieties which can be produced. In other words, there is a seemingly endless array of tastes to tempt the taste buds of even the most discerning beer lover. It can also be found in organic varieties and, less frequently but increasingly, in cans.

A Few Beer Basics

There are two basic types of beer, lager and ale. Lagers use yeasts which ferment on the bottom while ale ferments on the top. Beer is then divided into forty-four styles which refer to the process, ingredients, and flavor, with each having specific technical requirements: barley wine, extra special bitter, weizen, imperial, India pale ale, lambic, pale ale, pilsner, porter, steam beer, and stout, to name a few. Within each of these styles can be found such a vast diversity of flavors, one would wonder how they could possibly be related. Sampling ten pale ales, for instance, will in all probability result in ten very different tastes.

The wide varieties of tastes help to explain the large selection of beer available, which has led to businesses which promote themselves through an extensive variety of beers. Eugene boasts a store/pub which sells over 1000 varieties of beer. Not to be outdone, Portland's many sources include a tavern with more than 100 beers on tap and a beer store which stocks more than 1200 varieties of beer from around the world.

Brief History of Craft Beer in Oregon

After lobbying by local brewers, Oregon passed the brewpub law of 1985, which allowed the production, sale, and consumption of beer on the same premises. Previous to this law, distribution of products by small brewers was difficult. Shelf space is valuable in stores, not to be wasted on unknown beers. Pubs, taverns, and restaurants did not want to squander one of their few available taps on an unfamiliar

Beer display at Astoria Museum

beer. The new brewpub law provided an outlet for microbrews.

Of course, getting people to try this "odd" beer was a challenge. Frequently, brewpubs would provide a sample of their craft beer when a patron would order one of the traditional yellow beers. While initial thoughts on competition were negative, brewers soon found it led to increased sales and credibility as word traveled.

Oregon now boasts over 100 craft breweries, with more than thirty-five of them in Portland. In fact, more than twelve percent of the beer consumed in Oregon is brewed in Oregon. This is four times the national average.

Innovativeness has spurred the Oregon craft beer industry. Early microbreweries started with much of their equipment being jury-rigged. Widmer Brothers first tank was a shrimp cooker. Their first kettle was a kettle, which was never licensed or used, from the Pebble Springs Nuclear Plant. This attitude of repurposing continues in many Oregon craft breweries today.

The camaraderie found between the competing craft breweries is inspiring. Mention another Oregon city where a craft brewery is located while conversing with an Oregon brewmaster, and you will often be treated to observations, stories, and accolades. They know one another, their beers, and encourage patronage of competition.

Craft brews have become so mainstream they are now being imitated by major brewers. Careful examination of a few of the new "microbrews" appearing on store shelves will reveal they are actually a product of major breweries. Why should one care? Mass produced beers often use inferior hops and other ingredients, though this may or may not be the case with the "craft brews" produced by the major breweries. As with institutional food, production of large quantities may result in inferior taste. Rather than proudly displaying their "brand" name, the true identity of these mass produced "microbrews" is reserved for fine print. More importantly, Oregonians should support local Oregon brewers.

Support of local and small businesses is considered profitable for all concerned, with the economic impact of the Oregon brew industry being quite significant. Employing more than 4,700 Oregonians, the brew industry's estimated economic impact is $2.33 billion. Add to this, the generosity of Oregon brewers contributing an estimated $1.25 million to charities and non-profit organizations, and it definitely pays to support local breweries.

Take the Tour

After sampling beer all across the state, we learned it was not the size or complexity of the brewery, but the passion of the brewers that make the beer. Using the finest ingredients money can buy, such as locally grown hops and malted barley or obtaining ingredients from around the world to create the style of beer they prefer, Oregon brewers frequently went beyond using ingredients from around the world, to traveling the world, learning the art of brewing to bring with them to Oregon. It is all about quality and the quest to make the best beer possible.

Like the changing views across the state, there is a kaleidoscope of colors on sample trays in pubs throughout Oregon. You too, can pursue that perfect beer at the end of each sampler rainbow – but beware, it is elusive. Just as you imagine you have found the best, another contender materializes. You will learn, the true pot of gold is the experience itself. There is truly a view, an activity, a place, or a pint of beer for everyone in Oregon!

Bob's Point of View

Since the early 80s when I stumbled upon my first twenty-two ounce bottle of craft beer in a little Mom & Pop store in Nesika Beach, I was hooked. Then started the search...the hunt for new and exciting tasting beers.

In the '90s I learned I could make my own beer. From that first batch, when I held a handful of whole flower hops to my nose, breathing in the enticing aroma, adding it to the boiling wort, I began to appreciate the taste of hop's influence on beer, leading me to search out more and more heavily hopped IPA's.

As a person who has always enjoyed traveling, Oregon road trips have long provided opportunities for trying new beers. This is how the idea for this book arose. Knowing I am not the only person who enjoys tasting new beers, we decided others would appreciate a guide which would uncover the hidden gems available to connoisseurs everywhere. Though I was raised in Oregon, I was surprised by how many routes and small towns I had never seen. Some I had not even heard of. But hidden away in these small towns and lost in the twisted streets of the cities were cozy little pubs, with couches for seating; rocking sports bars with huge TV screens, pool tables and dart boards; and pizza parlors with breweries in the back. We found a purpose, a word to get out, people everywhere deserve to drink fine beer.

I have enjoyed many great beers across this state, but to write a book we needed to see the breweries and brewpubs, as well as talk to the brewers and owners. While this may sound easy enough, we both have full-time jobs, and live in the southwest corner of the state, so visiting over eighty breweries was no small task. This "grueling" adventure was filled with an exhausting and tight schedule. It would have been nice to linger or at least to have had a bathroom break scheduled in between interviews. Deb, who was not tasting, failed to consider when scheduling interviews, that what goes in must come out.

When we began our tour, I was seeking out that perfect IPA, and was not disappointed, though I was unable to narrow the field to just one; there are many impressive IPAs in Oregon. Some are well balanced, while others are over-the-top hoppy, but I enjoyed them all. I discovered and was able to identify how different hops created different flavors, with blending producing even more variety.

Keeping an open mind, I tried as many styles as I could. Soon, I found myself really taking a liking to Red Ales, which are lighter on the hops, but surprisingly, still possess a big, bold flavor. Next, I found a Belgium style beer that was incredible; the yeast that was used produced a flavor that I had never before experienced. Then along came a Pilsner. Though I had never thought of myself as a Pilsner fan – light in color, flavor, and hops just did not seem to be my style – but during our tour I tried many first-rate Pilsners and one that simply blew me away!

So I urge you, as you tour Oregon, to keep an open mind and let your tastes evolve. I will always appreciate an excellent IPA, but I await with enthusiasm the next opportunity to try a Belgium, a sour, a bourbon-barrel aged, or whatever other quality work of art these masters create.

Deb's Point of View

The odd thing about me co-authoring a book on beer is that I do not like beer. Maybe I should revise that to read - I *really* do not like beer. But Bob enjoys it immensely and I have found great enjoyment in searching Oregon for the perfect beer for him.

As a result of my distaste for beer, Bob takes great joy in what we call the "face test." He has discovered that the more extreme of a face I make when I taste a beer, the more he will enjoy it. Since I love to see his amusement over my beer faces, I "suffer" for his enjoyment.

As a non-beer person, one might ask what pleasure I could get from traveling throughout the state touring every brewery and brewpub we can find. Actually, I have had a blast! Seeing the different designs of the various brewpubs has been fascinating. From ultra modern, with clean, uncluttered lines, to old-world cozy with many touches of home, to big open gathering places for watching the latest sports, there is a pub somewhere in Oregon to satisfy everyone and every mood.

More surprising to me has been the variety of brewing equipment. Whether touring what appears to be not much more than a three-tier homebrew system, a converted dairy, or a state-of-the-art brewery, I have been heartened by the ingenuity and use of materials in both the brewery and the brewpub.

Most unforgettable have been the owner/brewers behind this brew revolution. From the dapper businessman, to the seventies hippy throwback, to barely old enough, to brewers with pink boots, to those long past retirement age, the people we have interviewed have been as varied as the establishments they operate. The common binding element has been an awe inspiring passion. Whether that passion is for beer, business, independence, or a combination of these, it is a compelling energy which is inspiring. Add to this the camaraderie among Oregon brewers and this is a group of people truly worthy of high regard.

In addition to acquiring a respectful admiration for this industrious group of people, I seem to have developed something akin to a motherly attachment to some of them. It has now been just over a year since the first of our interviews and it warms my heart to see the little guy is still in business. An odd sense of mourning seems to transpire when I discover one of "our" hopefuls has become one of the "fallen comrades." Excitement creeps in when one of my "babies" begins bottling.

Discovery of a new brewery means more than a new interview to do; it means the anticipation of seeing what they came up with, and what their angle is. While to Bob a new brewery represents tasting opportunities, to me it resembles looking forward to vacationing in a new place and anticipating the unknown.

Do I recommend the tour for the non-beer drinking tourist? Absolutely! Many breweries also make root beer; or if you prefer, many brewpubs also offer full bars. If you, like me, do not drink beer, *do* drink in the flavors, aromas, styles, sounds, and personalities found on the Oregon Brew Tour!

Responsible Touring

With this being a beer tour book, we felt it necessary to include a chapter on responsible drinking. Since "tour" implies that the reader will have a need to journey from place to place, the assumption may be made that this will, at times, include travel in a vehicle. Our position is clear, if you are going to drink, do not drive!

How much can you drink and still drive? One beer? Two? More? Our position is, if you are going to drink at all, do not operate a vehicle. Have a designated driver. Walk. Take a taxi. Take a bus. Call mom (friend, sibling, or even enemy). If you are planning a tour, plan your transportation first.

On our tours, the answer was obvious. Debra does not care for beer, Bob does. We knew when we left home; Debra would be driving the vast majority of the trip.

How much can a person drink and still drive? Oregon law says an adult is intoxicated at .08 percent or above, blood alcohol concentration (BAC). The .08 BAC limit is the standard measure of the "impaired" driver across the United States. In addition to the .08 limit, the State of Oregon has lower limits for commercial drivers (.04) and a .02 or Zero Tolerance limit for drivers under the age of 21.

So how much can an individual drink and remain below the legal limit? This has been the subject of much debate. How much do you weigh? What is the alcohol content of your drink? How long has it been between drinks? While there are charts to help you determine your blood alcohol using these questions, they cannot take into account all factors affecting your individual situation. For instance, have you eaten anything recently? If you plan for alternative transportation or a designated driver, there is no need to play blood alcohol roulette.

If you do choose to drink and drive, be prepared to suffer the legal consequences.

1st Drunk Driving Conviction
- DUI Diversion Program Possible
- Jail – 48 Hours Minimum up to 1 Year, or
- Community Service – 80 Hours
- Fine - $1,000 Minimum
- Fine - $2,000 Minimum (BAC .15 or Above)
- Fine – Up to $10,000 (If Child under 18 in Vehicle and was 3 Years Younger than Driver)
- Various DUII Fees – $300 Minimum
- License Suspension – 1 Year
- Ignition Interlock Device – For 1 Year after Suspension
- Complete Drug / Alcohol Treatment Program
- Participation in Victim-Impact Panel Program Required

2nd Drunk Driving Conviction
- Jail – Up to 1 Year
- Fine - $1,500 Minimum
- Fine - $2,000 Minimum (BAC .15 or Above)
- Fine – Up to $10,000 (If Child under 18 in Vehicle and was 3 Years Younger Than Driver)
- Various DUII Fees – $300 Minimum
- License Suspension – 3 Years (If Within 5 Years of Previous)
- Ignition Interlock Device – For 2 Years after Suspension
- Complete Drug / Alcohol Treatment Program
- Participation in Victim-Impact Panel Program Required

3rd Drunk Driving Conviction
- Class "C" Felony Offense (If Other Offenses within Last 10 Years)
- Jail – Up to 5 Years

- Fine - $2,000 Minimum
- Fine – Up to $10,000 (If Child under 18 in Vehicle and was 3 Years Younger Than Driver)
- Various DUII Fees – $300 Minimum
- License Suspension – Permanent Revocation
- Ignition Interlock Device – For 3 Years after Suspension
- Complete Drug / Alcohol Treatment Program
- Participation in Victim-Impact Panel Program Required

Additionally, all DUII convictions must receive a mandatory alcohol evaluation to determine the extent of their alcohol problems.

The preceding lists show what will happen if you are caught drinking and driving. Things get far worse if you are involved in an accident. If someone is injured or killed, life as you know it, is over. Plan on a new residence, one with bars. These bars have no beer involved. Once convicted, you will be a felon.

Do this the easy way, don't drink and drive…ever!

The Breweries

The next section includes write-ups on almost every brewery in the state, with the primary source of information being interviews. We would like to thank all the wonderful people who generously donated their time so that we might obtain the information to complete the upcoming section.

While every attempt possible was made to contact and conduct interviews, you may notice a few are missing. Though we regret this, considerable attempt was made to include each and every brewery.

For those with more than one location, we have included only one write-up. While it would have been wonderful to include all locations, the requirement of a wheelbarrow to transport a book of that size prevented this. Though we anticipate some will feel all write-ups should have been the same length, there simply would not be enough information to make some write-ups longer and excluding interesting items to make others shorter, for the sake of "fairness," would not be cool or interesting.

With more than eighty write-ups, we hope you will find the variety of topics we have chosen to write about amusing and inspiring. While reading and visiting, please keep in mind that due to the ever-evolving nature of the brewing industry, with new breweries starting every year, places changing, brewers moving, and breweries closing, you may find variations on the themes as written. It would be a good idea to check with the brewery before traveling significant distances to visit. In the same vein, your assistance in keeping an up-to-date listing for future editions would be appreciated.

A great deal of thought and stress was involved in determining the arrangement of the write-ups. By region? By city? By tour route? Each choice came with its own set of benefits and disadvantages. We finally settled on alphabetically by name. This not only satisfied my need for order, but it is simple. In answer to the need for the aforementioned possibilities, we have included four lists later in the book, by alpha, by city, by region, and by tour route. Surely, one of these lists will meet your needs. Included in the alphabetical list is an indication of type, family friendly or not, and if they currently bottle.

As an aid for locating the breweries, we have included a small Oregon map outline with stars showing the cities in which each brewery has a presence. For purposes of ease and simplicity, those locations in the Portland Metropolitan area, regardless of number, have only one star. Please be aware, the locations of the stars are approximate. These maps will be found on the lower right corner of the last page of each brewery's description.

Our hope is that as you visit the breweries and brewpubs in Oregon, you will make notes, rate the beers you try, get creative; allow this book to become a tool to enhance your tour experience.

4th Street Brewing Company

77 NE 4th Street
Gresham, Oregon 97030
503-669-0569
www.4thstreetbrewing.com

"4 the Beer, 4 the Food, 4 the Fun"

4th Street Brewing Company partners, Adam Klimek and Adam Roberts met in Green Bay, Wisconsin, before deciding to open their own brewing company in the best of brew places, Oregon. Choosing Gresham because it reminded them of Green Bay and they loved the history of the downtown area, the Adams actually found their original building on the internet.

Opening as Main Street Ale House in 2004, they changed the name to suit the location after purchasing the current property, knocking down the decaying old church which occupied it, and building the brand new pub. Built so the exterior harmonizes with the surrounding historical downtown buildings, 4th Street is quite contemporary inside.

The division of space has artfully created such distinct areas, that while enjoying one, patrons are completely unaware of the other. For a family atmosphere, the restaurant side features traditional booths in

Adam Roberts

Adam Klimek

a separate, yet open area. Cross over to the other side and enter a modern sports bar, complete with nine high-definition televisions, pool tables, and bar seating.

Also available are two meeting/party rooms. The enclosed Ale Room, which accommodates up to 48 people, includes a home theater system with Dolby surround sound and a seventy-eight inch projection screen. With an open balcony, the Lager room has capacity for 110, its own private bar, and a twenty-eight inch flat screen television.

While the Adams moved the rest of the brew equipment from the Main Street location, the landlord would not allow them to remove the old brewhouse from their previous location; resulting in the purchase a brand new brewhouse. This is one of the disadvantages of setting up in a leased location; the permanent installation required for a brewhouse converts the equipment to being part of the building.

View the brewery through windows from the sports bar

Brewing on a ten barrel system with a current annual output of 600 barrels, the entire brewery was designed by owner, Adam Roberts, who is also the brewer at 4th Street. An auger system moves the grist from the bomb-proof mill room, which was required by the city, to the brewery where Adam makes five standards, as well as many seasonals and one-offs to fill out their twelve taps.

After attending the Seibel Institute in Chicago, Adam brewed for a while in Missouri before partnering with Adam Klimek in Gresham. Adam Klimek serves as General Manager at 4th Street.

Though 4th Street has done a few festivals, it has been a while since they have participated in any competitions. Festivals and competitions take time, and Adam Roberts has been a bit busy with the birth of twins in mid 2010.

Sports Bar

Though previously, they had a few taps around town, during the time of our interview, 4th Street was searching for a new distributor, as their old one had failed to return their phone calls. Also up for consideration is the addition of bottles. Until then, you can enjoy a twenty ounce imperial pint at the brewpub or take your favorite 4th Street brew home in a growler.

Family Restaurant

Christmas at 4th Street

10 Barrel Brewing Company

1135 West Galveston
Bend, Oregon 97701
503-306-4488
www.10barrel.com

"Independently Handcrafted in the Northwest"

Changes happen at 10 Barrel Brewing, beginning with the name. Originally named Wildfire Brewing, they were compelled to change their name in 2008, two years into business, after receiving notification that they were in violation of a registered trademark. Oops! Rather than get involved in expensive and time-consuming litigation, the partners chose to relinquish the name to the Wildfire Restaurants chain of Illinois, a division of Lettus Entertain You Restaurants of Chicago.

The source of inspiration for the revised name is rather obvious to everyone; they brewed in a ten barrel brewhouse. Though some have thought this choice to be a mistake, equating it with "naming your dog, 'Dog'," we think it was an inspired selection. Basic, unpretentious, easy to remember, it is rather like "clean lines" in decorating.

Rebranding was not so basic. It meant changing their name on kegs, taps, and signs, to name a few items, as well as designing a new logo, plus getting the new name out to the public. All this re-naming cost the partners a reported $45,000. Though the publicity and its resulting write-ups generated by the name change may have provided a bit of free publicity, helping to assuage the cost a bit, that is a large sum to recoup through free publicity.

The question is, now that they have their new fifty barrel system with a projected 10,000 barrels to be produced in 2011, will another name change be forthcoming? Definitely not. But what about the ten barrel system that produced a respectable 2500 barrels in 2010? Housed right next to the larger system, it will allow for creative testing, without jumping in with both feet.

In order to house both these systems, 10 Barrel will be moving into a 22,000 square foot facility. Plans call for this new brewery to have over one hundred wooden barrels aging at all times. All these barrels will also allow

them to expand into sour beers, an eminent item on the to-do list. Also in the line-up for the new brewery location will be their own bottling line, a change from the mobile bottling service they have been using, with the possibility of cans later.

Partner, Chris Cox

Though the company began with five partners, at 10 Barrel, changes happen. With Paul Cook leaving to brew at Ninkasi, the four remaining partners are: twins, Chris and Jeremy Cox, Oregon State graduates in business who moved to Bend from their hometown of Lincoln City; and father and son, Brad and Garrett Wells, Bend natives. Add to this mix, the team of top brewers: head brewer, Dan Olson, formerly with Deschutes; Tom Tash, previously with Kona Brewing in Hawaii; and most recently, Jimmy Seifrit, another ex-Deschutes brewer considered by other brewers to be one of the top three brewers in the Northwest. Not to be outdone, the kitchen is now headed up by Chef Justin Hauson, a recent change after Chef Mike Moore, a one-time shoe salesman, became general manager.

Patio with firepit...and snow

10 Barrel began when twins, Chris and Jeremy, who co-owned JC's Bar & Grill in downtown Bend, decided they wanted to open a brewery. Starting as a production brewery, 10 Barrel had many taps in Bend and Portland, as well as beer available in about 300 locations around Oregon and Washington. The next big change came when, in March of 2010, 10 Barrel opened their pub in the building previously occupied by Di Lusso Bakery.

Extensive remodeling using local and reclaimed materials turned the one-time bakery into a modern, yet simple, hot-spot. The reclaimed barn wood siding gives the structure a rustic look, while the garage door opening onto the patio lends that trendy, airy touch coveted by many. More reclaimed wood provides magnificent table tops and chair seats that evoke a compelling desire to stroke them. Though the look is basic, this pub has been designed high-end with an eye toward giving the feel of a neighborhood gathering place.

Glorious wood tabletop

Though design is nice, beer is the thing. 10 Barrel proved they have the beer when they won the Bronze Medal at the 2009 Great American Beer Festival, in Denver, Colorado. S1NISTER Black Ale pulled the third place finish in the Out-of-Category Traditionally Brewed Beer, competing against 82 other entries. According to Chris, "S1NISTER put us on the map."

Summer Ale, a really light body IPA, has been well received by 10 Barrel fans. For those new to the world of craft beers, it provides an excellent transition; for enthusiasts, it is a refreshing reprieve from the highly-hopped beer so popular in the Northwest. But...as a company, those on the inside at 10 Barrel like the seasonal India Summer Ale (ISA) better. Ever open to change, 10 Barrel's Summer Ale will not be brewed in 2011.

"We don't have any attachments," Chris states, "This makes us different...we'll stop brewing a good seller when we get bored with brewing it."

Even with five standards and eight or more seasonals, creativity is important at 10 Barrel. To add an extra fun element, 10 Barrel has the Solera Project. The barrels for this project are visible high-up in the glassed-in tap room at the pub. This living beer begins with four barrels filled with a base beer, each "belonging" to a different brewer. Every six months five to six gallons of beer are removed from the barrel and replaced with an equal amount of a different beer of the brewer's choice. 10 Barrel has created a bit of a competition among the brewers for the best Solera, with the public voting on the best beer at the Solera Party.

Solera barrels near the ceiling in the tap room

"As a brewer the most important quality is the creative side," according to Chris; 10 Barrel strives to promote and encourage creativity.

This creativity is demonstrated in 10 Barrel's devotion to supporting the community. Each month 10 Barrel chooses a local charity to champion. A portion of proceeds from all "I Drink For Charity" tees

sold during that month are
donated to the charity. Then at
month-end, 10 Barrel hosts a
charity party, with all proceeds
going to the charity of the
month. A few of the past
charities which have benefited
from this unique fund-raising
approach are: Volunteers in
Medicine, Big Brothers/Big
Sisters, Bend Firefighter Foundation, Humane Society of Central
Oregon, Bend Parks and Recreation District, and Grandma's House-
where shelter, support, and guidance are provided for abused, pregnant,
and parenting teens.

One of the surprising things was that Bend is slow in the winter.
With all the skiing at Bachelor, we thought Bend would be a hopping
place. But, it seems 70% of sales are made during the summer, when the
place is bustling. Apparently not too many skiers make it into Bend. So
if you are like us and prefer less crowded conditions, grab your chains
and make the trek over the Cascades to Bend for a bit of winter
wonderland...and *Pray for Snow Strong Ale* at 10 Barrel Brewing.

Alameda Brewhouse

4765 NE Fremont Street
Portland, Oregon 97213
503-460-9025
www.alamedabrewhouse.com

"Beer brings people in, food and service bring them back"

Our interview at Alameda Brewhouse was one of those early morning things. Though we may have been feeling a bit slow, that didn't stop us from enjoying the luscious smell of freshly baking bread as we entered the building. Nor did it stop the exhausting energy in Matt Schumacher, who with partner, Peter Vernier, owns and operates Alameda Brewhouse.

Matt, a culinary school graduate and home brewer, takes pride in what they have created here. When they first opened in the summer of 1996, the neighborhood was different than it is now. As a twenty-seven year old, single father, he often wondered what he had done. Matt says the first four years were a struggle. Despite those early doubts, he was not surprised by them; things have transpired about as expected.

With an eye toward good food, good service, and of course, good beer, Alameda Brewhouse makes not only their own beer, but also their own bread, deserts, smoked meats, soups, and much more. If the hand-formed burgers are not your thing, they also make their own unique vegi-burgers. With a large and varied menu, there is sure to be something to entice you.

The restaurant's booths were designed by Mark Annen, of Annen Design Industries, an architectural and interior design professional, who grew up on a hop farm in Mt. Angel. The noteworthy design replicates hop poles. With subtle under-lighting, these modern booths help this large space feel personal. Added to each booth is a picture of his parent's hop farm, over which is hop bag art. Mark also created the impressive hop adorning the front of the building.

Another local artist, Brian Treleaven, created Alameda labels while he was still attending the Art

Institute of Portland. Being a forward thinker, Matt had him do many labels in advance for future use. Papa Noel, a special holiday ale, sports a label created by another artist.

Best known for their Black Bear XX Stout, winner of the Gold Medal at the 2003 & 2005 Great American Beer Festival in the Foreign-Style Stout category, Alameda sports a 5.5 barrel Brewhouse. With six standards, plus at least one seasonal and one on nitrogen, Alameda focuses on making beer other people want to drink.

Preceded by Craig, who was there for Alameda's opening, and John, who took them to another level, head brewer, Carston Haney, has never had to dump a batch,

saying, "I take every care I can." According to Matt, "He's great!" Carston, who has a bachelors in science, home brewed for five years before doing a two-year internship with a

Early morning in the dining room...with chairs still up for cleaning

brewer in Pennsylvania. Working without pay as an apprentice for a year, Carston was determined to become a brewer. He seems to have found his niche at Alameda, where he combines science and art to create new beers and stay on the cutting edge of the brewing industry.

When Alameda rented tank space, Carston was concerned that it

could affect consistency, but his apprehension was unfounded and it has worked out well. Moreover, it has freed space for the fun of creating specialty beers. Still, Carston finds himself working six days a week during the summer, yet unable to meet demand. Job security at its best!

Awards at Alameda

Alameda began bottling seriously in 2008, using a mobile bottler and hopes to eventually add a bottling line. With plans to open a brewery (as opposed to a brew pub) to alleviate the continuing problem of limited production, and possibly expand into the Washington market, Matt sees a good future for Alameda Brewing, despite growing competition. With recent brew production up twenty-five percent and restaurant business up ten percent, Alameda appears to be up and coming.

Ambacht Brewing

1055 NE 25th Avenue, Suite N
Hillsboro, Oregon 97124
503-828-1400
www.ambacht.us

"We're Oregon's only brewery without an IPA"

Belgian inspired ales, using local organic ingredients, are the exclusive focus of Ambacht Brewing (pronounced Ämbäkt – ä as in fäther). Unusual in Oregon/Northwest, in that they do not make an IPA, (nor do they intend to) Ambacht is looking to move beer to a new area of acceptance, closer to the chic style of wine.

While Ambacht beers are all organic, they are not certified organic. This allows them flexibility. If at some point the organic ingredients they need are unavailable, they will not be stuck. This also allows them to avoid the considerable expense of becoming certified.

This bottle-conditioned beer uses honey to prime the beer, which causes a second fermentation, resulting in carbonation. Because

Ambacht uses honey in their beers, they must have each recipe approved by the Alcohol and Tobacco Tax and Trade Bureau (TTB). The TTB has determined that Ambacht must include "Brewed with honey" on the label, which is technically incorrect. Rather than *brewed* with honey, Ambacht is *bottle conditioned* with honey. But hey, the feds say do it, it gets done, correct or not.

Ambacht is proud to use ingredients acquired locally. Malts are acquired from Great Western Malting Company in Vancouver, Washington. Founded in 1934, they are America's oldest malting company. Wyeast Labs in Odell, Oregon, supply their yeast. Hops come from nearby Silverton. Various Northwest sources

Partner, Tom Kramer

provide the honey used for conditioning Ambacht beers. Cherries for their Pie Cherry Beer are purchased direct from the grower in Yamhill.

Ambacht is the dream of brewer, Tom Kramer. Partnering with his wife's cousin, Bandy Grobart, the pair is very candid about their processes and the ingredients they use. Shamelessly admitting their beers are a bit inconsistent due to continual adjustments they are making, they say their beers mellow out and improve with age. Each beer they make is held a minimum of three months, with some being held up to eight months before being released.

Opening in January of 2010, the guys at Ambacht were proud to show us their first award, the first annual Monoco Cup. To win the cup, Ambacht's Golden Rose Ale was selected by Portland's Chef Andrew Garret of Café Nell to pair with his pork and beans. As for the other beers in the competition, Ambacht beat out such icons such as Ninkasi, Double

Brandy, showing off the loving cup from Ambacht's 1st place Monoco Cup win.

Mountain, Upright, Hopworks, and Heater Allen. Sponsored by Kimpton's Hotel Monoco Portland, six Portland chefs paired a dish with an Oregon beer of their choice; the winner was determined by attendee votes. A benefit for the United Way, the hotel expects to continue this successful fund raiser. Look for it in November.

According to Tom and Brandy, their beers pair well with food. In fact, they say the same Golden Rose Ale which won their award, is excellent paired with salmon.

Tom, previously an engineer with 3M Company, who was also an adjunct professor at Hamline University in physics, has homebrewed for over 20 years. His interest in including honey in his beers comes from his longtime hobby of beekeeping, though he has not yet used his own honey in making Ambacht beers.

Brandy, a carpenter with twenty years experience, who has also been a stay-at-home dad while his wife taught school, thus providing benefits, has been brewing for about seven years. While he had previously made wine, beer offered the benefit of year-round brewing. When we spoke with him, he said his

This one-time Tuck's brewery, now makes its home at Ambacht.

Blanketed

contractor's license would be good for another year before requiring renewal, but rather than renewing, he was hoping to be working full-time at Ambacht by then.

Brewing four barrel batches on a five barrel system allows head room for the Belgian strain of yeast used at Ambacht. The system was originally used by Tuck's Brewery where Tom was working as a "brewery slave" when they closed. When Kessler Israel, an orthodox shul, or synagogue, purchased the location, they had no use for the brewery equipment and put it up for auction. Though Tom really did not want the equipment because there is no bottom access for cleaning out the mash tun, he put a bid in anyway. When he was overbid, it was not a big deal, but then the winner of the bid withdrew and the equipment was on its way to Ambacht.

The name, Ambacht, a Dutch term meaning "handmade," is a fallback to the time Tom spent in the Netherlands following college.

Ambacht offer six-bottle bottle totes.

As stated earlier, the guys at Ambacht have no problem sharing information, including the fact that one of their more popular beers, Ambacht G++ Ale, a Belgian, strong, golden ale; was a total mistake. While their direct-fired kettle produces good carmelization, this batch had even more than planned. During our visit in December 2010, they had one remaining case, and then it would be gone. Let's see if it really goes away, or if they manage to repeat their "mistake."

Another unusual Belgian they make is the seasonal specialty beer, Ambacht Matzobraü. This curious beer is made from the unleavened bread, matzah, which is used during the Jewish holiday Passover, as commanded by God in remembrance of the death angle passing over the homes of the Jews during the final plague in Egypt. Gathering leftover matzah, still wrapped-of course, the guys include two pounds of crushed matzah to 18 pounds of grain in the mash, then bottle condition with honey, to produce a slightly sweet brew with an interesting beginning. Or is it an interesting history?

Brewing twice a month and producing 100 barrels in 2010, Ambacht self-distributes. Though still learning the workings of the retail end of brewing, they nevertheless had bottles in several bottle shops and markets around the Portland area. What surprised many Portland area residents was their presence at area farmers markets. Why not? We thought it was a wonderful and creative marketing idea. Additionally, it has been quite pleasing to many thirsty market patrons.

While Ambacht is available almost exclusively in bottles, as of this writing, they do have a tap at both Milo's City Café and Hawthorn Hophouse in Portland. Check their website or give them a call for current taps. Another option is to stop by the brewery, where they do tastings Thursday evenings, Sunday afternoons and by appointment. It may be advisable to call first, since these times can change. Also, keep an eye open for Ambacht at Portland area festivals. So far they have done the North American Organic Brew Fest, Zwikelmania, and Portland's Cheers to Belgian Beers. With an eye toward helping local charities, the pair enjoys doing fundraisers.

When asked what their wives thought of their new business, these cheerful, fun-loving guys smiled and said they are being patient, but are waiting to see the $$.

Brandy, in the Ambacht booth at a Portland farmers market.
Photo by Sanjay Reddy, used by permission

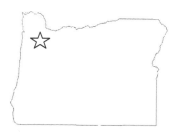

Amnesia Brewing

832 N Beech Street
Portland, Oregon 97227
503-281-7708
www.amnesiabrew.com

"It's a skill, it's a craft, it's a passion. You don't do it for the money."

Kevin King spent eight years as a homebrewer. Then, he worked at six different breweries in nine years, in hopes of learning and getting as much experience as possible, including McMenamins, Red Hook, Pyramid, The Ridge in Seattle, Far West in Ireland, and last of all, Rogue. Finally, in 2003, he and his wife, Kristina, moved to Portland to open their own dream, a brewery.

Their search for a location did not include strip malls, or fancy locations, their desire was for a simple warehouse setup. They found it at the Beech Street location. An empty warehouse when they took it over, they put everything in themselves, on what, in the brewing world, was a shoestring budget of ninety thousand dollars.

When they opened on May 21, 2003, the Beech Street area was

Owner/Brewer Kevin King

known for its gangs...a bad area. There was nothing there but a pizza place and a coffee shop. With assistance from the city, Beech Street is now a booming area. Full of small businesses, of which ninety percent are first-time business owners, the area includes no corporations.

When we asked Kevin how they decided on the name for their brewery, he said

he did not like it at first. He and Kristina had been in Amsterdam and saw a coffee shop named Amnesia. Kristina immediately felt it would be a great marketing name. Kevin, on the other hand, had his doubts. Thankfully, Kristina won that one, because it is a great name!

For the first three years, the pair did everything themselves. Kristina took care of the front of the house, while Kevin did all of the brewing, including the not-so-fun stuff like cleaning and scrubbing floors. While it was a lot of work, it was also a lot of fun; working for themselves was the way to go.

True to their plan, this pub is very unpretentious, there are no frills. Picnic tables, a few bar stools at a simple bar, with a bit of local artwork and posters on the walls, all say this is an easy-going place for adults to hang out. The frilliest item would be the candles at night. While there are two TVs, this is definitely not a sports bar. The simplicity continues as the mandatory garage doors open to the patio, which includes two portable

carports, with one closed in with blue tarps, which are removed during the summer. During less hospitable weather, there are outdoor propane heaters for comfort. Under the open carport, a couple of charcoal barbeque grills and a picnic cooler comprises the only cooking area at Amnesia.

While this may seem a bit too simple to some, rumor has it that Kevin, a trained chef who once worked at Marriott, can prepare some mean things on those grills, including the delicious house smoked pulled pork. Other items include  Burgers, both the meat and vegi varieties, including tofurky, chips, pickles, bar snacks, and sausages from Old Country Sausage on Sandy Boulevard, as well as fresh local bread. Remember, the key word here is simple.

As time went on and things got busier, Kevin hired Chris Spollen, a twelve-year veteran of Rogue, and Sean Thommen, who had just finished a two year Master Brewer's course at the Siebel Institute in Chicago and Europe. According to beer writer, John Foyston, these three "make some of the consistently best beer in Oregon, or the world, maybe."

Bob may agree. In addition to sampling some of the other beers, which were all fine beers, Kevin proudly handed Bob a glass of a Pilsner he had been lagering for several months, in preparation for the holiday season. Honestly, at the time, I did not pay that much attention, after all, Bob has been handed hundreds of glasses of beer to try while

Brewer Chris Spollen

doing interviews for this book. But my ears picked up after we left and Bob, who is not normally a pilsner fan, said, "If I thought all the beer was going to go away, that's the beer I would drink. I could drink that beer every day for the rest of my life. Super good taste!" Unfortunately, Precious Pils was just that, precious. A time and fermenter consuming brew, Kevin has no plans to make it a regular. *Rest of his life*, Kevin! Sounds to me like it is worth a tank, perhaps in the corner of the front...it would make a nice

Each tape is a little journal of the history of a brew

embellishment for the pub. Unfortunately, the seven barrel brewery and three fermenters at Amnesia are having difficulty keeping up with demand as it is. While Amnesia produced eight hundred barrels their first year, 2010 saw 1800 barrels brewed. Amnesia currently has 150 accounts they distribute to, and could add more if they could produce enough beer. Kevin says it would have been nice to have a larger system from the beginning, but...remember the shoestring starting budget. Regardless of the time crunch, Kevin says they never rush. "At Amnesia we use quality ingredients and take our time. We don't rush anything."

When asked about his dreams, Kevin would like to do a warehouse where they could regularly make Belgians and Lagers, as well as add a bottling line; with a tasting room included, of course. And... see all of Europe. We definitely have something in common.

While Amnesia does not always offer lagers, they have recently added a full bar, and they do offer a selection of Oregon wines. With eight taps, filled with six standards, there are always two seasonals available.

It is a comforting thing to see familiar faces when we visit a business, especially a pub. At Amnesia the crew sticks around. In fact, Kevin has not hired anyone new for three years.

Amnesia is right on the bus line, plus they have a bike rack which is full throughout the summer. While they may not be a sports bar, being Portlanders, they do offer happy hour prices during all Blazer games. This is a place where buddies meet, patrons work on their computers, and dogs are welcome, but beware, minors are not.

Crowded conditions

Astoria Brewing Company
Wet Dog Café & Saloon

144 11th Street
Astoria, OR 97103
503-325-6975

"Chill out, kick back, and enjoy"

Founded in 1995, Wet Dog Café is more than just a café. With a small stage for regular bands, All That Jazz was playing while we were there; a gift shop, which includes the necessary company tee shirts; and of course a bar, to serve and satiate, this relatively small café has a lot going on, including a full menu. The ambiance brings to mind the place you have expected to find next to the waterfront...forever. Step into the next room and see the Saloon portion of this establishment, with pool tables, a big screen TV, additional seating, and a window view of yet another space, the brewery. Astoria Brewing Company, located in a small room in the center of the "U" that is the rest of this busy concern, was added in 1997. Since then, they have undergone a few changes, including a new name, and several brewers, but patron enthusiasm has not diminished.

During our interview in November 2009, a changing of the guard was underway. Only in this case, rather than a change, it was more of a rerun. Brewer John Dalgren was in the process of brewing his first batch, though he had previously brewed many batches at Astoria Brewing. He had just returned after spending some time in the Portland brew scene.

With a style of his own, sporting a Fedora, or perhaps it was a

Brewer, John Dalgren

Bowler (anyway, it was a hat), John, a tall, skinny, Astoria native, who looks amazingly young, despite being in his thirties, says there had always been beer around while growing up. Admitting to sneaking more than one of his parent's beers, his passion was aroused when he swiped a microbrew from a friend at the tender age of fifteen. John discovered three things: he really enjoyed the bitterness of hops, a "buyer," and a tongue for flavors. At twenty-one and finally legal, John went to work for the Beer and Winehouse in Seaside.

It was about this time that John tried homebrewing. His first batch was…awful! But we know the old adage, *try and try again*. And he did. After John began working at Wet Dog Café as a cook, he kept pestering them to let him apprentice. Then luck smiled on him, a new brewer, an acquaintance, Chris, took over at Astoria Brewing. He allowed John to watch and learn.

Two and a half years later, when Chris left, John was asked how much he knew. Stretching the truth a bit, John told them he knew everything. That embellishment led to the job of head brewer. Excited and nervous, John set about brewing his first batch, an amber. Oops, it did not quite turn out to be what he had planned; but in the proverbial step in it and come out smelling like a rose, it did turn out to be a magnificent strong ale!

He must have figured out the key to getting those beers to turn out as planned, because six months later his Bitter Bitch IPA won the People's Choice for best overall beer and the Brewers' Choice for best IPA at the Spring Beer and Wine Festival in Portland. In fact, this ultra hoppy IPA won this event three years running.

Plenty of take-home choices

After a while, John left Astoria, venturing to Portland, hoping to add to his brewing knowledge. Used to being head brewer, it was certainly humbling and a bit frustrating, but John took a job at Hopworks, working on the bottling line and in the kitchen. During the six months there, he watched...and learned. Naturally, during this time, he continued to homebrew, working on recipes.

When Astoria Brewing asked him to come back, he was there five days later. Returning to some new equipment and a few leaking seals, John had some adjustments to make while getting to know the brewery again. But, as he said, he was "really excited" and felt "like a nervous new father." It brings back memories of when he first began as brewer with Astoria Brewing, only this time, he had recipes. With assistant brewer, Steve Allen, Jr. (son of the owner), who also assisted the previous brewer, they are keeping a close eye on this homecoming batch and are anxious to try some of John's new recipes.

Typical of the camaraderie among brewers, when asked about the competition up the hill at Fort George, John insists there is more of a team spirit than that of competitors. In fact, in commemoration of the twenty-fifth anniversary of the movie *Goonies*, which was filmed in Astoria, John paired with Fort George Brewery's, Jack Harris, to brew "Truffle Shuffle Stout." This tribute beer was made with seven ounces of black truffle mushrooms. Both breweries are hoping to turn Astoria into a beer destination.

Assistant Brewer, Steve Allen, Jr.

When asked to name a favorite of his own beers, John said, "It is rather like having kids, you just can't pick a favorite...I love beer more than anything on the planet and I have a hell of a sense of smell and taste." While John has, for years, been a hophead, his big interest is now Pilsners. Though a light beer, John says that hidden within are very complex flavors, if one has the refined tastes to find them.

At the time of our interview, Astoria Brewing was not yet bottling. However, future plans call for bottling, using a mobile bottling service. Seasonals and the more popular brews are likely candidates for bottling. This would add even more pressure to this eight barrel brewery where summers are staggeringly busy. Since he had just returned, John said he would be brewing daily until everything was full, then three to four times per week, and more in the summer.

As hard as John will need to work to keep up, the real effort comes from the yeast, according to John, "Yeast is the hardest working thing in this brewery; we put in some long days, but don't work as hard as the yeast." With an eye on consistency, Astoria Brewing limits the use of yeast to ten generations. This is important, since consistency is more of a challenge in a small brewery than in large breweries.

Owners Steve and Karen Allen purchased this former produce warehouse with partners, whom they later bought out. Steve, is a CPA and onetime tax auditor who quit because, "they didn't like beards and I didn't like ties." Steve, Jr. is not the only one of Steve and Karen's children to work at the café and brewery, all seven children have worked there at some time.

Named for their dog, who was always wet from swimming in the river, Wet Dog's high ceilings and floor-to-ceiling wall of windows offers spectacular views of the Columbia River and giant freighters as they pass. Also available is a front deck, which is open during the summer.

Originally, the brewery was named Pacific Rim Brewery, but in 2005 the name was changed to Astoria Brewing Company to commemorate Astoria's first brewery, which was established in 1872, but forced out of business by prohibition. A side trip to the local museum will reveal a fascinating local brewing history.

The cafe sports a full bar.

Barley Brown's Brew Pub
2190 Main Street
Baker City, Oregon 97814
541-523-4266
www.barleybrowns.com

*"Small batch hand-crafted beer, good food,
good company, good times..."*
Driving into Baker city, one is reminded of the town in the movie *Back to the Future*, primarily because of the city hall. This was one of the towns on our tour I wished we had to time to stay and investigate. It reminded us of small towns of the 1960s. Unfortunately, this was not to be, we had back to back interviews scheduled, with the only break being the drive from town to town. But be assured, we will return to explore.

With roots in the Civil War era 1860s, Baker City began as a gold rush town on the Oregon Trail, with a second surge in the 1890-1910 mining boom. At that time, its population of 6700 was greater than Boise or Spokane. With the financial advantages provided by gold mining, Baker city developed into a cultural oasis in Northeastern Oregon. This is apparent in the many elaborate historical buildings located there. Of course, mining was also synonymous with a colorful way of life, with many local saloons and brothels to service the miners, as well as the cowboys and sheepherders. Today, more than a century later, over 100 buildings are preserved. Many of them, like the city hall, are highly crafted and worth the tour.

1918 Postcard showing a birds-eye view of Baker City.

Like the rest of the town, the external appearance of Barley Brown's made us want to investigate the interior. On the National Register of Historic Places, the building began as Gwilliam Brothers Bakery in 1940. The thought put into the curb appeal in what could have  been just a boring brick building is obvious. Though we were there in November, web site pictures show they have very nice sidewalk seating for fifteen to twenty diners in the summer, which enhances the allure even more.

A family owned corporation that has evolved through time, we not only found the building and décor to be captivating, but met some very special people there. Tyler, part owner and manager, is known for doing the job, regardless of what it is. Shawn, the brew master, tells of how Tyler spent an entire summer washing dishes because they had been unable to find a reliable dishwasher. This is the mind-set of the entire family, they lead by example.

The building was purchased in 1976 by Tyler's parents, Judy and Bill Brown. At that time, half of it was a garage which was remodeled in 1983 to become part of the restaurant. It was at this time that the magnificent tin ceiling - which is new but used the original press - was installed. They initially tried their partner's idea of fine dining, but it just did not work. After their partner left, Judy and Bill went to Mexico, where they learned to make a few Mexican dishes which they served in their revamped, now Mexican, restaurant. In the late 1980's a Mexican family opened a restaurant in town prompting another Brown family eatery transformation. Because they also own Sumpter Junction Restaurant, renowned for its "G" gage model train running through the premises, consideration was given to selling, but the Brown's decided instead to grow the homebrew hobby of their son, Tyler.

Many in this small town did not feel Baker City could support a brew pub, but such pessimism did not deter this enterprising family. The capital for the pub venture came when a local bank went public and the initial stock offering doubled in one day. Despite an iffy first three years, after 11 years Barley Brown's has developed a solid clientele and established itself in the community. Initially, the pub was better known for its restaurant. Heidelberg & Keystone Light, which Barley Brown's did *not* serve, were the popular beers among locals, so education was required. Many samplers later, Barley Brown's Brews have not only made their mark on Baker City, but also introduced this isolated community to the full, rich flavors of craft beer. Despite this current acceptance, Barley Brown's is still more a restaurant than a "bar" to locals.

Many local and interesting resources have formed the pub into its current, and hopefully lasting, persona. The four barrel brewery was built by inmates at Monroe Correctional Center in Monroe, Washington. This pilot program was operated by a private company using inmate labor and paying a going wage to prevent unfair competition. Teaching inmates a trade, the program also allowed inmates to have funds to pay child support, attorney's fees, and needed capital upon release. The program was shut down when the new governor took office.

In the 1970s, after the courthouse got new jury chairs, Tyler's dad, Bill, strategically purchased the old chairs at auction and stored them in the basement until they were repurposed into bar stools for the new brewpub. By coincidence, there are twelve bar stools at the locally built bar, which Tyler, being a visual person, built out of cardboard appliance boxes before having it built by local craftsman at Moon Meadow Construction.

Décor which can keep you busy for some time, is a tasteful collection of random "treasures" collected over years. Many have stories of their own, such as the large striped bass, caught by a previous president of a local bank. After his wife would not allow it in their home, he donated it to the pub. Though it is found under a wonderful photo of an old fishing boat, they are unrelated, except for subject. The photo was taken in Alaska by Tyler's dad. Also found among the treasures in the pub are many books, including the obvious beer book. Though people sometimes borrow the books, they always come back, sometimes with friend-books. A worn dart board, an old coke machine, cans, pictures, a gigantic lobster claw about a foot long, and a big dough hook from the bakery which originally inhabited the building, artfully decorate the pleasant atmosphere of Barley Brown's.

One of the interesting aspects of the décor came about more by necessity than design. Due to the lack of grain storage, the bags of grain stacked against a back wall provide realistic ambiance. This openly conveys the need to expand the brewery. With increasing demand, more brew space is needed.

Storage Challenges

Barley Brown's currently brews one to three times per week. Brew master, Shawn Kelso, began by stopping by occasionally, to help Tyler brew. Though for a while Tyler had a female assistant, who had a fermentation science degree but no hands-on experience, he was unable to find anyone permanent until Shawn came to work. Shawn has been there for about nine years and now does 100% of the brewing. Barley Brown's brew masters have learned by trial and error without formal training.

After seeing a multitude of breweries, many begin to look similar, other than size. While at Barley Brown's we saw something we had not seen before...blue tape. At fist glance it looks like a rather odd paint job, but a closer look reveals it is strips of blue painters tape, a lot

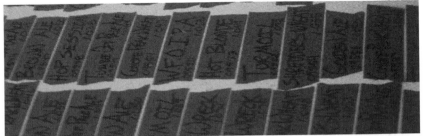

of them. These strips of tape catalog every batch of beer ever made at Barley Brown's. I like simple; this is simple.

At Barley Brown's brewing and cooking are both approached with the same attitude. *Use quality ingredients and a good recipe.* The restaurant uses Country Natural Beef and serves hand-cut fries, an almost unheard of extravagance in the restaurant business these days. The brewery welcomes different malts, allowing for a greater variety of taste in their beers.

Brewer, Shawn Kelso

Shawn is obviously happy in his position. To him, it is a hobby, what he does for fun. "There's not a day where I go 'uff – I gotta go to work.' I love coming to work." When he brews, he works to "keep it simple and clean, and a little over the top."

Whatever Shawn is doing must be working. Though Tyler had thought on a more local level, Shawn suggested they enter their beers in competitions. As the medals and pictures on the wall attest, they have done well. Despite this, they seem more excited about keeping it fun and experimental. In fact, Shawn does not know what beer will be entered in any competition until after they are entered. Shawn brews, both Tyler and Shawn taste, then Tyler chooses and enters the beer. Teamwork! At the Alpha King Competition, the competition for the hoppiest beer in the U.S., Barley Brown's Turmoil made it to the final round for the last three years. It is the only dark beer to make it to the final ground.

Though they do not bottle, Barley Brown's is developing a reputation outside of Baker City. The demand from the Portland area is adding pressure to their already strained brewing schedule. When we were there they were preparing to deliver to Belmont Station and Bailey's Taproom. Their appearance at "Meet the Brewers Night" at Belmont Station was the third largest night to date.

This family-friendly restaurant - kids are not allowed at the bar - was non-smoking long

Tyler Brown

before Oregon law prevented smoking at indoor public places. In fact, Baker was the second town in Oregon to pass a non-smoking initiative. Though Barley Brown's does not see themselves as a special occasion place, they do many parties, kids birthdays included. Some of this may be a result of their efforts to maintain the price-point to allow people to visit on a regular basis.

Despite not putting forth great effort to advertise, people find them. Tyler tends to be rather laid back, choosing not to make a big deal of promotion. His attitude seems to be, if we do really well with the regulars, the tourists will follow.

One of the rather odd things as we were opening the door to the restaurant was the broken door handle. For an establishment that was otherwise extremely tidy and well appointed, this was a bit of a surprise. It seems people are rather surprised they are not open for lunch and will keep pulling on the handle, eventually breaking it. It requires regular replacement.

Open from four to ten, Monday through Saturday, the Brown's feel there are plenty of lunch eateries in town, another was not necessary. Remember, Barley Brown's is also a brewery, whose primary goal is to sell beer. The decision to pass on the lunch crowd has been a good business decision. Due to the lag time between lunch and dinner, staffing can become problematic for restaurants serving both. Split shifts and part-time work are famous in the restaurant business. Dinner-only has allowed Barley Brown's to

get and retain good employees. The chef and bartender have both been there for ten years. Many servers are employed as a second job, including a second grade teacher. Another server worked her way through college at Barley Brown's and is now a first grade teacher.

Beware; Barley Brown's is closed holidays, New Years Day, Memorial Day, Labor Day, Thanksgiving, Christmas Eve, and Christmas. Don't be fooled by the activity within on those days, they are celebrating their family holiday dinners in the roomiest and most well equipped place available to them.

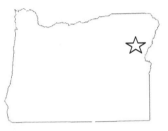

Beer Valley Brewing Company
937 S.E. 12th Avenue
Ontario, Oregon 97914
541-881-9088
www.beervalleybrewing.com

"We brew the hoppiest beer in Oregon"

Go east, way east…no further. Go on into a different time zone. Oregon's eastern most microbrewery is located in Ontario, the only place in Oregon in the Mountain Time Zone. About the north-south center of the state, Ontario is on the Oregon/Idaho border. For founder/owner/brewer, Pete Ricks, this is the best of places to open a brewery. An Idaho native, he grew up outside of Boise but said Oregon is the best brew state, the most conducive to craft beer.

Though he had a friend who homebrewed with extract, Pete had never seen himself as a brewer. Then his boss dragged him to a homebrew workshop. To his surprise, he enjoyed it and spent the next ten to twelve years homebrewing. After working in information technology for twenty years, Pete decided to make the jump to starting his own microbrewery in 2005. This meant leaving a six figure income and a nice house with a pool to pursue his dream. At that time he was in Arizona, which was not a good location for the new business, so when his youngest daughter graduated from high school, he moved the family to Ontario.

After looking for an industrial building that he could also do retail business from, Pete found a building with plenty of expansion room. Tucked back in an industrial area, we at first wondered if our GPS was leading us astray. Currently, Beer Valley is a 15 barrel brew house, using only a portion of the 6400 square foot building, but we will not be

surprised to see that change. Though the tasting room is currently in the large warehouse portion of the building, plans are to turn the office into a tasting room with hopes to eventually to open a pub.

The warehouse atmosphere does offer problems of its own. Pete needed to build a smaller, insulated, carbonation room which uses a space heater in the winter to obtain the 70° required for carbonation to take place. They even need to warm the *refrigeration* unit in the winter due to the extreme cold.

The eastern location does not appear to hurt distribution in the Western part of the state. One third of sales are to the west, both in bottled and draft forms, though mostly bottled. Beer Valley has been enthusiastically received in Portland, with Leafer Madness the favorite.

While Portland, Seattle, and Boise are the three main draft markets, Beer Valley can also be found in Arizona, California, Nevada, Idaho, and Pennsylvania. Expansion into Maryland and Washington DC are expected soon. To get the product to the distant markets they take

advantage of the ready availability of back haul in Ontario. Back haul is when a trucking company needs a load to get the driver back home and is normally less expensive.

It seems the toughest market has been their home town of Ontario. Accustomed to the light beers produced by the national breweries, locals, who said Beer Valley beers were too strong, are slowly becoming more open to the full flavors of microbrews. Created specifically to satisfy lighter tastes, Owyhee Amber, with its lower hop level, is the local favorite. Based off one of his homebrews, Pete created the recipe the night before brewing the first batch.

Beer Valley takes pride in their hoppy beers. Despite already producing the hoppy Black Flag and the even hoppier Leafer Madness, intentions are to produce even hoppier beers. Hopheads, keep on hoppin!

With Idaho thirty minutes away and an available supply of fresh hops during harvest, Beer Valley enthusiastically produces a fresh hop version of both Leafer Madness and Black Flag Imperial Stout. Pete jokes that they "had people fighting over the fresh hop products this year." Being the hophead that he is, Bob "really enjoyed the fresh

hop Leafer Madness and I highly recommend it to any hophead like myself."

Though he has been asked to brew an oaked version of Black Flag, Pete does not care for oaked brew and brews what he likes, so don't expect one. However, he is hoping to come out with a mead in the near future, making use of local products like apples and cherry. Also on the list of possibilities is root beer.

One unique aspect of Beer Valley is their beers are 100% bottle conditioned. According to Pete, this leads to a better shelf life. Four of the six beers produced are filtered. The two hoppier beers are not filtered in order to preserve the extreme flavors.

Bottling at Beer Valley is a tedious process. Using a six-head turbo gravity filler for bottling, Pete can bottle about four pallets per day if he pushes himself. The brew days, though, are like a weekend to Pete. "The rest of the stuff is what you have to do." This is a brewer who truly enjoys his craft and those associated with it. "You won't find an industry with better people," according to Pete. He believes beer is the most diverse beverage on the planet. At Beer Valley, quality is a necessity, requiring the use of the best ingredients possible.

Pete pours a sample

Pete is a self-taught brewer. He has not taken any classes beyond the initial homebrew workshop, though he did have two brewer friends in Arizona with whom he hung out and learned.

Pete likes to pay tribute through names. With his last location being Deer Valley, Arizona, he chose a more universal company name of Beer Valley as a tribute while making the drive back to visit his family while they were still there. Highway to Ale is a tribute beer to Oregon. The Oregon Trail is next to Ontario and was the highway of its day.

The artwork on the labels of Beer Valley Brewing is always an attraction. Artist Ward Hooper works with Pete to come up with Pete's vision of each label. For Leafer Maddness, Pete wanted the appearance of hops flowing out of the beer. You can see the Oregon Trail idea in Highway to Ale. The only exception to Ward Hooper as the artist is Gone Fishing,

the label was done by Pete's artist daughter, Christine, who also does the web site and promotional materials.

Beer Valley Brewing can be found at the annual Oregon Brewers Festival as well as the local Harvest Festival. According to Bob, it is worth a look-up whether at the festival, through a trip to Ontario, or a purchase at a local store. This beer is not watery; all have a good mouth feel, just a "dammed good beer."

Beetje Brewery

4206 SE Taggart Street
Portland, Oregon 97206
503-819-0758
www.beetjebrewery.com

"Little Bit"

Beetje, pronounced Bee-cha, is a Flemish word meaning "little bit." Owner/brewer, Mike Wright says he did not put a whole lot of thought into the name. It was inspired by his wife, Kaatje, who was born and raised in her early years in Belgium. He has, however, had a few second thoughts due to the constant pronunciation challenge. There is no denying it, the name fits.

Begun in late June, 2010, this one barrel brewery is literally a garage operation. Mike admits that he was a bit surprised – he did not anticipate being approved in the garage, through the process did take a full year. This garage operation has a couple of positive aspects to it: it creates a significantly lower financial risk and it is nice to be able to walk out the back door and be at work.

Beetje currently requires only about fifteen hours per week. Mike's day job as an IT Project Manager for Multnomah County takes him a bit farther away from home. Of course, in Mike's dreams, Beetje becomes a full-time job. But he is very cautious and does not want to get ahead of himself. He stresses that at this time, the point is to have fun. While the dream may be quite unattainable currently, we were quite impressed that at the early stage of six months into it, he had already stopped losing money in this venture.

In addition to two brand new one-barrel Blichmann kettles, Mike uses the "Lunar Lander." The Lander was at one time stored away in the Green Dragon building, the owner at the time, a friend of Mikes, found it. Unsure what its purpose was in its

Appropriately named "Lunar Lander"

previous life, a mere $150 turned it into a sixty gallon kettle.

Mike points out that the disadvantage of brewing one barrel at a time is that it is a lot of work for a small amount of beer. Though it had not occurred to us before, one barrel takes the same amount of time and goes through the same steps as ten barrels, only with less to show for your work. In contrast, experimentation on a one barrel system is easier, if for no other reason than the peace of mind, knowing you are not going to waste nearly as many ingredients if the batch is a flop.

At Beetje, consistent with the name origins, mostly Belgian style or Belgian-inspired Farmhouse ales are the focus. While Mike certainly does not rule out other beers, "If I have to have an IPA to fit in, it's going to be tough; there's a lot of great IPA's out there." He would rather focus on making beers that, "Reflect the way I like to drink beer, with friends and family." Beetje's B-side, a Farmhouse Ale, is an example of the session beers Mike expects to produce. But wait! Do not expect that all Beetje brews will be session beers; currently available is the 8.5% abv Little Brother, a Belgian dark ale.

With such a small system, Beetje does not have the level of sophistication to create the uniformity in beers which is found with the larger, push-button type craft breweries. While some may see this as a negative characteristic, Mike likens it to the variations in different vintages of wines and he intends to embrace this variability.

Unfortunately, with our interview at Beetje scheduled for 7 A.M., Bob did not get the opportunity to try any Beetje brews, but with his current fascination with Belgians, he will undoubtedly search out a Beetje tap on our next trip to Portland.

This is what owner/brewer, Mike Wright looks like at 7 AM (still dark outside).

Getting good feedback on his beers, Mike admits he still has a lot to learn. The selling and competition for taps are aspects he had not thoroughly thought through. Thankfully, there are places like Hawthorn Hophouse, who are quite open and encouraging to the small brewers. As a result, Mike has had to struggle to keep up with demand. This is one struggle he does not mind. The first time he saw his beer on tap was "super exciting – but nerve-wracking too."

We understood the feeling, the excitement of seeing our first book in print was something akin to seeing a newborn for the first time. Okay not even close, but babies only took nine months each to form, we have spent as long as two and a half years creating a book. This book, for instance, was approximately two years in

Beetje - behind the door is the insulated fermentation room, which can be kept warm in the winter with a heater and cool in the summer with an in-wall air conditioner.

the making, with the last year being more than a full time job.

Mike enjoys and is captivated by all aspects of the business. In the small raised beds in front of their house, he and Kaatje grow a few hops. Though they barely produce enough for one batch of beer, it is still way cool. The brewing process itself is a fascination for Mike, "The magic of fermentation is a blast to watch...trying to coral the yeast to do what you want."

Currently, Beetje is available only in kegs, Mike says many of his beers would do well bottled. Though he would love to be able to make use of Green Bottling, co-owner Mike Weksler is a friend, at this point it simply is not a possibility. Beetje's tiny brewery does not have the necessary pressure system and proper fill lines; and even if they did, with only a one barrel system, by the time it filled the lines, there would be nothing left to bottle. However, hand-bottling *is* high on the short list.

Bend Brewing Company

1019 NW Brooks Street
Bend, Oregon 97701
541-383-1599

www.bendbrewingco.com

"Fifteen years and counting"

While we were in Bend, the snow was there, but Bend Brewing was not. This was due to poor timing on our part. We were in Bend on the final day of the Holiday Ale Festival, in Portland. While we would have loved to attend, with limited time to do the tour, if we had gone, we would have missed many breweries.

After our return home, we were able to conduct a phone interview with owner, Wendi Day. While this is not ideal, and the exterior photo is the only one we were able to take, we were thankful for what we could get.

Bend Brewing Company (BBC) began in 1994 when Wendi's dad, Jerry Fox, a one-time partner at Bend Wood Products, and Dave Hill joined to create Bend's second brewpub. Opening February 27, 1995, BBC quickly became a favorite. Soon after opening, in May, Wendi began working at BBC as assistant manager. Then in 1999, Jerry Fox purchased Dave Hill's interest in the company. One year later, in 2000, Wendi purchased BBC from her dad.

Continuing with the family theme, at one time or another, Wendi's two daughters, her husband, and her sisters have all worked at BBC. In this family vein, minors are allowed at BBC until 9:30 P.M.

A great caveat for BBC was the day in 2002 when Wendi hired a new brewer, Tonya Cornett. Intrigued by the idea of homebrewing, Tonya began homebrewing in the mid-90s after

visiting a homebrew shop, where she purchased supplies, equipment, and *the Joy of Homebrewing*, in Fort Collins, Colorado, where she lived at that time. As the charm of brewing became more, Tonya wanted to brew professionally. Hoping to learn more and get her feet wet, Tonya took a position as a tour guide at a local brewery, where she would volunteer her time in the brewery, hoping to pick up any knowledge she could. After three years, it was time to take this brewing thing seriously, so Tonya enrolled in the Siebel Institute in Chicago and Munich. After  graduating, Tonya and husband, Mark, began searching the West Coast for a head brewer position. Through a coincidence of Mark being in the right place at the right time, Tonya landed the position with BBC, becoming Oregon's first female brewer.

Since that time, Tonya has racked up a collection of awards for Bend Brewing, as well as being named the 2008 World Beer Awards, Small Brewpub Brewer of the Year, the first female ever to receive this award.

While at the time of our interview, BBC bottled only two of their beers, Elk Lake IPA and a seasonal, Hop-Head IPA, which are available only at the pub, but they are hoping to bottle more 22 ounce beers in 2011, making them available in stores. As I write this I have noticed Lovely Cherry Baltic Porter and Dopplebock are available in limited 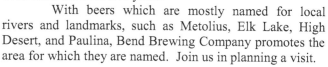 release bottles.

Brewing on a seven barrel system, Bend Brewing  has a capacity of twelve hundred barrels per year, and neared that capacity at 1000 barrels in 2010.

In the pub you will find a wide variety of food, from burgers, to tri-tip, to spinach salad, to chips and sandwiches, all of which are served by a friendly and knowledgeable staff. Employing thirty people, BBC has no trouble retaining help. The majority of the employees have been there for over five years.

With beers which are mostly named for local rivers and landmarks, such as Metolius, Elk Lake, High Desert, and Paulina, Bend Brewing Company promotes the area for which they are named. Join us in planning a visit.

Big Horse Brew Pub
Horsefeathers & Company
115 State Street
Hood River, Oregon 97031
503-386-4411

"Feels like hanging out at a family member's house."

We visited Big Horse Brew Pub twice on our tour. The first time we were there we had not been able to get in touch with them for an interview, so we stopped by in hopes of a meeting on the fly. Turned out the brewer was out of town, so we stayed for an enjoyable lunch with terrific views.

If you are unfamiliar with Hood River, it is in the Columbia River Gorge and is world-renowned as a premier windsurfing destination. It also serves as a gateway to Mount Hood and skiing. Additionally, there's fruit, wine, and of course, beer. Because Hood River is built on a hill, it seems as though it were on steps, and the views are great.

Big Horse Brew Pub is built into one of those hills, so be prepared for a hike up the stairs to get to the entrance, which is at the top.

By appearances it seems to be a converted home. In fact, the original house, which at one time housed a laundry, burned down, leaving only the stone foundation. Randy Rozeck, architect and owner of Horsefeathers & Company, designed and built the entire structure.

"Horsefeathers" was a last minute decision when the new company had to file their name. It's east coast slang for "bullshit." Just like the name of the company, most of the beer names are last minute decisions. There was a time when all the beers had names with a horse theme, but they have since shied away from that practice.

Thankfully, we passed through Hood River again on our way back from the Eastern corner of the state. This time we had that scheduled appointment. Our first sight of brewer, Jason Kahler, was as he was using a dolly to laboriously haul a keg of beer up the numerous stairs to the third level, in the same manner each and every keg arrives at the pub. Randy, why didn't you design a dumb-waiter or elevator into the building?

Like many brewers, Jason began as a homebrewer before getting his first brew job at the age of twenty-one in Minnesota, after attending the Siebel Institute of Technology & World Brewing in Chicago, Illinois. He went on to brew at Walking Man Brewing across the river in Washington and at fellow Hood River brewery, Full Sail Brewing, before coming to Big Horse Brewing in 2004.

As the only brewer at Big Horse, Jason has the freedom to create the beers he wants to brew, as long as they are good. This gives him the opportunity to make fifty different beers per year including four standards and several seasonals, which  assures the customers that the beer is always fresh. Working at capacity, with nine handles they run out of as much beer as he can make.

Despite the full-capacity production, there are no plans to expand this four barrel brewery, other than possibly adding a couple more bright tanks (where beer is conditioned) in order to maintain the space they have, though the recent addition of an on-demand water heater does make brewing easier. The brewery currently supplies only the restaurant and pub, with no taps at other locations. Don't expect this to change either; the brewery is in their 21st year.

Big Horse does not participate in competitions. Jason has judged them and is not a fan. They do, however, do a few festivals, such as the Hood River Hops Fest in October and Blues, Brews, and Barbeques in Stevenson, Washington, in June.

Being at capacity, they have no need to advertise. Nor do they bottle. Kegs are not sold to the public; after all, they can barely keep up with demand at the pub. Other than a rare keg sent for an occasional special event, Big Horse Brew is available at Big Horse Brew Pub and no where else. Sorry, folks. At least it makes a great excuse for a trip!

Brewer, Jason Kahler

Bill's Tavern & Brewhouse

188 N Hemlock Street
Cannon Beach, Oregon 97110
503-436-2202

"A local gathering place throughout the years"

We actually visited Bill's Tavern & Brewhouse in Cannon Beach on both of our long tours. Owner, Ken Campbell, had told us on our first tour that he would be out of town, but let his staff know we would be dropping by to take some photos. We tried again on our second trip through, and this time we got lucky.

Bill's Tavern originally opened as the Imperial Café in 1923, by then owner William (Bill) Gallagher, with help from his sister, Happy. After prohibition ended in 1933, they added alcohol. At some point Bill's was sold to the second Bill, Happy's husband, Bill Moore. Many successive owners and a change of name to Bill's Tavern later, the business was purchased in 1979, by Ken, a property appraiser.

Since that purchase, many changes have happened at Bill's. In 1984, Ken, along with Jim Oyala, the local jewelry store owner, partnered to purchase the land on which Bill's stood. Expanding that partnership to include the

Owner, Ken Campbell

Dining on the family side

Tavern in 1997 (and later the Jewelry store), changes had only just begun.

Celebrating the partnership, they demolished the old building in February 1997. While the community suffered pangs of nostalgia, the old building was without a foundation and in very poor condition. By November of that same year, the partners had built three new buildings in its place, including the new Bill's. Hands-on in the project, they participated fully in the carpentry of the new buildings.

Reopening in November to white walls around a stark interior, it took another year for the interior to be completed. The back bar, which had been in the old Bill's, is from Portland's old Benson Hotel, which had been torn down in 1953, gave them a good start. Architect, Tom Ayers designed the building so the

bright tanks are visible through the windows in the center of the building. A stove tucked in among the booths and across from the bar adds a warm feeling, both in ambiance and temperature, oft needed on the northern Oregon Coast.

Even before, in the old Bill's building, Bill's offered microbrews on tap, other breweries microbrews, that is. In fact, in the early '90's Bill's Tavern sold more MacTarnahan's per capita than anywhere in the world. But with the new building, adding their own brewery seemed a given.

Brewer, Dave Parker

Hiring brewer, Jack Harris, who admittedly embellished his experience a bit when he got the job, turned out to be a great boon to this fledgling brewery, where Jack established himself among brewers before moving on to open his own brewery, Fort George, in Astoria.

Dave Parker has worked at Bill's

for twenty years. For the first fifteen as a bartender, then, wanting to do something different, he interned with Jack as a brewer. With Jack's departure, Dave commendably stepped into the position of head brewer.

Originally thinking of a small system, maybe four barrels, Bill's ended up with a seven barrel steam jacketed brewhouse. Located upstairs, this all-in-one unit made by AAA Metal Fabrication in Beaverton, is barely able to keep up with the volume required by Bill's and their sister pub, the Warren House Pub.

While they may begin June with an excess, by August they are scrambling to keep up with demand. While Bill's is in a location which is hard to beat, Warren House, Ken's other pub, is in a completely different environment.

Local-made glass tap handles

The only other place to find Bill's brews, Warren House, which is not a clone of Bill's, is in the nearby Tolovana Park area of Cannon Beach.

Currently, Ken is nursing the idea of obtaining more fermenters. This would allow him to create a tasting/fermenting room in the building behind Bill's as well as facilitating the production of more lagers.

While some may remain nostalgic about the old Bill's, with its cork boot holes (logger's boots with spikes in the soles) and distinctive door noise, all agree, the new Bill's is great.

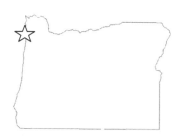

Block 15 Restaurant & Brewery

300 SW Jefferson
Corvallis, Oregon 97333
541-758-2077
www.block15.com

"Create something new based on age-old traditions---Belgian Brewers Philosophy"

Our timing for the beginning of our second long brew tour in Oregon seemed rather poor, considering it was the weekend of the Holiday Ale Festival in Portland. But it could not be helped; we both work full time and have to take time off for interviews when we can get it. Due to our schedule and beginning location, we were unable to start in Portland, which meant that a couple of our interviews were scheduled for a time when the brewers/owners were at the festival.

This was the case with Block 15's Nick and Kristen Arzner. However, Nick did make arrangements for us to meet with his lead cellar guy, Matt Williams. Matt, who has been with Block 15 since August of 2008, handles most of the conditioning and fermenting at Block 15, which in this case is actually downstairs – in the cellar. With Block 15 doing plenty of barrel aged beers, and sours on the horizon, Matt has plenty to keep him busy.

Lead cellar guy, Matt Williams

A graduate of Oregon State, with a degree in fermentation science, this is Matt's first position in the brewing industry. "I love it; it's a great job! Matt continues on to say there is always something to learn and that it is quite different than school. Though on campus students get a little practice, there is very little hands-on brewing experience. With competition for internships very tight, students ache for more practical experience.

To this end, Block 15 has plans in the works to have a "Brewed by Beavers" program. Fermentation science students, working in teams

Friendly service

of two, will be asked to submit an ale recipe. From the submissions, one will be chosen and the creators will be asked to visit Block 15 and will actually brew their recipe under the supervision of the Block 15 brewers. At the end of the month, the ale will be offered on tap in the pub. With this unique

Brewmaster, Steve Van Rossem

program, Block 15 will be going beyond the usual internship for students, which normally involves only the less interesting tasks, such as washing kegs and cleaning tanks, to giving students the opportunity for hands-on brewing experience in a professional environment. By the time you read this, this program should be going strong.

Brewmaster, Steve Van Rossem, has been with Block 15 since the beginning. He had been on hiatus since leaving McMenamins' High Street Brewery in Eugene when Nick sought him out for the position at Block 15. Steve is well-known as the brewer who made the porter which won a Gold Medal at the Great American Brew Festival when he worked for West Brothers Brewing in Eugene.

Housing a seven barrel brewhouse, with new tanks from Stromberg Tanks International in San Diego, California, Block 15 had a limited hand-bottling of their 2010 holiday ale, Figgy Pudding, but otherwise, does not bottle. A few taps can be found around Corvallis, Salem, Newport, and at Belmont Station in Portland. While they do an occasional brew festival (like the Holiday Ale Fest), they are still tossing around the idea of a GABF appearance.

Brewhouse

When Nick and Kirsten met at Indiana University, they soon found they had a lot in common, including a love of beer, a desire for entrepreneurship, and "green" goals. After moving to Corvallis, the pair was surprised at the lack of a locally owned brewpub. As homebrewers, this realization inspired a business plan. It took five years and some management experience at the local McMenamins, but in February 2008, they finally opened Block 15, two and a half months after brewing had begun.

With both the brewing and restaurant businesses traditionally producing a great deal of potential waste, at Block 15, sustainable practices are a focus, with a continuing eye toward new ecological ideas. In the brewery, efficient use of water through a clean in place (CIP) system, glycol cooling, recycling spent grains with local farmers, using

View from upstairs

local ingredients whenever possible, and turning used grain bags into things like curtains and grocery bags, helps to reduce the Block 15 footprint. These measures are also incorporated into the restaurant side of the business, where the staff is trained to conserve. Using efficient lighting that is on only when needed; serving water only when requested; turning on cooking elements only when required; recycling whenever possible, including sending used cooking oil to Enviofuel to become alternative fuel; using only compostable to-go containers (no Styrofoam); using organic as much as possible; and sending food waste for composting are all extra steps taken to reduce waste.

Originally built in 1926 for the Gazette-Times newspaper, the building has housed several businesses since their relocation. The Block 15 name is a fallback to the city map for Marysville, the original name of Corvallis, where 300 SW Jefferson was located in block fifteen.

Block 15 is family friendly until 9 P.M, though minors are not allowed in the game room, where shuffle board, darts, and television can be found. Wi-Fi is also available for all to use.

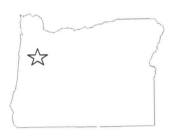

Blue House Café & Brewery

919 Bridge Street
Vernonia, Oregon 97064
503-429-4350
Find them on Facebook

"Mediterranean food, locally brewed beer, and live music"

We had not been able to contact Sam and Eleonora Semerjian, owners of Blue House Café & Brewery, so we decided to drop in on our way to the coast from Portland. Arriving in Vernonia shortly before Blue House opened, we discovered the very good reason we had not been able to get in touch with the Semerjians, they were out of town. Thankfully, they had left the café in the very capable and friendly hands of employee, Richard Harutunian, who kindly showed us around and answered numerous questions.

Blue House Café & Brewery originally opened in early 2007 on Nehalem Highway. That same year, on December 3rd, the storm came: hurricane-force winds, driving rains, and rivers at record-high levels. Vernonia will never be the same.

This was not the first time this small town in the coast range had endured a massive flood; 1996 saw a "once in a lifetime, 500 year flood," with waters exceeding the previous record set in 1895, by four feet. Only eleven years later, that never to be repeated event was surpassed, when in only four hours the waters rose to twelve inches higher than the 1996 levels. The flooding affected most of the major infrastructure of Vernonia, the senior center; the food bank; the health center; the waste water system; and not one, but all three schools, elementary, middle, and high school were all destroyed. Only city hall and the fire hall were spared. Federal Emergency Management Agency (FEMA) issued a decree, either elevate or evacuate within four years.

It is apparent as you drive into town that this resilient community of 2,370 weather-worn people refused to evacuate. House after house has or is in the process of having an elevated foundation fitted under it. While the state sent several modulars for classrooms after the flood, residents realized the six hundred students of Vernonia needed a real school. Passing a thirteen million dollar bond-an astounding number for a community this size, receiving fifteen million dollars in state and federal funds, and banking on ten million in donations, Vernonia is building a new $38 million school a half mile up the hill, well out of the flood plain.

This K-12 campus is an Oregon Solutions Project, whose mission is to "develop sustainable solutions to community-based problems that support economic, environmental, and community objectives and are built through the collaborative efforts of businesses, government, and non-profit organizations." This school of the future is lauded for its green/sustainable design/construction. Included will be an indoor/outdoor learning center, a natural resources center, and an innovative learning lab with connections to community colleges. This 100-year school (and beyond) is expected to provide huge long-term savings for the district. Moreover, it will be a source of pride and "home" for many "Loggers" (school mascot) for years to come. Expectations are for the new school to be student-ready for the 2012-13 school year. To donate go to http://www.vernoniaschools.org/get-involved/donate/ or contact Betsy Miller at 503-429-5891 for more information.

Markers are provided to write on the bathroom walls

When I was a sophomore in high school, the boy who sat behind me in math burned our school to the ground, leaving only four classrooms that had been added a couple of years before, four cottages, and two shops. Knowing how difficult it can be to attend school around town, without lockers, and without "a" school, my heart goes out to these kids. Our gym was completed just in time for my graduation, but my school is forever gone.

One of the buildings which flooded was Blue House Café & Brewery. Though the building was already somewhat elevated, water reached three feet up the walls before the flood waters receded. Spending over two months cleaning the mess, they reopened Valentine's Day, 2008. But the threat of flood remained, so April 2009 brought a move to the current Bridge Street location, which the Semerjian's had purchased as an investment to rebuild and sell, but when the county said they must open within four months or lose their licenses, they made the move, killing the proverbial two birds with one stone.

Brewery

Painted cobalt blue and yellow, Blue House is difficult to miss. In a building which at one time housed a bank, Blue House still includes a vault dating to the 1920s, which is now used to store the brewing malts. This spacious café is decorated by an eclectic array of items, local artwork, antiques, plants, and Eleonora's collection of cobalt glassware.

The Mediterranean food is lauded by all who partake, including us. Wanting an ethnic café which was not too ethnic, the Semerjians planned an inviting place, which would allow everyone to feel welcome. Though they hale from Armenia, they preferred to call it by the more generic term of Mediterranean, alleviating the problem of cultural exclusivity.

Blue House hosts a monthly food celebration, with a different country's foods featured as well as music and other

Fermenters

entertainment showcasing that country for a full day. A peak at their Facebook page shows recent months have featured Spain and Egypt.

With a focus on health, natural foods, organic whenever possible, are all made from scratch. There are no fried foods. There are no "diet" foods. There is no high fructose corn syrup. Many of the ingredients come from the owners own greenhouse and a local farmer. They roast their own coffee, peaberry beans, smaller than normal and grown on the top of the tree.

While there is a patio next to the Blue House Café, it belongs to the city, with rent costs prohibitive, so Blue House is looking into other outdoor seating options, perhaps a rooftop garden?

While Sam does not drink, he dislikes beer, there are no other businesses in town with a microbrewery, so adding a brewery seemed like a wise choice. In the old location the brewery consisted of two converted kegs. For the new location, Sam had a different looking custom built brewery made. This homemade system is about three barrels.

Brewing for Blue House is Brett Costly, a former Texan who began homebrewing in 1991. Previously employed by Compac, Brett moved to Oregon for his day job at Intel. A member of the community, Brett has also served on the city council. Specializing in session beers, Brett is most well known for his Blueberry Wheat.

While you will not find guest taps at Blue House, you will find a selection of wines available. Blue House brews are not available in bottles, though you can take a growler or a keg home.

This "little town that could," located out of the way in the mountains between Portland and the coast, once was home of the largest sawmill in the world, the Oregon-American Sawmill. By the 1950s the old-growth timber was gone and so was the sawmill. Though the timber has grown back, the sawmill did not return. One remnant of those old timber days is the counter, made from an old spar tree. A spar tree was used to provide lift as the steam donkey would pull the logs out of the "hole," before modern day towers were in use. But the "Loggers" live on.

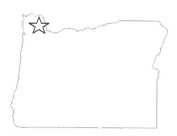

Boneyard Brewing

37 NW Lake Place, Suite B
Bend, Oregon 97701
541-323-2325
www.boneyardbeer.com

"Let it be known..."

What do you get when you throw together bits and pieces from thirteen breweries in five states and a lot of talent? Boneyard Brewing.

Tony Lawrence came from a mechanical background, he's been a lift operator and an auto mechanic, then lived as a snowboard bum with the Barfoot Snowboards Team, before renting a room from a fellow who worked in the kitchen at a brewery in Bend. Through this guy he began working in the kitchen at Deschutes.

At Deschutes, Tony found a fit. Gravitating from the kitchen to the brewery, Tony began working closely with renowned brewmaster, John Harris, who is now at Full Sail, eventually working his way to the position of Senior Brewer. During his time with Deschutes, Tony enhanced his brewing knowledge by attending The Siebel Institute in Chicago in 1999. Then, after twelve years with Deschutes, it was time to see what else the world had to offer.

Feeling there was much to learn from other breweries, Tony did a bit of brewery hopping, including stints at Firestone Walker Brewery in Paso Robles, California and Three Floyds Brewing in Chicago. It was through this experience that Tony honed his skills in building and fabricating breweries.

Returning to Bend in 2005, Tony founded Brewtal Industries, a brewery installation, fabrication, and consulting firm. In addition to developing deep connections in the brewing industry through Brewtal, Tony also amassed a collection of bits and pieces of breweries across the country, frequently trading labor for stainless.

Enter friends Clay and Mel Storey, who had worked in the construction business in Corvallis for seventeen years before the economy turned. The couple felt the time was right for opening a brewery, and Tony was the brewer to partner with to make it successful.

When the new partners found a warehouse location which had hops growing around it and up twenty feet in the back, they knew they had found their new brewery site.

The partners came up with the concept of a pull tab for their logo, an indication of their canning plans, then had a graphic artist do the artwork

Cobbling together, making repairs, and modifying all the pieces he had collected through the years, the three created a brewery. This

resurrected hodgepodge of equipment was only the beginning of the work for the partners. Doing everything in the brewery, from concrete work to building taps out of an old skateboard, the only thing they contracted out was the electrical controls.

Originally, the plan was to brew under the name Brewtal, but decided against it due to a potential name conflict. While Tony still consults as Brewtal Industries, the brewery built from castoff and inoperative leftover waste pieces opened with the appropriate name, Boneyard Brewing.

While many breweries on our tour had at least one used piece of equipment they had purchased from one, or maybe even two or three, breweries, these were almost always still working items which had simply been replaced. Boneyard, conversely, has been cobbled together from cast-off chunks of thirteen breweries in five different states. The main body of the brewery came from Three Floyds Brewing Company in Chicago, Illinois, and Munster, Indiana (both a five barrel brewhouse and a twenty barrel brewhouse came from them), tanks and other hodgepodge equipment came from such points as Cascade Lakes; Deschutes; Oakshire; Beer Valley; Silver Moon; Skagit River Brewing in Mount Vernon, Washington; Loan Peak Brewery in Big Sky, Montana; and Big Sky Brewing in Missoula, Montana. This diverse

Anywhere they could insert 13 into this brew, they did, including 13 ingredients and an ibu of 13

brewery even has one brand new tank, fabricated just for them.

What Boneyard now boasts is a twenty barrel brewery in a production facility. In 2010, their first year of production – they opened May 5, 2010 – Boneyard produced 750 barrels. Expecting up to fifteen hundred barrels to flow through Boneyard in 2011, this new Bend brewery has had a good beginning.

Though the folks at Boneyard have no interest in opening a pub, they do have a tasting room, which is open six days a week. While there, you can try their samplers and purchase growlers, they do not do pints. Also available on tap at select locations locally, Boneyard is just beginning to make the break into the coveted Portland market.

Focused on quality control and quality assurance, Boneyard would rather not jump the gun where growth is concerned. Though the public may have other ideas, as Boneyard has seen rapid growth and wide acclaim, these overworked partners have no regrets and have been rather surprised by the response.

Visiting on a snowy Bend day, we were unable to meet with Tony or his partners, but we were able to talk to him the next week by phone.

Boneyard fans and future fans should keep an eye open for Boneyard in sixteen-ounce cans. The machinery has already been purchased; they are just waiting for the aluminum to arrive. Hopes are to eventually distribute from Seattle to San Diego.

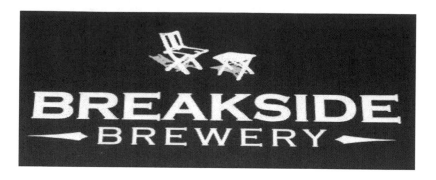

Breakside Brewery

820 NE Dekum Street
Portland, Oregon 97211
503-719-6475
www.breaksidebrews.com

"Great vibe"

While Scott Lawrence was in Juneau, Alaska on a kayaking trip, he was enjoying a beer at the Alaskan Brewery's Tasting Room. After a few beers, he realized he had discovered his dream and announced with a grin that he was going to open a brewery. After arriving home, he shared this revelation with everyone he knew, figuring it would have a better chance of passing the dream state if he voiced it.

One of those friends he told introduced him to Tony Petraglia, a fellow visionary and homebrewer who also had a desire to dream his way out of the corporate world. The two pooled their minimal financial resources and began learning and searching. Looking all over Portland for the right space, Scott saw the Dekum Street space on Craigslist. He jumped on his bike and was off to establish whether it would fit their needs. Drawn to more than the angled corner, Scott liked the welcoming feel of this promising neighborhood, both the businesses and the residents.

Location and the building shell was what this space had going for it, since that was all it was. Empty for ten years prior to Breakside, it lacked such basics as electrical or plumbing. Hoping for a light and airy neighborhood hangout experience, the design called for skylights, as well as a garage door on the corner, allowing an open sidewalk café feel when weather permits, integrating the ample, outdoor seating seamlessly.

Brewer, Ben Edmunds

As an enthusiast, Scott played on Ultimate Frisbee terminology when naming their new brewpub. "Breakside," in Ultimate Frisbee language, means "going against the flow or force." Adapting the meaning to become a bit more mainstream, the partners like the idea of a "take a break and enjoy life" theme. Breakside's logo, a camp chair and foot rest, exemplify this concept.

Through a friend in the Ultimate Frisbee community, Scott met brewer, Ben Edmunds. After showing him the space and talking about their plans for it, the partners offered Ben the position of head brewer. Conceding to Ben's superior knowledge of brewing, they granted him full reign in the design of the brewery, within their limited budget, of course.

Ben was a homebrewer in Colorado before the brew bug drew him to the Seibel Institute in Chicago. Participation in the Masters course led him to an internship at Doemens Academy, outside Munich, Germany. While Ben had plenty of formal training, he desired hands on work; this led him to Portland, aka, Beervanna.

Ben's other business

Excited to get started, and at the same time he was working to get Breakside up and going, Ben, Jason Yale, and Robert Bosworth founded the one-of-a-kind Portland L.L.C., Oregon Beer Odyssey (OBO), in early 2010, where they offer classes, tastings, and events designed to promote beer appreciation and education. Holding classes at various Portland locations, such as bottle shops and taprooms, OBO is dedicated to beer education by promoting appreciation and knowledge of craft beer through formal tastings and classes.

While Ben's training in Germany qualifies him to brew authentic German beers, he says German styles do not sell that well in Portland, but beginning in 2011, Breakside will be brewing an alternative Northwest style German beer.

While Breakside brews on a brand new, three barrel system, they still have a half barrel homebrew system to allow them

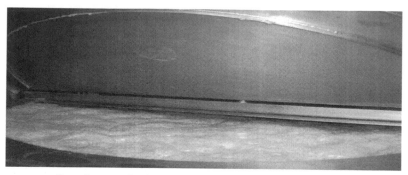

Open fermentation is an unusual aspect of brewing at Breakside.

to experiment. Taking advantage of these experimental beers, Breakside has found their distinctive feature. Each Wednesday at 3 P.M. Breakside taps one keg of an experimental batch of beer. When the keg is gone, it may never return, though a few have gone on to be a part of their regular line-up. Double IPA was an experimental which is now a seasonal. Fall of 2011 is expecting to see the former experimental, Imperial Cream Stout return. Some Wednesdays find the experimental keg tapped out within two hours, so stop in early.

Tony, as a homebrewer, assists in the brewing at Breakside. While the majority of the recipes are Ben's, Tony has added a few and likes to participate in the experimentals when not working his full-time job at Intel.

As a former homebrewer (truth-be-told, he still homebrews), Ben knows the itch of many homebrewers, wondering what it would be like to brew commercially. Breakside is hoping to begin a program which will allow a homebrewer to come in and brew with Ben. While plans have not yet been solidified, participation may be gained through a competition. The resulting beer would then be sold at the brewpub.

Breakside beers are not filtered. With no finings used, this means most of their beers are vegan friendly. Organic and vegetarian

dishes are also found in the pub. Most famous for their blue cheese infused burgers, which has received accolades by multiple reviewers, Breakside proudly states that their food is all made with pride, on site, not dumped out of plastic bags.

Obviously, the same pride was taken in the design of Breakside. A modern, yet cozy feel, with an abundance of ambiance and light, the unique design allows patrons to peak between the stairs at

Cupola

the brewery on the mezzanine level. On the main level, plenty of windows and a windowed garage door allow an open, light feeling regardless of the weather. Striking stairs lead to the upper level, where the most amazing feature is the cupola style skylight.

With the focus at Breakside good beer, good food, and good service, it is family friendly until 9 PM. Good service is a source of pride at Breakside. Scott, who manages the front of the house, has a relaxed, carefree approach focused on the customer. His goal is to provide a local gathering place which caters to customer needs and desires.

Currently, Breakside bottles only for competitions, though tentative plans call for bottling beginning summer 2011. Until then, you may take your Breakside beverage home in a growler. In addition to the brewpub, Breakside taps may be found at limited Portland locations. Not willing to compete for taps, Breakside has a laid-back attitude regarding that particular market. Dreams call for an eventual separate production brewery, with an eye toward making bottled Breakside brews available on grocery store shelves.

Looking at the main level from the upper level

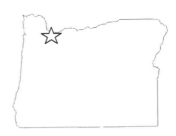

Brewers Union Local 180

14329 East 1st Street
Oakridge, Oregon 97463
541-782-2024
www.brewersunion.com

"We're Oregon's only real ale public house & brewery"

It may be a bit out of the way, but the short drive to Oakridge is well worth it. In a state filled with beautiful drives, this is among the best. While there are not necessarily great views of the distance, (too many trees for that), there is a wonderful relaxation among all those trees. Upon reaching Oakridge, you will be in one of two cities in Oregon completely surrounded by national forest.

This once thriving mill town has struggled to survive despite the down-turn of the timber industry. With the mills now a thing of the past, Oakridge has found a focus in the recreational advantages provided by nature and is becoming an outdoor enthusiast's destination. Whether you are into hiking, biking, birding, hunting, cross country skiing, equestrian activities, motorcycling, snowmobiling, fishing, or boating, the Oakridge area offers an abundance of outdoor activities. Now known as the mountain biking capital of the Northwest, the International Mountain Bicycling Association (IMBA) is building a ride center in Oakridge.

If indoor activities are more to your liking, or if you are ready to take a break from all that outdoor fun, step into another land and relax at Brewers Union Local 180. Patterned after a British Public House, with an American flair, the Local 180 is full of ambiance and comfortable nooks allowing one to spend hours curled up with a good book (books available) or deep in dialog with your favorite chum. If meeting your friends for a game of pool, foosball, darts, or a board game is more to your liking, play to your heart's content at no charge. A public computer is even available for patron's convenience. Designed as a place to stay as long as you wish, in the tradition of the old British Pub, I could easily wile away the hours in this cozy and inviting establishment.

With compartmentalized spaces, like any good English pub, in addition to the bar, Local 180 has a parlor (with couches), a music room, a billiards room, a reservable meeting room, and soon - an ice cream and soda bar in the family side. So if you are vacationing with the kids, bring them with you to the West side of the pub, which is open to minors until 9 P.M. and even provides a kid sized pool table for their amusement. Most Fridays and/or Saturdays you can enjoy a variety of live music including jazz, rhythm and blues, folk, funk, or rock, beginning at 7 P.M. Perhaps you would rather enjoy a quite game at "Scrabble Madness" on Mondays at 6:30 P.M., or open mic on the 2nd and 4th Thursdays from 7-10 P.M.

The brilliant design of this pub was not always there. Brewers Union Local 180 owner, Ted Sobel, quit his highly paid job as a software engineer, mortgaged his house, maxed his credit cards, and purchased the old Breaktime Tavern, which in his words, was a dirty, dingy, smoky, redneck joint. Gutting the building, except for the kitchen, the refrigerator, and the floor, which was from the old Mac Court in Eugene, Ted spent ten months completing the renovation. Using as many recycled materials as possible, including wainscoting made from the subfloor at the old Camp Adair north of Corvallis, Ted has created the "rooms" of Local 180 through clever use of old windows. Lamps, old bottles (beer, of course), books, and maps serve as accents which have useful purpose as well as providing a decorator's touch to this relaxed and informal environment.

Originally from upstate New York and Illinois, Ted and Patti Sobel (an artist) once back-packed and hitch-hiked around Oregon.

Just a few of Local 180's many seating options

When finally ready to settle down, they literally opened a map and looked for a small town in the woods near a college town. Oakridge was the town of choice.

Ted began homebrewing at the age of twenty-one and in 1997 investigated the possibility of opening a brewpub, but found that it was not a feasible idea at that time. Then in May of 2004, he traveled to England and trained in traditional brewing at the Woolpack Inn in the Lake District, now the Local 180's sister pub.

Deciding to "do this thing," in the fall he returned three times, learning the arts of brewing, cellaring, bartending, and what it means to be a good publican. The first time he went back was for ten days, increasing this to two weeks for the second trip. During this stay he was totally immersed in the reality of being a publican when the bartender broke his leg, needing Ted to cover for him while he was at the hospital. On his third trip (lasting one month), Ted stayed upstairs from the pub, with the owners leaving him in charge while they took a much needed, short vacation.

Brewmaster Ted Sobel behind the bar.

Real ale uses traditional ingredients and is served out of the container in which it ferments, the cask. There is no extraneous carbon dioxide used. It is served at cellar temperature, 55°. Served from traditional hand pulls, the long swan's neck extends to fill the glass from the bottom. The sparkler on the end of the swan's neck makes the ale creamier. Though regularly used in Northern England, in Southern England the sparkler is thought of as the Devil's work. Cask conditioned ale will change subtly from day to day. Care must be taken by the bartender to taste each ale every morning before opening, since cask conditioned ale can sour overnight. When a pint is pulled, a pint of air goes in to replace it.

When the Campaign for Real Ale (CAMRA) began in England in 1971, there were only four traditional breweries left in the United Kingdom. Still active, CAMRA continues to advocate for traditional beers, the local pub, value for your money, consumers rights, and improvements throughout the industry. To learn

more about real ale and how it is served, check out their web page: http://www.camra.org.uk/page.aspx?o=180651.

Naming the Local 180 was an international effort. When Ted would gather periodically with a group of home brewing friends, they would discuss how to sell their brews. They united together and did a 180° turnabout from home brewing to selling. In the United Kingdom and Ireland the "local" is "your" pub. Hence, the Brewers Union Local 180. One of those home brewing friends helped with the renovation of the pub and has a share in the business.

You will not find Local 180's ale in a bottle; that would be a harsh contradiction. Nor will you find it at other locations, unless Ted accompanies it as a guest brewer. Don't expect to purchase casks of it either. This is a "living product" and needs knowledgeable care. You will simply need to make the trip to Oakridge and get the full experience.

Bob & Ted in the brewery.

Using equipment that once belonged to fallen comrade, Hawks Brewing Company in Roseburg, Ted brews where the now demolished stage and karaoke bar once stood in the old tavern which previously occupied these premises. Additionally, he has designed and made some of the equipment himself, such as the handmade cooling coils and the converted garden sprinkler that works wonderfully as a rotating sparge. Ironically, the underbath is an old Budweiser keg (though you will find no yellow beers here). The on-demand hot water heater assures the ample supply of hot water needed by any brewery.

Kettle

Ted brews on demand, when he accumulates eight empty casks, which under "normal" conditions translates to usually once every week and a half. But during not-so-normal conditions, for instance, summer; an up-coming event like a festival, such as the Oakridge Keg & Cask

Festival; going on a guest brewer appearance; or an Oakridge mountain biking event which he sponsors and provides free beer to riders with a wrist band ID, brewing is, of necessity, more frequent, at least weekly.

Ted mostly adheres to traditional brews, but occasionally includes a mix of West coast ideas into his brew. He is a fan of session beers, which are low in alcohol (3.1%) so you can go to the pub and hang out with your mates all evening. Of course, this certainly does not mean he limits his brews to session beers.

As an officially certified purveyor of the Honest Pints Project, you may be assured that when you order your pint of ale at Local 180, you are getting at least a full pint. Served in a nonic glass, which is a traditional British shape with a hump toward the top, it includes half and full pint lines. These glasses are imperial pints, which serve 20 ounces, though they are actually 23 ounces to allow for head room. Sodas are served in a barrel shaped mug called a "jug."

Be sure to watch as Ted fills your pint. It is a process unlike any other pub, at least in Oregon. When he places the glass on the bar before you, get down and look at it. You can actually see the creaminess of the beer. It is fun to watch it "rise." Not being a beer connoisseur, I simply had not been able to understand how Bob could say some beers were creamy. They tasted anything but creamy to me. After seeing the creaminess and trying a small sip, I finally understand what "creamy" means in beer. The unexpected aspect of this is that when he convinces me to "just take a little taste" of other beers, I can actually tell now when it is creamy. The "real ale" taught me! Not only that, Ted even had a beer I might consider drinking, I actually rather liked it. However, I would still rather have a good root beer, but that just leaves more for you.

The Cellar, located behind the bar.

In addition to the authentic ale at Brewers Union Local 180, you can also partake of some traditional British pub fare. Bangers and mash (sausage and potatoes), as well as less British items such as French bread (made in house), Greek salad, and a good old fashioned American hamburger can be found on the menu. In this case, old fashioned means the burger is hand formed, which true burger buffs know makes a far better burger. As in any pub, "it's comfort food, it's not meant to be a restaurant." You will need to order at the bar, since this is a pub and they don't wait tables, but they do bring the food to your table.

Our prevailing thought as we left Brewers Union Local 180 was of the intense passion Ted has for his craft and the ale he creates. Though he says he hopes to open more "real ale" pubs in the future, his growing fear is that this could become a business rather than a passion. He hopes to find the right people to make any possible future pub a mom and pop operation. Until then, make the beautiful drive to Oakridge and find your new "local."

More seating

Bricktowne Brewing Company
3612 Calle Vista Drive
Medford, Oregon
541-941-0752
www.bricktownebeer.com

"Quality before cost"

After enjoying the Zwickelmania tour at Southern Oregon Brewing, we fell into conversation with Medford couple, Steve and Lauralynn Ferrell. Members of both the Hellgate Homebrewers and Rogue Valley Homebrewers clubs, they began telling us about Craig McPheeters, a Medford homebrewer who was in the process of going commercial. Many thanks to this wonderful couple who put us in touch with Craig, resulting in not one, but two additions to this book.

Sporting a brand new brew system for his fledgling brewery, Craig was brewing – still as a homebrewer – his first test batch in the new system just as we were learning of his existence. While the system is capable of thirty-one gallon batches, this initial test batch was only twenty gallons. Still awaiting his state and federal licenses, in February, Craig was not yet officially commercial.

The new one barrel system, with a stand built by Craig's dad, a master welder who is currently taking metallurgy classes.

Planning to self-distribute when he does become official, it should not be difficult to find Bricktowne brews, as Craig already has several places planning to provide

Bricktowne on tap: Shoji's, Jackson Creek Pizza, 4 Daughters Irish Pub, The Brick, and Ashland Resort Ski Lodge. Thankfully, being in Southern Oregon, where breweries are few, the fight for taps is not nearly the competitive crusade found in Portland, where breweries are prolific.

Rather than the usual half barrel keg, Craig has opted to use the smaller five gallon sanke keg, by Plastic Kegs of America, which is made of a high density polyethylene non-porous material, with stainless steel dip tube. The reasoning behind this decision was threefold. Plastic kegs typically do not

Craig McPheeters, in his brewery

have the theft appeal that all stainless kegs seem to garner. The initial cost for plastic kegs saves about $35 per keg. And lastly, most of the draft accounts Craig has spoken with can only accommodate the smaller kegs.

Still awaiting the arrival of Bricktowne taps and a small walk-in cooler, Craig is nearly ready for business, as soon as those licenses arrive.

Craig, originally from Bend, began homebrewing six years ago with his dad, and believes homebrew is one of the best beers you can drink. Brewing to style, as a certified Beer Judge Certification Program (BJCP) judge, he has the training and know-how to determine style. Craig feels his training as a judge makes him a better brewer, enabling him to distinguish flaws and flavors, though he does add that it also tends to spoil beer drinking for fun, since it is difficult to turn off the judge in himself.

The refrigerator/freezer has been converted to hold the fermenter, run by a Johnson controller, which turns it on and off as needed. Fermenting at too high a temperature causes strong fruity esters.

Bricktowne Brewing will soon be adding a small walk-in cooler.

Look for two beers to start, Siskiyou Pass English Ale and Table Rock Red Ale. Siskiyou Pass is described as the perfectly balanced bitter ale. While Table Rock Red Ale, named for the iconic Southern Oregon landmark (the huge flat rock, or mesa, just north of Medford), is a session beer that is considered easy drinking. For celiacs and FMer's who are intolerant of gluten, gluten-free beers are also planned. Barrel aged beers are also in the forecast, with Craig currently on the hunt for local winery barrels. Bricktowne Brewing also anticipates doing festivals and competitions in the future. Plans are in the works to do Hop Madness in August.

The brewery is currently located in a building behind the McPheeter's home. Previously Craig's man-cave, filled with slot cars, a recliner, rugs, and the flat screen TV which remains in the brewery today, its conversion to a brewery is okay with Craig.

Long-range plans are not terribly long-range. Hoping to open a tap house in Jacksonville in September or October 2011, Craig's parents, Denny and Jamie McPheeters, who recently sold their bar in Culver, outside Bend, and will be moving to Southern Oregon to run the establishment. If a Jacksonville location remains elusive, Bricktowne Taproom may locate in downtown Medford. While Medford would be a wonderful location, Bricktowne is named in celebration of Jacksonville - a city of total fascination for the McPheeters - in honor of their understanding of it having one of the first brick buildings in Oregon. So Jacksonville is the optimal, and hoped for, location.

Craig's parents make the *Monster Mash: The Original Insulator Blanket* and sell on the Bricktowne website.

Creating far too much spent grain for the bread, Bricktowne sends the remainder to a farm in Eagle Point.

A little farther down the timeline, Craig is not planning for a large increase in size, thinking of maybe a five or ten barrel system at most for the taproom in the far future. Consideration is also being given to the possibility of making Bricktowne available in cans. Seeing cans as the more mobile (camping, fishing, picnics, etc.) way to go, they also have the advantage of being easier to stack.

As a real estate appraiser, the havoc created by the economic recession created a financial upheaval in the life of the senior McPheeters. As a result, their running of the planned taproom creates a win-win situation for both Craig and his parents. Craig will get an experienced management team he can trust, while Denny and Jamie get a fresh start near their grandchildren. In fact, going commercial was originally Dad's idea.

In anticipation and preparation of opening the taproom, Craig's wife, Nicole, has purchased commercial bread making equipment and is busy perfecting bread made with the spent grain from the brewery. Knowing that beer imparts a wonderful flavor to bread, we are looking forward to stopping in when they open and sampling the bread. Also in the experimental stage are butters for use on that bread. Nicole and Craig are even testing a hop infused butter.

Being well aware of the importance and influence of homebrewing, Craig has determined to teach and train homebrewers in the art and science of brewing, especially from an all grain perspective. Craig offers all-grain homebrewing classes on a monthly basis for new brewers. As of this writing he is only

Keg

charging $15 to cover costs such as propane, printing, and heating, with each student taking home a large instructional packet and a Bricktowne Brewing glass. The classes are held in Craig's garage and he has retained his homebrew system for use in the classes. Also up for consideration is an advanced brewing science class. Sign-up is on the Bricktowne website.

When not brewing, Craig is a full time Board Certified Medical Dosimetrist, meaning he does radiation treatment planning for cancer patients. Wife Nicole is a Mamographer and Ultrasound Technician; both work for Providence Medford Medical Center.

Craig and Nicole are the proud parents of three children. With

Nicole being fortunate to have the ability to carry and deliver children easily, they feel that God has gifted her and it would be selfish not to use that gift through surrogacy. Currently undergoing testing in preparation for her second surrogate pregnancy, Nicole will soon be presenting a second baby to the same couple for

Craig shows Bob where he stores his kegs

whom she has already delivered one child. Retaining a friendship with the couple, who live in Seattle, Craig says he and Nicole just love them. Undoubtedly, the feeling is mutual. The father has an amazing story, raised as a Tibetan monk, at the age of sixteen he and eleven others walked twelve hundred miles to get out of Tibet through China. With the combination of harsh conditions and the murders of the Tibetans, he was one of only four to survive the trek.

A check just before publication told us that Bricktowne is now available!

Bridgeport Brewing Company

1313 NW Marshall Street
Portland, Oregon 97209
503-241-3612
www.bridgeportbrew.com

"Oregon's oldest existing craft brewery"

The historic building was built in 1886 for Portland Cordage Company as a hemp rope factory, where they made ropes used by the shipping industry until 1935. Relegated to the status of warehouse for the next forty-nine years, new life blossomed in 1984, for this National Register of Historic Places site when Richard and Nancy Ponzi, a local wine-making family, teamed up with brewmaster, Karl Ockert, to establish the Columbia River Brewery.

After Oregon's brewpub law of 1985 was enacted, the Ponzi's changed the name to Bridgeport Brewing Company in 1986, and opened the popular brewpub. Bottling followed in 1989, followed by another big change in the summer of 1990, a new brewmaster.

Brewmaster, Karl Ockert, who received his bachelor's in fermentation science from UC Davis and had built and run the brewery for the Ponzi's since its conception, decided he wanted to see what else the brewing industry had to offer. From there he went on to work at everything from a seven barrel brewery to the major nine billion barrel per year plant at Anheuser-Busch in New Jersey.

Change being constant, in 1995 the Ponzi's sold Bridgeport to The Gambrinus Company, based in San Antonio, Texas. Gambrinus immediately instituted several changes; the first was to bring Karl Ockert back to run the brewery. Investing $3.8 million in equipment, installing a new bottling line, installing a new laboratory, redesigning the packaging, and initiating a first-ever marketing campaign for Bridgeport, the Gambrinus Company has grown Bridgeport from its original 600 to over 100,000 barrels per year and is now in eighteen states.

In a more recent change, long-time, on-and-off again, original Master Brewer, Karl Ockert left Bridgeport

Gambrinus, legendary king of Flanders, is the unofficial patron saint of beer.

again on July 30, 2010, to serve in the position of Technical Director for the Master Brewers Association of the Americas (MBAA). Active in the MBAA since 1993, Karl had been serving as second vice president of the

organization prior to accepting the position as Technical Director. Karl has also served as chair of the MBAA Technical Committee and editor of the MBAA Practical Handbook for the Specialty Brewer series. Word has it that Karl and his family will remain in the Portland area.

Taking over the position of Master Brewer at Bridgeport is Jeff Edgerton. Jeff had previously served as assistant brewer at Bridgeport for six years and has also held the position of Quality Assurance Manager.

Master brewer, Jeff Edgerton leans on a bale of hops.

President of the local chapter of the Master Brewer's Association, Jeff had also worked for Blitz-Weinhard on Burnside as brewery microbiologist. After graduating from Canby High School, Jeff received his degree in microbiology from Oregon State. Later, he attended the Seibel Institute, taking their master brewers course. In all, Jeff has twenty-two years of experience in the brewing industry.

The original ten barrel system once stood where the restaurant's reception area is now located. Currently working on a seventy barrel system, Bridgeport has maxed out their brew space. Leasing the building, which covers three-quarters of the block, Bridgeport is unable to store all of their supplies on sight, so they have a warehouse on Columbia Boulevard, where they store all but their working supply.

This space problem is further evidenced at the loading dock. In this busy city location, trucks must load **The seventy barrel brewhouse at Bridgeport.** and unload off the side of the street, meaning time is a prime concern. While this is not an ideal situation, it is an inconvenience of which Portlanders are quite familiar.

Using both pelletized and whole hops in the brew process, they were preparing to dry hop when we were touring. From a layman's point of view, the dry hopping is essentially a vat of hops which is set up so the brewed beer can be sprinkled over and through the vat, rather than letting them soak in the beer, adding a fresh hop taste to the brew.

A new cellar, designed specifically to avoid the problem of hoses on the floor, except for cleaning the floor, is quite impressive. A series of pipes

The loading zone at Bridgeport

connected to the tanks show a well designed system which will move product in and out as needed, then will even clean itself and the tanks, leaving a floor that is clear of hoses and other clutter.

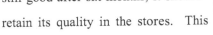

The new cellar relies on a series of pipes to keep things moving and hose-free.

A visit to the old cellar reveals what has been avoided through the design of the new cellar. With large hoses winding their way through the cellar and around the floor, watching your step is important. (This is not always an easy thing to do when trying to take notes and pictures at the same time.)

Quality control is of prime importance at Bridgeport. When one bad batch could ruin a reputation, it must be taken seriously. With a large quality control lab and attached testing lab, Bridgeport is serious about their beer

and reputation. Stacked in the lab is six months worth of beer batches. Six-packs and twenty-two ounce bottles, each labeled with batch information, are stacked along a wall as you walk into the lab. Exposed to the light of the lab as well as the room temperature conditions, if it is still good after six months, it should

retain its quality in the stores. This

The old cellar, with its maze of hoses

stack also serves the purpose of providing product to check if they were to receive a complaint.

Located in a city where there are many very well-educated beer people, who understand what beer is and should be, Bridgeport is aware of the importance of consistent product; if you drink a Hop Czar today, it should taste like the Hop Czar you drank six months ago.

Coupled with this is the need to stay fresh. Just because Bridgeport is Oregon's oldest brewery does not mean they are stale in their design of beers. Continuing on the edge of brewing, Bridgeport's special releases have included the bourbon oak-barrel aged Old Knucklehead and the blended Stumptown Tart, which was then aged in French Oak Pinot Noir barrels. Familiarity with Bridgeport will tell you that they do not rest on their laurels, regularly releasing new styles and specialty beers.

In the lab

Because Bridgeport brews on a seventy barrel system, experimentation without a smaller system could be quite costly. Being maxed out in their space, Bridgeport simply does not have room for a smaller, experimental brewery. For these trials, they take advantage of the fifty-five gallon pilot brewery at Oregon State, which is mutually beneficial for both parties. Using their system for pilot brews, commercial breweries, like Bridgeport, help to support Oregon State's eminent fermentation science program.

Jeff says it is still exciting to come to work each day and that the people at Bridgeport take pride in every drop that goes out the door. Feeling incredibly lucky to have a job he loves, where he

Ready to ship

gets to speak with people from around the world, strangely enough, as Brewmaster, Jeff actually does more overseeing than brewing. But as he opens the kettle and breaths in the aroma, the feeling of satisfaction showing on his face is quite apparent.

In addition to the brewery, but run separately, this location houses the Bridgeport Brewpub, a well designed space which has taken advantage of the warehouse atmosphere instead of trying to hide or work against it. A great deal of exposed brick, art, and steel all come together to somehow create a comfortable, upscale environment.

In the brewpub

Burnside Brewing Company

701 E Burnside
Portland, Oregon 97214
503-946-8151
www.burnsidebrewco.com

"Old world brewing craftsmanship blended with forward thinking recipes"

We had not been able to get in touch with the guys at Burnside Brewing to schedule an interview, so during our final tour we took a chance and dropped by the proposed location for this new brewpub. Brown paper covering the windows told us that they were still in the building stage. Experience and determination led us to knock on the door. With the work noises from within, we knew they would not hear the knock, so we banged on the door. Success!

After being admitted, we were led through the other exterior door to meet with Adam Cassie, co-owner in charge of operations, sales and also the brewer's assistant. We immediately felt rather guilty for interrupting; the poor man looked as though he had not slept in days. We know the pressure of trying to meet a deadline, and these guys were trying to get this place ready to open in eleven days. Obviously not having time for us, Adam graciously allowed us to take a few photos and asked that we send him an e-mail interview.

An exhausted Adam pauses for a photo

Burnside is the collaboration of Adam; with former homebrewer and fallen comrade, Roots founder/brewer, Jason McAdam; and Jay Gilbert, previously with Full Sail Brewing. Originally the

Fermenters

company went by Alchemy, but after discovering it was trademarked, they changed it to reflect their new location.

Led by their logo of Galena (which also happens to be the name of a hop variety), a dreamy hop nymph, a divine spirit who offers respite in the form of beer, the trio's idea is to provide "a remarkable brewpub experience in our space where the beer is present in all the food offerings and prompts the pub goer to say, 'wow, in a city like Portland where there's amazing food and beer, it's great to see them both happening under one roof!'"

To this end, Burnside will "strive for a balance of art and craft" in both their beers and their food. While offering standards, such as IPA, you will also find unusual beer offerings available, such as Sweet Heat, which incorporates apricots and Jamaican Scotch bonnet peppers. While the word "artisan" frequently gets batted around in brewing circles, it is usually used to refer to the beers. At Burnside, pride is taken in integrating this vision into the food. A brief glimpse of the starter menu is enough to reveal the difference. This is no ordinary pub food. Specializing in in-house smoking and pickling, with offerings like "duck" on the menu, the term "high-end" comes to mind. Thankfully, the price side does not follow. Offering "champaign (so-to-speak) on a beer budget," current offerings sell from four to sixteen dollars. Doable.

Burnside opened December 28, 2010, with a fifteen barrel brewery. Expecting to supply the Portland metro area in the beginning, with plans to begin bottling during summer of 2011, predictions call for 1200 barrels of beer from Burnside in 2011. Long range strategy is to eventually distribute throughout the Northwest region.

The Burnside Brewing building was built in 1926 after the Burnside Bridge was redone. Originally auto related, the building has seen many uses through the years, including a music store and most recently a dry cleaners. The building boasts huge beams which the partners have used to their advantage

Chairs and kegs await completion of the pub

by allowing them to highlight this modern, artistic space.

Burnside features a black walnut bar which is banded and inlaid with maple, and was designed and built by Troy Jordan. The walnut  came from a tree felled by a good friend of Jason's and has definitely been used to its best advantage.

We look forward to returning to Portland and seeing the finished Burnside brewing, sampling the beer (Bob), and trying some tempting cuisine.

Calapooia Brewing Company

140 Hill Street NE
Albany, Oregon 97321
541-928-1931
www.calapooiabrewing.com

"Great beer, good food, cool atmosphere!"

The Calapooia River is 72 miles long and runs through Crawfordsville and Brownsville before converging with the Willamette River near Albany. It is also the inspiration for the name chosen by husband and wife team, Mark Martin and Laura Bryngelson, for their brewpub, Calapooia Brewing, which also honors the area's native people, the Kalapooian Tribe.

Originally Oregon Trader Brewing, which was founded in 1993, Mark and Laura purchased the business in 2006. The brewery had already been through two owners; wanting to be sure the public knew it was a fresh start - a new beginning - they determined a name change was necessary. The additional problem that the name was continually mixed up with Oregon Trail Brewery, reiterated the need for a name change.

Many windows create a light pub (on the right), while the massive patio provides plenty of outdoor seating (on the left).

Many changes have occurred since the purchase. Originally, Mark and Laura purchased only the "blue sky," but then followed this with the acquisition of the building. While Oregon Trader had only one outside tap, Calapooia has grown to over sixty outside taps around the

Willamette Valley. Starting with a six and a half barrel Brewhouse, they now brew on a fifteen barrel system and are looking to purchase a 30 barrel system and two more fermenters. In the beginning, Mark and Laura did everything; now, eighteen employees are essential to keep this growing enterprise going. In addition to all of this, plans are in the works to begin bottling.

While it may have taken time for the regulars to accept some of the changes, it seems they have now embraced them. The brewpub has acquired the affectionate name of "Pooia." Welcoming the nickname, Mark is hoping to have the local area named the "Pooia District" of Albany.

Mark, who taught high school science for two years, has actually been in the beer industry for some time, as a doorman, a bar manager, and a distributor. After he and Laura married, he wanted to own his own business. When Oregon Trader became available, Mark quit his distributing job and started working as an intern for four months - for free - to learn how to brew. Though he had homebrewed previously, it was not terribly successful, so the training was a vital aspect of the purchase.

While Mark brews and handles sales, Laura is the business manager, making sure the operation runs smoothly and handling finances. This is all the more amazing when you realize Laura still has a part-time job as a software and database programmer with Benton Education Service District. This steady income helps to assure the bankers are happy when obtaining financing.

Just in case this enterprising couple is not busy enough, they also recently purchased Siletz Brewing Company. After a few months of trying to keep the business going in Siletz (NE of Newport), they regretfully made the decision to temporarily close the brewery and move it to Albany. By

Calapooia owners, Mark & Laura

the time you read this, Siletz beer should once again be available. Expectations are that production will be notably increased over previous years.

One would think that all of this would keep Mark and Laura quite busy, but instead of sitting back and relaxing, in February 2010, they also partnered with Tonya and Iain Duncan to open Flat Tail Brewing in Corvallis,

Brewing exclusively with whole hop flowers, Mark has been accused of clinging to the old school ways. While it would be cheaper to use hop pellets, as well as less cumbersome to store, he simply does not want to. "I just think there's something romantic about using whole flower hops."

Bales of whole hops and Calapooia kegs

Most famous for their Chili Beer, which has won several people's choice awards, including first place at the KLCC Microbrew Fest in 2007, second place at the Spring Beer and Wine Fest in 2007, third place at the HOTV Oregon Homebrew and Mircrobrew Fest in 2007 (tie), third place at the Spring Beer and Wine Fest in 2008 (tied with Ninkasi's Tricerihops Double IPA), and first place at Oregon Garden Microbrew Fest in both 2008 and 2009. Bob loves both hot stuff and beer, but he does not usually want the hot stuff in the beer. However, he suggested this great tasting beer would

make an exceptional red beer with a little tomato juice added, if you are into that sort of thing. Made with a blend of Jalapeño, Serrano, and Anaheim peppers, it is the best of its type that Bob has tried.

The Calapooia Brewing building was built in the 1950's and originally housed the Blitz-Weinhard distributor. This building has been about beer from the beginning. While the interior of the pub may not be too large, the building extends far beyond to include a sizable warehouse, two apartments, and an expansive covered patio.

Inside the pub, the bar covers a corner extending about half way across each adjacent wall. At one end of the bar is a wall with shelves

for the mug club mugs. All the mugs give a bit of a glass wall effect. The Pooia's mug club has eighty members with an extensive waiting list.

Three steel-tip dart boards line the half of another wall not covered by windows. Use of the

Mug club on the right, growlers in the center, and taps on the left.

dart boards is restricted to times when there is no band performing, since the staging area is directly in front of them. Pooia features local live music every Thursday and Saturday, with occasional Fridays thrown in. Less frequently, a Wednesday performance will be added. Every Sunday at 4 P.M. patrons are treated to a blues jam, where the Vicki Stevens Band is frequently featured.

During the day, the pub provides a light, cheery atmosphere. With windows along a full wall and half of two other walls, a variety of table types, and plants on the tables, Calapooia creates an approachable, daytime atmosphere acceptable for families until 8:00 P.M.

Outdoor seating is available on the covered patio – the "Atrium." The sprawling patio has been made intimate by adding

movable fencing to reduce the area. With the Atrium open year round, warmth is provided when needed through the use of propane patio heaters. A wide variety of seating is available here also, including picnic tables, wine barrel tables, or high bar tables.

Note the giant doors in the background which open to the warehouse

The fencing which surrounds the Atrium can be

moved, allowing expansion to the full patio to accommodate large groups. Also, the massive warehouse can be arranged to provide indoor capacity for numerous people. Huge doors open to allow the massive combined space of the warehouse and patio. In the past the space has comfortably held five hundred people. The warehouse recently provided venue for a wedding. With a space this size, the options are endless.

Mark describes his vision to Bob

Future plans for Calapooia's space are many and varied, though as yet, not set in concrete. Included is the possibly of installing skylights in the patio ceiling to allow even more light in this versatile space. Talk has been battered about of eventually expanding the pub into the warehouse space. Of less importance to pub patrons is the continuing upgrade of the adjacent apartments as money allows.

For this enterprising couple, I would say the sky is the limit. It will be entertaining to return periodically and discover what changes time generates. In the meantime, this is a nice, versatile place, run by two genuinely nice people.

Caldera Brewing Company
Caldera Tap House

31 Water Street
Ashland, Oregon 97520
541-482-4677
www.calderabrewing.com

"When in doubt, add more hops"

Located under a bridge and backed up to Lithia Creek, Caldera Tap House is Ashland, though and though. The look, the feel, the whole ambiance screams, "Yeah, I'm in Ashland!"

We arrived at Caldera just before it opened and took advantage of the emptiness to take several photos. Boasting the largest outdoor deck in Ashland, which is actually comprised of several decks on various levels, Caldera is inviting, both inside and out. Be sure to follow the walk around to the back entrance for a breathtaking view of Lithia Creek, with the walkways which cross over it, and feel transported to another land.

Step inside to a light and comfortable space that feels like a hip basement hangout. Complete with a comfy couch and chair facing the fireplace, which is flanked by a bookcase with games as well as reading material, this space says 'stay awhile.'

Black & white does not do this blown glass lamp justice.

Choose to sit at the pub height tables, traditional dining height tables, or just belly up to the bar on a bar stool. Wherever you sit, be sure to check out the beautiful blown glass lights made by local artisans, Scott Carlson and Keith Gabor, at Gathering Glass Studio. The raised wooden stage rounds out this well-designed space.

Incorporated March 12, 1996, owner/brewer Jim Mills brewed Caldera's first batch of beer on July 4, 1997, with the first keg going out the door August 28th. This ten barrel production brewery includes fermentation tanks ranging from ten barrels to sixty barrels, which are filled by brewing multiple batches.

After spending eight years as a draught-only beer, Caldera made history in June 2005 by becoming Oregon's first craft beer in cans. Why cans? According to the folks at Caldera,

Cindy pours the first beers of the day

Gift packs, hats, and tees available at the Tap House

"Cans are accepted in locations where bottles have long been banned, such as, golf courses, concert venues, beaches, and other places that do not usually mix with glass. The lightweight aluminum beer can is the package of choice for backpacking, fishing, hiking, camping, rafting, and to put in your refrigerator at home." Additionally, they say cans eliminate light and oxidation, chill quicker, stay cold longer, and are 100% recyclable.

While Caldera's line-up includes eleven year-round beers, plus several seasonals and specials, they currently "microcan" only three beers, Pale Ale, IPA, and Ashland Amber, but look for others in the more traditional 22-ounce bottle.

Caldera's brewery is currently situated in a 6000 square foot building which they are quickly outgrowing. However, Caldera is in the process of obtaining approval to build a new, 28,000 square foot brewery, which will include a tasting room. If approved, Caldera will expand from the current twenty employees

(brewery and Tap House combined) to as many as fifty employees within three years. Until then, remember, this is a production brewery with no tours offered.

Caldera Brewing Production Brewery

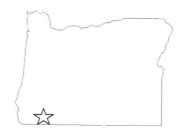

Lithia Creek behind Caldera Tap House

Captured by Porches
Brewing Company

40 Cowlitz, #B
St. Helens, Oregon 97051
971-207-3742
www.capturedbyporches.com

"Extraordinarily eclectic"

While we have run across a wide variety of breweries and brewpubs while writing this book, the most unusual one is assuredly Captured by Porches. From the name, to their business model, to their "pet," Captured by Porches is fascinating, distinctive, and avant-garde.

When owners, Suzanne Moodhe and Dylan Goldsmith met, what motivated each of them was quite dissimilar. As a Masters student, Suzanne was a single mom, with a young son, just trying to get by. Dylan, also a student, whose past jobs included postal employee and a paralegal, was a punk, living in a punk house, a type of communal-living arrangement, similar to the hippie crash pads of the 1960s. His focus was on living a simple life, an organic life, with a true disdain for waste. Sustainability was his motto.

Dylan was working as a baker for Delphina's Bakery, Portland's oldest artisan bakery. Due to his simple, uncluttered lifestyle, he was able to save much of his wages, which allowed him to take a year off to learn to brew beer. In brewing, Dylan had found his passion.

Dylan and Suzanne had rented an old house which had many porches. As an avid homebrewer, an eclectic homebrew club began gathering at their house in 2002, brewing, testing the various brews, engaging in stimulating conversation, and would joke that they were captured by the porches of the old house. After all, what was the motivation to leave?

When the pair decided it was time to take this brewing passion to the public, Captured by

Dylan & Suzanne
Photo courtesy Captured by Porches, used by permission

Porches was the obvious choice for the brewery's name.

Unfortunately, they had to move from the company's namesake. At first they rented a small space from Clinton Street Theater, where there was a small licensed area in the back. Dylan struck a deal with them to provide their house beers. Later, as he began to distribute, Captured by Porches needed more space.

Their search led them to an incredible old gas station on Highway 30. Living in their bus inside the station and showering at the local YMCA, the pair began the process of getting it licensed for a brewery. Unfortunately, with all the restrictions and requirements imposed by the City of Portland, the Department of Environmental Quality, and Oregon Department of Transportation, it would prove to be prohibitively expensive to complete the transition to a brewery.

**Captured by Porches tee-shirt,
which they print themselves**
Photo courtesy of Captured by Porches, used by permission

Finally locating near the waterfront in historic downtown St. Helens, which is close to their Scappoose home (there were no locations available in Scappoose), Dylan and Suzanne were pleased to have a

Dylan, making tee shirts
Photo courtesy of Captured by Porches, used by permission

home for all the various pieces of equipment they had collected, which came together to make up their eight barrel brewery. To have it in such a wonderful and family-friendly area is a definite bonus.

Collecting, restoring, and repurposing brewery pieces was only a part of the owners' of Captured by Porches quest for sustainability and wise use and reuse of resources. Since their union, Suzanne has embraced Dylan's disdain for waste, and together they "strive continuously to minimize our negative effect on the environment, both in our personal lives and in our production methods. Almost all of the waste generated by our brewing process is either eaten by animals, re-used, or recycled. Plus, we are the only NW brewing company at this time (that we know of) that is using

Reusable bottle
Photo courtesy
Captured by
Porches, used by
permission

only returnable bottles to distribute our product in." (Reusable bottles are also used at Standing Stone.)

When purchasing a bottle of Captured by Porches beer, you will be charged a $1 deposit. These reusable bottles with the ceramic caps are a source of pride for Suzanne and Dylan. While the bottles are definitely more work, they feel it is worth the effort. Customers also love the reusable bottles. As Suzanne said during our interview, "We're never going to stop doing returnable bottle unless the law says we can't (do them)...it's more responsible...we really, seriously need to change the way we're doing things...wish bigger breweries would do this...much more simple and close."

Ever on the lookout for ways to reuse everything in their lives, Suzanne has even discovered a way to reuse the labels after removing them from the bottles. Turning the labels into paper-mache' style birds, has also generated a new source of income for the family.

The bottles are only the beginning of things being done

The Mobile Public Haus
Photo courtesy Captured by Porches, used by permission

differently at Captured by Porches. Though at one time they had planned to open a tasting room, they have eschewed this traditional outlet for the more non-conventional bus. This green short-bus, dubbed the Mobile Public Haus, aka Guerrilla Public House, is currently parked at the D Street Noshery at 3221 S. E. Division Street in Portland, on a temporary vendor's license. Hopes are great that they will be able to obtain a year-round license, just as the food carts at that location have. In past years, you may have seen this same bus at Krugers Farm on Suavies Island.

The long bus in progress
Photo courtesy Captured by Porches, used by permission

Currently in the works is another bus, this time a long one. The interior has been gutted and Suzanne and Dylan hope to fix it up using used materials found locally. Plans call for possible inside seating and using this bus at Krugers Farm, where they will play vinyl records, and have six taps (4 beer, 1 kombucha, and 1 ginger ale). In addition to the buses, Captured by Porches has also acquired a 1946 Franz Bread truck, which they are prepping to become their next mobile beer cart at 23rd & Alberta in Portland, on the same lot as Burgers or Bust.

1946 Franz Bread Truck
Photo courtesy Captured by Porches, used by permission

If your question is the same as mine, "What is kombucha?" It is fermented tea. To make Invisible Alchemy Kombucha, Dylan and Suzanne partnered with long-time friend, Balam McNally. Balam had been homebrewing kombucha for twelve years, when Lindsay Lohan's love of the drink, combined with its slight alcohol content (a natural byproduct which will be found in any *real* kombucha after bottling), suddenly made

Invisible Alchemy Kombucha label
Photo courtesy Captured by Porches, used by

kombucha famous. The partnership combined Captured by Porches' brewing equipment and licenses with Balam's experience and recipes to create this popular drink (.5 to 1.5 abv). Add to this a great label designed by Balam's wife, Maeve Callahan, and you have a winner.

Some may think it odd that Captured by Porches should choose such a "troublesome" bird as the starling to grace their logo. The endearing story of this "pest" bird is sure to tug at even the most hardened heart, and is one that is very dear to the hearts of Suzanne, Dylan, and their family.

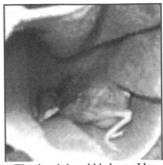

The tiny, injured bird saved by Dylan and Suzanne.
Photo courtesy Captured by Porches, used by permission

In May 2008, Suzanne and Dylan watched as a scrub jay stole a tiny, bald, baby starling from the nest, as its mother screeched and squawked in protest and mourning. As the jay landed on a nearby branch and began pecking at the helpless hatchling, Dylan ran to the branch, scaring the jay, who left his pray and flew away. The frail baby had been badly injured by its chicknapper, so Dylan cleaned its cuts and made him comfortable.

Peckers loving Suzanne
Photo courtesy Captured by Porches, used by permission

After researching how to care for the infant bird, the entire family watched over and cared for it, including feedings with a dropper every fifteen minutes. The weeks brought both strength and feathers to the tiny bird, who had been named Peckers. After misreading information on an internet website, Suzanne released Peckers outside their house, before being told that it was a drastic mistake because he had imprinted with people and would be killed in the wild.

But Peckers came and went, frequently singing in the tree in the backyard, sometimes leaving the yard, but always returning for love from his family. Then when the family planned a move 2½ miles away, they worried about Peckers, after all, he only knew the old place. The worry was unfounded; when Suzanne released him at the new house, Peckers left for a couple of days, but then continued to return home to his people.

With time, the family realized that Peckers was spending nights with his bird family at the old house. He was torn between two worlds. Gradually, Peckers came to

Peckers
Photo courtesy Captured by Porches, used by permission

The Captured by Porches delivery van, being painted by Dylan.
Photo courtesy Captured by Porches, used by permission

visit less and less, but continued to make occasional visits. A grown Starling, Peckers now cares for his own bird family. While his human family misses him, they are proud to have been a part of his life. (Peckers' story is a condensed version of "Meet Peckers," written by Suzanne Goldsmith, who gave me permission to adapt it for this book. Read the full "Peckers" story on the Captured by Porches website.)

This unusual and exceptional family is living their dream, in their way. Whether it is minimizing their negative impact on the environment, crafting incredible beers, designing unusual beer buses, or saving "pests" named Peckers, Captured by Porches is definitely fascinating.

Having recently contracted with a new distributor, Captured by Porches is now available by bottle throughout Oregon and may soon be available in Southern Washington. In addition to being available on tap at their buses (bring your own to-go container), Captured by Porches is also on tap at select Portland locations.

Cascade Brewing Company
Art Larrance's Raccoon Lodge & Brew Pub
7424 SW Beaverton-Hillsdale Hwy.
Portland, OR 97225
503-296-0110
www.raclodge.com

"Here to answer the question, 'What's new?'"

Opened December 11, 1998, the Raccoon Lodge & Brew Pub's interesting name is a tribute to the raccoons who once inhabited the lot on which it was built. An early plan for sleeping rooms on the third level contributed the "Lodge" portion of the name; though the idea for the rooms was abandoned, the name remained unchanged. Plans had begun in 1995, with ground breaking in 1997.

Owner, Art Larrance was one of the earliest entrants into the Oregon brewing scene as a co-founder of Oregon's fourth microbrewery, Portland Brewing Company. An even greater claim to fame would be his role as one of the principle organizers and originators of Oregon Brewers Festival, one of the nation's longest-running and most renowned brew festivals, where he currently holds the office of festival director.

Brewmaster and Oregon native, Ron Gansberg, began his brewing career at the age of 12, when he first began brewing root beer. In the early 70's he graduated to hard ciders and fruit wines. After several years in the Northwest wine industry, Ron went back to his roots and began brewing for Bridgeport Brewing Company in 1986, where he eventually changed to the equipment and

Brewmaster, Ron Gansberg

- 115 -

engineering end of the business, becoming the engineering manager. He then directed the design and installation of their 80 barrel brewhouse. Leaving Bridgeport to aid Art Larrance in the design and realization of Cascade Brewing and its state-of-the-art ten barrel system, Ron has been there since the beginning.

Brewhouse

Art and Ron knew they were a "tall tree in a forest of tall trees" and needed to distinguish themselves. Not willing to participate in the "hops arms race" for hoppier/hoppiest so popular in the Northwest, they looked instead for a style which would give an intense, savory experience as their unique distinction. After a look at potential ideas which would utilize area resources, they seized upon the inspired image of the availability of local fruit and the abundant supply of wine barrels from the region's wineries.

In 2005, they began collecting the oak wine barrels and by 2006 were producing the base beer that would then be aged up to a full year. After a trip to the Great American Beer Festival (GABF) in 2007 to taste other wood barrel aged beers similar to what they had planned, they were confident their idea was a winner. Cascade Brewing would specialize in *sour ales.*

If you have never tried a sour ale, don't let the name scare you away. I actually found them to be rather sweet, definitely something not to be missed. Bob compares them to wine coolers.

Cascade Brewing released the first of their sour beers in 2008, the same year they entered three of their sour beers at the GABF, winning a Bronze Medal for *Cascade Kriek* (Flemish for cherry) in the Wood and Barrel-Aged Sour Beer category, which had twenty-two other competitors. Buoyed by this success, they attained even more barrels and kept brewing. With their 2009 wins of a Gold Medal at GABF for *Bourbonic Plague* (which is aged in a bourbon barrel) as well as a Silver Medal for *Vlad the Imp Aler,* this little Portland brewery has become nationally known for their sour ales. Named as one of Draft Magazine's top twenty-five beers in 2008 for Apricot Ale, and in 2009 for Vlad the Imp Aler, Cascade Brewing is definitely receiving accolades for their efforts.

While most of the sour ales are barrel aged for up to and even over two years, these dry ales are also bottled. However, the bottling of these sour ales is very different than for that of regular ales, with a secondary fermentation required. Taking this extra step allows Cascade Brewing to sell their brainchild up and down the West coast as well as Boston, with recent distribution contracts into New York, Pennsylvania, the Carolinas, and Florida. At the time of our interview, they were bottling six sour ales, while only three were available on draft.

Choose the pub next to the brewery...

Ron has developed a true fondness for these sour beers, naming them as his favorite style. When asked what his favorite other Oregon beer is, he stated he has no time to drink the competition's brew. The man is loyal as well as enthusiastic about Cascade's sour ales. When not creating brews he finds time to play the guitar and sing bluegrass and folk. He states he also used to write adventure fantasy and sports as a hobby; though never published, he did have a New York literary agent.

In answer to the question that must be plaguing you, yes, Cascade Brewing does

or the restaurant upstairs...

make other beers, IPA's, wheats, Pales, all of the others in variety. All of their currently available brews, sour or not, may be enjoyed either in the family-friendly restaurant upstairs with its hunting lodge feel, high rough-hewn timbered ceilings, and massive rustic stone fireplace, or in the Den downstairs where you can play pool, lottery games, watch the projection HD television, or view the brewery below. Now you can also enjoy the brews at their new Cascade Brewing Barrel House on Belmont Street.

the choice is yours.

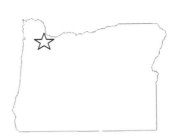

Cascade Lakes Brewing Company

1441 SW Chandler Ave Suite 100
Bend, Oregon 97702
541-388-4998
www.cascadelakes.com

"Proud to be Redmond's first and only brewery"

Chris Justema, one of four partners at Cascade Lakes Brewing Company, was busy tending bar the afternoon we interviewed him at their newest location, The Lodge. Chris joined the partnership in 2003, when Cascade Lakes Brewing Company purchased Tumalo Tavern, which Chris owned with Eric Hudson. Before purchasing Tumalo Tavern in 2002, Chris had worked in sales at Gallo winery, tended bar at Rogue Brewery at its original location in Ashland, and spent three years in high tech.

Founded in 1994 by three brothers who built most of the original equipment by hand, Cascade Lakes was a brewing company in an industrial area near the Redmond airport. In 2000 the brothers sold  the company to partners, Rick Orazetti and Doug Kutella, who have since added a forth partner, Ron Kutella, and five locations, all with their own special appeal. Not all partners are involved in all locations.

Each location is distinctive, appealing to different clientele. The brewery is still a brewery, no pub there. Using a twenty barrel system, Mark Henion heads up the brew crew. In 2006 a bottling line was added and 2009 it was reconfigured to allow for twenty-two ounce bottles. The two fifty barrel

fermenters and two new bright tanks added in 2005 apparently were not able to keep up, requiring Cascade Lakes to add two custom seventy barrel fermenters in 2007.

The 7th Street Brewhouse came about in 1997 because of the fantastic response to Cascade Lakes' brews. This family friendly pub offers pizza to go, horseshoe pits, garage doors leading to the patio, a mug club, taco Tuesdays, and a full bar.

Red Dog Depot, also in Redmond, is what Cascade Lakes refers to as their "dog bar." On the heated, dog-friendly patio, even the pooches are catered to. But from reading reviews, it is the amazing depot burger which is the human favorite. What I find fascinating is the history of the building. This 2,263 square-foot, stone building, which was built in 1912, was originally the Redmond Railroad depot. In 2004 Cascade Lakes had the building dismantled stone-by-stone and moved two miles down the road to its current location. Decorating every wall is a plethora of dog pictures, which have been enthusiastically donated by local pooch owners.

Cascade West is everything a bar should be. For those us who are history buffs, it has a long and varied history. Built in 1954 as a garage, at least three additions have increased its size to its current 4000 square feet. Lighted mostly by the forty neon point-of-sale signs on the walls and ceiling, there are also four pool tables (free on Sundays), two

Upstairs at the Lodge

The bar at the Lodge

Golden Tee golf machines, darts, six televisions, Oregon Lotto games, a fireplace, a full bar, and 32 beers on tap (the most in Central Oregon). In addition to all of this, in celebration of NASCAR, there is a model of Bud's #8 Dale Jr. car. Andy Dyke, one of CW's customers, built the car to NASCAR exterior specifications.

Tumalo Tavern, or T.T. as the locals call it, was built in the spring of 2002. Cascade Lakes considers this their honky-tonk. Besides Wednesday pool tournaments, the T.T. offers a full bar, pool tables, video games, Golden Tee, Oregon Lotto games, and free pool on Sundays.

The Lodge, where we met with Chris for our interview, is the most recent addition to the Cascade Lakes family of pubs. This 6000 square foot building capitalizes on the Bend ski and outdoor theme with its ski chalet feel. A two sided fireplace allows plenty of fireside dining. Pool tables, video machines, Oregon Lotto, and darts are all in the open upstairs, so the main floor

Fireside seating at the Lodge

allows for peaceful dining, with the full-service bar at one end of the room.

In addition to being the second brewery established in Central Oregon (Deschutes was the first), Cascade Lakes has ranked as the tenth largest brewery in Oregon for the last six years.

Winter ski conditions are available at the Lodge

Coalition Brewing Company

2724 SE Ankeny
Portland, Oregon 97214
503-894-8080
www.coalitionbrewing.com

*"Bringing the Community Together
Through Beer"*

It was serendipitous that brewer, Elan Walsky was working at F.H. Steinbart's on the same day that Kiley Hoyt, also a brewer, chose to shop there. Both brewers had attended the Sieble Institute in Chicago. Both were interested in starting a business. As they began chatting, they found their common background, goals, and even brewery name plans matched. One thing led to another and...you got it, Portland would have a new brewery!

Elan, a former insurance salesman, began homebrewing as a hobby to remain sane in the insurance business. While at F.H. Steinbart's shopping for brewing supplies, Elan overheard them talking about needing help; after boldly telling them he was the man for the job, they hired him. However, Elan's long-term goal was to open a brewery named Hobo Brewing.

Kiley, as distribution manager for a coffee company, had recently been transferred to Portland from the east coast. Eight days after arriving, they laid her off! She then took matters into her own hands and filed an LLC with the name Hobo Brewing Company, the first step in fulfilling her dream. As a person without a job, she felt Hobo was an applicable name. That is when she met Elan.

Kiley

The new partners began looking for a space to house their new business. Originally thinking they would start a production brewery, they were searching for a basement space. Then Kiley found the location on the corner of 28th and Ankeny. It had everything for a brewpub: garage door for opening to sidewalk seating, a loading dock, ventilation, the list goes on.

While original plans called for putting the brewery upstairs,  when they were submitted it was determined that the enormous weight of a brewery would be too much for the second story of the building. With this revelation, thoughts turned to the storage shed in the back of the business. Unfortunately, the $70,000 price tag to get water and sewer set up in it prohibited that idea from working. As a result, they crossed the street to a sight formerly occupied by a call center, which was a perfect space for the brewery.

The large brewery space also allowed them to exchange their initial plan to put in a 3.5 barrel brewery for a ten barrel brewery. A shiny new brewery purchased from JV Northwest, accentuated the extremely clean conditions in the brewery. Funny thing was, they told us we were there on a "dirty" day-Thursday, Friday was their "clean" day. I suggest sunglasses on Fridays.

A mutual friend suggested Elan and Kiley meet with brewer, Bruce McPhee. After working for Deschutes for more than ten years, Bruce was ready to either get out of brewing (which he really did not want) or move to a smaller, more hands on brewery. Though it was good training, hitting the "start" button and watching the beer be made was not his idea of brewing. He wanted to rediscover the "art" of brewing. The new partners were offering just the "out" he was looking for, and he took it. Though not a financial investor, Bruce is considered a partner, with a small percentage of the business, in recognition of his expertise and time investment.

Looking to advertise the new business, one of the first logo items they ordered was glasses. After their receipt, the next hurdle in getting the brewpub up and going presented itself, a lawsuit. Apparently, Hobo was already being used by a

Elan and Bruce

company in California.

This twist brought about the necessity of a different company name. Since the name was required before they could proceed with setting up the brewpub, time was of the essence. The three decided to go on a hike up a mountain and not come down until they had made a decision.

This need for a new name triggered a re-design of the business model. Their love of beer and the brewing process, coupled with their heart for, and beginnings as, homebrewers, provided the impetus for both the name and business plan, as well as one of the features that sets Coalition Brewing apart.

Coalator brews brewing

Coalition Brewing's Coalator program allows homebrewers the opportunity to brew with Coalition on their ten gallon pilot system. When ready, the Coalator beer is then served in the pub. This program has been received with enthusiasm by both homebrewers and Coalition patrons. While the previous record for the ten gallons of Coalator brew

Salvaged bar wood from 1920

to disappear when served at the pub was about two hours, it was soundly beaten by *New School Beer* blogger Ezra Johnson-Greenough's peanut butter/chocolate beer served on Halloween, which vanished in an astounding thirty minutes!

One of the few things Coalition did not have to work hard for was their bar. It was already in the building, left there by Noble Rot Wine Bar when they relocated. Like many bars, it has a story. In 1920 a ship loaded with timber and bound for Japan sank just outside Walapai Bay in Washington. There it remained until 1980 when it was salvaged. The top of the bar is made from that salvaged lumber.

While the set up of the brewery took on a life of its own, much bigger than originally planned, the trio have been so busy they have not had the time to stop and fret over it. Bruce, as head brewer, has taken Elan on as his intern, since he lacked professional hands-on experience.

From the sound of things, Elan is getting plenty of practice. The two put out over two hundred barrels of beer in their first five months of production. Just before our interview they had brewed twenty-three batches in succession.

In this brewpub besot with bumps in the road, the brewing was not without its own bump. On their first brew day, when all was ready, they filled the mill with grain, only to have it seize up. Turned out, the auger was rotating the wrong direction. Once again, the bump was traversed and things are going well.

Aside from the unusual names, including a red named for the neighborhood cat, a stout named for their general contractor (Hans Arenz, who they say was a gift, tolerant and helpful), a pale ale named Mr. Pigs, Coalition also makes a porter, Loving Cup Maple Porter which includes real Vermont maple syrup, which, as a Vermonter, is Kiley's favorite – she loves maple syrup more than anything.

In addition to enjoying experimentation in the brewery, and encouraging the Coalators to experiment, Coalition also supports experimentation in the kitchen. While we were there, one of the chefs, Jonathan Koreski came out with an artichoke dip with baked bagel slices that he had been working on for everyone to test. Yum...

Grain Mill

With no deep fryer by choice, Coalition serves simple pub food, though not the traditional pub choices. Pininis, finger foods, salads, and soups form the base of their menu, but remember, these are not necessarily in the conventional forms you may expect. Additionally, Coalition tries to incorporate wort, the liquid extraction from the mashing process of brewing, in several of their

Inside the Mash Tun

recipes. After all, this is a pub, shouldn't beer, or some form of it, be in nearly everything? Most unusual is the variety of homemade foods coming out of the kitchen, including jerky, sausage, and ice cream. Also, you may depend on all meats coming from "local, happy places. ☺"

What does coalition see down the road? Most immediately, they had an appointment after our interview with the folks at Laurelwood to learn about their work with Green Bottling Company. While they would like to eventually have distribution throughout the Northwest, they have no designs on going national.

Their focus is on the local neighborhood based brewpub, and the local Portland market. Hoping the community will see and sense their pride and passion, they said, "Our desire is to provide the best beer we can for the local market." Toward that end, an outdoor patio is in the works. Beyond that, the three

Coalition uses only whole flower hops.

see themselves down the road entering the craft spirits market. Coalition Rum? It has a ring to it!

This family-friendly pub wants the public to know "We're here. Come try our beer, because you'll be back."

**Columbia River Brewing
Company**

1728 NE 40th Avenue
Portland, OR 97203
503-810-7920
www.occidentalbrewing.com

*"Come try us out; everyone who has is
blown away"*

When Rick Burkhart makes a decision, things start happening. After working for Sears as a distribution business manager for thirty-seven years, he was done. He had spent the final two years of his tenure at Sears searching for the right location for his brewpub, when Laurelwood moved and their old location came available, he knew he had finally found it. He took ownership on July 7, 2010, hired a full staff, and opened July 9th. Wow!

This all started in the early 1970s when he went to England to visit his wife's family. While there, he fell in love with the beer. Talking to a pub owner, he learned about Free House, where the public can brew with a brewmaster. Rick spent almost half of their three week vacation brewing beer. He was hooked.

Upon their departure from England, his in-laws provided an old steamer trunk filled with hops, dry yeast, malts, and books – as well as two Wilkinson swords – as a gift. The trip through customs was termed as "quite interesting."

Rick was so hooked on brewing, he wanted to move to England. His wife, who had moved to the U.S. at the age of thirteen, said "No." With three children, they could not just uproot them to move to a different country.

With homebrewing not yet "available" in the States, when Rick ran out of ingredients he had no way to replenish them. Finally a beer supply store opened in San Jose - a full two years later. The store would special-order grain for Rick, which he would then crush using a rolling pin.

Time did not diminish Rick's

In our early morning interview, owner Rick Burkhart told us, "What separates us from the masses is not a unique style, but the way we build them."

enthusiasm for brewing. In 2006 Rick purchased a sixteen thousand dollar homebrew system which includes a microprocessor, a dump station, a complete sparge arm, and temperature control. This system is now used for experimental batches at Columbia River Brewing.

The old Laurelwood brew system came with the location.

A perfectionist, Rick works with a recipe until he has total control. Using just the right yeast and knowing what they do; maintaining constant mash temperatures; not adding additional sugars to raise gravity, which affects flavors; Rick tests and trials until he can embrace the resulting brew with enthusiasm and pride. But no brew is complete until it has passed the father-in-law test. As Rick's harshest critic, and British to boot, he is not one to hold back, he tells it like it is, so Rick runs everything by him first.

Columbia River Brewing's beers have been well received. According to Rick, when Portland beer writer, John Foyston visited and tried all twelve Columbia's standard beers, he could not find a flaw in any of them. The on-line reviews are also quite complementary. Additional evidence of this was received when at the December 1, 2010, Northwest Brewing News awards, held at Widmer Brewing, Columbia River received five awards: Best Golden/Light Ale, Best Belgian, a tie for Best Bock/Doppelbock, Best "Other" for their Ground & Pound, and Honorable Mention for their Wheat Ale. The Madagascar Chocolate Porter served at the Holiday Ale Festival also received accolades.

Perhaps the Belgian honor stems from the yeast strain Rick uses. A temperamental strain, used by very few brewers, Rick learned to control it years ago. Though many people think he adds spices to the Belgian, he does not; it is totally through control of the yeast.

With a seven barrel system, producing an anticipated 900 barrels in 2010, Rick hopes to begin bottling using a mobile

bottler sometime in 2011. There is nothing automated about the system at Columbia River. In fact, it requires paddle stirring, which Rick says has taken a total of forty-eight pounds off of him since he started brewing for Columbia River Brewing.

In charge of the kitchen is Rick's son-in-law, Josh Pickles. A Portland native, Josh attended culinary school at Western Culinary Institute in Portland where he completed a twelve month ACF accredited, Le Cordon Blue Culinary Arts program. Currently serving twists on fairly standard pub fare, the food has also received great reviews.

The décor at Columbia River has been there for some time. In the glassed-in brewery, there are faux Old World style blocks and ivy painted walls, left from the days when Old World Pub & Brewery was there. The basic bar and seating remain the same as when Laurelwood resided there. Remember, Columbia River Brewing opened two days after Rick took possession. Besides, this is a nice, comfortable environment the way it is.

After they began brewing, which took a few months, since they were still waiting on licenses when they opened (they served other beers to start), Rick was concerned when he could smell the brewery from the restaurant. It was then he discovered the glassed-in brewery walls were not completely closed in, allowing the aromas from the brewery to waft though the restaurant.

When it came time for tap handles, Rick ended up going all the way to Tennessee to find someone to make them to his specifications. These adorable handles are canoe paddles with the Columbia River logo.

Rick woke with the design for Columbia River Brewing logo in his head at 2 A.M. He then had a graphic artist do the work for it. We tend to think this logo qualifies as one of the prettiest in Oregon. Of course, it is hard to go wrong with Oregon's nature.

Deschutes Brewery

901 SW Simpson Avenue
Bend, Oregon 97702
541-385-8606
www.deschutesbrewery.com

"Consistently good beer"

We knew Deschutes Brewery would be large, but admittedly, we were a bit intimidated upon seeing this amazing facility. Built in 1993, and expanded in 1999, this is a local brew pub all grown up. Yes, Deschutes began as a local brew pub in 1988 when owner Gary Fish chose Bend to open his new business.

Though his parents were both from Oregon, Gary haled from the San Francisco Bay Area. He had been looking for a place in Northern California to open his brew pub, when his parents passed through Bend after attending a college reunion in Corvallis. Acting on their suggestion, he made the trip to Bend and, obviously, chose it for his new business.

Despite a bit of a rough beginning, with ten consecutive batches going bad due to a design flaw in the location of the grain mill - in addition to the nay-sayers who insisted it would never last - Deschutes finished their first year selling 310 barrels, well over the few Gary thought they would sell to local resorts. After that, as he told us, "We got caught up in the growth of the industry and the area. We didn't have to sell the first few years, people just bought!" As he further stated, "We were in the right place at the right time."

From the beginning Deschutes hired brew masters. With a background in restaurants, unlike many in the business, Gary did not start as a home brewer. In fact,

Owner, Gary Fish, showing us the brewery

he learned it as part of the business process. What he may have lacked in beer knowledge, he obviously made up for in business knowledge.

This privately owned company now employs 280 people, of which 100 are in Portland. At the time of our interview, Deschutes could be found in fourteen states, but according to Gary, "The adventure is not

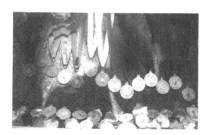

A few of the medals on desplay at Deschutes

over, in some ways it's just getting started." With an eye toward aggressive growth in the coming years, going national is a long-term goal. Gary's business expertise is exampled in the 1997 Oregonian interview when he was quoted as saying, "One of the mistakes that people in this industry made, I think, was that they tried to *create* national brands." (Italics ours) By taking it slowly and growing first locally, then regionally, Gary has shown himself as an astute businessman.

As we sat in his office, which by itself is larger than some of the breweries we toured, looking out at the amazing views, Gary told us Deschutes is more than just the way they make beer. Strong supporters of the community and the recipient of two community service awards, Deschutes has contributed more than $2.7 million to organizations in the communities where they do business. Acting as the pilot business for Volunteer Connect's Corporate Volunteer Program, Deschutes strongly encourages employees to volunteer. With more than 30 employees showing up to help build four houses for Habitat for Humanity, it seems the employees share the company community spirit.

Perhaps this shared spirit has to do with Gary's thoughts that the employees are not just employees, but co-workers; they work together as a group. All understand that while they may enjoy their work, this is not a game, it is serious business. It is the livelihood for many people and contributes a great deal to the economy.

Not a company which cuts corners based on cost, Deschutes has installed German state-of-the-art computer control technology. This gives ultimate control over everything, with consistency at a high level.

Believing that crystal clear filtration takes the flavor out of the beer, Deschutes achieves coarse filtration through the use of a centrifuge.

Using whole hops almost exclusively, which come primarily from Oregon and Washington, the number one concern at Deschutes is taste. After first developing the best beers they can, cost structure is then figured.

Quality control is taken seriously at Deschutes.

One of the areas we found intriguing during our tour was the quality control room. A small, plain, long room with several voting-style booths with stools, this is where their quality control taste testers work. Rough job, but somebody's got to do it. Tasters go through a week long training process to qualify for this hardest of jobs. Though we may speak lightly of it, this is one more example of how Deschutes takes their beer seriously. Perhaps this room and the people who work in it are why Deschutes is known for its consistently good beer.

As you enter the brewery, be sure to check out the art. Deschutes commissions a different Oregon artist to do

Each Jubelale label is, literally, a work of art.

Jubelale each year. Whether it's the art, the tasting room, the brewery, or the bottling plant, everything at Deschutes is done top-notch and is well worth the tour.

Tasting room at Deschutes

Double Mountain Brewery & Taproom
8 Fourth Street
Hood River, Oregon 97031
541-387-0042
www.doublemountainbrewery.com

"Mission Statement: Make great beer for craft beer fans."

We met with Matt Swihart early in the morning. It was a bit of a slow start for all of us. One thing about meeting early, everyone is pretty laid back and in no hurry. We did get the impression, though, that Matt is normally a fairly laid back kind of guy.

As an aerospace engineer, Matt started home brewing so he could have the beers he wanted after traveling Europe and enjoying beers there. Not finding his career in aerospace very satisfying, Matt went to work in a homebrew supply store teaching home brewing. While there, he saw an advertisement for the Siebel Institute, a brewing school in Chicago. You guessed it, Matt was off to Chicago.

It was while working at Full Sail for thirteen years that Matt met fellow employee Charlie Devereux. Charlie left Full Sail to go back East, but returned to complete his MBA at Portland State University. Like Matt had been, Charlie was unhappy in the work for which he had studied so long.

Obviously, Matt does not shy away from making big changes, so when he and Charlie would get together, they would inevitably end up discussing what Matt's next big step would be. They figured it out when Matt saw a "For Lease" sign in one of the storefronts in downtown Hood River that in times past had housed a used car sales and repair

Matt at an early morning interview

shop. With Charlie being the obvious choice for a business partner, they opened Double Mountain Brewery and Taproom just over a year later on St. Patrick's Day, 2007. Each year this anniversary/holiday is celebrated with a big party.

Focusing on creating beers they like to drink, all are non-filtered, taking a minimum of three weeks to brew, with up to a year of conditioning for some of the cask-conditioned beers before serving. Matt believes the more you filter a beer, the more you filter out the flavor. Determined to use only the finest ingredients available, Double Mountain beers are made with organic malt, which is 30-40% more expensive. The extra cost is well worth the better flavors and brewing performance obtained from organic malts, which is more the motive for their use than for the organicness. Unfortunately, Matt feels organic hops are usually of poor quality and hard to find so they are not necessarily used. However, during the hop harvest they make a point of traveling to Yakima to "rub" flowers from different fields, searching for the best aromas. According to their web site "Ours is a 'brewer's brewery,' with an uncompromising focus on quality." They must have it right; during our travels and interviews, when we asked brewers what their favorite "other" Oregon beers were, Double Mountain was overwhelmingly the most common response.

Talking grain storage

Like much of the equipment at many of the breweries, this twenty barrel brewery uses bits and pieces of many other breweries. With equipment once used at Widmer, Breckenridge, BridgePort, Great Divide, Terminal Gravity, an ice cream company in Eugene, and a company in Colorado, as well as new cylindrical fermentation vessels fabricated by AAA Metal Fabrication in The Dalles, Double Mountain should be set to meet market demand for quite some time. With a bit of help from their assistant, Kyle, a student doing distance learning at Edinburgh in Scotland, they get plenty of opportunity to do what they enjoy...brew beer. They are hoping to add bottling soon.

Charlie, originally from Connecticut, is a food guy, he loves to cook. He is responsible for not only the authentic New York style pizza, which according to Kevin King at Amnesia Brewing is the best Pizza in Oregon, but for the entire menu. The attitude for their food, like their beer, is to use the best ingredients and it will taste better.

Matt and Charlie have received a lot of encouragement and support from their old employer, Full Sail, as well as the other bigger brewers. According to Matt, a lot of this has to do

Mahogany & Copper Bar

with "People who work in and run breweries are really genuine people."

As we go from brewery to brewery, brewers speak of other brewers more as friends than competitors. These are people who are excited about their craft and happy to share it.

Inside the Taproom, there is a beautiful bar made with 100 year old mahogany and topped with copper. After finishing, the copper was rubbed with beer to create an instant aged look. Behind the bar is the obligatory mirror, wooden taps topped with a wooden hop, and a signed Buck Owens picture. The siding around the lower portion of the room is from a 15' x 20' mini building that was originally behind Double Mountain. Matt commented that he really likes the coziness of this place. Less cozy but full of fun is the large second room which still includes the original garage doors from the car repair shop, space

Originally a repair shop, the second room still includes the garage doors.

for a band, several tables, and couches. During good weather, a few tables may be found outside. Music varies: bluegrass, rock, jazz, and "bazooka band" are some of the styles that may be playing. With plenty of space for patrons, both local and the many tourists who pass through

Hood River, Double Mountain is there to stay. "A local offering," as Matt puts it.

Found on tap in most places in Hood River, Mt. Hood Meadows, and about 100 places in Portland and with nine to ten beers continually on tap in the taproom, Matt and Charlie try to keep things low-key. They concentrate on providing good beer and good pizza, then just let the product sell itself.

Draper Brewing
7752 Highway 42
Tenmile, Oregon 97481
541-580-5585

"Hand-made...artesian...small batches"

Surprisingly, our interview on December 3, 2010, with Sam Eslinger, owner/brewer of Draper Brewing in Tenmile, and the only brewer personally appearing at the Umpqua Brew Fest, was his first interview.

This thirty-three year old, like many, started as a homebrewer. After ten years, Sam's decision to make the leap to commercial brewing led him to employment at the Sacramento location of the chain BJ's Restaurant & Brewery. BJ's provided training for Sam through the American Brewer's Guild's intensive brewing science and engineering program where at thirty, he was actually considered the old guy in the class. After a six-month internship at Six Rivers Brewing in McKinleyville, California, Sam relocated to Lost Coast Brewery in Eureka, California.

It was encouragement from his parents that drove Sam to open Draper Brewing in July 2010. Their idea... move into the second house on their property in Tenmile, set up the brewery in the shop, and avoid many of the start-up costs and large loans that frequently hamper new breweries. This choice provided the advantage of ten acres of organically grown fruit trees, berry bushes and vines, as well as room to grow some of his own hops. Additionally, the spent grains from the brewery make great compost for the gardens.

The short answer when asked where the name "Draper" came from is that it is Sam's middle name. The

Sam Eslinger

more complete answer is that as his grandmother's maiden name, family tradition calls for one child in each generation to be given Draper as a middle name. Though Sam's initial idea was to name the brewery

Eslinger Brewing, there was an Esslinger Brewing in Pennsylvania from 1897 to 1964 and he was concerned about possible confusion and potential trademark violation, so rejected that plan in favor of Draper.

Continuing with the family theme in his design of the Draper label, Sam drew on the family crest for inspiration. The tortoise with wings means "patience," something Sam may have to draw on as a brewer.

At the time of our interview, Sam was still brewing on a three-tier, one

The "new" grundy.

barrel system. Though this system has been good for getting the Draper name out and experimenting with recipes, it will not pay the bills. Those bills may soon get easier to pay for this full-time brewer. Though he had only been selling Draper beers for three months, Sam was excited to show us his newly acquired equipment. When Umpqua Brewery went out of business, Steve at Harvest Store in Winston acquired their grundies. A local winery used them for a while, then Steve sold them to a potential brewery which fell through, leaving them sitting in storage until Sam started looking for equipment. The grundies with a history, as well as a heat exchanger that once called Seven Brides Brewery home, are now patiently waiting for Sam, who has a history in construction, to complete the walls for his new brew room.

While finding it difficult to build and brew at the same time, Sam is "having a blast." The evening we visited, he and a couple of friends were hand bottling his latest batch. According to his friends, there is a definite perk to helping Sam bottle...beer! Undoubtedly, good company is an additional bonus.

Until he gets the new equipment up and brewing, Draper is

Hand bottling at Draper

available only in bottles and can be found at Harvest Store in Winston, Pyrenees Vineyard & Cellars in Myrtle Creek, Belmont Station in Portland, and The Beer Stein in Eugene. While not yet comfortable with or ready to use a mobile bottling service, Sam sees it as a possibility on the horizon. Once

Ready to keg

the new equipment is brewing, Draper will be kegged, making it available on tap. Also a possibility in the future is 'Draper in a can,' an idea Sam says makes sense by reason of reduced light damage.

With Draper's location in the heart of Umpqua wine country, there is a wide availability of wine barrels for use in barrel aged beers. Sam has plans to take advantage of those barrels as well as the ready availability of fruits grown on the Eslinger property and around Douglas County. Leaning toward Belgium and esoteric beers such as barrel aged, fruit, and sour beers, Sam takes pride in the use of real ingredients in his beers, using no imitation flavorings. In addition to the readily available fresh fruits, Draper chocolate beers use real coco nibs.

Unlike many start-ups, Sam has no aspirations to become the next Deschutes or Ninkasi. Preferring to stay small, which allows him to play with flavors and avoid large loans, the possibility of an eventual tasting room in town does appeal to him. But for now he is content with the immediate plans to finish walls, to start brewing on the new equipment, to begin kegging, and to continue experimenting with recipes.

Barrel aging

Sam, serving samples at the Umpqua Brew Fest

Fanno Creek Brew Pub

12562 SW Main Street
Tigard, Oregon 97223
503-624-9400
www.maxsfannocreek.com

"Your community gathering place"

When Marvin Bowen retired from his work as a certified public accountant in 1990, he just could not stop; he had to keep doing something. Since then, he has found many things to do. By the Sea of Cortez in Mexico, he managed an art gallery. Then he spent some time remodeling houses. Working as the assistant superintendent for a construction company, he was involved in building the Nike expansion.

So how did this guy with such varied life experiences end up owning a brewpub? He has no idea! Though he had no experience in the restaurant business, during his time living and traveling in Mexico, where he has driven in twenty-nine of the thirty-one states, he and his wife

Marvin Bowen

learned to cook the food. Thinking they would open a Mexican restaurant, Marvin spent about three months negotiating a lease on a location only three blocks from their home. After finally coming to an agreement and signing a lease, Marvin returned to the new restaurant sight, only to discover that the owner had made many interior changes without notifying him, thus invalidating the lease.

Instead, they ended up leasing a former paint store, with only two little offices and a bathroom. By this time the Mexican restaurant idea had been abandoned, with a brewpub somehow taking its place. Did he have vast homebrew experience? No. In fact, his only foray into homebrewing was in college, when he and friends used a peculiar recipe which included brown sugar and sliced potatoes, which was bottled and caped within three hours and ready to drink four days later.

Turning the paint store into a brewpub was not an easy feat. With the only plumbing being to the small bathroom, they first had to cut out the concrete floor to add water and sewer. For breweries, this usually includes a drain trench in a sloped floor.

Installing a ten barrel JV system from outside of Dallas, Texas, where it was used by Big Horn Brewing Company, part of the Ram International Restaurant chain, and five fermenters,

Brewhouse

Marvin needed a brewer. He turned to Jason Webb, a German certified brewer with fourteen years brewing experience, the last six at Saxer Brewing in Portland (merged with MacTarnahan's and no longer produced) as head brewer. While Jason has since left Fanno Creek to open his own homebrew supply/pub with his dad, Portland U-Brew – aka P.U.B., most of the recipes used at Fanno Creek are still Jason's.

When we visited in December 2010, new brewer, Cole Hackbarth, had just started brewing for Fanno Creek. An Oregon State fermentation science graduate, Cole came to them from Full Sail Brewing in Hood River, where he had worked for three years.

New Brewer, Cole Hackbarth

Opening on May 3, 2007, Max's Fanno Creek Brew Pub is a family friendly restaurant all hours they are open and includes a children's play area, though children are not allowed around the bar, of course.

Marvin's easy going wife, Connie, runs the kitchen and is in charge of recipes and quality control, plus takes care of the office work, other than the accounting, which CPA Marvin does. Connie has the confidence it takes to manage both the kitchen and her strong-willed husband.

Looking for consistency in product, Fanno Creek purchases ingredients from restaurant supplier, Sysco. They also use trans fat-free vegetable oil, Painted Hills beef, and free range chicken. While Fanno Creek has a large standard pub menu, they occasionally serve Mexican food as nightly specials. When they served it for their anniversary, they were told by a patron that it was the best Mexican food they had ever tasted. One disadvantage of having nightly specials is that the customers keep wanting to see them added to the menu, which is how it has grown to its current size.

A comfortable conversation pit

Marvin says the restaurant is a jealous mistress. Though he and Connie used to travel a great deal, they have only left the state twice in the last four years. Nevertheless, they enjoy what they are doing. After a short period when staffing problems rocked the boat a bit, they now have a good staff in place, which brings back the fun.

In addition to the spacious restaurant, which seats 145, and outdoor seating for seventy-two, Fanno Creek has just opened a gathering room in the back, which seats fifty. Available for use without additional charge, a beautiful and unusual scenic mural adorns one wall. In this mural, by Catalina Cooper, a close look at the hops discloses that they are actually mugs of beer and a glance at the clouds reveals figures and the word

The gathering room and its mural

"beer."

The importance of art in the Bowens' lives is apparent throughout the restaurant. Additional murals, painted by Jai Ferrier, as well as another by Catalina Cooper cover the columns and a couple of walls. Unusual back-of-glass paintings by local artist, Ryan Burpot decorate the walls, and a bronze eagle-the symbol of freedom- guards the front entrance while an astounding bronze statue of children reflects the play area. Above the children's play area is a kite, but not just any kite. Marvin and Connie

were thrilled to find it laying on a bed at an auction. History buffs will appreciate the World War II target kite. Developed by Paul Garber to train fighter pilots, these maneuverable kites gave the ability to train pilots in aerial combat. This same Paul Garber had a significant role in the creation of the National Air and Space Museum, and was its first curator.

Another item of interest, with a history of its own, is the extraordinary bar. Made from 600 year old hemlock, which spent an

estimated one hundred years plus at the bottom of the Columbia River before being logged out by an underwater logging company, the wood is a sight to behold. With what looks like curly-cues interspersed throughout the wood, an aberration which is believed to be caused by a fungus, the bar was assembled with wooden doweling, there were no screws used. The purple heart trim, a hardwood from South America, serves as a fitting frame for this majestic piece of art. Master woodworker, Speed Carter, built this one-of-a-kind bar, though according to Marvin, his name is a bit of irony, as everything he does is slow.

Fanno Creek is known for its Nano Brewfest. Hosting two, one in the winter and one in the summer, they welcome some of the smaller breweries in the state to share their brews in a less crowded environment than can be found at some of the larger, more well known festivals.

While Fanno Creek may do a couple of festivals, competitions are not their thing,. "We have good beers, I know that." They do not feel the need to have that knowledge substantiated by awards.

By the way, while you are there, look for Sasquatch in the mural on the post.

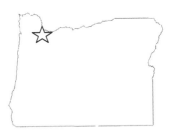

Fearless Brewing Company

326 S Broadway Street
Estacada, Oregon 97023
503-630-2337
www.fearless1.com

*"Made from the Magical waters of the
Clackamas River"*

ЬRЕШiПg СОМРАПУ

Ken Johnson's wife thought he spent too much time working and needed a hobby, so she bought him a homebrew kit for Christmas. It worked. Growing beyond the kit, soon Ken was winning every homebrew competition he entered.

As president of his own corporation, an automotive engine part distribution business, he began looking for a new line of work when people stopped having engines rebuilt. Engines then became his hobby. Although he tried for a job at many breweries, no one would hire him, he was simply too old, he says. They could not understand why the president of a corporation would want to scoop grain for seven dollars an hour.

At that time, in late 2002, many small breweries tried and failed, leaving an ample supply of used equipment available. Ken and his wife, Bennett, decided they would hire themselves...and Fearless Brewing Company was born.

While there are many who question if "Fearless" is an attitude, it was actually Ken's nickname as a child and

Fearless owner, Ken Johnson
Photo courtesy Fearless Brewing, used by permission

seemed the logical choice for the name of the new brewery. He had attached it to the front of each and every beer name when entering homebrew competitions and it had worked well.

Ken, a Scandinavian farm boy from Nebraska, says he is the first Johnson to have a "job" in two-hundred years. Coming from a long line of farmers – in fact, his grandfather died on the same farm on which he was born – he still misses farming. While he and his father had once farmed a thousand acres, most of which is now out of the family, suffering as many

Fearless fermentation tanks
Photo courtesy of Fearless Brewing, used by permission

farmers did in the early 1980s. Not all was lost though; Ken's sister still lives on the family's original 160 acre homestead.

As a boy, Ken was crazy about cars and drag racing. Though his mother begged him to go to college, he hated school and had no desire for college. A compromise was found in a tech school. In this way, Ken could follow his passion, go to school, and be able to use his expertise to keep the equipment running on the farm.

With the demise of the family farm, Ken chose the engine part business, which was a great way to supplement his drag-racing habit. Running the division-six circuit a couple of times a year kept him quite busy, but then Bennett had to go and buy that homebrew kit.

Fearless Brewing was, like many breweries, started on a shoestring. After incorporating on June 1, 2001, Ken began transforming the cast-off brewing equipment into a real brewery. After setting up shop in the old Ace Hardware building, the first Fearless batch was brewed on May 18, 2003, followed by the opening of the Fearless pub on June 6, 2003.

Brewing on a seven barrel system, it is surprising that as a homebrewer Ken entered many competitions, but as a professional Fearless enters no competitions. Maybe it has something to do with selling every drop he can make; maybe it is more that Ken *knows* he makes great

Fearless interior
Photo courtesy Fearless Brewing, used by permission

beer and does not need judges' opinions to tell him.

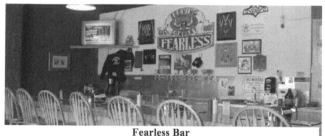

Fearless Bar
Photo courtesy of Fearless Brewing, used by permission

Being a generous person, Ken shares brewing responsibilities with brewer, Josh Riggs. Originally hailing from New York, Josh came to Fearless from Mt. Shasta Brewing Company, in Weed, California. Demand requires a sort of relay system as they brew six days per week at Fearless.

Embracing a style most brewers in the Northwest have eschewed, Fearless specialized in Scottish Ales. Never fear, Fearless still provides the usuals, like IPA. Unique because of the long boil of the mash, which creates carmelization, well-done Scottish ales have a big carmel body without being sweet. With hops not growing well in Scotland, Scottish ales are not highly hopped.

Ken's idea is that people approach craft beers in thousands of ways, from the artistic approach at one end, to the technical approach at the other. While the artist approaches brewing from a crafty standpoint,

Photo courtesy Fearless Brewing, used by permission

wanting to "create," the technician views brewing more from a scientific approach. Ken falls more on the technical end of the spectrum, expecting excellent and consistent beer every time he brews.

Available throughout the seven counties around Portland on tap and in cans, and in Eugene's better bottle shops, as well as Corvallis Brewing Supply, Fearless is looking to expand their distribution. A full list of locations carrying Fearless can be found on their website.

When asked why they chose to can, rather than bottle, their beer, Ken says it results in better beer, with no light damage, faster chilling, and less dissolved oxygen than bottles. Additionally, fully half the bottles in store coolers are not recyclable and those that are use four times the energy over cans for recycling. With all the cans being recyclable, they are a

Brewers Ken Johnson and Josh Riggs
Photo courtesy Fearless Brewing, used by permission

greener choice. One advantage of cans is initially a disadvantage: though canning is overall less expensive than bottling, start-up costs for canning can be quite expensive. Companies simply cannot purchase a few cases of cans, like they do with bottles. Cans must be purchased by the boxcar. Okay, you can get a half a boxcar if you want to pay a $1500 penalty. Then after you get the cans, there are storage issues; twelve pallets which are nine feet high take considerable storage space.

Gracing the front of Fearless cans is their logo, a Viking, in celebration of Ken's heritage. This Viking has a name, Sven. Named for Ken's childhood imaginary friend, Sven is a favorite among Fearless patrons. Keeping it in the family, the can label was designed by Ken's wife, Bennett.

Going for an old, family atmosphere in this family-friendly pub, and being on a constricted budget, the walls at Fearless are lined with family photos. All of the booths, the tables, and the bar were made by Ken. With chairs and couches forming seating groups, feel free to get comfortable and stay awhile.

Unlike the engine parts business, where he was rather isolated, Ken says the best thing about Fearless is meeting all the people and making them happy. "We would not exist if not for our fantastic customers."

When asked about his goal, Ken says "I want people to drink my beer and go…'Wow!' … I want them to be at work at the end of the day and be scared to death they are not going to get out of the building fast enough when coming to get that beer on the way home."

FIRE MOUNTAIN BREW HOUSE

Fire Mountain Brewery

10800 NW Rex Brown Road
Carlton, Oregon 97111
503-852-7378
www.firemountainbrewery.com

"Bottom line...do it for the people"

Hidden in the hills outside Carlton, Fire Mountain Brewery eluded Nuvi, our GPS. Oh, she knew where it was all right, but instead of taking us the shortest, most direct route, she took us over the mountain. We figured she had led us astray when we found ourselves on a logging road. Soon after Bob said we were going to come to a gate at any moment, we rounded a corner, and there it was, a locked gate! After turning around, we drove down the mountain, followed the picture on Nuvi, ignoring her insistence that we turn around, and discovered it should have been a short drive. In our comedy of errors, as we arrived, we learned that owner/brewer, Henry Gorgas had been called away on an

Fresh hops at Fire Mountain
Photo courtesy of Fire Mountain Brewing, used by permission

emergency, which actually was a relief, since by this time, we barely had enough time to make it to our next interview. Moral of the story, don't trust your GPS to lead you there when visiting Fire Mountain.

While still a homebrewer, Henry was attempting to come up with a name. He had narrowed the choices to three. Brewing outside, watching the boil, keeping an eye on the flame, yet still taking in the beautiful views from their mountain home, he knew he had the name when, prophetically, the song *Fire on the Mountain*, by the Grateful Dead came on the radio. It all fit. Henry had his brewery name, Fire Mountain.

As a custom airplane builder, Henry Gorgas was particular, meticulous, picky - okay, call a spade a spade - he was anal! This same trait came in "handy" when doing other creative things, like building his own log home. It followed that when he began homebrewing in 1999, this attribute would brew also.

Photo courtesy Fire Mountain Brewery, used by permission

While building the kitchen for their log home, Henry was discussing the granite countertops with the salesman when they began discussing the salesman's hobby, homebrewing. By the time he had those countertops, Henry also had a new hobby. Henry says his very first brew, all-grain, by-the-way, tasted very much like a Guinness Extra Stout. He was hooked.

Led by *The Big Book of Homebrewing*, by David Line, a new problem arose. Henry soon found the five gallon system he was brewing on was too small, so he upped it to a twenty-five gallon system. Before he knew it, he outgrew the newer, larger system. Friends advised him to sell his beer.

As those of us who are baby boomers know, the body just does not stay as young as the mind. Though Henry enjoyed building custom aircraft, it was becoming more and more difficult for him to do the physical maneuvering necessary for building aircraft.

With the encouragement from his friends added to the rebellion of an aging body, Henry spent 2006 considering the idea of going commercial. Making the decision in 2007, Henry began the mountains of paperwork required by the various agencies. In 2008, the used brew equipment arrived from New Mexico, in less than perfect condition. After doing a great many

Brewhouse
Photo courtesy Fire Mountain, used by permission

repairs, and armed with the many recipes he had written in the blank

Cool Growlers
Photo courtesy Fire Mountain, used by permission

spots in the "Big" book, Fire Mountain finally brewed their first commercial batch of beer.

Since that first "Big" book, Henry has referenced many brewing books. Though he may have grown past it, the *Big Book* is still with him as a keepsake. While he is continuously trying to learn more about his craft, what Henry has not done is take formal brewing classes. He is not interested in doing what everyone else does in the same way they do it. Likening it to hearing a song and picturing it however you wish, but then seeing the video and forevermore picturing the song as shown on video. He wants to create his own "video/beer," not someone elses.

Now brewing on a fifteen barrel system, with three fermenters, Henry and his assistant, Henry Dietzman, who has been there for every batch of Fire Mountain ever brewed, work well together. Until he can invest in more fermenters, brewing will be limited to one time per week, since Henry leaves all of his beers to ferment for two or three weeks before moving them to the bright tanks. With the way production has increased from year to year, Fire Mountain may soon need to obtain a forth fermenter. 2009 saw Fire Mountain produce thirty-nine barrels. 2010 followed with eighty-seven barrels. Henry expects 2011 production to double 2010.

Available in on tap and in bottles, Fire Mountain can be found at select locations from Portland to Ashland, plus in Long Beach, Washington. With Henry planning a trip to Vancouver the week after this writing, expectations are that it will be available in Vancouver by the time you read this. Longer range plans call for Fire Mountain to make its way to Seattle.

When we asked Henry what his dream is, he said "To be thirty years younger!" We know the feeling. More seriously, he just wants to make a living and put out a good beer.

That same sense of humor showed itself when we asked what makes Fire Mountain special. Henry's tongue-in-cheek answer, "I brew it!" Brewed by hand the old school way, with no buttons to push, Henry premixes the grain before putting it through the grinder to make stirring the mash easier. Leaving the mash longer, at a lower temperature than most, creates more grain flavor, according to Henry.

While Henry has learned that brewing is still a very physical job, he enjoys it immensely. Most amazing to him has been the calls he get from people who have tried Fire Mountain wanting to thank him for brewing it.

Tours are available Sundays 11-6. Perhaps you will be there in time to try Fire Mountain's newest brew, Bogart, which has a tagline of "Don't bogart the Bogart, share it with friends."

Flat Tail Brewing
202 SW 1st Street
Corvallis, Oregon 97333
541-758-2229
www.duncanculinary.com

"A home for Beaver believers"

The early morning interview was easy for us to remember, this was what the whole trip was about; but unfortunately, it was missed in Flat Tail Brewing partner, Iain Duncan's busy schedule. After leaving a note on the door, we continued on to our next interview. Thankfully, when Iain's wife and partner, Tonya, found the note, she called and we made arrangements to fit Flat Tail in. This was a challenge, since we were scheduled back to back, but we managed to work them back into the schedule, so we dropped back by for a micro-interview (pun intended). While it did make for a very short dialogue, Tonya certainly made up for it by sending us away with a couple of wonderful and tasty wraps for lunch.

Owners of three other restaurants in downtown Corvallis, and a trained Chef, Iain and Tonya have provided a diverse culinary selection for residents since 2005. With Le Bistro serving Country French cuisine, Terzo specializing in West Coast Italian, and Aqua serving Hawaiian Regional cuisine, they not only had enough to  keep them busy, but variety as well.

While renovating the Le Bistro location, the couple spent time at the Fox & Firkin, which was just across the alley. Iain was drawn to it and was amazed by the great location. Opportunity presented itself when Fox & Firkin closed their doors in January 2009.

Partnering with Laura Bryngelson and Mark Martin, owners of Calapooia Brewing Company and Siletz Brewing Company in Albany, Iain and Tonya purchased the 10,000 square foot building that summer. The English tavern look of the Fox & Firkin was soon transformed into an Oregon State sports theme. With plans to cater to University students, alumni, staff, and Beaver fans in general, the partners' plan was to turn Flat Tail into "Beaver Believer Central." With no other Beaver-oriented sports bars in this college town of almost 55,000, acceptance has been swift.

Even the exterior of Flat Tail has received a good reception. As a 2010 Downtown Corvallis Association Award recipient, the partners at Flat Tail received recognition for their efforts toward improving the downtown area. This seems to be par for the course, as the Duncans had previously received the same award for their efforts at Le Bistro.

Obviously, we cannot fail to mention that the building is not the only thing at Flat Tail winning awards. As the winners of the People's Choice Award at the 2011 KLCC Microbrew Festival, Flat Tail has proven that they are a contender in Oregon's brewing industry. Unfortunately, the beer that won the award, *Licentious Goat*, was a special, and according to their Facebook entry made just a few hours before I wrote this, the last keg in existence would be tapped at Belmont Station, in Portland, on April 30, 2011. Hopefully, the Goat will return.

Brewer, Dave Marliave

Return or not, kudos are definitely due to Flat Tail brewmaster, Dave Marliave. With Flat Tail since February 2010 (when they opened),

Dave brewed the first Flat Tail batch in July. Before that, Flat Tail was contract brewed by Calapooia Brewing in Albany.

Dave, at 23, is one of the youngest brewmasters in the state, and had completed three-fourths of his fermentation science degree at Oregon State before being offered a brewer's job at Oregon Trail Brewing. While he is a bit busy at Flat Tail these days, his pipe-dream is to complete that degree. In the meantime, he's living his dream. Along the way, he also helped get Fire Mountain Brew House up and going.

Brewing on a seven barrel system, tribute is paid to the building's origins as Corvallis Creamery (1897-1932) through use of an old dairy tank as a semi-open fermenter. The large space in Flat Tail's brewery allows for plenty of future expansion.

As we did our whirlwind interview, Flat Tail had just begun barrel-aging. Also ahead are plans for twenty-two ounce bottles, possibly by late 2011.

Until then, try a sampler paddle at Flat Tale brewpub. Take home a growler of your favorite Flat Tail brew. Cheer on a Beaver.

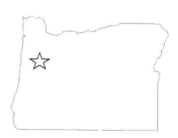

**Fort George
Brewery + Public House**

1483 Duane Street
Astoria, Oregon USA
97103
503-325-7468
www.fortgeorgebrewery.
com

"Astoria's own Brewery Block"

Founded in 1811, and originally named Fort Astoria, for John Jacob Astor of the Pacific Fur Company, this fort, built over a spring to provide water, was the first American-owned settlement on the Pacific Coast. After being sold to the British in 1813, it was renamed Fort George. Eventually declared booty of the war of 1812, the fort was returned to U.S. hands in 1818, never having been conquered.

The Fort George building was built in 1924 on the site of the old fort. Originally housing a Ford dealership and service station, the building had been vacant since the late 90s. When co-owner and brewer, Chris Nemlowill found the building, it was considered a public nuisance by the city in this once-neglected part of town. But Chris saw more than the many broken windows and pools of rancid rainwater on the floors; seeing the huge wooden beams, made from 400 year-old old-growth timber, he knew it could be exceptional.

After first asking him to consult, Chris got his actual desire

Chris was attracted to the ceilings of old-growth timber.

when he partnered with Jack Harris, who was brewmaster at Bill's Tavern in Cannon Beach. The two then leased the larger part of the ground floor of the building, with the other portion already being occupied by The Blue Scorcher, a bakery and coffee house. Assembling a group of local craftsmen and artisans, the two set about restoring the building and designing a brewpub which would exude an urban feel, while focusing on the theme of the wood that so attracted Chris.

The bar and tables were crafted by local carpenter, Barefoot Bill, using 2000 board feet of Alaskan cedar he found in a float shack near Brownsmead. Brought from Alaska with the intention of using it to

build a boat, the cedar laid unused for forty years because the builder wanted clear wood, this had knots. Bill negotiated with the owner and got it for $1500 and a bottle of Wild Turkey. Rather than using urethane, this wood is now lovingly cared for, with weekly oiling.

Interesting touches throughout the building indicate the thought put into the design of this public house. A peace sign crafted at a local forgery is of interest when one is aware that an old rifle was used to

Hand-Forged Bar Stools

make it. It would be difficult for anyone to miss the irony of a peace sign, made from a rifle, in a building which occupies the space on which a fort once stood. The stools are worth a second look. Crafted by Nathan Neil, the bottoms bear the raised likeness of the Fort George building with the business name around the edge of the iron.

An unusual recommendation on any tour, the restrooms are not

to be missed. Designed in a manner which commemorates the past, one is fashioned for the fort which once stood here, and the other celebrates the cars and auto shop which once occupied this very building. Be brave, open both doors.

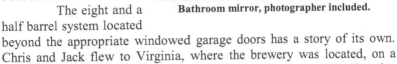

Bathroom mirror, photographer included.

The eight and a half barrel system located beyond the appropriate windowed garage doors has a story of its own. Chris and Jack flew to Virginia, where the brewery was located, on a Monday. The pair spent Tuesday figuring how to dismantle it. They dismantled it on Wednesday. Thursday it was loaded onto the U-Haul and a semi. By Friday they were on their way back to Oregon with their very own brewery. However, this trip was not meant to be so simple. On Saturday, the U-Haul started smoking and smelling like burning transmission fluid. When U-Haul sent a different truck, they had to move the entire load from a twenty-seven foot truck to a seventeen foot truck. Then, as they were driving through Nebraska, the emergency warning signal went off,

Honey, are you done taking pictures of the bathroom yet?

followed by golf ball sized hail. The sky was dark, with a green hue. Then came the funnel cloud, dyed brown from the pasture it had ripped through. Cars were stopping with the occupants taking cover in the ditch alongside the highway and the overpasses. The semi driver, who was hauling the large brew tanks, shouted to them on the CB to punch it! The next thing they knew the tornado hit the side

This brewery's been through a lot.

New artwork will greet you.

of the U-Haul. The straps on the tank broke loose and they danced on the foam that was between them. After the excitement was over, on Sunday the truck driver re-strapped the tanks and they continued their trip. Finally arriving in Astoria, after being the only brewery that has been through a tornado, it was only appropriate to christen their IPA, *Vortex*.

Using organic base malts and all organic natural yeast, many, though not all, of Fort George's brews are certified USDA organic. Though all could be, they just do not see the need to spend over $1000 per brew to get them certified. They make the best beers they can and making them organic is one way of making them better. Fort George also offers many organic foods, as well as homemade sausages from scratch, and local caught fresh fish. While we have all heard of beer samplers, Fort George also offers a sausage sampler.

Fort George has received tremendous local support since they opened March 11, 2007. In the 1970s and 80s, like many Oregon cities, this coastal town lost the mills on which they had thrived for so long.

After that, like the Fort George Building, much of the town withered. Since then, Astoria has focused on education, micro-manufacturing, and tourism. The addition of the growing microbrew industry is welcome. Fort George has recently added to the revitalization of this beautiful and historic city by purchasing the Fort George building they are housed in, as well as the adjoining property, and the adjacent 1921 Lovell Building, a 30,000 square foot building which once housed a

GM dealership. The purchase of their own "Brewery Block" was accomplished with $1.65 million, facilitated by Small Business Administration (SBA) loans.

Plans for Fort George are both long-term and extensive. Initially, they are focusing on turning the 8,000 square foot ground floor of the Lovell Building, a former repair shop, into a new production brewery and canning line. After receiving their canning line from Cask Systems in January, the first cans of Fort George's special Astoria Bicentennial beer, 1811 Lager, came off the line in March 2011. This was followed by a second canned beer, their famous Vortex IPA.

Artisan shops, including a glass blower and metal smith are planned for the second floor of the Lovell Building. Hopes for attracting like-minded businesses that will focus on the local community and history of Astoria are high. The second floor of the Fort George building

Owner/Brewer, Chris Nemlowill

will be fashioned into a barrel aging room and event space. An open-air beer garden and outdoor seating with a multi-level deck are planned for the outdoor space.

The new brewery will house a 30 barrel brew system from St. Arnold Brewing, in Houston, Texas. With a nearly fourfold increase in production capacity, Fort George should have no problem with production levels. The original Brewhouse, which survived the tornado, will remain in operation in the Fort George Building.

Chris is obviously going to have plenty of opportunity to put his degree in marketing to use. As a 2003 graduate of Southern Oregon University, he wanted to learn to brew. Like many brewers, he began by homebrewing. While studying in the Netherlands, he would go to school on Monday and Tuesday, and then spend the rest of the week researching breweries. After returning to Oregon, he brewed first at Bill's Tavern, then as head brewer at Astoria Brewing Company. Fort George Brewery + Public House is the culmination of a dream which is coming true, for Chris, for Jack, and for the city of Astoria.

Full Sail Brewing
506 Columbia Street
Hood River, Oregon 97031
541-386-2247
www.fullsailbrewing.com

"Stoked to Brew. Brewed to Stoke."

One of Oregon's oldest craft breweries, Full Sail, was founded in 1987 when a group of individuals purchased the old Diamond Fruit cannery which had stood abandoned since 1972. After fifteen years of vacancy in this old cannery, Full Sail began production and opened their taproom to patrons while still working on the renovation. While many drastic changes have occurred, much of the building still retaines the old cannery flavor.

The entrance corridor may evoke thoughts of the building's previous life as a cannery, but arrival in the Taproom will impress you with its diverse style. There is a brilliant design mixing the essence of the old cannery with a new elegance to arrive at a comfortable, up to date, yet almost stately situation, which entices patrons to relax and stay awhile. The one thing all will agree upon is that this room affords the occupants a magnificent view.

If you would rather feel a part of that glorious view, step outside to the courtyard, which is *next* to the taproom to avoid obstruction of the view. Though surrounded on three sides by building, it feels amazingly open. Perhaps this is achieved through the décor. From the impressive mosaic, to the chairs that give the appearance of sails, to the colorful three-dimensional sails on the simple mural, you are enveloped by the scenery of the Columbia and its famous wind surfing and kite boarding.

Beyond the beauty of its surroundings, Full Sail Brewing is outstanding in many ways. Ownership, environmental awareness, innovations, and awards all speak of the uniqueness of this company.

The courtyard at Full Sail offers remarkable views.

When some of the original partners chose to leave, they turned to the employees. In 1999 Full Sail became an independent, employee-owned company. Two of the original partners have remained as employee-owners, founder Irene Fermat and executive brew master James Emerson. Being employee-owned creates some unique challenges and opportunities. While there is not the access to the deep pockets (capital) that may be found in a corporate environment, these employee-owners have learned to look at efficiencies in a different way to save time and costs without sacrificing quality.

Whether as cost-cutting measures or as ecologically sound business, Full Sail has incorporated many green practices into their work and production. Though the maintenance staff works the traditional five eight-hour shifts, the brewing staff works three twelve hour shifts, with the rest of the staff working four ten-hour shifts. Not only do these non-traditional work weeks help reduce water, power, and gas consumption by 20%, but also allow employees more days off. Who wouldn't like that?

Stacks of beer, many cases high, use recycled paperboard.

Through energy efficient and saving efforts like purchasing wind energy; using recycled paperboard in packaging, glass, stretch wrap, and pallets; sending spent grain and yeast to farmers to use as feed and fertilizer; and the use of local ingredients – 85% of hops and 95% of barley come from Northwest farms, Full Sail is committed to "reducing the amount of waste and pollution that comes from running our brewery." Responsible environmental practices do not stop there. Breweries typically consume six to eight gallons of water for each gallon of beer produced; but

The Bar

not at Full Sail, where water usage has been reduced to an amazing 3.45 gallons. All of their water reduction practices have led to a savings of 3.1 million gallons of water per year. Wait, there's more! After saving all this water, Full Sail treats their own water before it goes out to the local treatment plant, reducing strain on the city sewer system.

All of this leads us to believe this employee-owned company when they say "We're dedicated to operating our brewery in the most socially and environmentally sustaining manner possible..." Their efforts have not gone unrecognized. Full Sail has received numerous awards for sustainability, including awards from the State of Oregon, Oregon Business Magazine, Treehugger.com, Recycleworks, City of Portland, Travel Oregon, and the Oregon Travel Commission.

In addition to their commitment to sustainability, Full Sail is also committed to the community. As a staunch supporter of local schools, Full Sail takes their community responsibilities seriously. This is understandable when you consider that this is an employee-owned company. These employees live in and raise their families in Hood River. Full Sail focuses this devotion locally, as a staunch supporter of over 300 charities and events.

Just a few of Full Sail's many awards

Sustainability awards are by no means the only awards garnered by Full Sail. Winner of 65 plus awards over the years, Full Sail has won several Gold Medals at the Great American Beer Festival and the Brewers Association World Beer Cup. Beginning in 1989 with their first gold medal for Full Sail Amber, which has been followed by another 13 through the years, recently their Session beers have proven to be a judge's favorite, reaping a gold collection of their own.

This hand-crafted beer is built in a 220 barrel system which uses 11-14 thousand pounds of material per batch. Brewers work in teams with one at the hot end and one at the other end on tasks such as cleaning tanks. This is done in two shifts on brew days, allowing for four brews each day. Full sail uses a centrifuge for primary clarification of the beer. They prefer this method over the use of diatomaceous earth, which creates a lot of waste. Just one more indication of their sustainability practices.

Most of their beers are produced in 7 ½ hours, start to finish, the fermentation cycle is usually 2-3 weeks, though some can take months. Porter and Top Sail are both aged in oak barrels.

Big brew kettle

Though they currently produce around 180 kegs per year, Full Sail showed their innovativeness early on, by not only by producing the first Amber here in Oregon, but also the first craft beer to be bottled, something thought nearly impossible at the time. From their early bottling efforts, Full Sail is now capable of bottling up to 600 bottles per minute. On these bottles you will also find a code date for optimum flavor. But that is not the only unusual thing you will find on a Full Sail bottle. Look under the cap of Session Lager to play "rock, paper, scissors."

Bottling Line

Lab at Full Sail

Full Sail also runs a small brewery on Montgomery in Portland which uses the original brewing system from the Hood River facility. Portland brew master, John Harris, was previously a brew master at Deschutes Brewery. This Portland branch of Full Sail runs a 70 barrel system. You can see this brewery through the window.

Full Sail in Hood River offers tours daily at 1:00, 2:00, 3:00, and 4:00, on the hour. Kids 12 and over are welcome when accompanied by a parent or guardian.

Whether you go for the tour, the scenery, the food pairings with the beer, or just out of curiosity, you will not be disappointed. You will find "Great beer, a great place, and great people."

**Now that's a bright tank!
...and Bob**

Gilgamesh Brewing

2953 Ridgeway Drive
Turner, Oregon 97392
503-779-9686
www.gilgameshbrewing.com

"A Beer for Everyone"

While looking for Gilgamesh Brewing, our GPS certainly came in handy. Located at the rural Turner home of the Radtke family, Gilgamesh is housed in the building near the same home where Lee and Eileen raised their three sons, Mike, Nick, and Matt.

Lee and Eileen lived in what is now the fermenting room while they built their beautiful log home out of trees, from Eastern Oregon, which they fell themselves. The only part of the home they contracted out was the massive fireplace.

The oldest brother, Mike, was the first of the three brothers to begin homebrewing. With time, the other two brothers and Dad joined in, and through the last twelve years they have all enjoyed experimenting with flavors and recipes. One of their more successful experiments has been their "hopless" beers. Technically a "malt beverage," the Radtkes will throw in a few hops to make it a beer-with a high alcohol content.

Mike has also been the backbone of the business. He got the business going. He championed it. He came up with the recipes. And, in the beginning, he was the main brewer. But, just as they say it takes a village to raise a child, it takes a family to create a brewery-at least at Gilgamesh.

After deciding to open the brewery, the three Radtke "boys" (at the time of our interview in December 2010, they were 33-Mike, 32-Nick, and 26-Matt) did what Radtkes do, they built the brewery themselves. Of course, Dad, as facilities manager, could not watch all that "fun" and not lend a hand. By the time you read this, they will have completed their winter project of expanding the brewery, necessary after only a year in business.

Though Mom, who helps with the bookwork, initially greeted the brewery idea with a bit of reluctance, after Mamba, one of the "hopless" beers, (previously known as Black Mamba) won the People's Choice Award at the 2010 Spring Beer & Wine Fest, where it broke a record for keg sales for the event; then followed that a week later with another People's Choice Award at the 2010 Oregon Garden Brewfest; Mom definitely climbed on board.

Matt Radtke, head brewer

These awards also gave the brothers the confidence to "go for it." Up to that time they had been brewing on a one barrel system. With

Justin, on-the-go in the brewery, made it difficult to get a picture

their newfound confidence came a seven barrel brewery. This self-reliant family has taken the whole process step-by-step, not acquiring loans, which relieves much of the financial pressures, but can be far more restrictive during times of growth. When we visited, their newest acquisition was a small bottling system.

The "new" seven barrel system came from Seven Brides Brewing in Silverton, who got it from Block 15 in Corvallis. Lee, a woodworker, traded his skills for it when he used reclaimed wood to build the striking bar which now graces Seven Brides.

Currently, Matt, also a woodworker, who used to build furniture for a living, is the only full-time Gilgamesh brother, with their sole employee - and friend - Justin, assisting. Mike's full-time job keeps him busy doing sleep studies, but when he's not studying sleep, he's probably wishing he could get more of it as he is in charge of sales and does much of the paperwork for Gilgamesh. Nick, who is in charge of marketing, also has a full-time outside job doing computer programming for manufacturers.

The name Gilgamesh is from the *Epic of Gilgamesh*, among the world's earliest works of literature from Sumaria, the most complete version of which is from the library collection of an 7th-century B.C. Assyrian king. Gilgamesh, who is thought to be an actual Sumarian king from the 27th-century B.C., and his friend Enkidu, who the gods created to be the equal of Gilgamesh, undertake dangerous quests that anger the gods. In the epic, the Sumarians, who worshipped the Fermentation Goddess, Ninkasi (also a Eugene brewery), made several references to beer.

"Eat the food, Enkidu, it is the way one lives.

Drink the beer, as is the custom of the land.

Enkidu ate the food until he was sated,

he drank the beer--seven jugs!

-- and became expansive and sang with joy!"

~*Epic of Gilgamesh*

Notice the Gilgamesh logo on this Sumerian beer recipe tablet

The Gilgamesh Brewing logo looks like an arrow, though it is actually the Sumerian word for beer, which symbolized their stone fermenters. Lowering reed straws into them to drink directly from the fermenters, the beer the Sumerians drank did not contain hops. Thus came the Radtkes' desire to follow that tradition.

With "hopless" beers being quite unique-and people sometimes being resistant to trying new things- they say "Just try it!" The biggest surprise at Gilgamesh has been the positive response of the public to their beers.

Matt told us the story of California honeymooners who showed up during a big disaster. Unfortunately, being upset, the brothers were "inventing several new words" as we say in our house. The couple tried a few samples and left. When Matt ran into the couple at a Belmont Station tasting, he began apologizing, but was stopped by the couple when they said that Gilgamesh beers had made their whole trip!

Gilgamesh creates their unique beers from locally grown ingredients:

- Glisan Backyard Pale Ale, a limited release no longer available, was made from hops Matt grew in his Portland backyard. An annual maybe?
- Pumphouse Copper Ale, the water is from the pump house next to the brewery, untainted by chlorine or other added chemicals

found in city water. (Was Exbeeramental #2, was so popular they made it a year-round brew.)

- Filbert Lager, Gilgamesh Exbeeramental #1, hand-chopped Oregon filberts from neighboring Scio are added to the boil along with the hops-eight pounds per barrel!
- Chocolate Mint Stout, uses locally grown mint along with Amano Chocolate nibs
- Cranberry Saison, another "hopless" beer, uses cranberries from Bandon, where the authors met, and is aged in Port Wine Barrels.
- Honey, when used, is obtained from Albany.
- Spent grain and hops are taken down the road where they are given to a local farmer, necessitating fending off the big longhorn bull when unloading.

Because the "boys" at Gilgamesh love to experiment, they

We were greeted enthusiastically by Ted, who is lying in front of the famous-and adorable- pumphouse.

occasionally produce "exbeeramental" batches, one-off releases. When these hard to catch batches are received with exceptional enthusiasm by the public, they may graduate to the regular line-up, as was the case with Pumphouse Copper Ale. Or perhaps as seasonals, as planned for the Filbert Lager.

Another unusual beer, Mega Monster XXX Imperial IPA, uses three pounds of humulus, hop pollen, in addition to a pound and a half of hops for every barrel produced. The humulus is what makes the hop bitter (Humulus is also the scientific genus of hops). This monster with a lasting "bite" was Exbeeramental #3. As of this writing it is unknown if it will rear its monstrous head again.

What do the "boys" at Gilgamesh see in their future? In the immediate future, they hope to continue to increase their presence in

Eugene, where there has been a good response to their "hopless" beers. They are looking forward to bottling and hope to first introduce into the small bottle stores, followed by supermarkets. We loved the idea of a holiday variety six-pack. A bit farther down the road, the plan is to add cans to their line-up. In two to three years they hope to move to the Salem-Turner area with a thirty barrel system and their own brewpub...maybe even one in Portland.

Please be aware, Gilgamesh Brewing is not open to the public. Though they do have a monthly open house, when you can have your growlers filled, they are hoping to change that to every Saturday. Otherwise, be sure to call for an appointment.

Find Gilgamesh at the Salem Public Market on Saturdays!

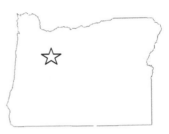

Golden Valley Brewery
Brewpub & Restaurant

980 NE 4th Street
McMinnville, Oregon 97128
503-472-2739
www.goldenvalleybrewery.com

*"People have forgotten the value of
real food – homemade food"*

In the early 1970s Peter Kircher worked restaurants in San Francisco, Texas, and Wisconsin, as a French chef. Then in 1976 he settled in Alaska, but this time he was a commercial fisherman. Finally, eleven years later, in 1987, it was time to go home; so he brought his boat with him and began fishing in Oregon. That same year, Peter purchased a seventy-six acre ranch near McMinnville, complete with a vineyard, which included pinot noir and chardonnay grapes. Finally, in 1993, Peter decided it was time to sell the boat and open a brewpub.

Originally, Peter and his wife, Celia, thought to open a big brewery with a small pub in Portland, but when the location of interest fell through, they decided to look around McMinnville, where their ranch was located. When a warehouse in the historic downtown district became available, it seemed the perfect choice.

Originally built in the 1920s as a storage warehouse for flour, it warehoused lumber in the 40's, and then became a Pepsi warehouse for a time. But in 1993, its warehouse days were over. Peter was amazed by the ancient, massive wood beams, as well as the substantial space. This would be the location for their new brewpub.

Peter Kircher

Celia, who is from Wales, helped inspire the name for the new enterprise. With family in Herefordshire's Golden Valley, Peter and Celia felt the Willamette Valley is golden/great, so they chose to draw on the name for the new brewpub. The Golden Valley of Wales has more in common than beauty with the Willamette Valley and Golden Valley Brewery. The River Dore runs through the valley, with Dore derived from the Welch word, "dwr," which means water. But the Normans confused it with the French word d'or, meaning "golden," thus, the valley became the Golden Valley. While the Willamette River's name may not have been confused with another language, it is frequently mispronounced,

The only small area in the building remaining as it was originally.

and it definitely runs through the valley. As for the brewery, what is a brewery without water? Plus, Golden Valley Brewery is unquestionably beautiful.

When Golden Valley first opened, it was not much more than a big warehouse with tables, but a lot has changed since then. In 2000 Peter and woodworker, Jim Curry, trimmed the whole place, resulting in a gorgeous restaurant, which looks like it has been well cared

Huge beams

for through decades, certainly never a warehouse. The centerpiece of this grand place is the bar.

When Peter heard about it from a contractor who was bidding on the interior work for the restaurant, he made a trip to the warehouse in Portland where it had been stored for years. Originally from the old Hoyt Hotel in Portland, this solid mahogany masterpiece stands fourteen feet high and is twenty-seven feet long. Included were the original stained glass and mirrors. When a woman who used to play piano at the Hoyt came into Golden Valley and saw this glorious relic, she was so moved she began crying.

In case you have not figured it out yet, the pub did not exactly stay small. With a seating capacity of forty in the pub, and an additional seventy in the banquet room, there is a total capacity of 300 at Golden Valley, for plenty of room in what is more of a restaurant than a pub or a

The glorious, solid mahogany bar

bar.

Serving a ratio of food to beer that is 75:25, while most pubs in Portland are 60:40, this is a family friendly restaurant where everything in the kitchen is made from scratch. There are no prepared sauces. "People have forgotten the value of real food – homemade food," Peter says. At Golden Valley they serve real food, much of it grown and produced by the Kircher family themselves.

Bob, enjoying a Golden Valley Pale Ale

The beef served at Golden Valley is raised on an all-natural program of spring-fed pastures and premium rations at the Kircher's Angus Springs Ranch, which is one of the oldest ranches in Oregon. Fed rations of spent grain from the brewery, with no hormones, antibiotic feeds, or animal by-products, these cattle are some of the finest beef in the Northwest. The beef is then processed in Carlton by Carlton Farms, who also make Golden Valley sausages from Golden Valley Brewery's own recipe.

Happy employees in a large, clean, well designed kitchen

With the restaurant going through vast quantities of food, they are unable to get all of it local, but they do know where it comes from, and as much as possible is local, including fresh vegetables from their own garden. In 2008 alone, the Kirchers provided 2,960 pounds of vegetables for Golden Valley from their own large, organic garden. The restaurant uses real butter from Rose Valley Creamery, right in McMinnville. A local woman supplies all of the berries used at Golden Valley. The breads used in the restaurant are supplied by Portland French Bakery.

As Peter says, "Good food doesn't have to be fancy, just real." If their burgers and fries are any indication, it qualifies. Golden Valley's reputation for great tasting food is well deserved.

Chef Greg Meixner

The Brewhouse at Golden Valley Brewing

The craft beers were a bit of a shock for the city of McMinnville, where microbrews were essentially unknown. Peter's friend, John Harris, brewmaster at Full Sail's Portland brewery, helped with the suggestion that if a customer ordered a Bud, bring them a Bud and a sample. Sometimes you just have to teach your customers.

Though Peter took the short course on brewing at the Sieble Institute, Brewmaster, Mark Vickery is a graduate of the Sieble Institute Masters course. But that was before coming to Golden Valley. Mark began at Bridgeport, but established a reputation during his ten years at Deschutes as the brewer of Mirror Pond and Black Butte Porter, both for which he won awards. Mark has been with Golden Valley since the beginning.

On the seven and a half barrel system at Golden Valley, they focus on producing traditional style ales and lagers. They enjoy creating balanced beer with complex malt components. While they strive for respect of the classic styles, they still enjoy trying new things at Golden Valley.

In the south of France, there is a brewery that makes beer using the 'champaign' method, though due to a 1994 ruling by the European Court of Justice, they are no longer allowed to use that term; now they must call it the 'traditional method.'

In this tradition, Golden Valley barrel aged an IPA, then took it to the winery in Dundee (down the road from McMinnville), where it was bottled in 'champaign' bottles, they then applied 'dosage,' the addition of yeast and fermenting sugars for a secondary fermentation, which raises the alcohol content. Later, they performed degorgement, freezing the neck of the bottle and pulling the yeast plug out. This very special beer was called Golden Valley IPA Brute. Unfortunately, it was very expensive so they no longer make it.

Entry

With five wineries within one and a half blocks of the restaurant, barrels are easy to get, so Golden Valley enjoys making barrel aged beers.

At Golden Valley, quality control is a prime focus. When Peter was at the Sieble Institute, they had a two-hour quality control class each morning during which time testing was performed each day. This was, of course, only a part of the 6:30 AM to 7 PM class schedule and two hours of homework each and every day. (And this was the short course!) Peter has brought this kind of conscientiousness to Golden Valley.

During our interview, Peter excused himself for a moment to seat some newly arrived customers. They had waited maybe twenty seconds, but Peter is, in his words, a freak for customer service. This is a man who cares...about the beer, about the food, about the restaurant, about the customer. Something very noticeable though, is that all this caring comes out not as stress, but very cheerfully. Throughout most of our interview, he was smiling a very natural and well-worn smile. This smile must be contagious, because we saw a lot of them on employees all over Golden Valley.

In addition to the brewery, Golden Valley Beers are available at all the grocery stores in McMinnville, many places in Portland and Salem, and on tap around Portland.

An older gentleman, with three tree farms in the area, chooses a tree for Golden Valley Brewing every Christmas, always a Turkish noble.

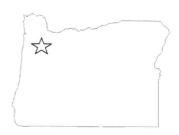

Good Life Brewing Company

1355 S.W. Commerce
Bend, Oregon 97213
541-440-5288
www.goodlifebrewing.com

"Good beer for good life"

We met with Good Life Brewing Company partners, Ty Barnett and Pratt Rather at Cascade Lakes Lodge, due to the fact that Good Life's brewery was still under construction. In fact, at that point it was pretty much an empty warehouse with a few tanks in it. Conservative estimates for opening say spring 2011. When we spoke, they were still waiting on construction permits. As of publication, the partners are saying June 1st, for sure.

Good Life Brewing is setting up in a leased 21,000 square foot building, part of the of the Bright Wood mill complex. Originally a toy factory, manufacturing balsawood airplanes, it converted to a specialty mill, manufacturing molding for doors and windows, after cheap toys began being outsourced to China. More recently, it served a short tenure as the West Bend Tennis Center, where three full-sized tennis courts easily fit inside the building.

Good Life's plans include a production brewery with a 30 barrel brewhouse, a small bottling line, and a kegging system. Expectations are for a maximum production capacity of 60,000 barrels per year. The idea is to have a tasting room with "in the brewery" décor: Bavarian style picnic tables, a bar, hor d'oeuvres, a television, with a half-wall to separate visitors from the brewery. The design should allow the sights, sounds, and smells of the brewery to envelop the tasters. Tours will, of course, be offered.

The trio hope to create a unique experience, Pratt traveled the country asking "Where's the brewpub?" Because of the experience, the team feels they have an exceptional perspective on what to offer. The plan is for a "unique facility that makes unique beer to supply anywhere that wants it."

Some of the

Partners Ty Barnett and Pratt Rather

Brewhouse at Good Life
Photo courtesy of Good Life Brewing, used by permission.

equipment - the brew system and two fermenters - will be brand new, manufactured at AAA Metal Fabrication in The Dalles. Additional used equipment once called Steamworks Brewing Company in Durango, Colorado, home. New Belgium Brewing in Fort Collins, Colorado was the source of the orange silo.

In addition to the space afforded by the building, the partners were attracted to the local business base in the area. According to Ty, they originally planned to be located on High Dessert Court, but the "Earlier location fell through and we thank God it did, because this is ideal!" It also has the advantage of a forward thinking landlord. As Pratt said, "My dream is to be a part of a community of businesses that relate to each other."

Ty Barnett, originally from Cannon Beach, and Curt Plants, who grew up in Bend, both attended college in Ashland, they even lived in the same dorm, but did not meet until they moved/returned to Bend and were introduced by mutual friends. At that time there were only four brewpubs in town, though McMinamens' Old St. Francis Pub opened soon after that.

When Ty, who has ten years experience in the restaurant business as a manager, trained in Texas for a management position, all he could

Good Life Brewing Company
Photo courtesy Good Life Brewing, used by permission

find were Bud Light and Michelob Amber Bock. This was quite a shock to the young man who had, prior to this experience, drunk only craft beers. Returning to Bend, Ty had a whole new appreciation for Oregon beers.

In 2004 Ty and Curt began dabbling in homebrewing. As they learned to make great beer, they began talking of opening a business together. Though Ty enjoyed the history behind beer, Curt's passion was the science of beer making.

This excitement led him to the Siebel Institute in Chicago. Though his plan was to continue his education hands-on working in breweries, he found himself in Munich, Germany,

Good Life Brew
Photo courtesy Good Life Brewing, used by permission

at the Doemans Academy, a premier training center for brewing which was founded in 1895 and is associated with the Siebel Institute. After Munich, Curt's training ground was at Rogue Brewery with his mentor, the great John "More Hops" Maier.

Pratt Rather, the third partner, and next door neighbor to Brett Joyce, president of Rogue Brewing, is a medical engineer for Medtronic and Biotronic and a member of one of the 1995 Race Across America teams, a 3000 mile timed bicycle race which runs coast to coast across the U.S. Despite this medical/engineering background, Pratt has plenty of experience with breweries, including part owner at Sweetwater Brewing-the second largest brewery in the Southeast-in Atlanta, Georgia, for which in 1994 he helped put together an investment group, as well as one other in Georgia. He is also a silent partner at Everybody's Brewing in White Salmon, Washington (an easy visit when in Hood River). This familiarity has come in handy when searching for investors to obtain the reported $900,000 in funds required to open Good Life Brewing. Unlike the other breweries, Pratt plans to take an active part in Good Life Brewing Company.

As the name of the company states, these partners have a great outlook; as Ty put it, "Good Life isn't just a name, it's the philosophy of our business." Their initial intention was noble, if a bit self-centered... to live in Bend. Of more interest to beer coinsurers, is a plan to use only the finest ingredients available. Probably the best demonstration of living the good life and of most interest to the people of Bend, is their desire to give back to the local community. "Good Life's goal is to donate a portion of our profits to local charities, perhaps in the form of a percentage of sales."

Hair of the Dog Brewing Company

61 S.E. Yamhill Street
Portland, OR 97202
503-232-6585
www.hairofthedog.com

"Beer of Kings"

We almost certainly requested our interview with Hair of the Dog owner, Alan Sprints, for the least convenient day possible for his schedule. Yet, he not only consented to the interview, but was a gracious, albeit somewhat (understandably) distracted, host. We met with Alan the day before the annual Hair of the Dog dock sale. At the time of our interview, this was the only occasion they sold directly to the public and hundreds attended each year-people would even fly into Portland to attend. More importantly, it was also the only day to obtain Michael, the barrel-aged Flanders red style ale named for the late Michael Jackson. (For those new to the world of fine beers, this is *not* the pop star, but the great British "Beer Hunter," and writer, who in 1977 first published *The World Guide to Beer*.) According to Alan, Michael (the beer) would be gone the next day and would not return until next year.

At that time they were still in their old, production-only location on 23rd Avenue, a former foundry. As we were doing interviews around Portland, brewers kept asking us if we had been to Hair of the Dog yet. We kept hearing "good luck finding it." Thankfully, Nuvi (our GPS) had

Alan, moving pallets of beer.

no problem, though we understand things like MapQuest would attempt to take followers over and through some interesting places.

The new, easier-to-find location - a 1935 industrial building - with over 10,000 square feet, more than double the old brewery, has a tasting room with a kitchen. Alan, a professional chef before becoming a brewer, expected to man the kitchen until finding a suitable chef. Plans were to begin with simple fare initially.

An avid homebrewer who was bored with his aerospace career, Alan had moved from Southern California to Portland to go to culinary school. After chefting at several different places while searching for a family-friendly schedule, which is notoriously difficult to come by for chefs, Alan switched to brewing professionally in 1991, when he began brewing for Widmer Brothers. Then in 1993, Alan left Widmer and started Hair of the Dog, brewing alone for ten years before finally hiring an assistant. After two decades, he still finds it to be pleasurable, "People enjoy

The bottling crew, hard at work.

what I make, that really makes it fun." Obvious to us throughout our interview, he also takes a great deal of pride in his craft. Specializing in strong beers, Alan produces at least one new beer each year. Now with the opening of the new tasting room, plans are in place to develop some lower alcohol beers.

Alan likes to name his beers for people who have been influential in his life. In addition to *Michael*, for Michael "Beer Hunter" Jackson, *Fred* was created as a tribute to beer writer and the first person to purchase Hair of the Dog beer (Adam), beer historian Fred Eckhardt. *Ruth* is named for, and inspired by, Alan's grandmother, in recognition and appreciation for her love and support. The name for bourbon barrel aged, *Eve*, simply makes since he had already produced Adam, a dessert beer and Hair of the Dog's first beer. Seemingly aptly named - Adam was the first man - this is in reality, a convenient coincidence, it was

actually named after the ancient beer Alan was attempting to recreate. Legend has it that Adambier, originally made in Dortmunder, Germany, was offered to King Fredrick William IV, as he was traveling around Bavaria; the King drank the stein in one long chug, then passed out for twenty-four hours. Upon awakening, the King proclaimed Adam his official beer.

Alan Sprints

In addition to making the beer of kings, Alan has also created a beer which has sold for the equal of about $3500 a six pack. "Dave" is a 1994 barleywine in twelve ounce bottles with enclosable caps and twenty-nine percent (yes, that's 29%!) alcohol which was not released until 1998, when Alan took it to the celebrated Toronado Barleywine Festival in San Francisco. After earning a Gold Medal, Alan named the champion brew after festival sponsor and Toronado Pub owner, David Keene. Alan brewed a mere 90 gallons of Dave and has sold only a few bottles. When he donated five bottles of the rare brew to the 2008 FredFest on-line charity auction, whose proceeds went to Parkinson's research, the bottles sold for astonishing prices ranging from $478 to $707 per bottle!

Despite these staggering auction prices, Alan is heedful of both the pricing of his beers and sustainability. In the summer of 2007 Alan switched the base malt used in all of his beers to Organic Pilsner malt. Not only is this improved sustainability, but always mindful of quality, he believes this change has imparted even better flavors and colors in Hair of the Dog beers.

Heater | Allen Brewing

Heater Allen
907 NE 10th Avenue
McMinnville, Oregon 97128
503-472-4898
www.heaterallen.com

"We're different, try craft lagers"

For thirty years, Rick Allen worked as an investment banker in Portland. Then in 2005, he decided he wanted out. After working in the wine industry in Palo Alto, California for a year, it was time to come back to Oregon. Positions in Oregon's wine industry did not seem to pay well, he feared saturation point for wineries was being reached, plus he felt there were issues involved which he did not wish to deal with, so he switched gears.

As a veteran homebrewer with twenty-two year's experience, Rick had entered a few homebrew competitions and had done well. While he had no formal beer brewing training, he had read a great deal and spoken with many in the craft brewing industry. He felt there was definitely room in Oregon for different styles of beer. The decision was made; Rick would start a craft brewery.

Deriving the brewing name from a combination of his wife's maiden name, Heater and their last name, Allen, the new brewery name of Heater Allen had a ring to it.

McMinnville was chosen due to the quality water it provides. They own their own watershed and have very soft water. The soft water makes a better pilsner, while harder water is desired for darker beers. Starting in 2007, the brewery was very small, with only a twenty gallon system. Though his brews were well received, if he was going to make a profit, he would

Rick Allen

need to get bigger. Bigger meant a beautiful six barrel copper brewhouse. The small system was sold to a homebrewing friend.

The classic British style of the new system posed a small problem. With its single infusion, the British system did not meet the requirements needed for the multi-step infusion used in the German style beers produced by Heater Allen. A suggestion made by an Oregon State fermentation science student (who is a friend of Rick's daughter) was to mash in the boil kettle.

Rick stirs the mash

This solution requires the laborious act of stirring the mash by hand, but it indeed solved the problem. With most beers taking three to four steps and wheat beers taking six, Rick gets plenty of stirring practice.

Having uncompromising standards, Rick had spent two and a half years before starting Heater Allen perfecting his recipes. A great deal of experimentation with different yeasts and malts transpired. Then, there were incidents like brewing fifteen batches of pilsner in a row before achieving the desired perfection.

A few fermenters

Unusual for the craft beer industry, Heater Allen produces only lagers, which Rick started brewing in 2000. "I make lagers because that is what I prefer to drink…and virtually no one else makes them." The main reason other breweries seldom make lagers is the long fermentation period required, which ties up fermentation tanks. Rick allows his lagers to ferment four to eight weeks before bottling.

True to his reputation for precision, Rick says, "I always try to have my lagers be the best in that category; whenever a new one (competitor's lager) comes out, I have to try it to see how they compare."

Heater Allen brews have that competitive edge; they are proud to be the recipients of two 2010 NW Brewing News People's Choice awards. One in the dark lager category, for Dunkel, and one in the Oktoberfest category, for Bobtoberfest.

Heater Allen has four standards: Pils, a Bohemian-style lager; Coastal, a Northwest amber lager, which is too flavorful and hoppy to be categorized as an American lager; Schwartz, a malty/espresso beer with a hint of smoke; and the award-winning Dunkel, rarely produced in the United States, is brewed in the tradition of Munich.

Additionally, Heater Allen makes five or six seasonals: the award-winning Bobtoberfest; Hugo, a bock; Sandy Paws, a Christmas beer; Mediator, a dopplebock; Smokey Bob, a specialty of NW Bavaria is Rauch, or smoked beer; and IsarWeizen, fruity wheat beer made from a recipe a friend brought from the Isar Brau Brew Pub in Munich.

Heater Allen beers usually fall between 4.5% and 5% ABV, though Mediator is around 7% ABV. Rick makes lower alcohol beers because "I like to drink beer and I like to drink more than one."

Heater Allen has one full-time employee, Rick's daughter, Lisa. In addition to providing whatever assistance Rick needs in the brewery, she acts as the event planner for Heater Allen. Together they produced 250 barrels in 2009, 425 barrels in 2010, and are projecting 550 barrels of beer in 2011.

Bottling using the mobile bottling service, Green Bottling, Rick says he doubts they could have been successful without their services. Bottles are available at the brewery and stores around Yamhill County and Portland.

Lisa, cleaning is a constant duty in a brewery

Heater Allen is also available on tap at restaurants and pubs in these areas. With shelf space in stores being competitive, if you do not see

Heater Allen on the shelf, be sure to ask the beer steward if they could stock it.

Heater Allen is hoping to add a tasting room soon, hopefully by summer.

When asked if he is enjoying commercial brewing, Rick said it is a different kind of fun professionally, but fun, nevertheless.

Rick keeps smiling, despite the physical strain of stirring the kettle.

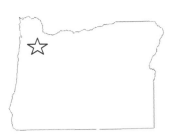

Hopworks Urban Brewery
HUB
2944 SE Powell Blvd
Portland, OR 97202
541-232-HOPS (4677)
www.hopworksbeer.com

"Portland's first Eco-Brewpub"

Hopworks Urban Brewery (HUB) is the dream-child of owner Christian Ettinger. Though born in San Francisco, he grew up in Lake Oswego. As the son of architect/builder Roy Ettinger, Chris learned to "shoot for the best!" Whether following his passions of bike riding, snowboarding, sustainability, organics, or brewing, Chris's enthusiasm is evident and has been the driving force behind this significant undertaking.

In college, at nineteen years of age, Chris studied for a term in Cologne, Germany, as an exchange student. While there, he fell in love with the history, culture, art, and craftsmanship of beer. The twenty-two brew pubs in Cologne were not enough for Chris, he also drug his friends to eight different countries in an attempt to satisfy Chris's need to investigate the European beer culture.

Owner/Brewmaster Chris Ettinger shows us around the brewery.

Though he had done a bit of homebrewing in his parent's kitchen before Germany, upon returning home, Chris began homebrewing in earnest. He had found his life's calling. While working toward a business degree at University of Oregon, Chris did an internship at Oregon Fields Brewery, a now-defunct Eugene brewery. After graduating, Chris spent the next three years at West Brothers Brewery, also in Eugene, and then headed south to complete the Intensive Brewing Science and Engineering course offered by the American Brewers Guild at Davis, California, where he studied under two great brewers.

After Davis, Chris returned to Oregon to work as head brewer at Old World Pub and Brewery in Portland. This position ended when a bounced paycheck and changed locks told him Old World had gone out of business. Interestingly, Chris then went to work at the same location for Laurelwood Brewing. It was during this time with Laurelwood that Chris was named the 2004 World Beer Cup Champion Brewmaster for small brewpubs (1-1,200 barrels per year). With this honor and six years as Laurelwood brewmaster, Chris decided it was time to open his own brewery.

Uncovering this amazing ceiling was a definite plus.

In June, 2006, the Hopworks Urban Brewery dream began when Chris's father-in-law, the major investor in HUB, purchased the old Sunset Fuel Company building and land. Built in 1948 to display and repair Caterpillar bulldozers, Sunset Fuel purchased the building in 1963 and remained headquartered there until 2004. Constructed entirely of reinforced concrete, this building, with its many hidden charms and possibilities, turned out to be perfect for Chris and his dreams.

Chris's dreams and plans included his passion for sustainability. By hiring Lovett Deconstruction to painstakingly dismantle the interior of the 16,800 square foot building, sorting and stacking lumber, drywall, and a vast array of fixtures over the course of a full month, Chris was able to assure that whatever was not salvaged was recycled. The only thing thrown away was the old insulation.

With his father as the architect, Chris acted as his own general contractor, saving as much as half of what it would have cost to complete this project, which is estimated to have cost two million dollars. As an admittedly picky person, in addition to the substantial savings of being his own general contractor, Chris was able to assure both construction and finishing were done to his own high standards.

Upon entering HUB there are many unusual things to notice in this intricate and remarkably designed building. When supplemented by knowledge of the origin of many of the materials used, this pub becomes a veritable treasure trove for both the antique buff and the most avid green enthusiast. Chris has exampled "reuse, reduce, and recycle" in every aspect of this amazing building, while clearly avoiding the "used" look one sometimes expects from these three R's.

Booths made from ceiling

Removal of the drop ceiling revealed one of the true beauties of this building, the amazing ceiling built with old-growth timbers. The use of environmentally safe cob blasting to remove decades of dirt and grime revealed a glorious amber colored ceiling which adds not just an accent to this amazing building, but is truly its crowning glory.

Whether you are sitting at the booths made from the old ceiling joists or the tables with tops acquired from Stanford's Restaurant & Bar's remodeling, you may be assured the furniture and fixtures have been reused or repurposed, not purchased new. Above the bar, which is built

An old bicycle wheel serves as the suspension mechanism for the lights.

of more ceiling material, old framing, and mahogany from the old office paneling, are the 44 old bike frames acquired from friends and local bike shops to create perhaps the most unusual light fixture we have seen yet. The effect is quite mesmerizing. At the foot of the bar, your feet will rest on the foot rail made from the old boiler pipe. Or perhaps you will choose to relax in the private booth, an old Mosler walk-in bank vault which is finished with the old ship-lap sheathing and includes a pedal-powered Lazy Susan and, of course, a *non*-locking door. While you are in one of the booths, be sure to look up at the top of the light fixture, it is suspended from an old bike wheel.

The eye is drawn to unique design features, such as the remarkable staircase, designed by Chris's dad, Roy. Built using traffic sign standards and industrial materials, it certainly provides the desired "wow" factor. The staircase leads to the mezzanine, which during the day is lighted partially by natural light entering through a skylight. There, in addition to a pinball machine and pool table, you will find seating for parties including up to 49 people.

Whether you choose to warm yourself in front of the unique "grundy tank" brew kettle gas fireplace; use the bicycle repair station with one of the free tire patches or a new tube purchased at HUB; or just to use the provided tire pump; there is no doubt about the inclusion of many features not normally found at a pub. Differences are noticed even before entering HUB: dedicated motorcycling parking and an abundance of bicycle parking.

Chris's passion for sustainability has led him to not make a single move without a full analysis of its impact on the environment. As a result, Hopworks is run quite differently. From the beer itself, to the energy used to make it, to building, to cleaning practices, Hopworks dares to make a difference by realizing that even small steps can make a large environmental difference when added together.

All Hopworks beers are USDA certified organic.

All Hopworks beers are certified organic. According to the Organic Trade Association, "Organic food production is based on a system of farming that maintains and replenishes soil fertility without the use of toxic and persistent pesticides and fertilizers. Organic foods are minimally processed without artificial ingredients, preservatives, or irradiation to maintain the integrity of the food." Certification means the growers and producers of the products have been through a rigorous inspection process to assure their product has been grown and produced according to strict uniform standards verified by independent state or private organizations and that the product contains at least 95% organic ingredients. By obtaining this certification, the USDA Organic seal may be displayed on qualifying products. Hopworks' pilsner, for example, is 99% organic. Going the extra mile to become certified, Hopworks gladly shells out more than a thousand dollars per year to cover the certification fee.

With a menu filled with organic, sustainable, and natural (meats), 50% of the produce used at HUB is organic and all of the proteins are hormone free. HUB cares about their patrons and the environment. Chris believes consuming poisons is making people ill and is doing what he can to stop the craziness of poisoning our food. By serving locally grown foods whenever possible, HUB is also doing their part to ease excess shipping.

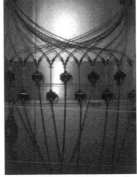

Everything at HUB is well organized, including how your beer gets to the tap.

If you take home a doggy bag or get food or drink to-go, be assured that it will travel in the most sustainable containers available. All to-go packaging is 100% post consumer and 100% recycled material including the use of compostable plastic to-go cups, which are corn based, and 100%

Everywhere you look, sustainability is evident.

recycled napkins. Whether making dressings from scratch, which results in less packaging, or recycling food waste for animal feed and composting, the attitude at HUB is sustainability throughout.

This attitude is carried throughout Hopworks, including the brewery. Whether with the biodiesel fired brew kettle-using HUB fryer oil, or the biodiesel powered delivery truck, Chris has tapped state-of-the-art sustainability practices to power his dream. From the utilization of the most energy efficient pipes available, to recovering hot water through the use of a wort heat exchanger, every possible step has been taken to preserve, conserve, and recover whenever possible.

Heading down into the brewery

With another basement space next door, which is the same size as the current brewery, this well-planned brewery has plenty of room for expansion. Thouhh it has been being used for storage, phase II of the project plans for opening into it soon. Every aspect of this business has been thoroughly designed, plotted, and planned. Chris's business plan must have taken volumes!

So when you visit HUB, passing the drought-resistant plantings, which are watered by rainwater off the roof contained in an 11,000 gallon "rain barrel," you will know that careful thought has gone into creating the most unusual, innovative, and sustainable brewpub possible. Take a look around. See what you could emulate. Have a brew.

Jacksonville Inn

175 E California Street
Jacksonville, Oregon
97530
541-899-1900
www.jacksonvilleinn.com

*"Award-winning restaurant &
inn now includes a brewery"*

During our interview with the newest brewery on our tour, Bricktown Brewing, owner/brewer Craig McPheeters told us about Jacksonville Inn's upcoming plans. So, of course, we made a quick phone call and added another stop to our Southern Oregon tour.

As the first city to be named as a National Historic Landmark on November 13, 1966, Jacksonville is also Oregon's only such city. Born when gold was discovered in 1851 by James Cluggage and John R. Poole, while digging a hole in hopes it would fill with enough water to allow their mules to have a drink, it grew into a bustling town of over two thousand people. Being bypassed by the railroad when it was built through Medford in 1884, taking with it much of the business, people, and the designation of county seat, Jacksonville remained essentially unchanged for many years. These unaltered commercial and residential buildings have created a unique and intact example of a late 1800's town.

One of the buildings which has been preserved is now known as

This b&w photo does not do justice to the historic elegance of the restaurant, where the subdued lighting is perfect and real gold flecks are visible in the walls, built from local sandstone.

the Jacksonville Inn. Built in 1861, with a foundation of locally quarried sandstone, it was repaired after a fire in 1873, and has served many purposes, including a general store and a livery stable.

Then, in 1968, Jerry and Linda Evans purchased and

renovated the building into the Jacksonville Inn. An eight- room period bed and breakfast, with an additional four luxurious cottages, which incorporate modern amenities such as steam showers, the Jacksonville Inn includes a gourmet restaurant and wine cellar featuring over 2,000 wines.

So what does all of this have to do with a beer tour? Chef Bill, a graduate of the California Culinary Academy, with 18 years experience as a chef (including places like Big Sur, Hawaii, and Carmel), has also been a homebrewer for the last fourteen years. After tasting Bill's brew, the wise people at Jacksonville Inn have decided to take advantage of this and have taken the necessary steps to obtain licenses to serve their own beer. Expectations are for the formalities to be complete and beer to begin flowing by April 2011.

Chef/Brewer Bill

In the beginning, Bill will be essentially running a homebrew operation in the Inn. Just as many homebrewers do, Bill will be brewing on the stove in the restaurant, in fifteen gallon

The winter bedded-down look does not do justice to this award-winning patio.

batches. Brewing around cooking sounds to us like a nightmare, but Bill thrives on demand and pressure.

Expecting to begin with a pale ale, something a bit subdued, and perhaps a brown with a bit more hops, Bill likes to layer different components in his beers, just as he does with food. His philosophy with the beer will be the same as with the food, "highlight the beer." Plans, of course, include food pairings.

Regardless of whether food or beer, Bill makes everything with love...from the heart. This gentle giant, aptly described by Host Gary as a "Mountain of a Man," says his primary goal is taking care of the people, making sure they have a wonderful experience. While we were a bit dubious when owner, Jerry,

At 6'9", Chef Bill covers much of the small pumphouse, which will serve as a fermenting room.

said we should talk to the chef, we understood once we met him. This is a person to whom you instantly feel a warmth and connection.

So whether you are there for the renowned Britt Festival, the outdoor adventures, the history, or the newest brew, you can find gold and beer at Jacksonville Inn.

Entering   Host Gary   The Inn includes a relaxed Bistro and Bar downstairs.

Kirsten mans the register in the gift shop, which includes an extensive wine selection and a modest craft beer assortment

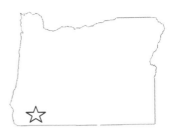

Klamath Basin Brewing Company
&
The Creamery Brewpub & Grill
1320 Main Street
Klamath Falls, OR 97601
541-273-5222
www.kbbrewing.com

"Our first interview"

When Lonnie Clemet, a Coors distributor, received a brew kit as a Christmas gift, the giver probably had no idea what they had started. This cute, relatively innocent gift snowballed into an interest that eventually led Lonnie, and friend Del Azevedo, to renovate half of Lonnie's garage into a licensed and permitted commercial brewery. But that was back in 2001. After purchasing the old Crater Lake Creamery building in Klamath Falls, circa 1935, they proceeded to renovate it into The Creamery Brewpub and Grill, a diverse and comfortable destination "sports bar" brewpub which opened in 2005. The famous "blue cow" neon sign from the creamery still welcomes patrons to the building.

Klamath Basin Brewing was the first of many interviews we did in preparation for this book. I shudder now to realize how little we actually knew then about the brewing industry, interviewing, and taking notes. Thanks to very helpful and understanding general manager, Jerry Rosterolla, we had a crash course in commercial brewing 411.

Party Pigs

While each of the breweries have their own unique bits and pieces, perhaps in location, pub style, history, equipment, or maybe philosophy, Klamath Basin Brewing has *multiple* distinctive features. Of all the interviews we have for this book, they are one of only two breweries offering party pigs. These 2.5 gallon reusable beer package/dispensers keep beer fresh and carbonated, while being easy to carry and fitting easily into home refrigerators. Not only that, they are rather cute. While they were not bottling at the time of our interview, Klamath Basin Brewing began bottling in May, 2010, and bottles are now available in select stores throughout the state. So whether a full keg, the cute little party pig, or a bottle, you have plenty of options with Klamath Basin Brews.

Geothermal Water Heater

If you are a fan of "green" efforts, Klamath Basin Brewing ranks high in this category. Using barley grown in the Klamath Basin and hops grown in the Northwest keeps things on a local level. While they use many types of yeast to gain diverse flavors in their beers, their favored yeast of choice is Wyeast from Hood River, Oregon.

Without doubt, Klamath Basin Brewing's most unique feature is their use of geothermally heated water for use in the brewing process. This water begins in the Cascades and Crater Lake, traveling through natural underground rivers to then be heated by geo-thermal hot springs. This naturally heated hot water is then added to the Klamath Basin grown barley to begin the brewing process.

Geothermally heated sidewalks in Klamath Falls keep the ice and snow at bay.
Slide 88 of 122, © 2000 Geothermal Education Office, used by permission.

The use of geothermal energy does not end with the beer. When visiting Klamath Basin Brewing during the winter, you will not need to worry about negotiating the snow on their geothermally-heated sidewalks. In Klamath Falls many downtown area sidewalks are heated with the use of tubing placed under the concrete of the sidewalks. In addition to being in front of businesses, these warmed walks can be found at city buildings, county buildings, and schools, such as Oregon Institute of Technology (OIT).

Though unknown in most of the country, geothermal energy produces 0.5 % of the energy in the United States. California is currently the largest producer of geothermal energy, although most of the western states are capable of producing it. With almost no emissions and a seemingly unlimited supply, this is truly an environmentalist's ideal energy source. According to City Manager, Jeff Ball, "We didn't know it was green; it just made sense."

Of course, the use of geothermal energy is not limited to sidewalks. Many Klamath Falls buildings are heated with this natural heat source, including the museum, public buildings, greenhouses, and of course, OIT. With the help of an $816,000 stimulus grant, the city is also building a geothermal generator for electricity like the one in use at OIT.

While visiting Klamath Basin Brewing and The Creamery Brewpub and Grill you will find a willingness to give tours of their easily visible brewery. You will find good food and an extensive menu. You will find a comfortable and versatile facility. You will find some nice people. You will find wine and cocktails. Mostly, you will find beer...be sure and try their sampler tray.

Bob and our son, Philip, enjoying a sampler tray and hummus.

Laurelwood Public House & Brewery

5115 NE Sandy Boulevard
Portland, Oregon 97213
503-282-0622
www.laurelwoodbrewpub.com

"A place where friends and family meet"

Mike De Kalb and his wife, Cathy Woo-De Kalb, had both worked in the food services industry for most of their lives. In addition to being in charge of the food services department at Portland Airport, Mike had run the Widmer Pub. In 2001 they decided it was time to open their own place.

Locating in the former Old World Pub and Brewery, where the brewery remained after Old World's sudden demise, Mike needed a brewer. He called the guys at Widmer, who said the former Old World brewer, Christian Ettinger, was great, so the new Laurelwood hired Christian.

In charge of the kitchen, Cathy developed most of Laurelwood's extensive selection of dessert recipes. In addition to using local organic foods as much as possible, with the realization that they produce a very diverse product, beer, they soon began incorporating it into everything they do; desserts, sauces, rib sauce, the list goes on. Discovering that stout adds a wonderful dimension to chocolate, all of Laurelwood's chocolate now includes stout.

One of the most important elements Mike and Cathy insisted on for the new brewpub was an environment which felt like home, where family, friends and children could meet and enjoy themselves. Having in mind a more European idea for pubs, Laurelwood would include dedicated play areas for the children, conversation areas with couches and comfy chairs, and no walled off non-family areas. While the bar remains somewhat separate, it is still open.

Mike and Christian worked together to develop an award-

Mike De Kalb

- 197 -

winning line-up of beers. Then in January 2003, assistant brewer Chad Kennedy, a former homebrewer, was added to the Laurelwood brewery. With Chad's assistance, Christian led Laurelwood to win the World Beer Cup World Champion Brewpub in 2004. Christian also received the World Champion Brewpub Brewmaster Award that same year.

World Champion Brewpub medal

When Christian left Laurelwood in 2006 to open his own brewpub, Hopworks Urban Brewery, Chad stepped up to the position of head brewer. As the former director for AM Todd Botanicals, in Eugene, he took a job in 2000 with Aria Imports - a Portland distributor of foreign beers - in order to follow his passion, beer. Working for Aria allowed Chad to meet plenty of

A wet December morning at Laurelwood's rooftop outdoor seating.

brewery owners and brewers, including the folks at Laurelwood. After learning that Laurelwood had an opening in the brewery, he knew he had found his "in."

With time, Mike and Cathy opened five more locations, including two at the Portland Airport, and turned the original location into a pizza pub. With their lease running out and landlord problems, they decided to close their original location, with Monday, July 5, 2010 being their final day in the Hollywood District location. Then in December 2010, Laurelwood announced the closure of their NW Public House location, sighting "declining sales and economic conditions in certain parts of town."

Brewers Lounge

Laurelwood still has hopes of opening a couple of other locations, possibly a new pizza pub, elsewhere in Portland in the next few years. At the time of our interview, Laurelwood was working to open a beer-only concession in the Rose Garden.

The bar, in the background, is separate, yet open.

All of Laurelwood's beers are organic, with four of them being certified organic. Laurelwood is committed to sustainable practices as stated by Mike in a BEF article, "Whether it's sourcing Organic ingredients for our beer, buying local produce for our kitchens, or sending food waste to the compost pile and not the municipal dump, our company is committed to helping make a positive difference in the communities in which we do business." To this end, in September, 2010, Laurelwood signed a three-year contract with the Bonneville Environmental Foundation (BEF) to support its Water Restoration Certificate program. It is said that this purchase will restore one million gallons of water to the Deschutes River.

More than one children's play area is available at Laurelwood

When asked if there have been surprises since starting Laurelwood, Mike names a few, including employee costs (many people are not aware an employee costs a company much more than the wages paid to the employee), and fluctuating costs of grain.

Brewing on a fifteen barrel system, Laurelwood produces 4,500 to 6,000 barrels per year. Available in bottles along the I-5 corridor throughout Oregon and in Southern Washington, as well as on draft, Laurelwood is gaining international acclaim as a result of their airport locations. Mike also expressed hopefulness that a Laurelwood production brewery would open soon, maybe in 2011, with an eye toward a production of thirty to forty thousand barrels per year.

Laurelwood offers a banquet area, a brewers lounge with its own bar and comfortable, couch seating; outdoor seating; and children's play areas. This award-winning brewpub also offers gift cards and a wide variety of Laurelwood accessories.

Plenty of brewware choices available

Lompoc

3901B North Williams Avenue
Portland, Oregon 97217
503-288-3996
www.newoldlompoc.com

"Badass Beers"

When we first entered Lompoc's 5th Quadrant (5Q), we were reminded of a '70's hippy hangout with a modern update twist. Being 70's oldsters, this meant we felt quite comfortable and at-home. Since it was past lunchtime and we were hungry, we decided before introducing ourselves we would try lunch. Besides some wonderful and relaxed service, we had a great meal. Nice thing for me, they offer their own root beer, which I later found out is made at New Old Lompoc across town. From the other food offerings we saw leaving the kitchen, we may have

to return to try more dishes. With Bob's enthusiasm for their beers, that should not be a problem.

We met Sam Orlanski, one of four brewers at Lompoc, as he was climbing out of the brew tank, part of the never-ending cleaning process. Sam attended UC Davis's master brewer program before doing his internship at BridgePort Brewing. This was quite a change for a guy who once sold mortgages. Sam's fellow brewers are: Bryan Keilty, who is also a chef who trained at the Culinary Institute of America in New York; Zach Bechwith, formerly an Arizona brewer; and head brewer, Dave "Chowdah" Fleming.

5Q brews daily; if the tanks are empty, their goal is to fill them. Since they are doing 22-27 seasonals plus seven brews on tap year-round,

this goal is understandable. Like many microbreweries, Lompoc beers are bottled by a mobile bottling company, specifically, Green Bottling.

According to Sam, Lompoc likes "to go over the top, big, badass beers." This can be seen in their C-Note, a hoppy "badass" beer which is hopped several times during the brewing process. It begins with the pelleted hops used by most breweries, but uses whole hops later in the process. Better yet, I can get one as a treat for Bob in our local grocery store over 250 miles away.

What many of the patrons at 5Q may not realize is there is a tasting room, Sidebar, adjacent to 5Q. The venue of choice for most of Lompoc's release parties, Sidebar is also available for private party rental. This is the only place you may enjoy a variety of barrel aged and seasonal specialty beers, which are available only in limited quantity. Lined with the oak bourbon barrels used

A handful of fresh hops.

for aging, Sidebar holds about fifty and includes its own bar. Remember, Sidebar has limited hours of Friday from 4-10 P.M. and Saturday from 2-10 P.M., and is for 21 and over only.

Sidebar, in the process of being set up for Halloween.

While in Sidebar, we met Lompoc owner, Jerry Fechter while he was enjoying some quiet time with family. Jerry, an employee of the old Lompoc, purchased Lompoc from the original owner, who did not care for craft beer and limited production to two or three styles. Like many brewers, Jerry began as a homebrewer. These days, Jerry leaves most of the brewing to Sam and the group, preferring to focus on the corporate end and expansion. His plan has included making each new location work in a year and a half. Having opened four in five years, I would guess his plan is on track. It will be interesting to see if he pulls off the two additional pubs planned for the next three to four years.

Though Jerry may be into expansion and corporate matters, when he starts talking about aging in bourbon barrels and specialty beers, the shine of excitement in his eyes is evident. According to Bob, this is quite

5Q's Patio

understandable after tasting the aged beer, "Wow! What a beer!" The oak barrels were originally used for bourbon, then purchased by Lompoc and used for three beer batches before being sold for planters and other repurposed

C-Note and a Sampler

uses. After three batches, they lose their flavor.

Lompoc began with a different label than is currently used. Then some guy by the name of Steve offered to make a new logo for $300 and a keg. Jerry told him to do something English. Yellow, English, and simple are the words I would use to describe this distinctive label.

Back in the 5Q pub, while Bob enjoyed a C-note and some samplers, one of the servers showed us the amazing booths. Initially, they appeared to be normal six person booths, but the center wall actually rises in the method of a guillotine to allow for one large booth for 12. There are two of these remarkable booths.

Outdoor seating may be found on the patio and in front of the building.

Guillotine booths allow seating for six to twelve

Long Brewing

29380 NE Owls Lane
Newberg, Oregon 97132
503-349-8341
www.longbrewing.com

"No Compromise"

Nestled on a rise, overlooking the beautiful Yamhill Valley, Long Brewing is located in the shop next to the home of Paul and Linda Long. Surrounded by vineyards, with quail in the yard, and pheasants flying up when startled, this location is one which cries out for peaceful relaxation and a fine, well balanced beer.

Fine beers which include layers, balance, proper aroma, and mouthfeel are not just goals, but a focus of passion at Long Brewing. For Paul Long, who has a background in wine and an extremely sophisticated palette, attempting to fill a nitch between today's craft brewing and wine making is an obsession. He speaks of his beers very differently than most brewers, using wine terms spoken with a cultured reverence. "I try to make beers more like wines, layer by layer, balanced."

You might say Paul was born to this business. Growing up on a farm, a hop farm to be exact, as a youngster he was a third generation hop farmer, literally in Hopville, Oregon, a micro-community near Corvallis. As an adult he became an electrical engineer in the high tech industry, where he developed the first microprocessor controlled defibulator. Never satisfied with good enough, he also acquired degrees in business and chemistry.

While working at Hewlett Packard, about the time the craft beer revolution first started, one of the engineers who worked for Paul was a homebrewer. Though he was more of a wine connoisseur, Paul thought he would like to try brewing beer – if he ever had the time.

As Paul says, "Am I overly anal?...yeah." Obviously, for him to homebrew would not mean just trying to come up with a

Paul Long

good beer. It would mean, as he says, "My goal is to make *the* very best beer you can,"

Toward this end, the very first year he homebrewed he took third in the nation for his IPA. Obviously, for a man like Paul, third was not the place to stop. Since then, five of his homebrew beers have taken first in the nation. Then in 2005 he was the recipient of the coveted Ninkasi award, which is given to the brewer who gains the most points in the second round of the National Homebrew Competition judged at the National Homebrewers Conference. Named in honor of Ninkasi, the Sumerian goddess of beer, the winner is widely considered the best homebrewer of the year.

2005 Ninkasi Award

Ten years after beginning homebrewing, Paul left the high-tech industry. For two years, Paul searched for the business model that would work for him. He felt it was time to make his award-winning beers available to the public.

A collage of the 1953 Independence Hop Growers' Association Annual Dinner includes Paul's dad, and is surrounded by Paul's medals and ribbons. At one time, Independence was the hop capital of the world.

Taking his time searching for a name for his new company, Paul looked for a title which would impart the flavor palette. Unable to unearth the desired term, he decided to draw on the family surname. This will also make it easy to someday pass the business on to his son, who is currently a business major at Oregon State and considering a minor in fermentation science.

The Long label is actually a reminiscence of Paul's boyhood. While working in the fields, he would see pheasants fly and get excited thinking about the end of harvest and going pheasant hunting. These thoughts relaxed him, just as a glass of fine beer does now.

A certified judge, Paul judges beer competitions a couple of times each year. His preference though, is to spend his judging time on his own beers. Enjoying the opinion of others, it is nice to sit with a friend, who also has refined taste, and judge each of his beers.

Paul, tasting, backed by awards
he has received

Paul has been blessed with a very refined palette. This important trait enables him to distinguish exactly what he likes and dislikes about a beer, which allows him to make the needed adjustments, honing each of the elements to perfection. When judging he will evaluate aroma, taste, appearance, and palette. Each of these categories has several characteristics which are evaluated, breaking the beer down to its most basic elements.

After searching the world for the finest ingredients, Paul looks to Europe, where they have been making malts much longer than we have in the United States, where Paul says we have trouble growing good malting barley. But when it comes to hops, especially for IPA's, the finest and best available are right here in the Northwest.

Paul explains that hops are a tool. He asks himself what hop he will need to use to get the flavor he is looking for when designing a beer. Using a variety of hops in a single beer allows a multiple release of flavors, with some hops emiting flavor early in a tasting while some delay the flavor release for a while.

For IPA's, Paul will go directly to the hop growers, choosing which pile he wants. Occasionally, the growers will even call and allow him to choose the hops he wants directly out of the field. Whether from a pile or from the field, Paul takes them immediately, vacuum-packing

Paul explains how he keeps a log book with tasting notes on every batch he makes.

and freezing them right away, allowing him to have the freshest hops possible throughout the year.

The hops Paul uses are all fresh and fresh frozen. Instantaneously able to discern a beer-by aroma-which has been brewed using hop pellets, Paul avoids their use. This would conflict with his goal of making beer with fresh off-the-kiln-flavor.

Paul rather snuck up on an IPA. He had no desire to create a beer where the drinker gets bowled over with bitterness. Desiring to craft an IPA with more flavor and less bitterness, he has come up with what he feels is his most special beer. "I don't think there's anything quite like it," he says.

Because of Bob enjoying the "face test," I have tasted many IPA's, which generally seem to be the gift which keeps giving. This is one of the reasons Bob gets such a kick out of the "face test," as the bitterness keeps giving, I keep reacting. As Paul spoke of his IPA, I could not resist, I had to try a sip from Bob's glass. Though Bob eagerly awaited the inevitable "face," he was quite disappointed; while I cannot comment on the "goodness" of the flavor (it all tastes bad to me) I do know the radical bitterness I associate with beer was not there. Even more surprisingly, I could discern the layers of flavor about which Paul spoke. Bob, who is far more qualified to comment on beer than I am, says it is a "Really clean IPA."

According to Paul, Allen Routt at the Painted Lady restaurant in Newberg, a culinary destination for fine dining, said about his IPA, "I've been waiting my whole life for a beer like this." Painted Lady, where they specialize in pairing

food with fine wines, departed on April 30, 2010, from their wine custom, offering a special night – pairing Long beers with a five course gourmet dinner.

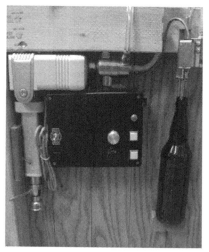

Additionally, Long offers Vienna, an elegant style beer; a nice blond, which is a soft, malty beer; a Porter, which is the only beer he makes that did not take a first in the nation when homebrewing; and a Kolch, a light beer with a pear/apple flavor and a soft feel, which is tart, rather than bitter. Paul suggests when on a wine-tasting tour, if your palette is done and can no longer distinguish, try a glass of the Kolch, it will cleanse the palette enabling you to return to wine tasting.

With Paul's extremely high standards, he will accept nothing less than the best for Long Brewing. Focused on truly artesian beers made with the best ingredients available, Paul notes that there is a steep learning curve in brewing quality beers. Then, once you have perfected a beer, it must be rebalanced each year to adjust for the difference in that year's hops. Add to this the tannin issues, which create a dry, pucker feeling in the mouth; tannin is especially problematic and must be dealt with when making soft/mild beers.

Long beers get a great deal of natural conditioning, though he does not bottle condition. Half to two-thirds of the carbonation in Long beers is from natural conditioning, which Paul tops off with just a bit of CO_2. But care must be taken; beer which is overly carbonated can give a carbonate bite, an obviously undesirable trait.

Long beers are bottled using a microprocessor controlled single bottle bottler, which Paul designed himself. (Being an electrical engineer does come in handy.)

So far, Long Brewing is restricted by their small size. Selling all he could make at the time of our interview, two to two and a half barrels per

Microprocessor controlled bottler, designed by Paul

month, Long is too small to produce enough to participate in festivals

This kettle was soon to be a thing of the past.

yet. Although as production increases, Paul hopes to do a couple of local festivals.

Paul has also been waiting to increase his volume before entering Long beers in commercial competitions. It is a given that this competitive, particular man is looking forward to entering the arena of professional contests. Never one to think small, another goal on Paul's list is to win the World Cup with his IPA.

Hopefully, some of Paul's volume problems will soon be a thing of the past. He had designed a new system and was awaiting its arrival when we interviewed him. Requirements for the unique processes used at Long Brewing dictated the need for a specially designed system; mainstream commercial systems simply would not allow him the tannin management abilities he demands. Tannin management is tops for Paul. Arrival of the new system should increase Long's output to three and half to four barrels per month.

While Paul would like to eventually try his hand at barrel aged beers, they are not yet on the agenda at Long Brewing. Concerned that a lot of oak aged beers are rather heavy handed, he has not been able to get too excited about them. Admitting that it would be fun to find out what he could do with them, perhaps layer different malts to get full complexity from the beer, Paul's eyes brighten a bit at the idea of the challenge.

While Long beers may be at the top end of the price curve, $8 - $22 per

The corner with all these signs is about a mile from Long Brewing.

bottle, the argument may be made that you get what you pay for. Tastings are available at the brewery by appointment only. One note about tastings, this high-end beer is served in a tulip glass, for full aromatic enjoyment.

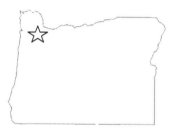

Lucky Labrador
Brewing Company

915 SE Hawthorne Blvd.
Portland, OR 97214
(503) 236-3555
www.luckylab.com

"2005 Best Dog Friendly Restaurant"

With a patio in back which welcomes pooches and an obviously dog-friendly name, Lucky Labrador goes beyond giving their four-legged patrons a treat. As the sponsor of several events to raise funds for the Dove Lewis Emergency Animal Hospital, Lucky Lab's heart for helping their canine friends also results in some sparkling clean pups. In addition to the Multnomah Days Dogwash, there is also Dogtoberfest, both offer a dog wash for a suggested donation of $10. Also earning funds for the animal hospital is the Tour de Lab, a cycling event which allows riders to choose the flat route or the hilly route. Either

way, a stop at each of the four Lucky Lab locations is sure to extinguish the thirst fired by the ride.

You will find no televisions, lottery machines, or pool tables at Lucky Lab. What you will find are people talking-and dart boards. As a

Many bulletin boards full of patron's dog pictures line the entry.

place which prides itself on focusing on the beer, this Portland icon prefers to keep the food simple and inexpensive. Among the eleven taps, plus one nitro and one cask, and an ever changing selection, you will find a guest tap which will usually be occupied by another Oregon brew, or at least a Northwest brew.

Also of note are bulletin boards covered with photos of patron's dogs. Interestingly, this was not part of the planned décor. As people randomly began posting their dog's photos, the idea multiplied. Now displaying several boards of pups, most of them labs, a quick count when we visited showed approximately 300 canine darlings.

Gary, showing us around

Except for a few charitable events and the Oregon Brewers Festival, Lucky Lab does not do many festivals. Nor do they participate in competitions, "Beer is a little bit like art, we kind of avoid all the beer competitions." Other than a few special releases, only three of the Lab's brews are bottled, and these are sold mostly out of the pubs. More bottling would involve more marketing, and this would take the fun out of it, so unless this changes, it is best not to count on finding a bottle of Lucky Lab in your local store. This works out well since they try to specialize in more complex beers specific to Portland tastes. According to Bob, this is too bad since they make a "…really good IPA…they could bottle and sell it anywhere." While they do distribute kegs to other pubs, your best option is to stop by one of the four locations.

First opened October 15, 1994, by partners Gary Geist and Alex Stiles (with the help of many investors) the Lucky Labrador building, circa 1923, was previously home to a roofing and sheet metal warehouse. Despite the slow and laborious process, Gary and Alex obtained a Small Business Administration (SBA) loan to purchase the building. With this and $190 thousand initial investment attained though talking to family, friends, friends of friends, and whoever else would listen, the two did much of the

remodeling themselves. After the remodeling and instillation of brewing equipment acquired from Cross Brewing Equipment in Springville, California, they were flat broke, but they had a brewpub!

The Lucky Labrador had become a dream after a post-college back-packing trip to Europe and exposure to various styles of beers. After returning, Gary worked behind the bar at Bridgeport Brewpub for a year and a half. About the time he left Bridgeport, Alex began brewing there. The two let the idea of their own brewpub ferment for a while, then began talking more seriously about it before doing a six-month feasibility study.

With Alex brewing, aided by two assistants, Lucky Lab uses a 14 barrel system at each of three locations (there is no brewing at the Tap Room). The addition of a solar thermal hot water system, made affordable by tax credits and installed by Ra Energy of Portland, is not only expected to save about $600 per month in energy costs, but also over 1700 pounds of carbon dioxide emissions. The initial cost of about $70,000 was reduced to approximately $5000 after rebates and tax incentives. With all the hot water needed for a brewery, it sounds like this is not only a great marketing advantage, but also a financially sound decision.

Gary, who is a father of three, an avid runner, and a surfer, believes there is "...a time and a place for every beer." He says this business is a lot of work, especially when you don't have much money. But with things getting easier as he learns to be a better trouble-shooter, perhaps he will have more time to dedicate to his other interests, or just to stop and enjoy a beer.

The Mash Tun Brewpub

2404 NE Alberta Street
Portland, Oregon 97211
503-548-4491
www.themashtunbrewpub.com

"Hand-made in small batches"

In the area of Portland known as the Alberta Arts District, The Mash Tun Brewpub sits just off Alberta Street. This place, which you somehow know feels comfortable within an artsy area; is simple, yet alive; relaxed, yet detailed; providing for the masses, yet catering to the individual.

When Christian Bravard first moved into this area in 1997, it was a different place. With active gangs, Alberta Street was not a place to walk at night. There were many boarded up businesses; It was what one would call a "bad" neighborhood.

Over the next eight years, Alberta changed, for the good. Artists began moving into the area in the late nineties, and it acquired the unofficial nickname, Alberta Arts District. A funky area, reminiscent of the 70's, a grass roots movement of change brought this once dying neighborhood back to life and respectability. Now hosting art walks that draw up to forty thousand people, Alberta Street has shed its "bad" image.

Christian had started as a restaurant cook at the tender age of fifteen. After homebrewing for six years, he decided it was time to put his vast restaurant experience to use and began looking for a space to take his brewing to the commercial level.

By that time, in 2005, Alberta Street was more of an up-and-coming area, though there were still many commercial spaces available. Drawn to the current location by the high ceilings and garage doors, which would create a nice patio for summers, Christian was in the process of adding an outdoor beer garden when we visited in December 2010.

Christian Bravard

The longer we were there, the more we realized that while this brewpub may seem simple at first glance, there is actually a great deal to

Board games are also available for your gaming pleasure.

take in, it is in the details. A large space with many tables, a pool table, and a juke box, we quickly noticed the many plants that add a warmth to such a large, high ceilinged space. Looking closer at the artwork on the wall showed they are all for sale. Christian tells us the art changes each month. An antique Hoosier cabinet displays hand-blown tumblers made in Wallowa County, which are also for sale. One of the more unique features was the door surrounded by coasters. As patrons began drawing on the backs of coasters, Christian, amazed by the artistry in some of them, started displaying them. Visiting the restroom reveals chalkboard walls, chalk included.

Doing the majority of the work on the building himself, we were impressed to hear that Christian built the bar. The ingenuity of repurposing reveals itself as he tells how he built it using wooden panel doors from Home Depot. That beautiful bar top is Douglas fir flooring. By thinking outside the box, Christian built a beautiful, functional, and solid bar at a reasonable price.

Hoosier cabinet with tumblers inside

A step out to the "patio" reveals a large space with plenty of seating and a can't-miss mural.

Bob and Christian chat at the bar.

Shortly after Mash Tun opened, a girl came to Christian and told him she had a dream that she had painted a mural for him, so she did...for free! This amazing artist was Molly Lowe.

The outdoor beer garden was nearing completion when we visited. With this addition, patrons will have plenty of options to choose from at

Mash Tun; indoors, covered indoor/outdoor patio, or outdoors. Located behind the building, the beer garden is expected to give Mash Tun more Alberta Street exposure through its perpendicular alignment with Alberta.

While Mash Tun possesses an Alberta Street Address, it is actually just off Alberta Street on 22nd Street.

Molly's mural in the background of the patio, where the garage door (right) was closed during our early morning interview.

This is Christian's regret. He would love to have Mash Tun directly on Alberta. At one time he had hoped to be able to rent the building next to Mash Tun, which does open onto Alberta, and expand into it, but unfortunately, that negotiation fell through. So remember, it's just around the corner!

The beer garden was a work in progress at the time of our visit.

Brewing on a 3.5 barrel system and having trouble keeping up with demand, Christian had just hired an assistant brewer. Mash Tun beers are unfiltered, unpasteurized, unprocessed, and served directly from the holding tanks. This all-electric brewery relies on 100% renewable energy, avoiding use of fossil fuels.

Available only at the brewpub, Mash Tun does not yet bottle, though bottles and cans are both part of the future vision. Christian hopes to provide cans to allow convenience for outdoor activities such as camping and fishing. Mash Tun is not available in kegs, meaning there are no Mash Tun taps around town. The exception would be for brew festivals, after all, there must be a mode of transport. Take heart though, you can get your corny keg filled and Mash Tun offers growlers for beer to-go.

Food at Mash Tun is not just something they have to do, not just a sideline, it is taken as seriously as the beer. Using high-quality ingredients,

In the brewery, the "mash tun" is on the far right.

which are local and organic whenever possible, Christian believes any food can be gourmet if made well, using good ingredients. With all-natural meats and organic tempeh and tofu, Mash Tun fulfills patron's dietary needs regardless of preference.

Being conscious of the importance of sustainability, Mash Tun goes beyond recycling and sending spent grain to local farmers. They also donate their used cooking oil to Mike Parziale's Grease Bus. The Grease Bus, run

Coaster art

exclusively on waste vegetable oil, has traveled the country for years and is now offering shuttle services from Portland to Mt. Hood.

Family-friendly until 9 P.M., Mash Tun offers free wi-fi, free juke box, free pool, and free darts.

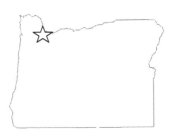

McMenamins Pubs & Breweries

430 N Killingsworth Street
Portland, Oregon 97217
503-286-0372
www.mcmenamins.com

"A place for family and friends..."

As we toured around Oregon, meeting various owners and brewers, we kept hearing one thing when the topic of the camaraderie and friendship among Oregon brewers came up, the McMenamin brothers are fun. As a result, we were looking forward to our interview with Brian McMenamin. However, despite the number of interviews we have done, we still find interviewing the "big guys" a bit intimidating. We are here to say, there was no need to feel intimidated with Brian McMenamin.

Growing up in Northeast Portland, neither Brian, nor older brother Mike said "I want to own a brewpub/hotel/theater empire when I grow up." The sons of an attorney, the late Robert McMenamin, both brothers thought they were aspiring attorneys.

After attending Madeleine Catholic Grade School, Mike, the older of the two by six years, graduated from Jesuit High School with a football scholarship to Oregon State. Though he did not yet know what he wanted to do with his life, Mike knew playing football was not it, so he quit football after his freshman year.

Taking a job at the Corvallis icon, Togo's, a submarine-type sandwich shop, Mike fell in love with the food business. But it was not until 1973 when he and his wife, Mary Ann, toured Europe in a Volkswagen bus with a foam mattress in the back and a Bunsen burner

Brian McMenamin

for cooking, that he was drawn to the pubs. Unlike the darkened taverns in Oregon, the pubs of Europe were family gathering places. This was when the idea for McMenamins was born.

After graduating from Oregon State in 1974 with a degree in political science, Mike took a job working at a produce warehouse in southeast Portland. Across from the warehouse was a small café with a "For Sale" sign. Partnering with two friends, Mike bought it, serving Togo's style food and beer. The café, Produce Row, was later joined by four other pubs, Bogart's Joint, Stockyard Café, McMenamin's Pub, and Westhill's Market & Deli.

Brian and Mike McMenamin
Photo courtesy McMenamins, used by permission

In those days, it was difficult to find beers other than the standard yellow beers put out by the major beer companies, so Mike decided to open a distributorship, focusing on imported beers. Finding it a challenge to run both types of business, Mike decided to sell the pubs and focus on the distributorship.

Brian worked in the kitchens of Mike's pubs from the time he was sixteen. After turning twenty-one, he even managed one for a while. With the same education as Mike, including a degree in political science from Oregon State in 1980, Brian could not see himself spending another three years in law school, the passion just was not there.

After the distributorship failed, Mike was driving by the Little Fat Rooster bar in Southeast Portland in 1983, at which he had spent some time in the past, and noticed it had recently closed. Going in to talk with the landlord, who was cleaning the place, Mike had leased the place by the time he left. After all, he was out of work and had three children, he needed an income.

Renaming it the Barley Mill and bringing Brian on as partner, Mike gathered eight friends and wrestled the mammoth sized barley mill he had purchased on impulse from a defunct brewery, through the front window of the newly acquired place to serve as a centerpiece in its namesake.

Explore McMenamins' website. Like the pubs, it is different, special. Delve deeply and discover its intricacies.
Photo courtesy of McMenamins, used by permission

When asked if they had any idea what they had started when they opened the Barley Mill, Brian says they really had no expectations; they just started simply and kept

Pipe angles come alive at McMenamins, where no detail is too small.

going. Regarding the earlier pubs, Brian says they "did them on the cheap," choosing old taverns, but things have changed through the years, these days, the McMenamin brothers are known for saving historical old buildings by turning them into light, family-friendly pubs, brewpubs, hotels, theaters, resorts, and any combination of the above.

By the time of our interview, McMenamins had a total of fifty-five locations in Oregon and Washington, with another six in process. Eight of those locations include movie theaters, eight include hotel accommodations, twenty-four include breweries, one includes both a winery and a distillery, one hosts two 3-par golf courses, and all are open to families. Additionally, McMenamins roasts their own coffee at their coffee roastery.

For those unfamiliar (yes, there are such people) with McMenamins, these are not the typical cookie-cutter chain brewpubs. Each and every McMenamins has its own unique design, size, history, and atmosphere. The common denominators being beer, food, family, and fun!

The location for our interview with Brian was Chapel Pub, which also serves as company headquarters. Extolled as "an architectural gem that ranks as one of Portland's finest" when it was built in 1932 at an amount that during the depression was an exorbitant sum, $40,000, this building spent the next

We enjoyed the sign pointing to several of the McMenamins locations.

The sign above the offices was designed with aging in mind. The steel was expected to rust to a streaky reddish-brown, allowing the blue weld joints to show and highlighting the painted lettering.

seventy-three years as a funeral home. First named Wilson-Chambers Mortuary, the name was changed to Little Chapel of the Chimes after chimes were added in

Iron work by O.B. Dawson, who also did the ironwork at Timberline Lodge. In the background is accounting, where the casket showroom once was. Offices are also located in the old embalming room and crematorium.

the late 30s. Organ and chimes concerts, worship services, and weddings were held in the chapel until 2005 when corporate owners decided to sell the property.

In stepped the McMenamins. Notably, there was still a working crematorium when they first toured the place. Location, historic relevance, and architecture drew them to this amazing site. In 2006, the same year it was inducted into the National Register of Historic Places, the long-time funeral home was renovated to become the newest McMenamins pub, as well as company headquarters. The Chapel was reluctant to give up its past, with the small congregation continuing to hold services there for a couple of years after the new pub opened.

As we toured, the history of the place was riveting, the respect for the past apparent, and the elements of whimsy around every corner reminded everyone not to take life too seriously. Whether through the Thursday evening organ concerts, the historical photos or the fanciful artwork, the McMenamin's enjoyment of life and history, along with their desire to share it, comes through. At McMenamins, history is treated as the fourth dimension, celebrating community.

With the passage of the 1985 Oregon Brewpub Law - the McMenamins were instrumental lobbyist - the brothers hired brewer, Conrad Santos, and opened Oregon's first brewpub, crafting their earliest beer in October 1985. Since Mike had done a bit of homebrewing, he and

At Chapel Pub, patrons now eat where the drive-through for the hearse used to be.

- 221 -

Conrad worked together on the initial batches of McMenamins beers.

With the brewpub concept increasing the fun, McMenamins has worked since 1985 to de-mystify the brewing process, going so far as to install open fermenters in their Lighthouse Brewpub location in Lincoln City (our first visit to a McMenamins was at this

The original organ is still played on Thursday evenings.

location). Open fermenters are rare in the brewing industry due to increased contamination risks, which would consign the entire batch down the drain, but for the few who assume the risk, it makes for quite a show.

With McMenamins beers being unfiltered, the bartenders originally thought no one would drink it, after all, you could not even see through it! How things have changed.

The year 1986 was the year the McMenamins began to submit to their love of history, purchasing a 125 year-old farmhouse on six acres, which they

Cornelius Pass Roadhouse
Photo courtesy of McMenamins, used by permission

proceeded to turn into Cornelius Pass Roadhouse. This Hillsboro piece of history was originally a 634-acre tract settled in 1843 by eighteen year old Kentucky native, Edward Henry Lenox, who traveled with the first major emigrant party over the Oregon Trail. In the 1850s the property was acquired by Robert Imbrie, who then built the three-story, gabled farmhouse in the 1860's. Before that, Imbrie had built the granary which still stands on the property and eventually housed the barley which Imbrie began selling to Blitz-Weinhard in 1933. Six generations of Imbries lived there until it was converted to a restaurant in 1977 by Gary Imbrie. When developers threatened the structures, McMenamins

Never take yourself too seriously, even in the brewery.
Photo courtesy of McMenamins, used by permission

stepped in to assure its preservation. The property now also boasts the Imbrie Hall Pub, which was built using timbers from Portland's Henry Weinhard's brewery.

From this first step into history, McMenamins has expanded their historical renovation to offer more than the average brewpub. In 1987, they converted the 1890s Swedish Tabernacle, a church-turned-union hall in Northwestern Portland, into the state's first theater pub, Mission Theater and Pub. A building with a long and varied history, it started as a place for missionaries to plan mission trips to Asia. After they left, it flip-flopped to a Long Shoreman's Hall. Eventually, McMenamins attained it for their wild experiment, a movie theater pub. Originally showing older movies at no charge, the Mission switched to second run movies for $2 when it was determined the older movies were not terribly successful. The second run movies must be a hit, considering McMenamins has followed this initial experiment with seven more theater pubs.

Then in 1987, the brothers saved Edgefield, in Troutdale, from sure destruction. This amazing place, built in 1911 as the county poor farm, housed as many as six hundred residents, called inmates, during the depression era. Residents, encompassing a varied range of occupations, races, religions, and ages, worked at what was at that time a more than 300 acre farm. This gave them a "leg-up" until better times would come. With the

Edgefield had to be saved.
Photo courtesy of McMenamins, used by permission

start of World War II and its accompanying jobs, most residents left Edgefield, leaving mostly the aged and incapacitated. It was at that time that Edgefield took on more of a nursing home/rehab center role until 1982, when the shrinking population and aging buildings forced transfer of the last of the patients to other locations.

For the next five years, the Troutdale Historical Society fought to save the stately old place. When given one more year to find a buyer, the Historical Society appealed to the McMenamin brothers. The seventy-four acre property with its wonderful buildings captivated the brothers, leading them to begin work on their first resort, which eventually blossomed into 100 European-style guest rooms and hostel accommodations, restaurants, bars, pubs, two three-par golf courses, a winery, a distillery, a spa, a gift shop, a movie theater, a glass blower, a potter... Brian described it as a "Disneyland for beer drinkers." Personally, I don't drink beer, but I still want to go there!

Chapel Pub

In addition to saving wonderful old buildings, this historical trek at McMenamins has added much to the communities in which these buildings are found. McMinnville saw a marked increase in business for their community, after their completion of Hotel Oregon, where the forth and top story, had never been completed before it became a McMenamins. As is their custom, McMenamins rejoices in what some would term "obscure," such as the annual UFO Festival. A celebration of the famous 1950 Trent sightings, when two local citizens photographed a UFO, McMinnville celebrated their twelfth annual UFO festival in 2010.

A fireplace at Chapel Pub

According to *Paranormal Underground's* January 2009 edition, there are those who say a few of the McMenamins' properties are haunted. Apparently, all are friendly ghosts, including a child who serenades guests with nursery rhymes and then wants them to play with her. Other reports include cold spots, footsteps, opened doors, and a woman who wakes people by shaking their feet. Whether there is any merit to the stories or not, it definitely adds to the fun, fulfilling the motto at

McMenamins, "It's got to be fun."

When McMenamins modeled John Barleycorns after a building they liked in Hawaii, it turned out beautiful. Imagine their surprise when they discovered the building in Hawaii they had thought was a pumphouse was actually a sewage treatment plant. But in typical McMenamin good humor, they laugh and tell the amusing story.

A large, old Dick & Jane book greeted us as we stepped into the McMenamins offices.

When asked if he has a favorite McMenamins, Brian diplomatically says he likes them all, but admits he gets attached to their current project. Brian and Mike do all the design themselves; they get involved in the surrounding community, being very hands-on. When visiting the various pubs, they become nostalgic, remembering when that particular place was their current project.

Rumor has it that a few have complained that some of the whimsy in the McMenamins renovations is irreverent. As a history buff,

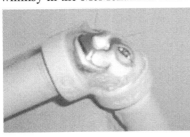

Irreverence? Or art which future generations will work to preserve?

I say, buildings evolve. Changes are continually made to buildings, even when they remain with the same people/business through the years. The changes McMenamins make are part of that progression. Hopefully, fifty or a hundred years from now, the changes McMenamins has made will be part of the revered past, protected for future generations the way Mike and Brian have now preserved them.

These are people who care about keeping history alive for the generations. In fact, an extremely unusual aspect of McMenamins is the two historians they have on staff. Additionally, managers are trained to identify visitors who have a history at that location, pre-McMenamins. Add to this, several staff artists, who work with the historians to create the artwork they refer to as embellishments.

Historical photos line the employee halls at McMenamins

Employees are exposed to and encouraged to learn the history behind each location. Historical photos adorn the walls and are available to view in the offices, to allow staff to relate to the history.

When speaking with Brian, his enthusiasm increases as he shows us pictures and tells us the history behind them. As we spoke of the 1912 Roseburg Station, he showed us pictures of the 1959 blast when a truck loaded with two tons of dynamite and 4.5 tons of nitro carbo nitrate was ignited by a structure fire. The ensuing blast blew a hole in the ground that was fifty-two feet wide and twenty feet deep. The explosion and consequent fire destroyed every structure within an eight block area and damaged buildings throughout the surrounding thirty blocks. Killing 14 and injuring 125, damages were estimated at up to $12 million. The blast pulled bolts into the trusses of what was then the train station, trying to blow the roof off the structure. Growing up in Sutherlin, I remember the newspaper clipping my dad saved about the blast. While I was a

Roseburg Station-saved by McMenamins
Photo courtesy Laura Ledford

toddler at the time, Dad had excellent memories of the occurrence.

While working on the Kennedy School reconstruction for McMenamins, one of the construction workers realized the picture

Roseburg Station features many lights
Photo courtesy Laura Ledford

showing the children exiting the school on its last day before closing permanently, included him. Imagine his surprise.

Brian says it best, "The history is fun; it brings the places to life."

In addition to the pubs each being different, the food at each McMenamins is different, but whether pizza,

- 226 -

burgers, or gourmet, you may depend upon the finest local ingredients available, with some organic and/or grown on sight.

While there are standard brews at McMenamins, you may find their taste slightly different depending on which of the twenty-four breweries they were brewed at. In addition to the standards, each brewery creates their own brews. In fact,

High Street Brewery & Cafe was the first brewery in Eugene since prohibition.

McMenamins hosts several of their own brew festivals for competition between the various McMenamins breweries. Collectively, McMenamins produces over two hundred recipes of beer and has handcrafted more than 54 thousand batches of beer!

McMenamins beers, wines, and spirits are available only at McMenamins.

Step out the back door at High Street and you will find outdoor cozy. In addition to a deck with plenty of seating, the backyard has been filled with patio, which is surrounded by hedges and trees to create a private outdoor pub experience. Complete with a fire pit, there are plenty of picnic tables to relax around while enjoying your brew, meal, and occasional entertainment at High Street's beer garden.

More fun on a tank at Roseburg Station
Photo courtesy of Laura Ledford

However, you can take it home in bottles, mason jars, growlers, and kegs. So take your time, explore, enjoy, and have fun at McMenamins. Who knows, maybe someday you will be the one to say "I remember when..."

Mia & Pia's Pizzeria and Brewhouse
3545 Summers Lane
Klamath Falls, OR 97601
Phone: 541-884-4880
& 541-884-0949
www.miapia.com

This family-friendly pizzeria has history behind it. Originally dairy farmers, with 135 milking cows, Don and Nancy Kucera and family delivered milk to local stores and outlying areas of Medford, Lakeview, and Bend on a daily basis. As the first dairy in the area with a concrete floor, the Kuceras showed they were open to new ideas. Dairy production ended when the government bought it out in a program to reduce availability.

In 1987, the Kuceras opened a pizza parlor in Keno. After purchasing a one-time grocery store/laundry on Summers Lane in 1988, they moved their pizza operation to Klamath Falls and became a pizza parlor/laundry.

After many years as a professional rodeo bull-rider, their son, Rod, heard an ad on the radio for the Northwest Microbrew Festival (now the KLCC Festival). While at the festival, where Rod found 72 beers on tap, he attended a homebrew session. He discovered making beer on a professional scale would require stainless steel tanks, with a good source being old dairies. "The light came on," according to Rod.

After arriving back in Klamath Falls, Rod built a three-tiered system, affectionately known as Buffalo Bill's Book. From the beginning, he used all grain, skipping the common new brewer's step of using extract. He was hooked!

In 1995, Brewing Techniques magazine had a symposium in conjunction with Oregon Brewer's Festival. They even included a seminar on "how to make a brewery with milk tanks." Obviously, Rod was there. He took several copies of the floor plan for his dairy/brewery and passed them out to other brewers at the festival. Showing the comradery for which Oregon brewers are famous, Rod's plans were accepted with enthusiasm.

After devoting all year to converting the old dairy to a brewery, utilizing much of the dairy equipment and hardware, Rod managed to produce his first six commercial barrels in December 1996, becoming

Klamath Falls first microbrewery. 1997 brought Rod's first full year of production as well as the change of the family pizza parlor from a pizza/laundry to Mia & Pia's Pizzeria and Brewhouse. Goodbye laundry! From this determined beginning, production has risen to the current 500 barrels annually, still using some of the same old dairy/brew tanks. Obviously, along the way somewhere, he found the answer to his number one question, "How do you get the beer inside that keg?"

Kegs at Mia & Pia's brewery

Mia & Pia's Pizzeria and Brewhouse is found in two separate locations. All brewing is done at the brewery on the old dairy farm. The Pizzeria and pub are located on Summers Lane.

Though the exterior may lack pizzazz in curb appeal, Mia & Pia's Pizzeria and Brewhouse caught my attention from my first look through the windows at the interesting lighting. Like most farmers, repurposing is the name of the game. Those interesting lights are fashioned out of the old milking machines. The mug rack, which holds the mug club members mugs, is the old 5-section harrow. For those uninitiated in farming, horses would drag the harrow through the field to break up the dirt clods.

Milking machine lights

Rod also traveled off the farm for equipment for the ex-laundry, now pub. In August of 1997 the Elks Club in Eugene had to move so the county could build a juvenile detention center. A large auction was held to sell many of the items from the old facility, including the large bar, which was split in two for the sale. Rod purchased one section for $50, which included the compressors. He followed this with the long bar for $75. The cherry paneling on the bar was produced by Weyerhaeuser. The old bar with its harrow mug club rack is an attraction in itself. Rod's auction travels and great buys did not end with the bar. The tables came from an auction in Jacksonville. The

Harrow mug rack with 206 mugs

chairs were previously used in the Hungry Woodsman in Medford.

Reuse, reduce, and recycle may be modern "green" terminology, but to a family used to the hard work, long hours, and making due, it's just another day on the farm...uh, at the brewery/pizzeria. With many farm antiques and repurposed items adding a decorative touch, there is plenty to keep the eye busy while at the pizzeria/pub.

The bar is not only beautiful, but historical and inexpensive.

Back on the farm...brewery, by outside appearances it still looks like a farm. However, there seems to be an extreme shortage of the expected animals... oh yes, it's a brewery. The solar panels on top of the ~~barn~~ brewery are another indication of the transition which has taken place at this family farm. The old 1964 milk truck the family purchased in 1967, when they first bought the farm, is still there. With a bit of repurposing it

Solar Panels help power the brewery.

has become a beer truck, including six taps on the outside for serving at beer gardens. One gets the feeling Rod has had a great time conceiving innovative uses for old equipment.

Next to the parking area is a well maintained "square" of lawn, bordered by beds which are the home to a small crop of hops when in season. A space like this cries out to be used for events, which is exactly its purpose. The yearly Mug Club Party is held here for mug club members. The anniversary party on the third weekend in August makes its home there (of course). Mostly this space is rented out for weddings, company parties, birthdays and other events, with the pasture being temporarily repurposed as a parking

Event space at the farm/brewery

lot. As I gazed out at the surrounding organic farmlands and distant mountains, it struck me as a wonderfully relaxing venue.

Though many of the items in the brewery are repurposed from the farm, "new" items are also seen. New, of course, means new to the Kucera family. "We never buy anything new." For example, the "new" chiller, bought at auction when a pub went out of business, would have cost $22 thousand unused-new...Rod got it for a bid of $5,000. Okay, he did have to fix it, but with a $17,000 savings, I would say he made pretty good repairman wages.

This solar heated brewery can brew two batches per day in the converted milk tanks. When we talked to Rod, they were brewing weekly.

In the brew room, Rod tells of how he used to milk cows, three at a time, in this room. But the story does not end there. When in high school he would slip in here to sneak a beer. Rather prophetic, I would say.

The brewery has some growth potential, after some renovating. Perhaps conical tanks would fit in. They are actually nicer because it makes re-harvesting the yeast much easier. Rod is concerned with quality and consistency. With no lab he must purchase new yeast every eight to ten generations. This creates more expense, but he feels it is worth the cost. Did I just say "new" yeast? Gotcha, Rod. Perhaps if he renovated, he could include a lab in the renovation. But, alas, there are no current renovation plans.

Brewer, Rod Kucera, now brews where as a teen he would sneak a beer.

Rod bottles only for contests, but you can purchase half gallon growlers to take home. He seems to be doing well at the contests, having made it to the final round at the Great American Beer Festival in Denver.

Back at the Mia & Pia's, named after the first grandson's names for "grandpa and grandma" when he couldn't yet say the words, you will need to get on a waiting list if you want to join the mug club here. The club is limited to 206 members, this number determined by the number of hooks on the harrow/mug rack. There are usually ten to 15 new

Patio at Mia & Pia's

members every year after others move or go into the military. Membership includes privileges such as special pricing, personalized engraved mugs to keep at year-end when the new mugs arrive, and special events for mug club members only-such as the 4th of July party.

If you are looking to have an event at the pizzeria, there are two options. An enclosed party room allows for privacy for the partiers and peace for the rest of the premises. Outside there is a fenced patio with a serving window, which will hold about one hundred people. Events such as rehearsal dinners and informal reunions are commonly held here.

Mia & Pia's offers an open jam on Tuesday nights and an open microphone the first Saturday of every month for the musically inclined and those who enjoy listening. If you are lucky, you may catch farmer/bull rider/brewmeister, Rod, on the harmonica or vocals.

Bob, enjoying a taster and pizza at Mia & Pia's

Migration Brewing Company

2828 NE Glisan Street
Portland, Oregon 97213
503-206-5221
www.migrationbrewing.com

"Newcomers from all walks of life migrated from far and away
places seeking new beginnings to fulfill their dreams"

The prominent garage door in the front of Migration Brewing, coupled with the picnic tables on the patio, spoke of an inviting spring day during our rainy December visit to Migration Brewing Company. Once inside we were greeted by a warmth which was due to more than temperature.

It was quickly obvious that this brewpub was a strong supporter of the local Portland Trailblazers basketball team, as evidenced by the display of jerseys and the banner on the olive green wall, right next to the big screen television. In fact, Migration would love to develop the reputation of being a Blazer supporter. So far, the following for their Blazer theme is not bad.

In addition to Blazer games, that TV is known for cult movies, documentaries, other sports...It is about the customer, whatever they want.

Named for the melting pot nature of Portland, Migration Brewing celebrates the diverse roots of the community. This is what Migration wishes to emulate.

Not desiring to be cubbyholed as a certain "type" of pub, the wish at Migration is to be known as everyone's home. Whether sports enthusiast, family (minors until 8 PM), students, business people, young, or old, Migration's goal is to embrace and provide comfort.

Comfortable seating available

After returning from Argentina in 2007, partner Colin Rath had an idea for a coffee shop. Shortly after he bounced the idea off buddy McKean Banzer-Lausberg, they got together again and did some brainstorming; a couple of months

Eric, burning logos into tap handles

later the idea for a brewpub stuck. McKean had managed one and Colin had spent a lot of time at Lucky Lab, so it is surprising it took them so long to come to the brewpub conclusion. Additionally, Colin and friend, Mike Branes, had done some homebrewing while rooming together, so Colin told McKean he knew the perfect brewer. By September 2008, the three were forming a business plan.

Colin, a Portland State communications development graduate, says his major comes in handy working the front of the pub. McKean's experience as a web-developer certainly comes in handy in this Internet-oriented age. Additionally, Mike's brew experience, plus his past working for a beer and wine distributor, are definite pluses.

Colin Rath

The partners were searching for the ideal location when Colin spotted an empty building with a perfect set-up, while riding past on his bicycle. This 1940s era building's previous life was as Decker's Radiator Shop, until they closed in October 2009. Its rebirth as a pub took sixteen hour days and a great deal of hands-on work by the partners who had more ambition than cash. Digging trenches, hauling wiring, installing plumbing, and HVAC, they did it all, and did it well.

McKean Banzer-Lausberg

The bar top and sides, tap handles, table tops, and trim they installed all came from wood made from old boom sticks which had long ago fallen to the bottom of the Columbia River and had recently been logged out of it. The wood is also all green-certified.

As we entered we could see employee, friend, and unofficial partner, Eric Haglund, who worked for Columbia Distributors for four years, burning the Migration Logo on tap handles for use by various accounts; they had about fifteen around Portland when we were there. The logo's wings represent the migratory nature of the area, while the red arrow, dubbed "Charlie" points to Migration Brewing. Sarah Osborn designed this impressive logo.

On the wall down from the Trailblazer layout is a mural which

Mural by Mickey Peterson

is clearly representative of Portland. Painted by artist, Mickey Peterson, this whimsical piece somehow still captures the beauty of the area. Gracing the small window next to the front door is a stained glass representation of the logo. This piece was made by Robert Rath, Colin's grandfather, who fills his retirement time by making stained glass creations.

Migration Brewing tries to support local ventures whenever possible. Rotating art is displayed and Mike's girlfriend, Heidi Waltemeyer, makes soap, which is available at Migration. Their desire to be supportive results in Migration taking no percentage from the art sold there.

After two wine bars on the block closed, the partners added a wine selection. In addition to supporting local wineries, it fills the niche left by the departing wine bars. Many of Migration's patrons come in specifically to appreciate their wine selection. Besides local wines,

Migration also has a selection of Argentinean wines available, in support of local friends who import them.

The seven barrel brewhouse was custom built by, and a first for, Metalcraft Fabrication in Portland. Though they had previously built fermenters

and other brew equipment, this was the first full brewhouse they built. The brewery included three fermenters. Unfortunately the forth one they had purchased did not work; after returning it, the partners decided they would make do with three for a while. The money cushion the refund provided felt too good. One of the three they have came from Lucky Labrador.

While the partners would love to have found used equipment, it may be located across country, which would mean additional cost in both time and money to inspect

those available and then have one shipped. The partners concluded that unless equipment was readily available, such as the fermenter from Lucky Lab, it would be more cost-effective to purchase new.

While Mike did homebrew with Colin, his professional experience began in 2003 at Barley John's in Minneapolis. Growing up

with his father drinking craft beers, he had long been exposed to them. When he began brewing, it became Mike's dream to open a brewpub.

One of the greatest challenges for Migration has been acquiring kegs; they are quite expensive, the shells run $150 each. When Mike found used kegs listed on-line for a price of $90 each, he called eight minutes after they were posted, they had already been sold. The seller told Mike he had twelve calls in the first five minutes after listing them. At the time of our interview, the guys at Migration had acquired sixty kegs and were hoping to attain 150 by summer 2011. With

Brewer, Mike Branes

many kegs being out where taps are; plus full kegs; dirty kegs; clean kegs; and empty kegs, waiting to be filled, a brewery requires a lot of kegs to keep production going.

With the Northwest so heavy with hops, many have said they would like a beer that is tailored back a bit, thus was born Migration's MPA, Migration Pale Ale. A "combination" IPA and Pale Ale, this flagship ale is representative of the "for everyone" attitude at Migration.

When we asked about regrets, they had to say the Belgium took top billing. Taste was not the problem; the problem arose when it locked up a fermenter for two months. Another fermenter was being repaired, so they were left with only one for brewing. This was a big set-back and a mistake which will not be repeated. So do not expect to see a Belgian from Migration until they acquire additional fermenters. Ditto for all lagers.

In the cooler with the bright tanks, Mike models the back of one of Migrations hoodies.

Though not currently bottling because space and beer quantity are a problem, it is a possibility in the future. Growlers are available for your take-home convenience for now.

In the pub, there are usually three guest taps and a cider. Food consists of soups, salads, sandwiches and finger foods. Simplicity and comfort are the buzzwords at Migration.

One unique find that we loved at Migration is their U.S map. Though I must admit, I expect to

Mark your spot on Migration's map

see them need to add a world map. This map is not beautiful, detailed, nor exceptional in any way, except perhaps its total simplicity and size. What is unusual is its purpose. Migration sells little red arrow stickers, the arrow from the logo, for $1. The purchaser may then put their arrow on the map to show where their home is. Every bit of the money raised from this is donated to International Community Development Fund (ICDF). This non-profit program works to improve social and productive infrastructure in South and Central America. Colin participated in this program, traveling to Central America with the man who runs it and works pro-bono, receiving no salary for his contributions.

In an ongoing effort to keep things fresh, amusing, and fun, Migration has just initiated Bingo Tuesdays. Every Tuesday for a $2 buy-in, patrons can enjoy some good-old-fashioned Bingo from 6-8 P.M. The good part...the winner takes the pot!

In commemoration of their anniversary, Migration is opening Charlie's Chug Club, which is their name for a mug club. Funds gained from the mug club memberships will be used to purchase a new seven barrel fermentation tank, allowing them to expand flavors and increase local keg distribution.

This brewpub has achieved and learned a lot since opening on February 19, 2010. As I write this, they will be celebrating their one-year anniversary tomorrow. Happy anniversary, Migration!

Mt. Emily Ale House

1202 Adams Avenue
La Grande, Oregon 97850
541-962-7711
www.mtemilyalehouse.com

"Bringing back a tradition of small local breweries producing fresh brewed beer...and specializing in gourmet pizza"

Jerry Grant loved beer and was just looking to save some money by brewing his own while in grad school in 1992. Additionally, it sounded fun. After receiving his Bachelor's and Master's degrees in biology, Jerry went on to earn his PhD in Fisheries Biology. As a Fisheries Biologist for the Oregon Department of Fish & Wildlife, he worked on the large hatchery and salmon program. The problem was, he was so good at his job they kept promoting him. Before he knew it, he was no longer involved in the biology he loved, he was too busy managing.

In 2006, he lost his mom; as often happens, this prompted changes in Jerry's life. Our time on earth is just too short, we should follow our dreams. So in 2007, Jerry enrolled in the Master Brewers Program at UC Davis.

After completion, Jerry searched La Grande for the perfect location, deciding to bank on the old U.S. Bank building. Built in 1900, this corner location's exterior is typical of the banks of the era. Inside, the original working vault still remains in the basement. More recently, the building has housed two jewelry stores, a clothing store, and a lending corporation.

Owner, Jerry Grant, at his hopyard
Photo courtesy Mt. Emily Ale House, used by permission

After originally opening in February 2009 with a partner, Bob Kidney, Jerry is now sole owner. The years spent dreaming and the months spent planning have culminated in a modern commercial look with a warm, relaxed, family-friendly atmosphere.

Mt. Emily, named for the local mountain, has a business plan focused on the new trend toward localism. Before prohibition, many bars and taverns brewed their own beer, it was the norm. Excited about the growing movement to bring this localism back to small

communities throughout the country, Jerry says there is a great phenomenon occurring, fresh locally brewed beer, like before prohibition.

The safe is still there
Photo courtesy Mt. Emily Ale House, used by permission

While Mt. Emily offers a varied menu, their food specialty is pizza. Also on the menu are sandwiches, seafood, salad, and obviously, Mt. Emily brews. They even make their own root beer.

Stop by on Saturdays and you will be treated to a variety of live music. Depending upon the week, you may be treated to folk, rock, country, reggae, or a local musician. Live music is also featured on occasional Thursdays. More than a brewery, Jerry's goal has been to make Mt. Emily a cultural activity center in La Grande.

Mt. Emily brews on a seven barrel brewhouse obtained from Sebastopol Brewing Company in Sebastopol, California, after they chose to transform into a wine bar. With seven standards, plus seasonals, Mt. Emily is currently available only at the brewpub, though they have begun looking to place taps all around Union, Baker, and Wallowa counties. Specializing in English style ales, their line-up also includes some Northwest style IPAs.

Brewhouse
Photo courtesy Mt. Emily Ale House, used by permission

With continued, steady growth, Mt. Emily is just beginning to hand bottle. Initially, expect to find Mt. Emily bottles available only at

Photo courtesy Mt. Emily Ale House, used by permission

the brewpub. However, with a soon-to-be-found four-head bottler, hopes are that by 2012, Mt. Emily ales will be available at small retailers within the three county area.

Having just completed the transition, all Mt. Emily beers are now organic (though certification is still pending). The beer you drink at Mt. Emily may contain hops grown in Jerry's own hopyard. With four varieties and 1000 plants, approximately 30% of Mt. Emily's beers contain Mt. Emily's hops.

In fact, Mt. Emily strives to use local ingredients whenever possible, and does with their beers. Unfortunately, with such a short growing season, the exclusive use of locally grown fresh vegetables for the restaurant is next to impossible, but it is still a dream. Supporting local businesses is important at Mt. Emily.

New on the Mt. Emily team is Matt Baxter, who will head up marketing and sales. Actually, Matt is a returning member of the team who served as the restaurant manager before quitting to complete a cross-country bike ride to the Florida keys, on a fixed-gear bike, as part of his MBA thesis.

Stop in at Mt. Emily, have a beer...or a root beer, enjoy a pizza, and a tour.

Photo courtesy Mt. Emily Ale House, used by permission

Mt. Hood Brewing Company
Ice Axe Grill

87304 E Government Camp Loop
Government Camp, Oregon 97028
503-662-0724
www.iceaxegrill.com

*"...Small, hand-crafted batches; with the highest
quality ingredients obtainable; sold for consumption very close to its source"*

Mt. Hood, a relatively short drive from Portland, greeted us with a beautiful snow storm when we visited on an early December evening. It felt right. I found myself wishing we had brought boots and snow clothes so we could take a walk. But with a 7A.M. interview in Portland the next morning, it probably would not have been wise.

Located in Government Camp, Mt. Hood Brewing Company and Ice Axe Grill are in a skier's Mecca. With four different ski resorts being only minutes away, this is not only a winter paradise, but also reportedly offers the only summer skiing in the U.S. Traditional summer activities are also available in abundance: hiking, rafting, camping, and biking, to name a few.

Ice Axe Grill, established in 1990, is a family restaurant with a lodge feel. The building originally served as a ski rental/gift shop/rock shop/café in the '60's and 70's. Some of the walls are made from flagstone which includes fossilized worm casings and was quarried from Oregon's High Dessert, while other walls are knotty pine and spruce.

Added in January 1991, Mt. Hood Brewing Company initially began by serving

Snowing at Mt. Hood at night

locally produced beers. By October 1992, the brewery was complete, the beer brewed, and Mt. Hood began serving their own beers.

While Mt Hood was initially under the watchful eye of Brewmaster, Jon B. Graber, he has long since moved on. At Mt. Hood from the beginning, Brewer Tom Rydzewski had long been a homebrewer before working with mentor Dave Logsdon, owner and founder of Wyeast Labs and one of the founders and the original brewer at Full Sail. In addition to mentoring with Dave, Tom has also taken a couple of the short brewing courses and currently works with one assistant.

Fermenters downstairs at Mt. Hood

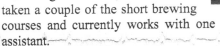

Tom helped install the custom JV Northwest system, built to fit the limited space, including a very shallow cone on one of the fermenters. This ten barrel brewery is currently producing twelve hundred barrels of brew per year. Brewing with distinctive water from a private, untreated well, it is "truly all about the water." Mt. Hood, who has between fifty and sixty accounts, distributes kegs throughout Oregon. While bottling would certainly be a possibility, it is not likely. Logistics would require more space allowing for

Brewer, Tom Rydzewski

greater production capacity.

The brewery is upstairs, visible through windows in the restaurant. After brewing, the beer is then piped downstairs to the fermentation tanks, where it is also

kegged for serving.

Tom is given full reign within certain guidelines at Mt. Hood and is welcome to brew special releases. Though Tom started with the standard recipes, he has manipulated them enough to now call them his own. Mt. Hood brews mostly ales, once again due to the space issues and the necessary lagering times required for lagers. They are most well known for their flagship beer, Ice Axe, a traditional British style IPA.

Originally from Tucson, Arizona, Tom moved to Portland to attend culinary school at Western Culinary Institute (now Le Cordon Bleu College of Culinary Arts), which he followed with an internship at Timberline Lodge. Tom followed the experience at Timberline by seeing the world while working on a couple of different cruise ships in Europe and Asia.

Ice Axe

One ship he worked on was Song of Flower, a Seven Seas (now Radisson) liner, which has since been decommissioned. As the only American to ever work in the Galley – he was hired out of Europe – he says it was quite interesting being yelled at in three languages.

An avid skier and cyclist who also enjoys telemark, Tom says he is quite content here, rooted enough to own his own home in nearby Welches (yes, he does get stuck at the brewery occasionally during snowstorms). At the time of our interview, he was unmarried, available, and loved where he lived.

Scheduling help for the pub can be a challenge, says manager, Leslie Skellenger. Because the weather is such a primary determiner of business at Mt. Hood, one almost needs to be clairvoyant at certain times of year. While summers are steady, things slow down significantly in October until the snow flies. Winters are, of course, their busiest time of year, with Christmas break being absolute craziness. In Spring, the weather once again determines business. During the summers the population of Government Camp gets crazy, mostly with vacationers, largely due to the summer snow skiing.

This family friendly restaurant can be cozy in the winter with its fireplace, or a great place to relax in the summer with a deck to enjoy the great outdoors.

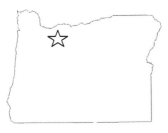

Mutiny Brewing Company
600 N. Main Street
Joseph, Oregon 97415
541-432-5274
mutinybrewing.blogspot.com

"Stop in and see what is brewing!"

Breathtakingly beautiful scenery alone would make the journey to Joseph worth the trip. Then there is the amazing local history. Add to that the true, old fashioned, small town atmosphere which can only be found in such an isolated place, and you will not regret the trip to this Northeast corner of the state. An added bonus upon arrival is the wide variety of recreational activities and events.

Before our tour, neither of us had seen this far corner of the state. We were curious and wanted to, but kept wondering what we would do when we got there, and it had not been high enough on our list of priorities to check the Internet. When deciding if it would be worth the time it would take to make the trip to the Eastern edge of the state to check out the breweries located there – we live in the opposite corner of the state - we realized we now had an excuse for the trip. What we found is definitely worth every mile and every minute. Joseph was amazing!

Nestled among the mountains, shops, and quaintness of this memorable local is Mutiny Brewing Company, whose owner and founder is as surprising as the surroundings. Twenty-eight year old (at the time of our interview) Kari Gjerdingen is not the typical brew master. This energetic and determined woman is making her dream a reality in a predominantly male profession. A member of the Pink Boots

Society, whose purpose is to "inspire, encourage and empower women to become professionals and advance their careers in the Beer Industry, mainly through education," Kari is making a great start toward filling those boots.

Starting in the brewing industry at barely twenty-one, Kari hales from Bloomington, Indiana. The stage was set for Kari's future when as a young girl, she enjoyed making ice cream, focusing on one thing and experimenting until she got the desired results. At twenty years of age, she journeyed to Belgium with her

Brewer Kari Gjerdingen

brother, where he made the monumental and prophetic declaration that she should become a brewer. After graduating from Wellesley College, whose mission is to "provide an ...education for women who will make a difference in the world," where they encourage women to go into non-traditional occupations, Kari did a six-month brewer's program at UC Davis. She followed that with a year and a half working for Upland Brewing Company in Bloomington, where she learned brewing, as well as worked the bottling line.

Due to her experiences, Kari actually brewed on a thirty barrel system before a five-gallon system. After trying a five-gallon home brewing system in a friend's garage, she said "home brewing is hard," and confined her home brew efforts to what she could do at breweries. All the necessary cleaning is much easier in a brewery.

Moving to Portland left her wondering which friend to stay with, the obvious choice became – the one closest to a brewery! This ambitious brewer would not be a house-guest for long. After three months in Portland, Kari attended a Master Brewers Association meeting in Bend where she met Steve Comer, owner of Terminal Gravity in Enterprise, who hired her as production manager.

While working for Terminal Gravity, besides managing, Kari naturally helped brew and order supplies. "Great group!" she says of the crew at TG, adding that Steve has been very supportive of her new venture.

After purchasing the site of a wholesale bakery, which had closed their restaurant portion two years earlier, Kari did extensive remodeling, including gutting and expanding the kitchen. A new addition to the side of the building houses the brewery and exhibits the thought she put into her design in the form of large garage doors in the front and back of the brewery. We have spoken with many who have had to tackle the problem of how to get the large tanks into their buildings, but this is not a problem Mutiny will encounter. Another demonstration of the preparation at Mutiny is the on-demand hot water heater, which will easily supply the thousands of gallons of hot water needed to produce batch after batch of beer.

Although the restaurant opened in June 2009, the brewery was just nearing completion when we visited in November. In fact, the final building inspection for the addition was scheduled for the day after our visit. Boasting what looks like brand new tanks still wrapped in their shipping plastic, the majority of her equipment was actually purchased used from Jason Ager, at Ager Tank & Equipment Company in Portland. Watching Kari look at

her new brewery leaves no doubt she is excited and proud of her new venture. She has a right to be; she has a wonderful place.

Mutiny is what I would describe as modern cozy. It has the clean lines of modern design, while at the same time giving the feeling it would be a wonderful place to cozy up on a cold winter evening. Even as I write this I realize it also easily lends itself to the refreshing feeling of a warm summer day in its light, airiness. Let's face it, it's nice and it's versatile. While the simplicity of design is what I first noticed, as I looked around I realized there were many intricate details. Intricate wood carved hops and barley by local craftsman Steve Armel embellish corners and edges. Amazing art by Debbie Keifer graces the walls. Multihued blown-glass tumblers capture your fancy.

Woodwork by Steve Armel

The glasses, made by local craftsmen, Jake Kurts and Russell Ford, are available for purchase. As Mutiny's version of a mug club, you may leave them there for your drinking pleasure, or you may take them

Bob relaxes at Mutiny's bar

home. We took ours home. Because Kari has plans to feature rotating artists, you may not be lucky enough to view Debbie's work, but there will undoubtedly be an artist worthy of consideration. In addition to the carvings, Steve Armel also built the bar and the "Mutiny is brewing" sign in front of the business; all are worth seeing. Kari was also searching for a local artist to make tap handles.

Unfortunately, Bob was unable to sample Mutiny's brew, as Kari did not expect to begin brewing for another month. Word has it that as of January, she expected suds within the week. Pressure is rather high, as are expectations. Kari will have brewed three batches before she is able to taste the first. With locals frequently asking her "where's the beer?" she is aware there is a lot riding on getting it right. Though the restaurant is doing well, this is a brewery, which requires beer, good beer.

Kari's goal is a one woman (person) brewery. Something tells me when she makes up her mind to something, there is little that will prevent her from accomplishing what she sets out to do. Her ideas are unique among many of the brewers we

spoke with. While many talk of lighter or sweeter beers for the women, Kari says her beers are gender neutral, they just taste different. She has plans for experimenting with adjuncts such as honey and lavender. Also

in the plans are chandis, which is beer combined with another drink, such as lemonade. Purists may relax, the standards will always be available.

With any luck, we may be able to take some home. Intentions are to hand bottle summer and winter seasonals to sell out of the brewery. Eventually, Kari hopes to self-distribute within the county. Of course she has dreams of expanding, but the logistics of production brewing are difficult and right now her focus is on establishing her new business in Joseph. There is no rush; "I've started early enough in time that I can take my time."

When asked about the Mutiny name, Kari says it is real. Her mutiny is against the big three as well as the constrictions placed on beer in judging – the standards. Judging is something quite familiar to Kari. While she first judged at the Indiana State Fair, she went on to win a Bronze Medal as a judge at the World Beer Cup and a Silver Medal at the Great American Beer Festival.

View from Mutiny's porch

From a simple and reasonably priced menu, Mutiny serves lunch and dinner Tuesday through Sunday with breakfast on weekends. As a parent with many children (all now grown) I was thrilled to see this kid-friendly restaurant offers a kid's menu with "big kids" and "little kids" sizes. Dining is also available outside on the porch or at the picnic tables on the lawn. Regardless of whether you choose to sit indoors or out, you will be blessed with amazing views of the Wallowa Mountains.

Natian Brewery

1321 N.E. Couch Street
Portland, Oregon 97232
Corner of NE Sandy & Couch
<u>www.natianbrewery.com</u>

*"We're like the Millenium Falcon, 'We may not be
much to look at but we got it where it counts, kid.'"*

One of the smallest breweries we toured was Natian Brewery, a start-up which is actually referred to as a nanobrewery, not yet big enough to be a microbrewery. In October 2009, when we met Ian, he had only been in business a few months, since August.

Originally from the east coast, Ian spent time in Albuquerque, New Mexico. When looking for ways to save money, he tried growing his food, specifically pinto beans, but discovered this was not cost-effective in an area where water is at a premium. After trying to discern what food he could plant that would pay, and not finding an answer, he changed his question to "What can I *make* that would save me money?" The answer... beer.

Like many home brewers, Ian began brewing with an extract kit in his mom's kitchen. That was around '96 or '97. After home brewing off and on, he purchased a twenty-gallon system listed on e-bay to aid in his homebrew efforts. This was quite a find for his first time on e-bay. With the common bigger-is-better notion getting the best of him, he upgraded to a forty-gallon system a year later. Though not yet aware of it, Ian was on his way.

When the business partner of a friend discovered Ian was

Ian, working in his brewery.

Storage at Natian Brewing, great views of included.

brewing, he showed Ian a label he had designed of a naked woman, suggesting Ian use it to sell his beer. Thankfully, Ian was wise enough to decline the offer. But it did start him thinking...

One question he had to ask himself was if Portland had reached a saturation point. Could it handle another brewery? In a city with thirty-odd breweries, more than any city in the world, and three new breweries starting every year, it was a good question. But considering Portland also has the largest craft beer market in the US, he felt it *could* use another brewery.

Knowing he made great beer, Ian figured if he began slowly, without going into debt, he could take that step from home brewer to commercial brewmaster. But what worked for his homebrew location, his garage, would not be acceptable for a commercial operation. A security system would be required to obtain a commercial license; that was beyond Ian's start-up budget and rather impractical. Then Ian had an epiphany, his day job is that of quality control manager at Portland Bottling, where there *is* a security system. Ian discussed the proposal with his boss. As long as it would be acceptable with the authorities, it was a go! Ian set up Natian Brewing in the glassed corner of Portland Bottling at NE Sandy and Couch, the old bottling room.

Natian got its name when Ian and partner/girlfriend Natalia Laird combined their names, Nat+Ian= *Natian*. With a name, a logo designed by Natalia, who works for Fast Signs in Tigard, and a location, Natian Brewing was ready for business. Okay, Natian had some legal hoops to jump through first, but let's not go there. Ian was also quick to give many thanks for the support Fast Signs has shown to his new venture.

Currently, Natian Brewing is available in kegs only. Since they are not a brewpub, Natian can only be found as a rotational tap in area bars; they are not standardized in any one place. Check their website for current tap locations. In consideration is the possibility of Natian in a can. With Portland Bottling, who actually cans rather than bottles, looking into an OLCC license, the possibility of canning is definitely

Natian Brewmaster, Ian McGuinness, loves what he does.

close-by (in-house). According to Ian, Portland Bottling started getting calls for canning as soon as they applied for the license.

Though some craft brewers are concerned about cans interfering with the flavor of the beer, Ian, as a professional in the canning business, has no worries about that. The cans are lined to prevent tainting. He pointed out that Fat Tire in a can has changed the image of beer in a can; it does not change it or taste bad. For cans, according to Ian, timing is everything.

In the summer, Ian is limited to producing about 10 barrels per month, but with things slowing in his day job during the winter, he is able to up this to 20-30 barrels. These numbers give the impression that Ian must have busted butt to keep up his orders for kegs from local bars and still manage to have the 29 kegs available that Natian Brewing served at the 2010 Oregon Beer Festival.

When asked what his beer is about, Ian responded that they are "transcending the whole craft beer/micro beer thing and getting to the domestic drinkers – a true 'bi-partisan' beer. You *can* have a unique craft beer that speaks to the average beer drinker. It's the 'gateway beer.'"

With their two year-round beers, Natian Brewing seems to be fulfilling Ian's "transcending" thing. Destination Honey Red (5.1%), according to Ian, is a balance between sweetness and roast that is light and easy to drink, which domestic beer drinkers love. The Everyday IPA (7.3%) is a good IPA for those who enjoy the bitter aftertaste of an IPA but don't care for the heavy hops of most IPAs. A person can easily drink more than one of this rare IPA. Natian also brews a selection of seasonal beers.

Ian wants to brew beers he can stand behind. Beers that sell without having to sell like a used car

Brewery, Natian style.

salesman. "I don't want to make beer that's popular for popularity's sake, or crazy for crazy's sake. I'm trying to go for nice, clean beers."

Ian is a homebrewers dream-come-true. Everything he knows about brewing he has learned from books or the internet – no mentor, no seminars, no schooling. He thinks it is too bad there are not more text books for brewing, books beyond the beginning brewing books for home brewing. In his dream of dreams he will grow to be one of the big boys, going nationwide, or maybe Natian-wide. After all, if he were doing this *just* for the love of beer, he would be doing it at home. At the very least, he has the ultimate home brew setup. When asked if he is having fun, his response is, "Absolutely!"

Ninkasi Brewing Company
272 Van Buren Street
Eugene, Oregon 97402
541-344-2739
www.ninkasibrewing.com

"Goddess of fermentation"

We had hoped to secure an interview at Ninkasi during our November 2009 tour. However, the day we were in Eugene, they were preparing for a company party that evening to celebrate the completion of their new tasting room, and therefore were unable to meet with us. By catching them during our December, 2010 tour, they had the time to complete not only the tasting room, but also the outdoor seating and fire-pit. It was worth the wait.

The tasting room at Ninkasi is a stunning, modern combination of steel, wood, and the trademark colors of black and teal. With large windows, which provide a view of the generous patio seating area, this light, airy space easily reminds patrons that this is a tasting room, not a pub. Though the expansive patio can best be described as solid, it is by no means clunky; in fact, this contemporary space is as inviting as it is beautiful. Featuring a black, concrete, gas fire-pit, which is filled with shades of teal glass; a seating bench and planters along the concrete wall; and astonishingly comfortable-looking concrete picnic tables; all sitting on brick pavers, there is plenty of space to enjoy a Ninkasi beer paired

Ninkasi tasting room

Patio

with a lunch obtained from one the rotating food carts, which visit the tasting room Tuesday through Saturday.

Focused on production, Ninkasi has no interest in opening a brewpub. With product quality at the top of their priority list, getting sidetracked with a pub does not hold appeal for this rising star in the brewing world.

While traveling in a Ninkasi sweatshirt, the comment was made by the uninitiated that the name sounds Japanese. Perhaps, but Ninkasi, meaning "lady who fills the mouth," is actually the Ancient Sumerian goddess of beer (or fermentation, brewing, alcohol) and head brewer to the gods. "Given birth by the flowing water," Ninkasi is the daughter of the god of water, Enki, and the birth goddess, Ninti. She and her seven siblings were created to heal Enki's eight wounds.

Ninkasi Brewing Company began on June 6, 2006, in a leased space in the back of the (now closed) Springfield German restaurant, Sofia's, which was equipped with a fifteen barrel brew house as a consequence of once housing a brewery (now the location of Hop Valley Brewing). After seventeen hours of brewing, the first commercial batch of Total Domination IPA began what would be a meteoric rise in popularity for this relatively new brewery.

Founders Nikos Ridge and Jamie Floyd met in Eugene in 2005 through mutual friends. Jamie, ready to start his own brewery, had spent eleven years at Steelhead Brewery in Eugene and had dreamed of

Co-founder, Nikos Ridge

his own brewery for much longer. As a sociology major at University of Oregon, this self-described over-achiever frequently worked two jobs while carrying eighteen credits. Somehow finding time, Jamie homebrewed with a friend in the campus co-op where he lived. After graduating, he amused himself for a while working as a cook at Steelhead Brewery in Eugene. Suddenly, Jamie's brewing hobby became his

Ninkasi gate

obsession. After taking every one-day brewing class Oregon State University offered, Jamie eventually made assistant brewer, though he had not yet fully worked his way out of the kitchen. The 70 hour weeks eventually landed him the position of head brewer.

Nikos, who was raised in Eugene, received his economics degree from New York University before working the floor of the New York Stock Exchange for over ten years. Glad to return to Eugene, Nikos finds a business with a tangible and enjoyable product refreshing after the years spent working in the intangible financial industry.

Capitalizing on their mutually beneficial backgrounds, Jamie and Nikos have brought Ninkasi from a concept, past microbrew, to regional brewery in just over four years. In Oregon, where great brews abound, this accomplishment took more than just good beer, the pair credit Ninkasi growth to good timing and good distribution.

Keeping things fun, when employees requested a slide off the brewhouse, they got it.

Though Jamie keeps a hand in the brewing development, Ninkasi now has a full team of brewers. This allows Jamie to spend much of his time traveling to promote Ninkasi outside Eugene or even outside Oregon. Currently found in Washington, Idaho, Alaska, the San Francisco Bay area of California, and obviously, Oregon, Ninkasi seems to have arrived, with their inclusion in Costco.

With Ninkasi available in kegs and twenty-two ounce bottles, they are not content to settle, as demonstrated by the twelve ounce bottles released in 2011. Though the current focus is on the Northwest, growth has a way of happening. With Ninkasi, things seem to happen quickly, as exampled by the increase in production from 1600 barrels in 2006 to 36,000 barrels in 2010. Wow! But according to Nikos, maintaining a small distribution footprint within the Northwest is helping to keep things manageable.

Located in the old Vos Plumbing building in the historic Whieaker Neighborhood, there is currently plenty of expansion room. On the day we toured, they were setting in two new 240 barrel fermenters and expecting to get two more of them. Additionally, they were excited about their "new" bottling line, whose previous home was with Sierra Nevada Brewing Company, of Chico, California. Bottling 140 bottles per minute, the line also sterilizes bottles, labels the beers, and assembles and fills the boxes. Fully automatic, Ninkasi can now bottle and case beer without touching the bottles. With many moving parts, the line still requires five or six employees to keep it running.

Notice the man installing the new fermentation tanks

Conscientious of the environment, Ninkasi looks as much as possible to local suppliers for their ingredients, with most coming from the Northwest. At the other end of the production line, in 2010 over ten million pounds of spent grain was "upcycled" to Oregon Natural Meats where it was then fed to pasture raised beef-cattle, suitable for locavores (people who attempt to buy and eat only foods grown, produced and processed close to their home).

"New" bottling line

On the bottling line

When you tour Ninkasi, you may not get to see how they set in huge fermentation tanks, but it is possible you may get to try a one-of-a-kind batch of beer. This unconventional method allows Ninkasi to try new recipes and enjoy experimentation. These single batches are never bottled, only kegged. Though occasionally they will be used for special occasions, like festivals, their primary use is at the tasting room. Or, on rare occasion, it may be chosen as the next great Ninkasi beer.

More than 27,000 pounds of spent grain per day were "upcycled" in 2010

Keg Lifter

OakShire Brewing

1055 Madera Street
Eugene, Oregon 97402
541-688-4555
www.oakbrew.com

"Humble brewers of delicious beer"

We thought sure Nuvi (GPS) had led us astray while on our way to OakShire Brewing. First we were on the edge of a neighborhood, then we were obviously in an industrial district of the warehouse/railroad type. Even when Nuvi put it right in front of our faces, we would have missed it if we had not seen someone through the warehouse door tasting a beer. Yes, we apologized to Nuvi for doubting her. Moral of the story, trust your GPS, at least when searching for beer. In case you have not deduced this, we talk to our electronics; in fact, I keep telling Bob I am going to report him for abusing Houston, his aging radar detector. He occasionally beeps continuously at nothing until Bob smashes him against the steering wheel. After that, Houston is quite well behaved for weeks. Poor Houston.

Anyway, back at OakShire…according to partner/brewer, Jeff Althouse, "The hobby got out of control." Together with his brother, Chris, he started OakShire brewing in 2006. Both are self-taught brewers. Committed to operating their business

"The hobby got out of control."

based on quality and service to their customers, they use only quality ingredients and never rush the process.

Jeff, previously a public school teacher with a math degree, said they focus on hiring the right people to help them succeed. To this end, early in 2010, they hired the very talented and knowledgeable brew master, Matt Van Wyk. Winner of the Small Brewpub Company Brewer of the Year award at the 2006 Great American Beer Festival, Matt is considered quite a coup for OakShire. Matt and the rest of the crew must be helping them in a good way; OakShire won their first medal, a Silver, at the 2009 Great American Brew Festival (GABF) in Denver, Colorado. Though this may be a first for OakShire, with Matt brewing it is a good bet there will be more to follow; it is his tenth medal from the GABF.

Previously known as Willamette Brewery, The Althouse brothers changed the name when they discovered Willamette Valley Vineyards own the name "Willamette." With their recent success, it seems the change was a good one. The name OakShire represents strength, independence, community and bioregion, values held by the owners and the employees.

Despite shiny new tanks that give the capacity to triple production with plenty of room to expand even more, there is still a small

Homebrew at Oakshire

three tier system in the middle of the tasting room. Used some Saturdays and on game days (Ducks), Jeff says keeping the home brew system helps them stay creative and close to those who know beer best...the consumer. Additionally, the three-tier system allows for home brew demonstrations and classes.

Remember, this is a brewery, not a brew pub. There is a tasting room with four ounce samples. When you find the one you just can't resist, there are picnic tables outside where you can sit to drink the pints available. You can even have lunch when the Devour Lunch Wagon shows up with Panini sandwiches and other lunch offerings. Also available on Saturdays are tours at 1, 2, and 3 P.M. While there you can pick up your case or keg, have your growler filled, or purchase some of their OakShire merchandise.

While you are getting those samples, take a look at the bar. It is a converted deep freezer with taps. The bar top opens to reveal the inside of the "freezer" with the kegs inside. Quite ingenious!

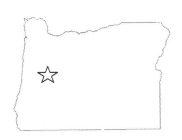

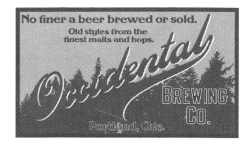

Occidental Brewing

6635 N Baltimore Street
Portland, OR 97203
503-810-7920
www.occidentalbrewing.com

"Portland's newest brewery"

The newest brewery we visited was still a shell of a building, with trenches dug in the concrete and not a single tank in sight. While many have speculated regarding this "planned" brewery and if it would ever open, there was a lot of work happening at a very early hour (7:30 AM) for this brewery not to open. While at the time of our interview they were saying "sometime in 2011, hopefully February," as of this book's publication, their website says "Spring 2011."

It was quite fascinating to see the brewery at this stage. We have now seen enough breweries to realize that most have grilled trenches for draining; here we were able to see the trench as nothing more than a line dug in the concrete and dirt underneath. The tremendous amount of work still required when we were there in December 2010, was quite evident.

At the center of all this work are partners Dan Engler and his nephew, Ben Engler. Though the early hour could have been the culprit, our own experience says the weariness visible in their eyes was indicative of the extreme hours the two have been investing in this new venture. Working twenty hour days each weekend and twelve hour days through the week, these two are definitely burning the candle at both ends.

Ben & Dan on Occidental's poster
Photo courtesy Occidental Brewing, used by permission

After Ben was laid off at his job with Weyerhaeuser, where he had worked in their marketing department, he and Dan began discussing the possibility of starting their own brewery. Then in June 2009, they passed the discussion stage and began forming a business plan while simultaneously initiating fund-raising efforts for start-up costs. By September, they had accumulated enough money for the building, though it took until April 2010, to find the right space.

The dirt patch in the corner is the future brewhouse location.

Dan had been a homebrewer for eighteen years and taught Ben the art. For Occidental, Dan will assume the position of head brewer. Assisting him, Ben will also take on the less desirable jobs; keg mover and washer, delivery truck driver, clean-up, what-ever it takes.

Planning to continue his day job as an attorney – a

Future drain trenches

public defender - Dan received his law degree in 2006, after graduating from Willamette University College of Law in Salem.

Ben currently owns a draft line cleaning business, meaning he has many ready-made contacts in the business, so expect to see taps showing up around Portland as soon as the beer begins flowing at Occidental. They are also hoping to stretch to cities outside Portland where breweries and brewpubs are not so readily available.

German-style beers will be the focus at Occidental, giving them a touch of uniqueness in a market where most beers are English Ales. Occidental will be available in kegs, the only visible evidence of this future brewery during our visit. Initially, plans include some hand bottling, with eventual utilization of mobile bottling.

Occidental is located across the street from Cathedral Park, and near the base of St. Johns Bridge, where opening the back garage door provides a wonderful view of both. It is truly a pity the door opens right onto the road; it could have made an incredible deck area.

A couple of months later, the trenches are complete.
Photo courtesy Occidental Brewing, used by permission

A cloudy morning view out the back doors of Occidental.

Occidental will be a production brewery, with a small tasting room included. Hoping to create the world's smallest beer museum, the Englers have been collecting old beer cans to include in the décor. The bar will be topped with bottle caps, and a liquor license from 1906 will adorn the wall.

We look forward to returning to the completed Occidental and viewing the changes. Bob, of course, looks forward to the beers.

The front of Occidental with St. Johns Bridge behind. We spoke with Dan just before publication, and the garage door is now a nice glass door.

Kegs await completion of Occidental

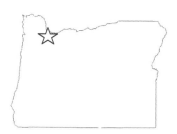

Oregon Trail Brewery
341 SW 2nd Street
Corvallis, Oregon 97333
541-758-3527
www.oregontrailbrewery.com

*"Distinctive Ales Brewed in the True Pioneer
Spirit of the Oregon Territory"*

Owner of Oregon Trail Brewery, Dave Wills, was out of town the day we were going to be in Corvallis, so he arranged for us to meet with brewer, Terry Butler. While we were sorry not to meet Dave, Terry was a great host.

Oregon Trail can be found inside Old World Center, a small shopping mall with a European atmosphere and a unique brick floor, best known for the Old World Deli, a Corvallis tradition since 1977.

Renowned for great sandwiches, lasagna, enchiladas, and their chili, which has been the Corvallis chili champion since 1996, Old World also offers belly dancing on Wednesdays, occasional live music, and of course, Oregon Trail Beers.

Terry had just been back with Oregon Trail a little over a month when we

Old World Center

met with him. Shear persistence won Terry his first brewing job at Wild Duck Brewing in Eugene, where he stayed for five years, until they closed in 2003. He then spent a year at Oregon Trail before moving on to another year at Rogue. While at Rogue, Terry reports he brewed a record 387 barrels in one run. After a year there he made Snipes Mountain Brewing in Sunnyside, Washington, home for three years. When he saw an ad for a start-up needing a brewer, Terry began e-mailing them, asking about such things as snow conditions. After shipping some of his brews for them to sample, he was offered the position of head brewer at the new Aspen Brewing Company, which quickly became an Aspen standard. When, in October 2010, it was time to return to Oregon, Terry landed back at one of his old pit-stops, Oregon Trail

Brewer, Terry Butler (left), with "Pigmeister" Todd Henderson, who has been with Oregon Trail since 2000

Brewing.

This seven barrel brewery must be one of the tightest fits we have seen, when you compare space available to brew capacity. In its back corner of Old World Center, the space seems more vertical than horizontal. Though two stories, it seems like three, due to the use of a stair landing as kettle space.

Oregon Trail Brewery has a long history. With Bridgeport, Full Sail, and Widmer the only other craft beers in Oregon at that time, they helped with the initial introduction of these strange, new beers. Initially founded by Jerry Shadomy, an award-winning homebrewer, in 1987, Oregon

Filling the kettle with hot water in the morning takes the chill off the brewery.

Trail did well at first. When their brown ale was named the 1989 Beer of

The lab at Oregon Trail

the Year, by legendary Oregonian beer columnist, Fred Eckhardt, they seemed to be on their way to success. Sadly, a combination of personal problems and a recurring bacterial infection took their toll. By 1992, the bank was ready to foreclose. This is when Dave Wills entered the picture.

Dave already owned Freshops, a mail-order business based in Philomath, which sells whole hops and rhizomes (root starts), but hated to see Oregon Trail die. So with new partner Jerry Brockmore (who is no longer with Oregon Trail), who had previously worked as a brewer for Hart Brewing (now Pyramid) out of Washington, they convinced the bank to allow them

Terry shows us the grain bin

Cask & Keg Storage

time to obtain financing to pay off the loan.

With $43,000 in capital raised from selling shares and $40,000 of Dave's own money, Dave and Jerry paid the loan and by January 1993, were ready to begin salvaging Oregon Trail Brewery.

After a meticulous cleaning and a lot of rearranging, Jerry began brewing. Then came the challenging task of convincing pub owners and beer drinkers that Oregon Trail could now be trusted to be a consistently good beer. Even medals from the Great American Beer Festival, a Silver in each of 1994 and 1995 for Oregon Trail Brown Ale and a Bronze in 1995 for Pete's Wicked Ale, did not seem to speed up the slow process. With shelf space in stores a bit easier to obtain at that time than taps, Oregon Trail introduced their twenty-two ounce screen-printed bottles.

Poster from the original 1987 Grand Opening

Today, only the barrel-aged beers are bottled. With some of the sours being aged three to five years, these bottles can be rare and difficult to locate. But taps are located in several places around the area and a few in Eugene. Even better, Oregon Trail pigs can be found at co-ops in both Corvallis and Eugene, enabling you to have fresh draft beer at home.

With no expansion room and unable to keep up with demand during summer months, Oregon Trail may rent additional space for storage. This would allow them to purchase a larger system. When we were there, Dave was looking at a fifteen barrel tank at California Brewing in Redding, hoping to bring it home in his truck. It would be a tight squeeze but we have no doubt they would find room in the brewery for it.

Dave, a Santa Paula, California native, originally moved

Dusty, screen-printed bottles

to Corvallis to attend Oregon State's agriculture program. While visiting the USDA Agricultural Station, he was impressed by the quality of the hops produced there. Aware that the majority of hops available to homebrewers were of inferior quality, Dave had an idea. In 1982, he purchased two hundred pounds of hops and began selling them to home brewers. Freshops was born and thrived.

In 1986 Dave and his partner, Laura Lee, a head-start teacher, purchased property in Wren, a rural "spot" outside Philomath. With a shop for a processing plant and plenty of land for hops, Dave not only has space for Freshops, but he also grows Christmas trees, which he harvests each year and sells in his hometown of Santa Paula.

Filling a pig

Taps at the brewery

Pale Horse Brewing

2359 Hyacinth Street NE
Salem, Oregon 97301
503-364-3610
www.palehorsebrewing.com

"We just want to be known for making good beers"

Way back in 2001, Dennis Clack was looking around the local ShopKo and saw a Mr. Beer® brewing kit. Taking it home, Dennis brewed his first batch of beer. For a guy who had not drunk beer since his army days, this was major. After the kit, Dennis graduated to all grain brewing; he was hooked.

Winning Second place in the homebrew competition at the Oregon State Fair with his very first all-grain batch, fueled Dennis's competition fever. He continued to enter and do well in homebrew competitions.

Then his brother, Sid, planted the seed of going commercial. After a homebrew competition judge told Dennis he should market Hillbilly Blond, thoughts of commercial brewing began to get serious. Six years after purchasing that Mr. Beer® kit, Dennis partnered with his wife and brother, Sid, to register Pale Horse Brewing with the state. Commercial brewing began in October of 2008, with the first keg sold in January 2009.

Sid believed so strongly in his brother's brewing abilities that he sold his home for start-up capital. His faith appears to have been well-founded; the company started with one bay in an industrial complex that

Brothers, Dennis and Sid Clack

looks like overgrown storage units but now occupy three, and need a forth. In fact, the pair are hoping to find their own property soon, which would allow them much-needed expansion space and a tasting room.

Named with Dennis's favorite movie in mind, Clint Eastwood's *Pale Rider*, Dennis also designed the logo. The labels are a collaboration of design by Dennis and a lady in Portland.

While the company self-distributes in the Salem/Portland areas, they use a distributing company for sales elsewhere. In fact, the big distributors are beginning to take notice. When we were there in December 2010, they were just completing details for expanded distribution and can now be found in Washington, with California soon to be added. Talks have been in the works with a distributor in Arkansas and requests have come in from Pale Horse Gastropub in West Chester, Pennsylvania.

Dominic handles marketing & sales

We originally made the appointment for our interview at Pale Horse with Sid. When we arrived, Sid was not there and Dennis and Dominic (nephew who handles marketing and sales) were not aware of the interview. Yet, both stopped what they were doing and graciously allowed us to interview them. Sid arrived about fifteen minutes into the interview...oops, he kind of forgot.

This was one of those rare interviews where we feel as though we are pulling teeth. The Clacks are quiet, rather shy gentlemen, and seemed very uncomfortable with the idea that anyone would want to interview them. Because our interview style is not a question/answer format, but more of a "tell us your story" system, which then discloses what questions we should be asking, interviewing those who are not natural story-tellers can be a bit uncomfortable for everyone. Thankfully, by the time we visited Pale Horse we had enough interview experience to know how to handle the reserved interviewee. We asked for a tour of the brewery.

While this always produces results, the transformation at Pale Horse was astonishing. In the office, these brothers seemed rather blasé or maybe even indifferent to the whole business, but it was when we began the tour that we realized these quiet guys were just not natural talkers. Once in the brewery, they were like kids with new toys, excitedly telling us everything we wanted to know. These guys definitely have a passion for this business.

When we asked

what Pale Horse's unique thunder is, Sid and Dominic smiled and said it is Dennis. Starting a business requiring intense amounts of time and labor at a time in life when most of his contemporaries are relaxing and enjoying their retirement, Dennis is indeed, unique. Retired from *Birds Eye Foods*, where he did tank work in the production facilities, Dennis says you "Just gotta find your niche and go with it." It seems he has found his niche, though he does add, "I didn't think I had it in me!"

Everything Dennis has learned came from books and reading directions. His favorite book is *Practical Handbook for the Specialty Brewer (Volume 2): Fermentation, Cellaring, and Packaging Operations* by Karl Ockert (original Bridgeport brew master).

What do the other guys do? Sid, besides believing in his brother's brewing abilities, is the company treasurer. A retired electrical engineer, his skills undoubtedly come in handy. Dominic, the nephew who is in charge of marketing and sales, was a manager at a tire store before getting his feet wet in the brewing business. Also helping out at Pale Horse is Joshua Frank,

Back in the office, Dennis shows us his favorite book.

who is employed as an intern and is an Oregon State University fermentation science major.

According to Dominic, he makes a lot of cold calls, 20% of which result in a new bar tap. In addition to cold calls, Dominic spends a great deal of time visiting potential tap sites. "We've been taking tap handles from the big guys," he says with pride. But with Pale Horse you

are not limited to locating a tap; Pale Horse also bottles.

Currently, Pale Horse offers four standard choices: Hillbilly Blond, Hopyard Dog, Mystic Wolf Amber, and Pale Horse Export Stout. Also offered is one seasonal, Pale Horse Winter Seasonal. This 9% ABV beer is described as "heavy in body and smoky sweet over the tongue." According to Sid, he and his wife have a small glass of it for dessert each night after dinner.

The filters   **The filters, air drying**   **The dried filters staying fresh in the freezer along with hops**

Tours are available at Pale Horse Monday through Friday from 8-5. They only sell kegs out of the brewery at this time, but bottles can be found at many stores around Salem, including Bi-Mart, Roth's, and Fred Meyer.

Panty Dropper Ale

Aloha, Oregon

"Homebrewers who perfected one recipe"

While we made countless attempts to contact Panty Dropper Ale, we simply could not connect with them. Not wanting to exclude them, and finding their story interesting, we have compiled what we could learn.

This LLC, owned by Aloha couple, Linda and Denny Hansen, came about when these homebrewers perfected one beer recipe. When they let a friend try it, he exclaimed, "Wow! What a panty dropper!" The Hansens got such a kick out of the proclamation, they christened their homebrew, Panty Dropper Ale.

Though this couple is busy with four children and careers (Linda is an oncology RN and Denny is a brick mason), they decided to form an LLC, obtain the necessary licenses, and market Panty Dropper in 2004. Initially brewing in their garage to supply three pubs, they soon graduated to the shop, then a bigger shop, until they eventually cried uncle over the late night brew sessions and turned to contract brewing. First contracting with Tucks Brewery, Panty Dropper was forced to find a new contract home when Tucks closed. After a great deal of searching and many phone calls, the trail finally led Panty Dropper to Silver Moon Brewing in Bend.

According to Tyler Reichert, owner at Silver Moon, the original request was to brew Panty Dropper for a couple of months. When the Hansens left, Tyler looked at his head brewer, Tyler West, and said they would be making it for years. It has, as of this writing, been over three years and it has been a beneficial relationship for both companies. Silver Moon brews Panty Dropper in twenty barrel batches. In 2008, Panty Dropper made their ale available in 22 ounce bottles.

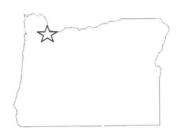

This self-distributed ale has done well, including winning a Bronze medal at the 2009 Great American Beer Festival. We say, "Well done Panty Dropper!"

Photo courtesy of Pelican Pub & Brewery, used by permission

Pelican Pub & Brewery

33180 Cape Kiwanda Drive
Pacific City, Oregon 97135
503-965-7007
www.yourlittlebeachtown.com/pelican

"Come for the beer, stay for the storms"

Unable to contact Pelican Pub & Brewery owners, Jeff Schons and Mary Jones, we decided to drop in and see what we could get. We were glad we did. Though Jeff and Mary were in Australia at a beer competition (maybe that is why we could not contact them), their staff greeted us as if we had an appointment and could not have been friendlier or more helpful.

When Jeff and Mary moved to Pacific City in 1990, they knew they were home. Since then they have created a destination at Cape Kiwanda. Whether you are looking for a selection of award winning beers, mouthwatering meals, an overnight stay, a vacation rental, or a shared property, Jeff and Mary have created all of them amongst great beaches and amazing views.

'On the beach' would better describe Pelican Pub & Brewery. So much so that the company needs to hire an excavating company periodically, so the sand does not take over the parking lot. This means in the summer the outdoor seating is second-to-none. And, as long as

Jeff & Mary
Photo courtesy of Pelican Pub & Brewery, used by permission

- 275 -

you keep Fido on the sand, your dog is welcome also.

Be forewarned, this is a very seasonal area. Though we were there during December, when it was wonderfully quiet, summers can be quite packed. While Pacific City boasts a population of just over one thousand, they welcome over six hundred thousand visitors each year. With plenty of recreation in the area, much of it comes to Cape Kawanda and Pelican Pub, such as the long board surfing contest, which happens every August and is into its twelfth year at Cape Kawanda.

Offering meeting rooms which can accommodate up to 200 people, Pelican Pub & Brewery is the setting for many weddings. In fact, there was a wedding in progress while we were there. With glass doors that open onto the patio, a giant gas fireplace, a screen for multimedia needs, and views to win the day, one would think this place has it all for a wedding or other special occasion. But just in case

this does not take care of your needs, Pelican also offers a large tent for outdoors, partitions for the rooms, catering services, and even event planning services.

Pelican includes a well-stocked gift shop

When Jeff and Mary decided to open a brewpub in 1995 in an old brick building on the beach, which they had purchased, they attended a Craft Brewers conference in Portland.

After seeing a 3x5 card left on the bulletin board by Jeff and Mary, brewer Darron Welch was hired, moved to Pacific City, and began brewing test batches in a storage unit while the pub was under construction.

Like a number of other brewers, Darron fell in love with beer while in Germany for a year as a student. After returning to the States, Darron became an avid homebrewer. Less than a year after landing a professional brewing position at Appleton Brewing Company, in Wisconsin, Darron saw the 3x5 card that changed his life and relocated him back to his home state of Oregon.

On May 4, 1996 Pelican Pub and Brewery opened their doors with their first brew, Doryman's Dark, an adaptation of one of Darron's favorite homebrew recipes and the first Pelican GABF medal winner.

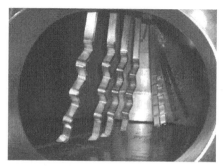

To break up dough-balls which form in the mash

Pelican boasts a beautiful copper-clad, steam-fired, three-vessel, fifteen barrel system that was custom built by Pub Brewing Systems in Santa Rosa, California, as well as four fifteen barrel fermenters and two thirty barrel fermenters. Top all this off with four fifteen barrel, one seven barrel and one three barrel serving tank, and this is quite an impressive brewery, especially in a one horse town.

In addition to the eighteen taps in the pub, and a beer engine on the back wall, serving five standards, plus specials and seasonals, you will find only Pelican brews at Pelican. Of course, there is an exception

to every rule. In this case, the exception comes in the form of beverages Pelican does not make, Redstone Mead from Boulder, Colorado, and Wandering Aengus Hard Cider from Salem.

From the beginning, Pelican brewery has included two bottling lines. The larger, more automated bottling line, purchased from Avery Brewing in Boulder, Colorado, is capable of completing sixty cases per hour. The smaller, more hand intensive bottler can complete up to fifteen cases per hour, depending upon the operator. This system is used for specialty beers and is hand labeled, while the regular line-up of bottles features printed bottles.

While visiting Pelican, be sure to saunter down the hall toward the restrooms. If Pelican keeps up at this rate, they will need to build more hallways to house all the awards adorning the walls. Notable among many notables is the 2005 Great American Beer Festival Small Brewpub of the

Year Award. Or perhaps you might find the fact that Pelican is the only brewer to have a beer, Kiwanda Cream Ale, in Draft Magazine's Top 25 for three years in a row – 2008, 2009, & 2010.

While this entire brewpub, contents, and its surroundings was quite impressive, we must say, it was the people we found to be most amazing. Friendly, accommodating, and right there, even before they knew we were writing a book, the staff at Pelican showed a passion for

their work. Saying Pelican is a great place to work, they stress the family feel at Pelican. Whether greeting you upon entry, helping with selections, or polishing the brewery (which the brew staff was doing when we arrived), all take and show pride in their work and company.

Assistant Managers, Justin Hite and Andria Thomas

Two of Pelican's five brewers, Mike Johnson and Daniel Pollard

Portland U-Brew & Pub
P.U.B.

6237 SW Milwaukie Avenue
Portland, Oregon 97202
541-432-9746
www.portlandubrewandpub.com

"Hey, I made this beer!"

One of Portland's newest brewpubs is more than that. Whether you want to try brewing just to see how it is done, lack the space and equipment at home, want some professional guidance, or simply like the company, Portland U-Brew & Pub not only makes and serves their own beer, you can also be the brewer at P.U.B. This is truly one-stop shopping for the beer fan.

When owner, Jason Webb, visited family in England in 1990, he was privileged to drink some of the beers made by his grandfather, who had homebrewed for forty years. Inspired, Jason and his brother returned to Oregon and brewed their first batch of beer, diving straight into ten gallon all-grain batches.

After a tour at Saxer Brewing Company (now defunct) in 1994, Jason, who at that time built houses with his brother, supplied brewmaster Tony Gomes with a sample of his homebrew and an application. Getting hired as Tony's apprentice came with an education; every morning he taught Jason the science of brewing for thirty minutes. As a brewmaster with a five-year diploma from Doemens Academy in Munich, Germany, Tony was more than qualified as an instructor.

In addition to apprenticing and working with Tony for six years, Jason has also worked at Portland Brewing; Mac & Jacks in Redmond, Washington; Cascade Lakes Brewing, Silver Moon, McMenamins Lighthouse, and Fanno Creek during the last seventeen years.

Finally, in 2010 Jason and his family decided it was time to open their own brewpub. But this could not be the typical brewpub. This one needed to cater to the customer on a greater level than simply selling the beer and food; you might say Jason plans to "pay-it-forward" for the time Tony spent with him.

Opening in an old office building with a bit of an English Tudor appearance, P.U.B. will have three distinct sections, the brewery downstairs, the brewpub upstairs, and next door the homebrew supply shop, complete with a separate entrance. Expect a hippy/British feel with several murals in this all-inclusive addition to Portland's brew scene.

P.U.B. will be brewing on a 3.5 barrel system with a four barrel fermenter and expect to brew around 200 barrels per year. Plans call for distribution to local small restaurants and several pubs. Hopes are to someday distribute through the state, and maybe more.

Additionally, they have six 20 gallon kettles for the U-Brew portion of the business. During their interview with NewSchool blogger, Ezra John-Greenough, Aaron Gillham, manager at P.U.B.'s homebrew shop is quoted describing how the U-Brew will work, "A customer will book a date, time, and tell us the size batch they wish to make. They will come in and get together all the grains, and grind it in our mill upstairs which comes out downstairs into a bucket. They'll take their crushed grains over to a "keggle" and mash in there. After saccharification we'll vorlauf, and pump the wort into a 20 gal. steam jacketed kettle. The customers can choose the hops and hopping schedule if they wish, or just use one of our in house recipes. After that we'll pump it through the heat exchange into carboys, and add yeast of the customer's choice. Then they'll come back after fermentation is complete, and bottle or keg their beer. All the fun of brewing without all the work...which is where we come in."

Three of the six twenty-gallon, copper-clad kettles for U-Brew
Photo courtesy P.U.B., used by permission

With all this homebrewing going on, expect homebrew competitions to be a regular event at P.U.B. Jason's desire is to make P.U.B. into a "mini beer mecca," a fun/kickback kind of place, within the greater beer mecca called Portland.

Look for P.U.B. brews at festivals and competitions also. Jason is no stranger to awards. While working for Saxer, they received many awards at the G.A.B.F. and fully expect to follow with P.U.B. brews.

Jason says the idea for the name just popped into his head one night. He loves the acronym being the word "pub." Oregon has

Owner Jason Webb on right
Photo courtesy P.U.B., used by permission

embraced the pub concept, and Jason expects them to embrace P.U.B.'s concept as well. By the time you read this, P.U.B. will already be open.

Prodigal Son Brewery & Pub

230 SE Court Avenue
Pendleton, Oregon 97801
541-276-6090
www.prodigalsonbrewery.com

"Live music and a theater room."

While it was unfortunate that we were unable to personally visit Prodigal Son, they opened April 15, 2010 (after our Eastern Oregon tour), we were pleased to be able to interview them by e-mail. While this is not the ideal method, it makes it tough to get a "feel" for the brewery and the people, it does allow some information and inclusion in the write-ups.

Prodigal son is named for the Bible parable of the prodigal son, who chose to take his inheritance early, went out into the world, partied and squandered it all, then returned home expecting to become a servant in his father's house, but instead was greeted and welcomed home with love and acceptance. While the owners may not have squandered their inheritances as the biblical son did, they did return home, to an apparent wholehearted welcome by the Pendleton community.

Having grown up in this Eastern Oregon community, famous for their Pendleton Roundup, Tim Guenther, Brian Harder, and Matthew Barnes left their hometown as soon as possible, with no intentions of ever returning to live. But time has a way of changing perspectives and priorities, and eventually saw Tim return to Pendleton, along with his wife, Jennifer, a newcomer to the area.

Photo courtesy of Prodigal Son, used by permission

While Pendleton was home to several traditional taverns, there were no pubs where families could gather with the focus on food and quality beer. Although Pendleton was once the home to at least two large breweries, they were better known for selling large quantities of Pendleton Blended Canadian Whisky, a product of Hood River Distillers, in Hood River, due to the name and, of course, the Roundup. Pendleton, despite its Oregon location, had become a place of traditional yellow beers.

The Guenthers were determined to revive the brewing tradition in Pendleton. Turning first to the Small Business Development Center for assistance in developing a business plan, Tim and Jennifer felt the time spent learning and developing the plan was invaluable. Though it may have been a time-consuming process, they felt it saved a great deal of time and money through preventing expensive learning experiences.

Tim began talking with his younger brother's childhood friend, Brian Harder, who was working as a brewer at Rogue, in Newport. Brian was immediately on board. While the other partners worked toward turning the plan into a reality, Brian's task was to add a bit of formal education to his years of brewing experience. This was accomplished through the Siebel Institute in Chicago and its international program at the Doemens Academy, in Germany.

With a brewer secured, Tim turned to an old friend, classmate, and ex-Pendletonian, Matthew Barnes. While Matthew was excited about the idea, and more than happy to consult on the project, he liked his life in Southeast Portland and thought he was not interested in returning to Pendleton. With a bit of time and convincing, this Portland chef left the big city and returned to his hometown as the forth partner of Prodigal Son.

With Pendleton looking to revive the downtown area and many old downtown buildings which would make a great pub, finding a location was more a matter of which one, rather than where. Choosing a building which was built to house a Packard auto dealership in 1914, and later sold GMCs, Buicks, and Studebakers until the 1950s, meant plenty of space for this fledgling brewpub. Heavy farm equipment was then sold out of the old building until a second hand store was housed there.

Prodigal Son, just after being painted

Long neglected, the plan was to clean it up and take advantage of the brick, the wood columns, and the open rafter ceiling. Power-washing the brick, with the intention of removing all the layers of old paint to expose the raw brick, the partners were amazed to find a mural underneath all that old paint. An original 100 plus year-old advertising mural all along one wall (100 feet long) says "Albers Cereal Foods - At the Housewife's Fingertips" with a picture of a woman's hand holding a box of rolled oats 'for breakfast and dessert' from the 'Albers Brothers Milling Co., Portland, Ore.' - the brand still exists today. Before their building was built, this wall was the exterior wall of the neighboring building, a bakery, and this mural was the first thing

Dining Room with Portion of Mural
Photo courtesy of Prodigal Son, used by permission

people saw as they entered Pendleton. Preserved for the past ninety years indoors, this magnificent find created a truly historic backdrop for Prodigal Son.

When the partners began using pre-1950s mismatched furniture and chandeliers, the community got into the spirit of the project and began bringing in pieces to add to the collection, each with a story to tell. With three seven-thousand square foot stories, there was plenty of room for Prodigal son to incorporate each addition to the collection. They are currently working on a walking tour of the building for folks who want to know all the details. We have to go see this!

The logo was designed by another Pendleton prodigal, this time a daughter, Amy Rogers of Tumbleweed Creative. The partners were pleased by the simple design, with the circle representative of the full circle of the area natives leaving then coming home again. The nostalgic touch of it fit with the design theme of the pub. Reminiscent of an old gas station logo, it suits the automotive history of the building.

Brewing on a ten barrel system which once called the now fallen Bell Tower Brewery in Vancouver, Washington, home, Prodigal Son can currently be found in limited small towns in Eastern Oregon as well as a few Portland locations. You can also look for them at the Oregon Brewers Festival in Portland during the last full weekend of July.

While they have not had the opportunity to enter competitions as of this writing, Beervanna writer, Jeff Alworth did give their Bruce/Lee Porter his Satori Award - best new beer of 2010. Prodigal Son is also a certified "Honest Pint" purveyor.

While we are not able to write about Prodigal Son from personal experience, time will definitely lead us there. We look forward to meeting you and say, "Welcome home, prodigals everywhere!"

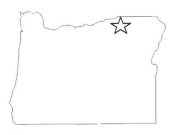

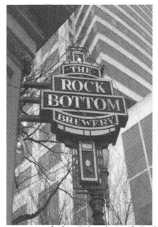

Rock Bottom Brewery

206 SW Morrison Street
Portland, Oregon 97204
503-796-2739
www.rockbottom.com

"Serious about our food, crazy about our beer"

Rock Bottom Brewery was a part of a group of breweries that suddenly became large. Started in Colorado and now in thirty-five states and the District of Columbia, it had just been purchased by a large corporation, CraftWorks Restaurants & Breweries, Inc., one month (November 15, 2010) before our interview. This same group also recently purchased the Gordon Biersch Brewery Restaurants, own Old Chicago, and are now the world's leading operator of brewery restaurants. They are headquartered in both Chattanooga, Tennessee, and Louisville, Colorado.

Portland's Rock Bottom opened in 1989, in what had been an old warehouse in historic downtown Portland. Unfortunately, the original use of the building has been lost to time. The building had been empty for a year before Rock Bottom set up house, with the most recent function having been as the location for the Portland Democratic headquarters. The area has changed a great deal since Rock Bottom first took up residence. In 1989, there was a methadone clinic across the street. Even now, that same building has been vacant for fourteen years – odd - considering its location in this busy, modern downtown area.

Known as being a great place for a beer after work where the businessman in the suit will sit at the bar, have a beer, and talk with the guy from the car garage, Portland's Rock Bottom suits patrons of many tastes and styles. Actually a very quiet and peaceful place between 1:30 and 4:00 P.M., Rock Bottom has always offered a lot of specialty beers, with ten taps, eight of them exclusively Rock Bottom brews, plus two cask beers.

Though about twenty percent of their sales are beer, Rock Bottom is a full service restaurant, with a menu to please. They also list nutritional and food sensitivity information on-line. Unfortunately for me, they do not have information for those with fructose malabsorption. But, hey, it is a good start.

Master brewer, Van Havig, had been at the Portland Rock Bottom since June 2000, making the beers

Hopefully, the bourbon barrel aged beers will continue, one of many specialty beers made at Rock Bottom. With bourbon makers only able to use a barrel one time by law, they then sell them to scotch makers, making them more difficult for beer brewers to get.

that answer the unique needs of the Portland market. With new owners, he had just learned that all Rock Bottom Breweries would be required to make four standard beers. Understandably a bit nervous at that point about what other changes might come, he was anxiously waiting for word that they would be able to brew the rest of their beers to answer the distinctive tastes of the local market.

In his anxiety, Van was quite outspoken about being told what to brew. This candidness led to his being let go from Rock Bottom on January 2, 2011. While we were not at all surprised at this turn of events, we were saddened that this personable man, who is admired as a first-class brewer, was not shown the respect merited by his years with Rock Bottom coupled with his talents and esteem within the brewing community. Will Rock Bottom survive without him? I have no doubt. Will Van survive without Rock Bottom? Definitely!

Van talks with his hands a lot.

Growing up in Massachusetts and California, Van first moved to Portland when he attended Reed College for his degree in economics. Later, when he was in Minnesota working on his PhD, he realized he really was not interested in completing it. Taking a job at the Minnesota Brewing Company, he later moved on to Rock Bottom after his then girlfriend/now wife got a job at Johns Hopkins. While there he took some classes at the Seibel Institute. After opening a Rock Bottom in Bethesda, Maryland, Van transferred to Rock Bottom in Portland.

Van is actually rather unusual in the brewing industry. In a

business with brewers whose job is a consuming passion, he readily admits it is not an obsession for him; it is a job. He enjoys the process. His excitement enters when he talks about cars, he loves them and enjoys a bit of small-time car racing; Bird hunting and his two

Upstairs a relaxed atmosphere includes pool tables.

Australian sheppards are other items of interest. Oh, he also likes to hang out with friends and drink...you guessed it...beer.

Enjoying the smell of Michelob, Van says it brings back cookies and ice cream memories of childhood. It is what his dad drank. But to Van, "Get a beer" means pale ale, though he does enjoy cask ale, saying Brewers Union Local 180's British style cask ale is the best in Oregon.

When Van called and told his dad he had been fired for speaking his mind and was most definitely his father's son, his dad agreed, after all that was how he lost a couple of jobs himself. At the time of this writing, Van is still researching his options. Though he had already worked on a deal to partner the beginning of a Ninkasi-type production brewery, that fell through, so we will just have to wait to see where Van lands. Undoubtedly, this one-time Oregon Brewer's Association president will land on his feet and come up brewing.

Word has it that one-time Astoria Brewing brewer, Bolt Minister, will assume the position as head brewer at Rock Bottom.

Note: Just before publication, it was announced that Van Havig will be opening his own brewery, specializing in Gose, a beer made with 50% of the grain being malted wheat. The new brewery will occupy the former Coca Cola bottling plant on N.E. 28th.

Rogue Brewery
1339 NW Flanders
Portland, OR 97209
(503) 222-5910
http://www.rogue.com/

"Rogue is a small revolution"

After introducing ourselves at Rogue in Portland, we were led to a back room of the restaurant where we found company president, Brett Joyce, at work in his "office," a table tucked away in a back corner. With papers spread across the table and the floor around him, dressed in jeans, and obviously comfortable with the casual environment, Brett quickly put any feelings of intimidation we may have had about interviewing the head of this internationally known brew to rest. While he may lead a "nation," he is as down-to-earth and easy to talk to as any of the "little" guys we interviewed. Realizing they will not "win" by having fancy offices, there are no closed office doors at Rogue.

Brett, son of founder, Jack Joyce, only recently assumed leadership at Rogue. Though he had worked waiting tables, cleaning kegs, and pulling mash when younger, he had been away for ten years while working as Director of Footwear for Adidas golf. Then in 2006, the board of directors asked him to come back to Rogue. With no guarantee of assuming the presidency, Brett joined the Rogue team's pursuit of their revolutionary mission.

That revolution began in 1988 when Jack Joyce decided to make yet another major career change. As a lawyer, he had practiced construction litigation for fifteen years but it was when he left the law

Brett, in his "office" at Rogue in Portland.

and went to work in marketing for Nike that he learned to work as a member of a team. Nike also taught him to make a world class product if you wish to succeed, plus the importance of branding, known at Rogue as unique thunder.

Together with his old friend, U of O fraternity brother and fellow Nike employee, Bob Woodall, and a third Nike employee, Rob Strasser, the Rogue idea brewed after being approached by Jack's friend and accountant, Jeff Schultz, an avid homebrewer. Despite Jeff being the only partner with any knowledge of brewing and none of them knowing anything about the restaurant business, this led to an investment in a brewpub next to beautiful Lithia Creek in Ashland, and the beginning of Rogue Brewing Company.

With the sixty seat pub upstairs and the ten barrel brewery in the basement, Rogue struggled on despite a flood in the brewery. But they were not thriving in Ashland and began the search for a new home. One of the partners suggested Jack talk with Mo Niemi, of famed Mo's Restaurant chain, in Newport, who had a property at the waterfront near the original Mo's restaurant, which she thought would be a good location for a brewpub. With legend being that Jack was snowed in for four days during a freak Newport snowstorm, he and Mo made the deal, despite Jack's initial uncertainty. With a few odd lease conditions, including the stipulation that an early nude picture of Mo in a bathtub must be displayed on the wall of the pub, Rogue made the move to Newport in 1989. Mo's likeness graces the label of MoM Half-e-Weizen, formerly known as Mo Ale.

With the Newport location being an instant hit, it was not long, (circa 93/94) before it became necessary to relocate the brewery across the bay to its current OSU Drive location, a former old ship storage building (yes, it's big), which now includes a pub and has plenty of expansion room. The Rogue Ales Public House remains at the same location on Bay Drive which Mo had insisted would be a great brewpub. Patrons now play pool where the brewery once stood.

When Brett first told us that Rogue started in Ashland, I thought that explained the name, after all, Ashland is part of the Rogue Valley. But he was quick to let us know that Rogue is a spirit, not a place. The dictionary defines rogue as "unorthodox and unpredictable." This rather defines the attitude at Rogue. According to Brett, there are not three, five, or ten-year plans; "we do well to have a one-year plan...we aren't in the beer business,

Names, labels, and colors all serve to market Rogue.

we're in the change business...to bring variety to the customer."

In the early days of Rogue, with no funds for promotion, they decided to let it promote itself. With a world class product - deserving of special packaging - the bottles on the shelves could promote themselves. Is there anyone who has not been attracted by Rogue's extraordinary names and labels? Bob was certainly attracted to the Dead Guy label when he purchased it as his very first microbrew many years ago; it remains one of his favorites to this day. For twenty years the artist behind those creative labels has been the imaginative Penny Murie. Rather than sticking with the conventional promotional items of coasters and signs, Rogue has added items like yo-yos, Mr. Bendy, and

At the brewery in Newport

brewshoes. It figures the guys who worked for shoe companies would promote their product with shoes.

According to Brett, Rogue is "a mile wide and an inch deep," meaning they are in all fifty states and twenty-one countries, but not heavily anywhere. Perhaps this is the result of rather than

Aging barrels and storage at the brewery in Newport.

building a brewery for shareholders, accountants, or ... Rogue focused on building for the consumer. Going the opposite, an inch wide and a mile deep may have satisfied the accountants, but think of all the consumers who would have would not have had access to Rogue if they had a different attitude.

Brewing a total of about 80,000 barrels annually at four of their pubs, Rogue is considered a mid-size brewery. With four brewpubs, six pubs, and 252 employees, many who are long-term, Rogue can be found from Issaquah, Washington, to San Francisco, California. Of the four brewpubs, the brewery in Newport brews the majority of Rogue brews. The Green Dragon in Southeast Portland also has a small brewery. Issaquah Brewhouse brews under the Frog brand, including such choices as Menage-a-Frog, Hippie Frog, and MacFrog. At the Eugene Brewery, they are busy brewing under the Track-Town brand, which is appropriate.

Award medals shoved in a messy storeroom is an indication of priorities at rogue...move on and create more greatness rather than dwell on past successes.

- 294 -

In addition to the four breweries, two Rogue locations include distilleries. The Flanders location in Portland has a rum distillery in what feels like, but really is not, the attic. Rogue House of Spirits on Marine

Rogue has a wide variety of three-dimensional tap handles.

Drive in Newport, on the other hand, is a dedicated distillery, distilling a variety of spirits: rum, whisky, vodka, and gin. At this location you can also enjoy brews, wine, and a limited food selection.

Rogue has expanded into a well-rounded "nation." Not stopping with only the brewing end of beer, at Rogue Farms Micro Hopyard, in Independence, on the Willamette River north of Albany, Rogue Nation's own Department of Agriculture has entered into a strategic alliance with Heritage Hop Growers, aka, the Coleman family. With seven varieties of hops; farming equipment; a farm pond, complete with large-mouthed bass; as well as corn and grass fields, this forty-two acre farm sits at the end of a dead-end road, creating the classic "farm" feel.

To enjoy the feel of Independence, perhaps a stay at Rogue Hop 'N Bed farmhouse will suit. Once used as a boardinghouse for children of

Beautiful amber colored spiced rum at Rogue.

hop farm workers, with the Willamette River only steps away and the Chatoe Rogue Tasting Room right across the driveway, you can enjoy Rogue's GYO (grow your own) Chatoe series ales, dawn a hickory shirt, and feel the tranquility of farm

Rogue sampler

life.

As we all know, Oregon has plenty of great water, the first ingredient for beer. With Rogue Farms Micro Hopyard, the second ingredient is covered. But there is a third ingredient in beer, barley, which Rogue has covered also. The Rogue Barley Farm grows 265 acres of Dare and Risk malting barley on the Tgyh Valley Bench in Eastern Oregon. Barley is only a portion of the crop on this 3800 acre farm. Grapes, apples, and plums round out the crops at this eastern location where guests can tour in the four-seater Rogue Mobile.

Surprised with the diversity of Rogue Nation, Brett says "if an idea makes us smile, we'll do it." Of course, this means a few bad ideas make their way through upon occasion, such as garlic beer. Being a beer connoisseur *and* a garlic-head, this would have interested Bob, but according to Brett, some things just should not be mixed. Hiring a band to play at South Beach, who had the name of Cherry Poppin' Daddies, did not go over well. People were outraged!

But these debacles can be countered with the numerous good/great ideas. For instance, there were those who said the twenty-two ounce bottle would not sell. Imagine! We particularly like the listing of ingredients on

Bottles are labeled with many languages

Mo's picture still graces the Newport plant

Rogue bottles as well as product specifications, dedications, and other fun stuff, like food pairings.

I wonder what brewmaster, John "More Hops" Maier, thought of the idea of that garlic beer- or was it his? As a senior electronic technician at Hughes Aircraft, John worked on the F-14 Radar System. Then in the fall of 1986, John attended the Siebel Institute of Technology, graduating from their 50th course in Brewing Technology. That same year, this talented brewmaster brewed a barleywine that won the American Homebrewer Association's Homebrewer of the Year Award. This was followed by a job offer from Alaska Brewery in March 1987, to be their assistant brewmaster. He left in 1989 when he became brewmaster at Rogue, just in time to brew the first batch at the Newport location. Since then his ales have garnered over 500 awards for Rogue.

Considered an artist, John says "You gotta like a lot of hops if you're going to drink our beer." Given the freedom to brew what he wants, without restriction, the accountants do not dictate to John. Price is figured after John creates. Though the higher prices this creates may be a point of contention to some consumers, it has not stopped them from becoming known and enjoyed worldwide. John loves his work and plans to continue forever.

Dead Guy dressed for Christmas

Night at the Nation

Passion is evident when speaking to those at this Nation of Rogue. Respect for those who have come before is evident. Jack Joyce is still active, despite relinquishing the presidency to son, Brett. He now holds the title of CWO, Chief Wisdom Officer.

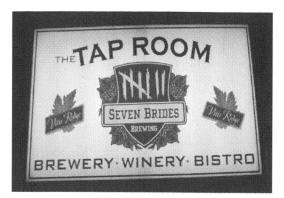

**Seven Brides
Brewing**

990 N 1st Street
Silverton, Oregon
97381
503-874-4677

www.sevenbridesbrewing.com

"Come and enjoy Seven Brides beer, food, atmosphere, and all Silverton has to offer"

Seven Brides got its name from three dads and two uncles who could not *buy* a "Y" chromosome, is the tongue-in-cheek reply to how they got their name.

It all started when partner, Phill Knoll began homebrewing in his garage about seventeen years ago. Soon, Josiah Kelly, Karl Knoll, and Ken DeSantis got involved. Though Jeff DeSantis was not a beer-drinker in those days, he wanted to play too. After all, there was talk of elk hunting, and other "manly" things.

Brewing on a fifteen gallon system for five guys to share was just not enough, so they transitioned to a thirty-five gallon system (otherwise known as one barrel). At one time they had even made beer in a square sausage cooker.

When friends started wanting their brew for weddings and other events, Josiah-the lawyer's son- said "Not legal!" So the five spent the next year making it legal.

The three dads in the group had six daughters: Josiah had two, Phill had two, and Jeff had two. Out of this they came up with the very cool name of Six Chicks Brewing. Then Josiah had to go and ruin it by having another girl. Thankfully, he was vindicated when his wife, Shannon, walked in and said,

Ken DeSantis standing next to the original 35 gallon brew kettle.

The seven "brides"
Photo courtesy Seven Brides Brewing, used by permission

"Well, there are seven daughters, they are all going to need weddings, so how about Seven Brides?" Wise woman! What would they do without us?

The partners each contribute an important element to the company:

- Josiah, president of the company, is a master of all trades, having spent 20 years fabricating industrial equipment worldwide. He helps with the brewing when needed.
- Phill, head brewer, works part-time for the company around his position as head of a chemistry department.
- Karl is assistant brewer and plant manager.
- Ken, head of accounting, is also vice president of DeSantis Landscapes, named a 2009 Oregon Best Green company by Oregon Business Magazine.
- Jeff serves as sales and marketing director, having worked in sales for over sixteen years. He is also the resident expert on heavy equipment.

Josiah Kelley

When it came time to design a logo, Ken insisted that with a name like Seven Brides, there had to be a shield or

The display in the taproom with "the picture"

something manly on it. While the graphic designer they worked with said to write down their ideas and he would come up with something in a week or two, the partners wanted to work together with him. So he plugged in his computer…two hours later there was the logo. As soon as the partners saw it, all five said "That's it!" That was on Friday. On Saturday, the partners picked up the T-shirts with the logo on them. Then on Sunday morning they took the photo which would symbolize their name.

When the commercial brewery opened in 2008, it was located in Jeff's two thousand square foot shop. Then the wife said, "Out!" The proclamation forced a move to a 1300-square foot facility that, interestingly enough, had once housed Victory Prints, the printer who dropped everything and did the hurry-up work for them on the Saturday after the logo was finally ready. The partners figured this place would house them for a good five years. But...Jeff decided they needed a tasting room...strictly

a place for locals to have a beer, a sort of testing ground...they now say with a smile.

Initially, the search for a new space led them to a 4500 square foot building. "Sometimes when you have to work too hard to get something, you realize it is not meant to be." Then the property where they were meant to be came available. With 17,500 square feet, it should sustain anything they can dream up for some time to come-I think.

Built in 1979, to house Copeland Lumber, it later became Keith Brown Lumber, before becoming Traeger Grills, manufactures of smokers, grills, and barbeque products using wood pellets for fuel.

With a wonderful landlord who took care of the outside renovations, Seven Brides handled the inside transformation. With the building basically a shell, there was plenty to do. The front of the building had five rotting telephone poles, which held up support beams, and had to be replaced. The partners insolated the entire building.

The design vision was Jeff's; "Trust me," he said. Jeff, being a visual person, actually laid everything out in blue painter's tape so he could "see" it better. A retired friend, who would come in on a weekly basis and acted as consultant, occasionally had to adjust Jeff's "vision," but in the end, little adjustment was needed. The taproom may have come in at three times the amount budgeted, but since completion, everyone has said, "Wow!"

The tomorrow Bar

All the molding is original to the building, it was stripped and refinished. Rite Way Electric, in Albany, provided all the wonderful lighting. The wood logo above the inside of the entrance door was burned by Rich Aschrel of Aschrel Industries.

The bar, known as Tomorrow Bar, so-called because when it did not arrive until a couple of weeks after the tap room opened, patrons kept asking when the bar was going to come. The stock answer was "tomorrow." This gorgeous work was made by Lee Radtke, whose family owns Gilgamesh Brewing, from reclaimed wood, which was sitting in the barn of a buddy of the partners. Roughly four hundred years old, the wood was originally beams at Silver Falls Lumber Company in Silverton.

Silver Falls Lumber Company was, in 1924, the largest operating lumber company in the world. An interesting note is that in the early 1920s, Silverton, Portland, and Oregon City each had about the same population of 10-15 thousand people. (2009 populations: Silverton-9,781; Portland-582,130: and Oregon City-31,826) The Father of a couple who visited the taproom, worked at the old mill and had an original panoramic picture of it. They graciously allowed Seven Brides to have a sizable copy made of the picture. This amazingly detailed picture will be displayed in the taproom. Legend has it that one of the men in the photo is Clark Gable, who worked for the mill at that time.

When they started the business, the partners decided to name the beer after the "brides." Phil's goal was to be sure all seven girls had a beer named for them. Now, with about fifteen beers to their name, they

Seven Brides had just received the large copy of the old mill picture when we interviewed them. They graciously rolled it out on the bar for us to photograph.

are needing to tap into the names of cousins and other girls. "Bride," Lilly, at five years old, is competitive. She wants her beer to sell the most. Ironically, the biggest beer, a dopplebock called Weezin-ator, is named for the smallest girl.

Opening weekend the partners were hoping for a thousand people. Instead, four thousand participated in the festivities, which included $20 helicopter tours around Silverton, the hop fields, and Oregon Gardens. (None of the proceeds went to Seven Brides.) The partners were quite proud of their staff, who performed brilliantly.

In the seven months since opening (at the time of our interview), only one staff member has left; for anyone who has ever worked in the restaurant business, this is amazing and says a great deal about working for Seven Brides. According to the partners, the staff has taken ownership-and the partners have given it to them-since day one.

This is understandable when they see all five partners and their families pitch in wherever needed, whether its mopping floors, clearing tables, or washing dishes, whatever needs to be done, the staff knows the owners will step in to do it.

Three dads and two uncles
Photo courtesy Seven Brides, used by permission

An extra benefit of working for Seven Brides is that all staff are encouraged to sign up with Josiah for a brew day, when they get to help in the brewery.

All of the partners grew up in Silverton, went to school there, and are proud this is home. This pride was displayed when they used a 1911 downtown Silverton picture on their first labels. They figure if Seven Brides can bring visitors to town, it will benefit everyone. With 30-40 percent of their current business out-of-towners, I would say they are making good progress toward this goal. Silverton

This 30 barrel brewhouse originally came from Montana to the last Seven Brides facility before being moved to Seven Brides' current location.

feels the same about Seven Brides. Since the May 2010 opening of the taproom, they have wholeheartedly embraced it as "their" brewery.

Silverton and Seven Brides have good reasons to be proud of their city. Beautiful views, plenty of recreational choices, and a slow enough pace to provide the small town feel, yet with added pockets of culture, this is an area to appeal to all tastes. Add to all of this a top rate brewery and taproom, local wineries, one of the premier parks in the state, and a full service resort with gardens to please, and who wouldn't be proud?

Silver Falls State Park

Silver Falls State Park, just outside Silverton, is renowned as one of the most beautiful in the state, with "10 majestic waterfalls, ranging from the grand South Falls (177 feet), to the delicate Drake Falls

(27 feet). Four of these falls have an amphitheater-like surrounding where you can walk behind the falls and feel the misty spray."

Oregon Gardens and Resort is beauty and luxury combined. Featuring more than twenty specialty gardens and features, the Gardens are a favorite venue for events. Weddings, birthdays, reunions, and tours are all favorites in the Gardens. They even host their own

Our room at Oregon Gardens Resort

Brewfest in April. Add to all this, a Resort which provides well appointed rooms featuring fireplaces and private patios or balconies. Both the restaurant and lounge, located in the main lodge, feature Seven Brides Beers and local wines, as well as superb dining. Also available are a heated outdoor pool, hot tub, and a day spa. As if this were not enough, Oregon Gardens also features the Gordon House, Oregon's only house designed by famed architect, Frank Lloyd Wright.

Back at the brewpub, events are also common, with Seven Brides providing a venue for events at an average of one per week. With five thousand square feet dedicated to restaurant, there is plenty of space, including a banquet room, in which the largest party so far was 300 people, with space for many more. Additionally, Seven Brides hosts five-course beer pairing dinners every six to eight weeks.

Eighty-five to ninety percent of the festivals Seven Brides participates in are family-friendly events. They have found they actually sell more beer and have more fun when they are not at a segregated "beer garden." "We would much rather sell two hundred guys one glass than fifty guys four glasses." While

The "no parking" square

the total amount sold may be the same, they enjoy the relaxed family atmosphere of integrated events. Offering food and carding everyone they serve, the assimilation works and is approved by officials. "By being more inclusive, smarter decisions are made by families."

One of these events is the Silverton Fine Arts Festival, an event for the public where local artists are invited by invitation only to exhibit and sell their art. Acknowledging the "art" of brewing, invitees include the local winery and Seven Brides Brewing, where this is the largest local event they do.

While some have commented that the parking situation is a bit odd, the partners had patrons in mind when planning it. There is no parking right next to the building to prevent headlights from shining through the large windows into the restaurant. Every thought has been given to the comfort of their customers.

When we visited Seven Brides Brewing it was at five o'clock on a Monday night in December. Though the taproom was closed, three of the five partners were busy setting up for their first annual Men's Night Out.

It was an idea born from wives doing Tupperware and other home parties. With men generally notorious for not enjoying shopping and the hustle and bustle of stores during the Christmas season, Seven Brides arranged for multiple vendors to be on hand to allow the gentlemen to complete all their shopping in one fell swoop.

On December 8, 2010, for the cost of a $10 ticket each man attending received two pints of beer, plenty of vendor tables at which to shop for their loved ones, entry into door prize drawings, and, to make the significant other happy, entry into a drawing for a half-carat diamond (did I say ½ carat diamond?!). Plus, there was sports on the big screen TV, more beer on tap, and all the male

bonding they could desire.

The idea was welcomed by both the men in the area and the local merchants. The only cost to the merchants to take part was for them to bring one gift, something the men would want themselves, for the hourly door prize drawings. With more than twenty merchants in attendance, Seven Brides finally had to turn away vendors for lack of space. For those local vendors unable to set up at the Tap Room, participation was still made possible through the use of the Silver Trolly shuttle, which took shoppers downtown and back to the Tap Room every half hour. After the men in attendance chose their gifts, there were no worries about wrapping, with complimentary gift wrapping services provided by Ken McGee from Aflac.

While Seven Brides thought this was a good idea, the response was phenomenal! Plans are to make it an annual event. We would not be surprised to see this idea catch on in other areas.

The Tap Room is family-friendly until 8 P.M. You will find no fried food in this bistro-style restaurant. A variety of reasonably priced offerings by Chef Jake include vegetarian options and a willingness to work with special dietary or children's needs. When they first opened, there were only five items on the menu-but they did them well! With more than five times that available today, they are still doing them well. In addition to the Seven Brides brews, you will find a selection of Vitis Ridge Wines available. Vitis Ridge is also available to purchase by bottle or case, since they lease space from Seven Brides.

Seven Brides has an eye and a heart for sustainable practices. All of the tables and chairs are from other closed restaurants rather than purchasing new. All spent grain and hops go to local farmers for feed or fertilizer. All pork and beef come from local farms where they ate the spent grain from the brewery.

In 2008, Seven Brides first year of operation, they produced 55 barrels of brew. They followed that the next year with 215. In 2010, production almost hit 1000 barrels. The partners are projecting up to 2000 barrels for 2011. I anticipate they will do at least that.

In addition to the Tap Room, Seven Brides can be found on tap at about forty (as of this writing) pubs from Eugene to Portland to Bend. Also available in bottles, Seven Brides has recently expanded distribution.

Barrel Aging

What do they see in their future? Most immediately, the first barrel aged beer from Seven Brides, a lager, which has aged in a cabernet wine barrel, and is picking up the red tones of the wine was expected be

released for Valentine's Day 2011. In the near future, plans call for the purchase of a bottling line within two years, which will replace the mobile bottler they currently use. In the far future, who knows, maybe more tap rooms. With a desire to minimize the debt load, they are in no hurry.

Currently, the Tap Room is open Thursday through Sunday. They close Monday through Wednesday because they are slow days in Silverton. However, this may change during the summer when tourists are more active, so call or check the web site for current days and hours.

When we asked if the partners had ever dreamed Seven Brides would be this successful, the answer was varying degrees of "no." Except for the guy with a vision - Jeff had no doubts. We say...it could not happen to a nicer group of guys.

Silver Moon Brewing
24 NW Greenwood Avenue
Bend, Oregon 97701
541-388-8331
www.silvermoonbrewing.com

"I'd rather do without than eat crappy food and low quality beer"

Tyler Reichert, owner at Silver Moon Brewing, headed west from Vermont in 1994. As a forester in Vermont, Tyler had lived in a farmhouse deep in the forest. With no road to the old farmhouse available, he was required to haul everything home by foot.

When a friend introduced him to homebrewing, Tyler had to try it; so he packed in homebrew supplies. Before long, fellow foresters were enjoying the results of Tyler's efforts.

Deciding to move west, Tyler knew he would live in a location with skiing available. After living in Missoula, Montana, and Jackson, Wyoming, he landed in Bend.

Subsequent to a few odd jobs in forestry, he purchased a homebrew supply store in 1998, which was in a leased building. The next year, he obtained his brew license and began brewing in a 1.5 barrel system, selling his brew out of his store, as well as at a few local pubs.

Hiring Tyler West as assistant brewer in 2003, Tyler Reichert continued as head brewer, also running the supply store until 2004 when he made West head brewer. These days, West has his own assistant.

Owner, Tyler Reichert, in the cooler

The brewhouse at Silver Moon

When, in 2005, Tyler was ready to increase the size of his system, he knew it was time to find a bigger shop to purchase. The larger system would require permanent installation, which could mean it would then be a part of the building, which he did not own; with the cost of brew equipment, that was a risk he was not willing to take. Things were a bit rough at the Silver Moon when they first opened in their newly acquired location, paying rent on the old location and payments at the new became too expensive to allow for plenty of time to ready the new building. Time has definitely eliminated any roughness.

When a Bandon brewery went out of business, an attorney there somehow ended up owning the equipment, which was being stored in a Bandon Dunes maintenance shed. Amid a lot of dickering, the attorney suddenly became amiable, Tyler got the ten barrel system for one-third of the original asking price, with one stipulation, he had to take it immediately.

A friend with a fifth wheel, twenty-one foot trailer generously agreed to help him move the system to Bend. Considering it was February, with four inches of fresh snow in the pass, he must have been a good friend.

Arriving in Bandon, they saw they the storage shed was filled wall-to-wall with equipment and supplies, much of it small stuff. Tyler suggested they get the major equipment and he could return for the bits and pieces. His buddy would have none of that, "We aren't leaving anything behind." After a trip to the store for tarps, ropes, and bungee cords, it was all loaded. "The Beverly Hillbillies had nothing on us," Tyler says. "I kicked myself later for not taking a picture."

With a storm scheduled to come into Oregon that night, and two mountain ranges to traverse, the pair were ready to depart Bandon at 7:30 P.M. Thankfully, a quick check of the

Unusual items available at Silver Moon include branded leather gloves

Much better in color

weather showed a high pressure system had settled over Oregon, while California got hit with the expected storm.

"It was still white-knuckle the whole drive…we were so heavy we weren't slipping…if we stopped we were done," are comments Tyler made regarding the trip over Highway 138 past Mount Theilson and Crater Lake. On the highway, as they came out of a group of trees, the full moon was rising over the horizon and it was like daylight. They arrived in Bend at 4:00 A.M, to a temperature of 17°, Tyler said "the moon guided us home and it is like this a lot in Bend, so I'll name the taproom after it."

With slow, steady growth in the brewery, Tyler decided in 2007 to sell the homebrew supply store, which, under new ownership, is now back at the original location on Division Street.

With the supply store gone, Tyler has been able to focus on the taproom. And focus he has. A great deal of time, effort, and thought has gone into this versatile atmosphere.

A magnificent mural graces the wall behind the sometimes stage, other times table area. Another mural on the other end of the same wall may require a second look to realize it is not a window showing the brewery (see picture at the beginning of this chapter). It is actually a mural of the brewery, which can be found behind the adjacent wall. Both murals are by David Kinker, an award winning local artist, who also happens to be a homebrewer. Tyler had wanted to have him do one in

Artwork, awards, bottles, and murals

the old location, but murals are expensive and it was a rental, so he decided to wait until he purchased his own building. Definitely worth the wait!

Gracing the walls are an assortment of works by local artists, which are for sale. While we were there, popular Bend artist, Francisco, was being highlighted.

Boxes of pelletized hops & bales of fresh hops

The family side – minors are allowed until 6:30 P.M. – of Silver Moon was designed so that it could be easily and quickly rearranged when there is live music. The small tables come off the

Tyler points out boxes of pellet hops versus bales of fresh hops. One box is the equivalent of four bales.

"stage," a carpeted portion of the floor which is one step higher than the rest; the large wine barrel table, which is on casters to allow for easy mobility, is moved to the side; and voila', instant dance floor!

Recently chosen as Bend's best indoor music venue, Silver Moon offers a wide variety of live music every weekend and occasional week nights. "We proudly present a diverse array of entertainment... nationally-touring acts, local acts, slam poetry, belly dancing, pub theater and more." With a sound system designed for quality shows, Silver Moon is able to attract quality shows like Grammy award winner, John Cruz.

Capitalizing on this excellent venue, Silver Moon hosts many parties. Other than the obvious New Year's and Halloween parties, one of their favorites is their Blue Moon parties. Using the popular definition of "a second full moon in a calendar month," they change all the lights to blue bulbs, with a blue light on a disco ball for this appropriate party for Silver Moon's cousin moon.

About the design of Silver Moon, Tyler says "I just designed this pub to be the most comfortable feeling place I could imagine." When he envisioned the room, he wanted it to be dynamic, to

accommodate both the restaurant and a music/dance venue. This is also a durable space which was designed to endure the punishment frequently imposed by its versatile use.

Of Silver Moon's five signature beers and up to fifteen seasonals, eighty-five percent of what is produced is on draft, available at many locations around Bend and a few in Portland and Eugene. Also available are twenty-two ounce bottles, which are bottled on Silver Moon's own equipment and can currently be found at various places in Bend and surrounding areas, Market of Choice in Ashland, Corvallis Brewing Supply in Corvallis, Cornucopia and Market of Choice in Eugene, Whole Foods and the major bottle shops in Portland, and even a few in Seattle.

Food at the Silver Moon may not be the usual pub fare. Due to a lack of a type-one hood with fire suppression, they are unable to grill raw meat. As a result, meat will be found in offerings like stew and chili. When we visited, they were offering organic beef chili.

Tyler says there really is not anything he wishes he had done differently, "if I had done them differently, I wouldn't have learned what I've learned." He adds that he has been able to apply lessons learned from the small rental building to the current location he now owns.

Breweries have a very distinctive aroma, hops. But Silver Moon brewery just smells clean. There is never any concern when inspectors drop in unexpectedly.

Southern Oregon Brewing Company

1922 United Way
Medford, Oregon
97213
541-776-9898
www.sobrewing.com

"Make Amazing Beer, Have Fun, Take Care of Your People"

We were at Southern Oregon Brewing for the Zwickelmania tour, along with about thirty-five others. While we have toured nearly every brewery in the state, this was the only public tour we joined. Being in the second tour with a group who were all part of the local homebrewing association, perhaps it was not representative of the typical tour group, with everyone present being fairly knowledgeable of the brewing process, but it was fun. Definitely rowdier than the private tours we have taken, but that just added to the fun.

Leading the tour was Dr. Tom Hammond, Medford Anesthesiologist and owner of Southern Oregon Brewing. As part of his eighty to one hundred hour work week, Tom makes sure he is available on Saturdays to personally guide the 4 P.M. tour.

Tom, whose undergraduate degree in is biochemistry, attended college and medical school in the Seattle area in the early 1980's. In that time and place craft beers were getting their big start in the area, and Tom was hooked. Additionally, Tom has been a homebrewer for five years.

After he began looking for something to do outside of the medical field, he lost a good friend to cancer. The friend had been an avid home baker of artisan breads, who had

Owner, Dr. Tom Hammond, describes the workings of the grain mill, which breaks the grain open, rather than crushing it, with rollers set 1/64 inch apart.

wanted to start a business, The Bread Man. As Tom was in the church during the funeral, he decided he should follow his own dream and open a brewery.

Smart enough to realize he would need to hire a brewer, Tom turned to Anders Johansen, whose past experience includes Deschutes and Pyramid. Tom gave Anders full control over the design of the brewery; after all, he was the expert. Shying away from the potential headaches of used equipment, they installed all new steam driven brewing equipment, which allows for even heating. Most of it was purchased from AAA Metal Fabrication in The Dalles, though the horizontal tanks came from JV Northwest in Canby.

This was the only brewery where we have seen horizontal tanks used, other than converted milk tanks. The horizontal tanks are used for lagers, with their bottom fermenting yeast. With less vertical fall, the beer tends to be brighter than with vertical tanks. Beers are lagered at SOB for a period of ten days to three months, depending on the lager.

Unlike most start-up breweries, SOB jumped in with both feet, going bigger than needed initially. Installing a twenty barrel brewhouse and four vessel system

Unusual horizontal tanks used to ferment lagers

with an annual capacity of forty thousand barrels, SOB has a long way to go before reaching that number; 2010 saw production of sixteen hundred barrels.

Bottling with the assistance of mobile bottler, Green Bottling,

SOB definitely gets the prize for the coolest growlers, which they have shipped from Germany. Love that handle.

during the last two years, SOB plans call for purchasing their own bottling line in the spring of 2011. With distribution expanding into Washington State, expectations are for up to sixty percent growth this year.

Also in the brewery is an unusual and rather rough floor. This floor serves three functions: the roughness is slip resistant, which is a definite advantage in a brewery; the surface is bullet proof, meaning it will withstand the rigors of a production brewery; and there are no seems or breaks, which helps prevent infection problems.

Another item we found at SOB that not many other breweries use is the kegs, which have polyurethane exteriors and stainless steel interiors. Lower theft risk is the largest reason for using these modern adaptations.

After getting the brewery up and going, and staying the committed two years, Anders left SOB in the capable hands of brewer Scott Sanders, who had brewed

Bartender, Jason Leusch fills a growler

with Anders at Deschutes. Anders has returned to Dolmen Distillery in McMinnville as planned.

This Mail Tribune 2010 Readers' Choice "Best Local Microbrew" winner makes no fruit beers, gives tours every Saturday at 4 P.M., and serves no food in the taproom – though you can have food delivered to your table from your choice of twenty-seven local restaurants.

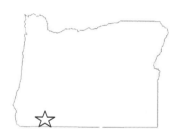

Standing Stone Brewing Company

101 Oak Street
Ashland, Oregon 97520
541-482-2448
www.standingstonebrewing.com

*"Real people working hard to give the
community a great place to eat and drink"*

The fire resistant, reinforced concrete, Whittle Garage Building was built for a sum of $6,000 in 1923, by Floyd Whittle, using the false front form, which was long a popular method for hiding the roof and making the building appear larger than it was. For the next twenty years, the building served as Morris's Oak Street Garage. The building's use history for the next ten years has been obscured over time, though some speculate Lithia Motors may have used it for repairs at one time. In 1953, a fire at the Busch Motors Building spread and damaged the Whittle Garage Building. During the repair, Pioneer Glass and Cabinet Shop was hired to replace the windows. In need of additional space, Pioneer rented the building, where it remained, albeit with two different sets of owners, until it closed in 1994.

1996: Enter the three Amarotico brothers. Alex Amarotico had passed Whittle Garage Building and realized it would be ideal. Alex, a homebrewer, had an idea to open a brewpub. With one brother a contractor and another a trained chef, it seemed the perfect collaboration.

Respecting the history of the building, which is on the National Register of Historic Places, the new brewpub was brilliantly designed to appear as though it were simply tucked into the original building. With

The large, dark beam on the right and the black steel on the left are the original track for moving things about the garage.

the exterior front appearing virtually the same as it did when built, the design allowed for meeting current codes while retaining historic integrity. Seismic requirements, American Disability Act codes, and other code requirements, such as sanitation were incorporated in a manner which would not detract from the original building.

One of the first things we noticed was the floor. The

Looking down at the restaurant from the brewery

Amaroticos kept the original cement floor, first cleaning it thoroughly, then sanding down high spots and finally allowing the low spots to fill in with the same clear polymer used to seal the entire floor. This process has created an interesting floor, which is durable as well as beautiful.

Of course this is not to say anyone could miss the unique brewery location. Raised, steel girders provide a second level which houses the brewery, mill, and grain storage. Open to full view, with no walls or glass separating the brewery from the restaurant, patrons of the pub are treated to all the sights, sounds, and aromas of a brewery on brewing days. Due to the difficult assent and confined space, tours of the brewery are not available to the public. As a lifelong acrophobic (it has taken years for me to graduate to six-foot step ladders), our tour made me more than a little nervous, no walls and too steep steps. But it is these same open conditions which provide patrons wishing to watch the brew process or have a view of the brewery the ability to choose brewside seating.

Beautifully coordinated with the glossy black steel of the brewery level, the original brick and concrete walls remain exposed. Be sure to look up, the original open truss system is also in view. I enjoyed the way they chose to leave the trusses and ceiling white, a

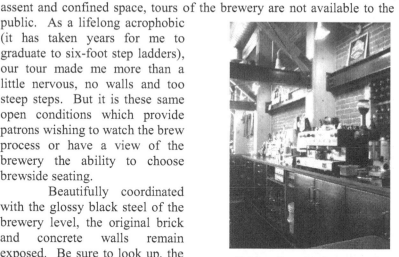

Brick walls, concrete posts, and black steel combine to create an amazing effect.

stark contrast to the rest of the brewpub, to accentuate them. Standing Stone also chose to leave the original beam and the track it ran along, allowing for easy movement of engines when this building was a garage. Also preserved were the original garage doors. Used as a decorative element, with one at the front and one at the back of the restaurant, and now painted green, preservation of the doors exemplifies the commitment to historical preservation at Standing Stone.

Outdoor seating

The original wooden storage deck was demolished by the city of Ashland in the early 1980's in an attempt to discourage indigent congregation. However, Standing Stone has rebuilt the deck, providing fantastic outdoor seating with views of Ashland's hills.

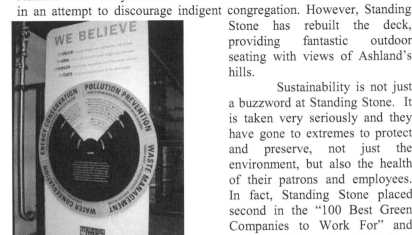

Turn the eco-wheel to see how Standing Stone rethinks everything for sustainability.

Sustainability is not just a buzzword at Standing Stone. It is taken very seriously and they have gone to extremes to protect and preserve, not just the environment, but also the health of their patrons and employees. In fact, Standing Stone placed second in the "100 Best Green Companies to Work For" and twenty-eighth in the "100 Best Green Companies" rankings by *Oregon Business* magazine.

Standing Stone's sustainability commitment begins with the building.

➢ The roof is topped with solar panels, which produce 7,800 kWh of electricity.

➢ The energy-saving hood runs only during operating hours using sensors which turn it on only when needed. This saves a reported 22% over standard restaurant hoods.

➢ The innovative heat-recovery system uses waste heat from the air to produce energy for the water heater, brewing, heating, and air conditioning.

➢ The adjustable, louvered deck awning limits the concrete building's absorption of heat during the summer months, reducing air-conditioning costs.

This dedication to the environment and public health continues in the kitchen with Standing Stone's food choices, both pre and post serving.

Standing Stone's laying hens
Photo courtesy of Standing Stone Brewing Co
Used by permission

➤ Standing Stone keeps a flock of sixty free-range chickens, without using antibiotics or hormones, to provide fresh, local eggs for the restaurant.

➤ Beef comes from Valley View Beef in Ashland, three miles from the restaurant, where they graze on chemical-free pastures exclusively, and receive no hormones or antibiotics.

➤ Recently, Standing Stone was granted a lease to use over two hundred acres of city property to raise poultry for in-house use; five thousand chickens are expected to be raised chemical-free each year, allowing for local, healthy poultry.

➤ Standing Stone serves certified organic buffalo which is from Full Circle Bison Ranch in nearby Williams Valley.

➤ Whenever possible, Standing Stone purchases local organic produce, with the chef frequenting the Growers Market, to obtain the freshest local produce.

➤ Pre-consumer waste is fed to the Standing Stone chickens.

➤ Post-consumer waste is always composted.

➤ Standing Stone serves equitably traded coffee, which is locally roasted at Noble Coffee, just a few blocks away.

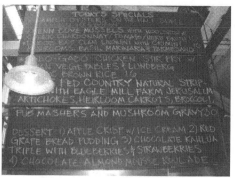

Daily specials using current available products

➤ All to-go containers are recycled, compostable materials.

➤ Reusable items are all that are used, including napkins and water bottles.

➤ All cardboard, paper, etc. is recycled

This commitment to sustainability and using local products results in an occasional irritable customer because Standing Stone uses no fresh tomatoes on anything until they are available locally in August, though the majority respect this commitment to avoid long-distance transport whenever possible. In answer to the desire for tomatoes, they have developed a smoked tomato relish which is served on their Standing Stone burger. A large chalk-board at the edge of the open kitchen announces specials made from locally grown items which are currently available.

In-house made bread and spreads , served with water in reusable bottles water

Standing Stone's commitment to sustainability continues in the brewery.

➤ Whenever in season, Standing Stone purchases organic locally grown hops from Alpha Beta Hops Farm, where they use wind power.

➤ Committed to using organics whenever possible, 90% of the grains used at Standing Stone are organic.

➤ Spent grains are fed to Standing Stone's own chickens.

➤ Distribution is limited to "dolly-able" locations. If they can wheel the keg on a dolly to the location, they will distribute. The one exception to this was when Crater Lake National Park wanted to carry Standing Stone brews; they simply could not pass up the honor.

Space is well planned in the brewery

➤ Bottles are reusable and ceramic capped. While recycling saves, reusing saves more.

At Standing Stone the commitment to the environment and people extends to the employees, where they not only offer health insurance and a 401K plan with match (very unusual benefits in the restaurant industry) but encourage employees to stay healthy and protect the environment in several ways. Free yoga classes are provided for employees, with a free yoga mat after attending twelve classes.

Employees with their free bikes and tees
Photo courtesy Standing Stone Brewing Co.
Used by permission

Most amazing and unusual is the RPM bike commuting program. Any employee who works there for a total of one thousand hours (equal to twenty-five forty hour weeks) and agrees to commute at least forty-five times within a year receives a free Kona commuter bike and tee-shirt. Inspired by this program, the folks at Rogue Creamery have also initiated a bike commuting program.

Standing Stone also encourages employees to find ways to apply their talents and abilities within the company. Whether through graphic design, flower arranging, or researching breeds for the chicken farm, utilization and recognition of employees' unique contributions is beneficial for both the employee and the company. It was through this utilization that the yoga program began.

As a self-taught homebrewer, Alex Amarotico served as Standing Stone's only brewer for the first five years before hiring an assistant. Then in January 2010, they hired brewer Larry Chase to take over the head brewer position. A graduate of American Brewers Guild with fourteen years professional brewing experience, Larry was moved to become a brewer after an eight-month European tour allowed him to taste beer throughout Europe.

Brewing on the ten barrel brewery above the restaurant, which includes eight fermenters, Standing Stone brews about five hundred barrels annually.

As the only brother actively involved in this privately-held corporation, Alex now serves as general manager. Also active at Standing Stone is Alex's wife, Danielle, who is in charge of hiring and service. This is no small job for a brewpub with forty-five to sixty

Solar panels on the roof
Photo courtesy of Standing Stone Brewing Co.
Used by permission

employees, depending on the season.

Plans originally called for Standing Stone to be named Pilot Rock Brewing, after the local landmark, but decided they want to use something a bit more innovative, after learning the Tekelma Indians used to call Pilot Rock "Stone that Stands," they realized they had their name.

Standing Stone tap handles

This same history, along with the building's history, is reflected in Standing Stone's tap handles. Look at the bottom and you will see a bolt, with the name on the head of the bolt. Then top the bolt with a three-D likeness of Pilot Rock and you have an ingenious design for a tap handle.

While they used to do many festivals, going as far as Portland for the Oregon Brewers Festival, the people at Standing Stone came to realize all that travel to participate messed with their local philosophy, so these days, find them in Ashland.

Standing Stone also owns the adjacent building, which they are in the process of refurbishing to house the upcoming kitchen expansion. With only twenty percent of their business beer and ten percent other beverages (they have a full bar), this means seventy percent of their

business is food, and food needs space.

Whether there for the beer, the food, the wonderful house-made breads and desserts, or the history and beauty of Standing Stone, visit the dedicated and sustainable Standing Stone while in Ashland.

Danielle Amarotico, seven months pregnant, showing us the "heart of Standing Stone," the recycle center out back.

Steelhead Brewing Company

199 East 5th Avenue
Eugene, Oregon 97401
(541) 686-2739
Keg Hotline: (541) 341-1330
http://www.steelheadbrewery.com/eugene.htm

"Relax while you sip"

Whether you are looking for a place to watch the Ducks latest game or to just relax and enjoy yourself, Steelhead Brewing Company offers both. A sports bar done with the styling of an English pub, a variety of seating choices await you with space for 152 patrons inside and another 40 outside. Whether you want to unwind on one of the wing-back chairs or couches, check out the place while seated at a tall table, or just gather around a table with your friends, there are plenty of large screen T.V.'s for viewing the big game.

Though we are not personally fans of sports bars, they tend to be a bit noisy for our taste, we know many of you enjoy them. This one is great in that they apparently have some good acoustical structure. Despite there being a Ducks game on while we were there, we could still comfortably carry on a conversation. Admittedly, I would find this an ideal place to watch the civil war game, though I might get thrown out, since I tend to root for both teams. I'm a life-long Ducks fan who spent

many years living in the Corvallis area. How could I not become a Beaver believer? Let's be honest, they are equally Oregon, we love them both.

Instead of the usual mirror behind the long, cherry-stained mahogany bar, there is a large picture window, allowing you to watch the brew process as you enjoy your beer. This state-of-the-art 10 barrel brewery began production in December 1990, opening their doors to the public in January 1991. With a 130 barrel capacity per month, you will have plenty of opportunity to watch them brew. If watching through the glass is not enough, tours are available by appointment.

Steelhead offers two kinds of root beer for those of us who are driving or just plain prefer it. Steelhead Original Spicy Draft packs a punch, so unless you are a big fan of strong root beer, ask for a sample first. I hear it makes a great root beer float. I really enjoyed the Honey Vanilla Root Beer. This smooth and mellow root beer is served in bottles with a glass on the side. Neither root beer contains high fructose corn syrup. If you are looking for something a bit stronger, Steelhead bar is full service, offering your choice of cocktails.

For your eating pleasure, Steelhead has a full-service restaurant with an extensive menu. I had them leave the menu so I could finish reading it; they have included a description of the brewing process on it.

Add to all of this plenty of free parking in this downtown location and you have a great place to eat, drink, and join your friends in cheering on the game of the hour.

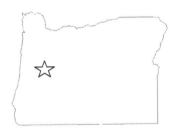

Terminal Gravity Brewing
803 S.E. School Street
Enterprise, Oregon 97828
Pub: 541-426-3000
Brewery: 541-426-0158

terminalgravitybrewing.com

"No fruit, no honey, no wheat, and no damn marketing department!"

Terminal Gravity Brewery and Public House (TG) is deceptive. By all appearances from the front and inside, it is a small, quaint, pub. In reality, the maze of this little converted house, which was built in 1883, actually seems to be the Eastern Oregon version of the Winchester Mystery House. On just under three out-of-the-way acres, this location in Enterprise was chosen for the quality of life in the area, after a search of thirteen small towns in the Western U.S.

It must have been a good business decision also, since TG is the busiest restaurant in Enterprise. The inside seems too small to get very busy, but additional seating can be found upstairs, though in the summer, the majority of patrons enjoy outdoor seating next to the creek. This was one of the main reasons TG was not located along a main street, the desire for outdoor seating, as well as a view.

Upon entering the pub, all of you science fiction / fantasy fans will love the screen door; antique buffs, you will like the ancient dairy cooler refrigerator, which came  with the building. Then you notice the bar, which dominates the room, accompanied by only three tables. The interesting signs and décor, the rustic carved tables, benches, and taps and several items for sell, such as hand blown glasses (made by an employee) and carved wooden bottle openers, keep your attention until learning there is more seating upstairs. Though the upstairs is more functional than decorative, it does provide needed space.

Serving appetizers; salads; sandwiches, including a buffalo burger; and pastas, TG also offers a kids' menu. Big screen TV, foosball, occasional entertainment, volleyball, darts, and monthly open-mike are some of the pastimes found at TG. But for most, the big draw is the beer. After all, it is a brewery.

The man responsible for all of this is Steve Comer, primary owner and head brewer. Though he's quite focused on his brew craft, he has many activities which hold his interest. His is passionate about mountain and ice climbing, though age seems to be intruding on that passion, as age has a way of doing. A one-time avid white-water rafter, sadly, the death of his daughter in a rafting accident understandably ended his rafting interest. As a primitive racer, also known as rally racing, he teaches rally and cross country racing in Hillsboro. Unfortunately, at the time of our interview his race car had a blown ring, though not for long, I would wager.

Owner, Steve Comer

After college, Steve ran a restaurant before working in construction. From all the additions built at TG, it seems both occupations were good training for his future brew pub. In 1989 he began his home brew venture, followed by a job at Bridgeport in Portland in '91. Then, in 1997 this motivated brewer began Terminal Gravity Brewing.

Named by Steve's ex-wife, Debra, terminal gravity refers to the gravity at which fermentation stops. The difference between the starting gravity (starting sugar content) and the terminal gravity (ending sugar content) tells how much alcohol is in the beer, since the yeast eats the sugar and their byproduct is alcohol and CO_2. Good name.

Steve is a fairly laid back, quiet sort of guy. He was not a big

talker, but definite sparks were seen when I referred to his beer as "product." He made it clear, he does not make a product, he makes *beer*, which is a living thing. It requires art and science. His focus, indeed, his passion, is quality. The beer comes first.

This is why you will find no marketing department at TG, nor do they enter their beers in competitions. In fact, as a member of the Oregon Brewers Association, the only festival TG participates in is the Oregon Brewers Festival in Portland. Terminal Gravity is growing slowly, and Steve is quite happy with that. He is not *pushing* growth or his beer; he just lets it sell itself. It must be doing an excellent job since

TG is the eighth largest beer in Oregon and the second largest microbrew, outsold only by Ninsaki of Eugene. ...Since I originally wrote this, Ninkasi brewed 18,000 barrels in 2009, putting them out of the official microbrew category, making TG the largest *microbrewery* in Oregon.

All this slow growth and no advertising budget has allowed TG not to accumulate debt, allowing them to afford to support the community and to purchase better quality ingredients. Though 60% of their malt is from the U.S. and Canada, the rest comes from England. The pelletized hops they use allows for consistency.

As Steve showed us around, introducing us to different employees, his respect for his crew was evident. He cares for his employees and wants them to be happy. Some of that care shows in the names of his tanks. Each of the brew tanks are named for people who have been there for a while.

Terminal Gravity tanks include many they built themselves, though most of those have been sold. Steve's ex-brother-in-law, who is an employee, still works one of them. Double Mountain in Hood River has four of their old tanks. New and old are mixed in the TG brewery. After the bottles go through the brand new bottler, they

I especially liked this tank

get their label from a 1950's era labeler. Soon they will be getting a new keg line to their list of "new" items. After speaking with many brewers, I now understand this means one of the other Oregon breweries will probably get their old keg line.

All this new equipment helps to supply Portland's insatiable appetite for Terminal Gravity. Eighty percent of their current sales are there, with sales of 6000 barrels (12,000 kegs) per year. But Portland, eat your heart out...TG will soon have oak barrel aged beer, but it will only be used for special occasions for the restaurant.

TG is summed up by their company statement, "No fruit, no honey, no wheat, and no damn marketing department!" Marketing department or not, I just wish I had purchased that cute little blue hand blown shot glass when I was there.

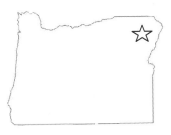

Three Creeks Brewing Company
721 Desperado Court
Sisters, Oregon 97759
541-549-1963
www.threecreeksbrewing.com

"We're Making Northwest Beers with Attitude"

A drive though Sisters might give one the impression they have transported to an 1880s western town. An ordinance passed in the early 1970s requiring all businesses to adopt the 1880s western style store fronts has turned this growing Central Oregon town into a hot-spot for tourists.

Capitalizing on this theme, Three Creeks Brewing Company is a refreshing blend of the Old West coupled with modern clean lines and simplicity. Though this all-new establishment has been designed inside and out with the Sister's "West" in mind, it is not over-the-top. Instead, the design is tasteful, clean, and open.

Located across the parking lot from the Sister's Movie House, Three Creeks Brewing might be easy to miss while driving though town due to the positioning of the building. The shape of the property dictated the building be designed so the side of the building faces the highway. Thankfully, Five Pine Plaza, the business development in which Three Creeks Brewing Company is found, is easy to spot. In addition to the brewing company and the Movie House, Five Pine Plaza

Hand -forged door handles by Jeff Webster at Ponderosa Forge

also hosts Five Pine Lodge, a highly rated hotel, giving the plaza a bit of a resort feel and making it quite convenient.

Local artisan touches are a noticeable feature at Three Creeks from the moment of arrival. Opening the entry doors with the hand forged beer stein handles provides a first impression that no expense was spared in creating this modern piece of the Old West. One look at the hand carved fireplace mantles made from an over 400 year-old juniper tree, reinforces this supposition. A local photographer's work graces many of the walls. The tap handles were created by another local. Whether building, branding, or merchandising, Three Creeks attempts to support locals whenever possible.

This family friendly establishment is divided down the middle. On the left is the unpretentious, family-friendly restaurant. On the right, pass through the Western style saloon doors to the adults-only modern-day saloon for a game of pool, a look at the shiny brewery, or a seat at the copper bar. The flat-panel TVs above the bar keep tabs on the sporting events of the moment.

Three Creeks Brewing Company opened in July 2008, after a great deal of research and planning by general manager and lead partner, Wade Underwood. Originally from Beaverton, Wade received his MBA from the University of Oregon in Eugene. After meeting his wife in California and spending some time in Arizona, the Underwoods chose to move to Sisters.

For a year, Wade researched to determine the best business to open in Sisters. Having been impressed by the business model at McMenamins, as well as a long-time microbrew fan, Wade realized the brewpub idea fit well into the Old West theme. Like the saloons of the 1800's, who made their own brew on site, Three Creeks Brewing Company would do that and more. Knowing many in this industry fail due to undercapitalization, he set out to locate prospective partners. He found the right one, who now fills the position of assistant manager.

Buying land, designing and building the brewpub, hiring the brewer, chef, and front house manager were just the beginning for this busy and enterprising hands-on owner/manager. He set out to hire the

best staff possible. "Hiring good people is the difference; I don't worry about the place when I'm not here."

Wade Underwood is proud of the experience they've created at Three Creeks Brewing Company. His pride was evident as he showed us around and told us about the different artisans, the brewery, and the relaxed atmosphere. He's proud of creating a community hub where anyone, from the businessman in a suit and tie, to the soot-covered fireman, can come in and feel comfortable. He's especially proud of the large high-gloss hand-made wooden table with the Three Creeks logo in

the center, located in the saloon, which was made by his father. Equally proud, he points to the extensive hand quilting on wall-hanging quilt depicting the Three Creeks logo, made by his mother. It is obvious by the remarkable amount of time, expertise, and work put into both these pieces, his parents are extremely proud of his accomplishments.

When asked if he would do anything differently, Wade admits he should have made the windows facing the highway larger. Since this is where the sparkling clean and all new brewery is located, larger windows may have helped attract the eye of passers-by. After all, they have a beautiful ten-barrel brewery, designed by JV Northwest, Inc., why not show it off? Thankfully, included are large windows between the brewery and the saloon, allowing adult patrons to have a brew and observe the process simultaneously.

The small menu at Three Creeks Brewing Company is amazingly varied, offering vegetarian, meat, seafood, pasta, and a children's selection. For those wishing to have an outdoor experience, there is patio seating available. With great views of the pines and cabins of the nearby Five Pine Lodge, an extended visit is tempting.

With beer names inspired by the Old West theme, Three Creeks brews six regular offerings: Knotty Blond, Anvil Amber, Stonefly Rye, Firestorm Red, 8 Second IPA, and Old Prospector Pale. Additionally, seasonal specialty beers are produced. Though a long-time IPA fan, Bob recommends to be sure you taste the Red. He's become a fan.

Three Creeks Brewing Company can be found at all Oregon brewers' events. They currently have fifty handles, or taps, at various locations around Bend, Portland, and Eugene. Taking advantage of a mobile bottling plant, Three Creeks bottles seasonally. Unfortunately, we missed their Christmas bottling by one week.

Tugboat Brewing Company

711 SW Ankeny Street
Portland, OR 97225
503-226-2508
www.d2m.com/Tugwebsite

"Good people making great beer and serving it to fun customers"

Megan McEnroe-Nelson began homebrewing with her dad at the tender age of about eight. Then when she opened her brewpub, he went to work for her tending bar and she fired him, twice. He just kept coming back, though Dad is now retired and no longer involved in the business. Megan says about Tugboat, "This is my kid. I don't have children, so this is my baby. It takes time…"

This pint sized, hole-in-the-wall pub is everything I would want my cozy, community pub to be. With carpet on the floor and books on the shelves to act as a sound buffer, as well as lamps on the tables, low light, pictures on the walls, and a selection of games to play, I felt quite at home here. It has a bit of a coffeehouse feel. Not being a jazz fan, I would need to vacate during the nightly jazz, but then, nobody's perfect. Who knows, maybe I could learn to like it.

With seating for up to fifty, this pub would be crowded if full. But this can be a bit of a relief from the large sports-bar atmosphere so prevalent these days. To Megan, it is perfection. She likes it just as it is. Though sports-bar fans would not feel at home here, according to Megan, Tugboat has a diverse group of people as regulars and irregulars. From Delta pilots to house sitters, they come.

Amazingly,

Megan and husband Terry have managed to fit a brewery into this petite pub. And they have been brewing in it since 1993. With a second floor, better named a balcony, used for part of the brewing process, they have utilized every square inch of space. Somehow they keep producing 120 gallons of non-filtered beer at a time. Terry, who brews full-time now, will make three or four batches back to back, then may wait as long as two weeks before brewing again.

Owner, Megan McEnroe-Nelson

Megan loves sharing Portland with travelers and those new to the area. A friendly, outgoing, yet laid back personality, it is easy to imagine her imparting Portland's virtues with a newbie. Portland must love sharing Tugboat also, since many of the patrons find it through word of mouth.

In the many years since opening Tugboat, Megan has been given literally thousands of surprises, and has made some mistakes, though she really does not know that she has any regrets. She gives one the impression she is the "roll with the punches" type. She certainly is versatile and open to ideas. Not long before our visit to Tugboat, she had a pajama party for a friend. Her philosophy is "do it the way you want and like where you're at."

With a simple, bar food type, easy to prepare, and inexpensive menu, Tugboat may not be gourmet, but this is where you go for beer,

company, and music, the food is just an extra so you don't have to leave.

Cash only – No minors

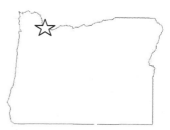

Upright Brewing

240 N Broadway, Suite 2
Portland, Oregon 97227
503-735-5337
www.uprightbrewing.com

*"Specializing in farmhouse inspired beers with a
Pacific Northwest twist "*

Finding Upright Brewing is quite easy; finding parking to visit Upright is another story. We drove around the "block" (which in the city means several blocks) three times before we finally found a place. Granted, it was unfamiliar, dark and raining hard, which made the task even more difficult, but the reputation is there, nevertheless.

Located on the mezzanine (basement) level of the Leftbank Project, just down the stairs from Stumptown Coffee Roasters, Upright Brewing is the dreamchild of Alex Ganum.

Several years ago Alex went to culinary school, but after he began homebrewing during that same time, he realized the brewer lifestyle appealed to him more. He says they are more relaxed, while cooks tend to be uptight. If you have ever worked in a restaurant, you understand why. After graduating culinary school, Alex went to work at Ommegang Brewery in Cooperstown, New York.

Then in 2002, Alex moved to Portland. After searching for a "gig" there, he went to work at BJ's for three years as an assistant brewer, learning a lot during this time. When the head brewer left, Alex held the position of head brewer for six months. Then he hurt his back in a hit and run car accident. After taking some time off to heal and get directional, Alex began planning Upright Brewing.

Opening in March 2009, Upright offers a relaxed tasting room where the official game is Rack-O; you are welcome to walk around the brewery; live '20s and '30s

Alex Ganum

Tasting Room

style blues is performed by Steve Cheseborough on most Sundays; you may purchase bottles, order kegs, and refill growlers; try a sampler or a pint; enjoy local art; and is family-friendly. This is a tasting room where you feel a part of the action, surrounded by barrels of aging beer, with the open brewery just steps away. Usually available, you may wish to try a one-off or some experimental while there. In addition to the hops art by Kim Hamblin, I was drawn to the unusual barrel tables, made by Brendan Alvistur, who also created the lovely live-edge table as well as the taps for Upright.

In addition to showcasing his favorite style of music, Alex honored musician Charles Mingus when he named the Brewery. It is a reference to his favorite instrument, the upright bass.

Specializing in rustic French & Belgian farmhouse style beers with a Pacific Northwest twist, Upright has quickly gained notoriety among

Upright Bottle Display

the beer community. Their uses of a special French Saison yeast lends toward the farmhouse style, which involves methods making the beer dryer and more drinkable; while the open fermenters, avoided by most due to contamination risks, simply jive more with the old style of doing beer. Alex enjoys brewing Belgian style beers because they are all about individuality. With no strict guidelines, they are open to interpretation. While Alex appreciates tradition, he does not feel bound to it.

Bottling by hand in the unusual 750 ml bottles, which are available from as far north as Seattle and as of the day before our interview, as far south as San

Bottling Station

Brewhouse

Francisco, Upright is also available on tap around Portland, with a few in Eugene and Bend. Bottles comprise about 35% of Upright's sales. Those great labels are the work of Ezra Johnson-Greenough, aka, Samurai Artist and *New School Beer* blogger.

Brewing every weekday, Alex had been struggling to keep up with demand on Upright's ten barrel brewery. Intern Gerritt Ill has helped since the beginning, with Alex just bringing him on as a full-fledged part-time employee a few days before our interview. Word has it, Gerritt has recently become full-time. Before going full-time, Gerritt had also assisted Ben at Breakside Brewing on a part-time basis.

Plenty of barrels aging at Upright

The week after we visited, Upright was scheduled to install three more fermentation tanks, hopefully easing some of their struggles, though Alex was eyeing them for use in making German style pilsners. As Alex phrased it, his pilsners are more happy than most pilsners, as well as being pretty dry.

In the Belgian tradition, all

A mirror is installed to allow you to see the fermentation process in the open fermenter, this is through a window looking into the closed fermentation room.

four of Upright's standard beers are known by numbers, Four, Five, Six, and Seven. These numbers represent their starting gravity – which is density, or pre-fermentation sugar content – in Belgian brewing degrees. Also currently planned are eight seasonals, including Oyster Stout at 6.25% abv, Four Play, which spends a year aging in pinot noir barrels with Oregon cherries; and Billy the Mountain, a deep malt with fruit flavors and 9.1% abv. Additionally, Upright brews probably forty different beers per year to assure that small batch beers are available for the tasting room.

The unusual barrel tables in the tasting room are surrounded by barrels of aging beer.

While Alex readily admits that he came into the brewing business quite cocky, he also acknowledges that it is harder than he thought. As a sole proprietor, in addition to brewing, there is the business end to deal with, financial management, accounting, promotions; it has all been a bit of a surprise. One of the drawbacks to a small production brewery is that there is not a lot of extra money, meaning after you are finished brewing, there's plenty of business stuff to do. Add to this, Alex receives twenty to thirty e-mails each day asking questions. It has been a challenge to find a balance between the production work, the non-production work, and fitting in some sort of personal life.

The tasting room includes one guest tap.

Despite this full schedule, Alex has partnered with two friends, the awesome chef, Ben Meyer, and restaurant and kitchen designer, Marcus Hoover, to open the Grain & Gristle Pub. At least one of Grain & Gristle's eight taps is always an Upright brew with the others showcasing breweries of the region.

Grain & Gristle

The limited selection is Grain & Gristle's trademark, simplicity. With a menu which changes on a monthly basis, the Grain & Gristle features homemade charcuterie, which is prepared meats, such as sausage, pastrami, and pâté. Featuring a wooden interior which is highlighted by an incredible maple "live edge" bar, this new pub opened in December 2010.

Amazingly, this industrious brewer is still thinking of, and looking forward to, other projects.

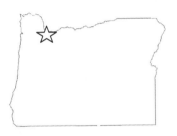

Vertigo Brewing

21420 NW Nicholas
Court, Suite D-7
Hillsboro, Oregon
97124
503-645-6644
www.vertigobrew.com

"Dizzyingly great handcrafted ales from our brewery to your glass"

When two Mikes began brewing at Beaverton's Westside U-Brew in 1995, they had no idea this new hobby idea would develop into a passion which would have a dizzying ability to consume them. After only a few times at U-Brew, the Mikes decided they could do better at home, where there would be more flexibility and they would have control beyond what the generic U-Brew could allow. Plus, they realized their brewing bills at U-Brew could pay for a nice little homebrew system.

After purchasing a homebrew set-up, several how-to-brew books, and some extract, the Mikes became homebrewers. Brewing five gallons at a time, the pair entered a few competitions and began refining their process. Going from a five gallon, extract brew, to a 15 gallon, all-grain brew within a year, the duo continuously experimented, read, and adjusted.

Then, in May 2008, they moved their brewery out of the home to their current warehouse space, which allowed them an address so they could begin the arduous process of becoming a licensed brewery.

Mike Haines

Receiving their license in September, 2008, the Mikes brewed their first commercial batch of beer in October.

Mike Haines, an electromagnetic compatibility engineer who has been with Intel for twenty-eight years, has spent the last year and a half working two full-time jobs, Intel and Vertigo. Despite his many hours away from home, Mike has had the full support of his wife, Barbara. In fact, as a graphic designer, Barbara created Vertigo's tap handles. Her only stipulation when they originally set up their homebrew operation in the family's garage, was that they had to make a beer she liked, which is how they began developing fruit beers.

Mike Kinion, also an employee at Intel for the past twenty-seven years, performs acceleratur for new laptops. With a wife who is also away a lot for her job with the school district, this busy couple are like the proverbial ships in the night.

When we visited in December 2010, Vertigo had just purchased a used, seven barrel system from Ager Tank and Equipment Company in Portland, where it had arrived from San Juan Brewing Company in Friday Harbor, Washington. Just beginning to put it to use, the Mikes

Mike Kinion

Arrival of the new 7 barrel system.
Photo provide courtesy of Vertigo Brewing, used by permission

are looking forward to the new system making a big difference in this little brewery.

Up until the purchase of this seven barrel system, Vertigo had still been brewing on a one barrel system. Brewing daily, this had not stopped them from producing as much beer as some seven barrel breweries. For example, Vertigo brewed thirty-one barrels in

November, 2010, more than one per day! full time jobs at Intel.

Despite this demanding schedule, the motto at Vertigo is "All about quality, not quantity." Combine this with their resolve to maintain consistency from batch to batch, and maybe it helps explain why the Mikes have had to work so hard to keep up with demand.

All this from two guys with

The old, one barrel system

Vertigo's first barrel of barrel-aged beer, made the day of our interview.
Photo provided courtesy of Vertigo Brewing.

With the new system, Vertigo is now able to branch out a bit and try their hand at barrel aging. In fact, their first batch of whisky aged beer had just gone into the barrel on the day of our interview. The pair do not have far to go to obtain their barrels, with a whisky blender only two doors down from Vertigo.

With the fermentation room kept at ale temperature, Vertigo brews only ales. Brewing to style, but to the ends of style, the Mikes brew what they like to drink.

While this brewery is receiving a great deal of notoriety for their good beers, brewer Mike Haynes says he tried brewing "many-many" years ago, resulting in something undrinkable. Through the years, he must have found whatever he was missing in that first, sorry attempt. Maybe he just needed a buddy named Mike to help.

Vertigo was the second name the Mikes had given to their beer while still homebrewing. Originally entering homebrew contests under the name Clear Brook, after the street where their garage operation was located, they had to choose a different name after discovering there is a Clear Brook Brewing in Abbotsford, British Columbia, in Canada. Since Vertigo had been their other option when naming their homebrew operation, Vertigo it became.

A couple of the many homebrew awards at Vertigo

Both Mikes brew. They work together to engineer new recipes. Each shares the cleaning. But, the Mikes have found their partnership works well due to each Mike having his own talent for the business end of this dizzying, full-time "hobby." While Haines watches over the financial end of the business, Kinion's talent lies in generating business, getting those tap handles that keep Vertigo going for this self-distributing business.

Kinion must be doing a good job. In the six weeks between our interview and writing this, their number of taps has increased from sixteen to twenty-three. The best way to discover where Vertigo's current taps are is to check their website. They have a great map system to show where to find Vertigo taps, with the information on the location provided when the pointer is placed on top of the location. Portland, Hillsboro, Beaverton, Dallas, Seaside, and Mt. Hood are current cities with taps, with more on the way. Kegs and growlers are also available at the brewery.

As of this writing, Vertigo is not yet available in bottles. While the Mikes' plan is to contract with Green Bottling, with the unexpected rapid growth Vertigo has experienced, this has not yet been a possibility. Keep an eye open for them; Vertigo hopes to be available in bottles this year.

Dreams for Vertigo? A paycheck would be cool, they say with a laugh. Not thinking nationally, their goal is simply to be thought of as a nice, little brewery in the region. They hope for good reviews; the ones I have read say they are doing well in this area.

The Mikes have no interest in opening a pub and getting into food service, they are brewers, though serious consideration is being given to the possibility of a tasting room. At this time, they are still working on the brewery itself; remember, they just upgraded from one barrel to a seven barrel system, while still holding full time jobs at Intel.

When asked if they have any regrets, Haines replies with "No regrets," but Kinion's regret is time...they need more hours in the day. In answer to "What are you most proud of?" Haines takes pride in Vertigo's speedy growth, while Kinion's pride is in the public's positive response to Vertigo's beers.

The recipe for one of those beers, Friar Mike's IPA, was developed with the assistance of another friend, named "Mike," of course. Friend Mike, an internet-ordained friar, actually named the brewery a church. In addition to

Named a church by Friar Mike

assisting with the recipe for Friar Mike's, he also bought their first commercial keg of beer. So the honor of the IPA went to Friar Mike.

For Vertigo's two very busy Mikes, success is on the horizon; and, as they say, it could not happen to two nicer guys. Growing beyond their many homebrewing medals, Vertigo is garnering acceptance and respect in the craft beer circles.

Wakonda Brewing Company

1725 Kingwood #4
Florence, Oregon 97439
541-991-0694
Find them on Facebook

Sasquatch on the bar

"Off the grid, but worth finding"

Wakonda was at the very end of a long day which began with a 7 A.M. interview in Portland. Several interviews and fourteen hours later, we were diligently searching for Wakonda. Nuvi (GPS) seemed to have led us astray this time. All we could see where she led under her guidance were industrial buildings, certainly no tasting room. We decided to look around...no luck. We called Juanita, at Wakonda, turns out Nuvi had been correct (sorry we doubted you), Wakonda *is* in that industrial park on the left side of the street, on the left side of the parking lot. The only sign is the stenciling on the glass door, the neon 'Open' sign in the window, and the small flag hanging from the hedge which says 'Come on in.'

This obscure front was even more difficult to locate at night.

Walking in, we felt like we had been transported back to the perfect '70s hang-out. Several comfy couches and chairs, a foosball table, some great batik on the walls, posters, and even a mannequin biker-babe...this had definitely been decorated by a person of our generation. In fact, the furniture had come from Juanita's house.

The bar, while it had had been at Juanita's house, had changed forms. It was originally her son's skate ramp. Made from an old growth tree, cut in 1934, the top has since been sanded and lacquered. The sides are of the same wood, but have been left rough, with a weathered driftwood look.

Juanita liked the name, Wakonda, in Ken Kesey's novel, *Sometimes a Great Notion,* which also happens to be one of Bob's favorite movies. When Juanita contacted the Kesey family for permission to use it, she was told that Kesey, whose family farm was in Pleasant Hill, got the name from Wakonda Beach, just south of Waldport.

For their logo, both Ron and Juanita wanted the Haida Salmon incorporated into it. Going to a graphic artist, they asked for the salmon with three eyes, for the three remaining Wakonda partners. The eyes were artfully incorporated into the eye (that was an easy one), the dorsal fin, and the tail. Totum maker, Steven Benson, made the wooden plaque bearing the logo, which is located on the wall behind the bar, from Alaskan cedar.

Tap handles in the beer business identify who you are, so Wakonda wanted something special, though it took the inspiration of a friend to realize it. Suggesting they make glass tap handles, they turned to Dave Tipton, of Trepid Glass, who, coincidentally, served as a Ken Kesey bus mechanic. While we have seen a few glass tap handles, these were ingeniously topped with a metal plate, which allows Wakonda to place the proper magnetic label for whatever beer is being served, onto it. Kudos, Wakonda!

Wakonda was started in 2004 by four partners who all

Comfy seating

Style - mannequin style

homebrewed. They lost one partner as soon as the first of the bills began arriving. Another left after three years. While the remaining two partners, Juanita Kirkham and Dr. Ron Shearer both brewed, the former third partner had done the majority of the brewing. With his departure the remaining partners hired Paul Pierson to brew for Wakonda. With Paul's move to Rogue, Wakonda went through one more brewer before the position was taken over, after Ron's tutoring, by Juanita's son, Henry Royal Schueneman with his

assistant and friend, Perry Ames. Both are students at Lane Community College, and make the trip to Florence each weekend to brew. Henry, an avid snowboarder, is actually planning a career in forestry. Perry through, will be attending Oregon State for their fermentation science program beginning fall 2011.

Wakonda's brewery is located at a different location without public flow and where land use regulations would not allow a tasting room, so they sublet the current facility for the purpose of receiving and storage. Then the party they sublet from did not pay the rent, which left Wakonda with three tons of grain inside with no other place to store it. While they really did not want the warehouse, leasing it themselves was the obvious answer.

While many in the Old Town Florence community were hoping

Wakonda would open a tasting room in Old Town, the partners felt rents there to be prohibitively expensive, meaning they would not survive financially by moving there. So, in 2008 Wakonda turned most of the warehouse into a tasting room – just in time for the downturn in the economy. While Old Town may still want Wakonda to set up house with them, they are happy where they are; 'off the grid' suits them…so does being debt-free, which they are.

Wakonda is a hang-out, a mellow, enjoyable, relaxing place and its clientele insist on a certain atmosphere. As Juanita says, "We are the 'Cheers' of Florence, everybody knows your name." If someone comes in and no one knows them, the regulars will introduce themselves…now they are friends. Wakonda apparently also has something in common with Las Vegas, since Juanita also tells us that "What happens in Wakonda, stays in Wakonda." No stories there, remember, what happens… As a place where local doctors, professionals, coast guard members, and teachers congregate, it is important that they can relax, hang out, unwind, and just be "regular" people.

A notable and essential-to-know item about Wakonda is that they do not accept credit cards, *so bring your cash.* And, being a tasting room, Wakonda does not offer food, except perhaps free peanuts or maybe chips. However, they do call in an order to the local Sushi place, Aloha Sushi, at about six each Thursday evening, to be delivered right to your table at about seven.

A regular feature at Wakonda is the music. A local blues band plays there twice a month, though style at Wakonda is certainly not limited to blues. Also featured are infrequent open mike nights; with a lot of good local talent, this can make for special entertainment and some surprises. When a young man from Ireland came in to play, it turned out Irish music was not on the menu, but instead, American rock, with a great accent.

It may not be up-scale, but it is comfortable.

Wakonda is also active in the community. Sponsors of Habitat for Humanity, the food co-op, and many local fundraisers, as a doctor and a teacher, Ron and Juanita know the importance of a helping hand.

Juanita's long-term dream was to own a pub. She loves bartending. As a super-social person, it fits her to a tee. While she may only put in forty hours per week at her teaching job, this busy woman adds another fifty hours at Wakonda, but says it is fun. To keep her family life intact with these horrendous hours, it has been made into a family affair, with daughter tending bar, her son the brewer, and her

Tees and hoodies are available.

husband the very necessary jack-of-all-trades. With only five years to go, she says Wakonda will be a great "retirement."

When we asked why Ron, who takes care of the administrative duties now that he is not brewing, does this, Juanita said it simply, "Because he loves beer."

Wakonda brews on a seven barrel system, but are in the process of increasing that. Consideration is being given to having a piece of custom equipment made, and they have written two economic grants in hopes of getting a new, larger system.

Also being mulled over is the possibility of bottling. At the time of our interview, it had not yet been decided whether they would turn to hand bottling or a mobile bottler. Until then, there are always growlers available. If you cannot make it to Florence, check for taps at many of the usual rotating tap locations. Also look for Wakonda at Lane County and Coastal brewfests; hopefully they will even make it up to Oregon Brewers Festival in 2011.

Sneaker Wave, one of the beers for which Wakonda is most renowned, takes a full four months to make. Thankfully their first brew, Beachcomber Creams, did not take this long. One of the more unusual

Signs of warehouse

offerings at Wakonda is Firthur Pale Ale, which contains real Douglas Fir. While we were there, they were working a Black Cream by combining cream ale and Black Stout.

While Juanita says it would be wonderful to see Wakonda become a destination, they have no goals of it becoming the next Rogue or Ninkasi. "We are the local. We love the beach. We love being here."

Photo courtesy Walkabout Brewery,
used by permission

Walkabout Brewery

921 Mason Way
Medford, Oregon
541-6647763
find them on facebook

"An Oregon Brewery...by a local Aussie"

Due to scheduling difficulties, Walkabout Brewery was one of the few interviews we did by phone. Normally I really dislike doing interviews in this manner; it makes it difficult to get a "feel" for the brewer/person. Finding an "angle" can a bit difficult over the phone. However, let's face it, Walkabout has a built-in angle.

Owner/brewer Ross Litton, a native of Perth, Australia, moved to the States after he had done some traveling and liked it here. Coming to Oregon in 1990 to serve as caretaker of a Hollywood producer's Rogue River home, Ross began homebrewing as an alternative to standard American beers, which he found very disappointing.

Realizing early-on that there were not a lot of great jobs in the area if you worked for someone else, Ross spent five years assembling a brewery in his garage, with plans to eventually go commercial. Multiple homebrew awards, including several Best of Show, helped to validate these plans. It was during this time that Ross gained commercial experience working for Rogue Brewery, while still located in Ashland. Ross was working there when the location flooded.

With the brewery complete, Ross decided 1997 was the year to open his own brewery. Working full-time from the beginning, he jumped in with both feet. As a self-distributed brew, Walkabout gained taps in many restaurants and bars throughout the Southern Oregon area. Currently, Walkabout produces four standard beers and two seasonals.

Most recently, distribution was expanded north as far a Portland. In addition to rotating handles in many of the standard

Ross Litton
Photo courtesy Walkabout Brewery,
used by permission

Walkabout Taps

places, such as Belmont Station and Beer Mongers, Walkabout has also gained stable taps at Woodstock's Pizza in Corvallis and Ship Ahoy Tavern in Portland. In the past, Walkabout has done only local festivals; with the expanded distribution to the north, Ross hopes to begin doing more festivals around the state.

Then in April 2010, with the assistance of Green Bottling, Walkabout began bottling Workers Pale Ale. With the success of Workers in a bottle, on February 17, 2011, the day before our interview, Walkabout had their first bottling of Jabberwocky Strong Ale. This long-

Walkabout Brewery's future location

awaited event has been received with enthusiasm by Walkabout fans. Look for additional beers to be bottled in the future.

While the extremely well-designed garage location has worked admirably, with expanded distribution, bottling, and increased sales, it is time to make a move. The morning of our interview, Ross had signed the papers purchasing Walkabout's new brewery sight, a four thousand square foot building on a full acre of land, allowing for possible later potential expansion. While transforming the new building to a brewery and moving will take a bit of time, Ross is looking forward to the additional space.

Plans include moving the beautiful, wood-sided, seven barrel brewhouse, the fourteen barrel fermenter, and the fourteen barrel bright tank to the new location, as well as adding additional fermenters and conditioning tanks. With the additional tanks, Ross expects to increase annual

Ross, with wife, Dana

production from the current level of nine hundred barrels to as much as three thousand barrels, as demand requires.

The new location will include a few firsts for Walkabout, including a tasting room and one-offs, which are single-batch experimental brews. Also added with the new location will be two employees, with

Ross's daughter dances in front of the brewhouse at Walkabout
Photo courtesy Walkabout Brewery, used by permission

one person full-time and one part-time, to help in this growing business.

When asked what his dream of dreams is, Ross said he would realistically like to remain fairly small, perhaps distributing throughout the Northwest region.

Walkabout focuses on the details. Looking for drinkability, a balanced malt and hop profile blend is of primary importance. While many in Oregon are running the hops race, Ross feels it is still essential for the hops to maintain a balance with the malts in order to have a truly good beer and not just the next over-the-top hopped brew. Mostly, at Walkabout, Ross brews what he likes to drink.

Portland Monthly named Worker's Pale Ale one of the top 48 craft brews in the state on their 7/2010 issue.
Photo courtesy Walkabout Brewery, used by permission

After twenty-one years, Ross's Australian accent is still quite evident. He returns for a visit to Australia and New Zealand every couple of years, visiting family, who all thoroughly enjoy Walkabout beer.

When asked about problems, Ross admits the Walkabout name creates confusion. Many are unaware that Walkabout is an Oregon brewery, assuming

the beer is an import. For those looking to drink only Oregon beers, and those who are conscientious of sustainability practices, avoiding imports, this may have caused them to avoid Walkabout. With expanded distribution, Walkabout is looking to get the word out... a made in *Oregon* beer.

Widmer Brothers Brewing

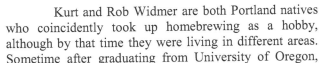

4765 NE Fremont Street
Portland, Oregon 97213
503-460-9025
www.alamedabrewhouse.com

"Quality is tops, if you ever let them down, they may not come back"

Kurt and Rob Widmer are both Portland natives who coincidently took up homebrewing as a hobby, although by that time they were living in different areas. Sometime after graduating from University of Oregon, Kurt spent two years traveling Germany, where he sampled beer throughout the country. Returning home to Portland he took an administrative job with a pharmaceutical company. By that time Rob, an Oregon State University graduate, had tried many things and was working in Seattle as a candy maker.

Then in 1984, Kurt called Rob and suggested they start their own brewery. The brothers were 32 and 28 respectively. Neither were married, nor had family to support at the time.

During a trip back to Germany, Kurt studied recipes at one of the many breweries in Düsseldorf. When he returned, he brought with him a unique yeast strain from the world-renowned Brewing Research Institute in Weihenstephan, Bavaria, which is still maintained in Widmer labs today and is an intrigal part of the Widmer brewing process. It was then that Rob quit his job and moved home to Portland.

Though neither had ever worked in a commercial brewery nor ran a business, they had been given an old fashioned work ethic by their dad, who had sold farm machinery for a living. When it came time to set up the brewery and get the business going, Dad was there to lend a hand, and there he stayed until two months before his death.

Starting with fifty thousand dollars and many I.O.U.s, the brothers turned to Schnitzer Steel to

Rob Widmer

find salvage tanks at a price they could afford. While some of the tanks they found were the usual restaurant and milk tanks, two of them were originally built for the Pebble Springs nuclear plant, but never used. Using one as a kettle, they soon discovered they were built too thickly, causing heat transfer problems. As a result, they were unable to get a boil going. After building a very large burner, a gentleman from the gas company spent a great deal of time with them to make the needed adjustments, which enabled the brothers to attain a boil. As Rob says, "We were quite relieved, for a period of time we

Display of history in the Widmer sales room

thought…this kettle is not going to work and there's no way we could afford another one, we're going under."

According to Rob, such things happen on a daily basis, even today. Surprisingly, Rob is still waiting for the "made it!" moment. When we expressed surprise, he thoughtfully stated that they were just wired that way. Their dad always thought he could lose his job. Let's face it, though it might take a pretty big blow at this point, with the way the economy has gone the last couple of years, many companies have surprised us and gone under.

A full sales room provides many Widmer choices.

While Rob should relax and finally realize he is "there," in the beginning the brothers rode the razor's edge. Their wildest dream was to brew enough to sell in Portland and be able to make a living. As Rob puts it, they could not have picked a better place and time. While they had no idea how their beer would do, the people in the Pacific Northwest welcomed them wholeheartedly.

Doing everything themselves when they first started; sales, advertising, accounting, they did it all. In those days they did not bottle, that began in 1996, but kegs were keeping them busy. Using a 1970 Datsun pickup as a delivery truck, the brothers brewed in the A.M. and delivered in the P.M. They still have that truck today, though of course it no longer serves as a delivery truck.

Rob states that if they had known how much they did not know when they first began, Widmer Brewing may have never gotten started. As they say, ignorance is bliss. (We say the same thing about this book.) Neither brother was an engineer; they just did what they had done at home, in a larger version.

When asked if he had any regrets, Rob quickly, yet peacefully answered "No. Every day we remind ourselves how lucky we are. At some point I think everyone would like to make a living from their hobby – we are lucky enough to do so."

The amusing thing is, the brothers have not homebrewed a day since they started the business. While they think about it occasionally,

they then realize it would be much easier at the brewery, but somehow never get to it. Along this line, they are considering installing a homebrew set-up at the plant for employees to use. Maybe for their use also?

They have come a long way since the early days of nuclear kettles. Widmer now has a 250 barrel Brewhouse and produced 300,000 barrels of beer in 2010. According to one list I found, they

Tap handles available from Widmer

rank number seven for craft beer sales in the nation and number two in Oregon (Deschutes is number one).

When Widmer first started, the Blitz-Weinhard brewery helped them out with some lab analysis, now Widmer does this for the little guys. Giving back is important. These are guys who remember their roots and are there to encourage and assist. "Kurt and I feel like we got a hand up back then and it's good for all of us to help others."

In 1990, Widmer opened their new brewery/headquarters facility, in the Smithson and McKay Brothers Block buildings. These National Register of Historic Places buildings were built in 1890 and 1887 respectively. The two buildings originally housed businesses on the ground level and apartments upstairs, frequently used by workers who built ships on Swan Island. The corner now occupied by Widmer's

Gasthaus Pub, originally housed an Italian restaurant; later the Interstate Tavern; then in 1969 a renegade company of free-lance Portland theater artists opened the avant-garde, experimental theater, Storefront Theater. While at one time there had been many of these buildings in this neighborhood, urban renewal of the 1960s resulted in many of them being torn down.

The Smithson and McKay Block buildings were headed for sure destruction when the Widmers stepped in. Bank owned at that point, the bank had a buyer who wanted to raze the buildings. Kurt and Rob, on the other hand, were looking to rebuild and restore these salvage buildings. Due to the buildings being listed on the Historic Registry, the bank sold it to the Widmers, since restoration takes presidence over destruction.

Wonderful woodwork at Widmer surround Rob

While the buildings had the advantages of no asbestos, no oil tanks, and no PCB's, there was still a great deal of work to be done. Bringing such buildings up to today's code is no small task with changes such as Seismic stabilization to be done. Though the Smithson building was in pretty good condition, the engineer described the McKay building as a "house of cards" and said he was nervous just being in it. Though he then challenged himself by saying the building had been there for over a hundred years and maybe the engineers back then knew more than he did.

Restoration of the buildings was not an inexpensive undertaking. As Rob says, "We could probably have knocked it down and built it to look just like it does now, much cheaper." Ah, but then it would not have that wonderful history and the Widmers would not be heros to historical buffs. Though the woodwork in McKay was either destroyed or missing, Smithson still had all of its woodwork – all clear fir. Old fir like this becomes very brittle, so while some of it was able to be used in the restoration, some of it split, necessitating the use of new wood. It remains a work in progress. Though the second floor location of our interview was quite wonderful, Rob told us work on the third floor is still ongoing. Chances are the third floor will house offices upon its completion.

Frustration enters in when we discuss continued attempts to raise taxes on Oregon beer. Rob believes the message to the legislators who would raise beer taxes, hurting Oregon breweries, is to remember that the Oregon beer industry is one of the bright spots in today's economy. While they are using tax credits to attempt to entice other  industries to Oregon, remember, the beer industry is not asking for credits, "we are already here, just leave us alone." This is an industry which is clean, put Oregon on the map, is a tourist attraction, creates five thousand direct jobs, and it is not asking for anything. While the legislature should be falling all over the beer industry, instead they are constantly trying to tax and hamper them. "Honestly, what else do we have in Oregon right now that's growing?"

In 1997 the Widmers sold a 27% stake in the company to Anheuser-Busch, which enabled them to take advantage of the vast distribution network of Anheuser-Busch. Then in 2004, along with Redhook Ale Brewery of Washington and New Hampshire, Kona Brewing Company of Hawaii, and Goose Island Beer Company of Illinois, they formed the Craft Brewers Alliance, Inc. This publicly held company/alliance stock symbol is currently HOOK, but is expected to change to BREW. The alliance allows for an easier and more sustainable distribution/brewing network. For instance, Widmer brews and distributes Kona beers as part of the alliance, much easier than shipping it from Hawaii.

When we asked what they would like people to know about Widmer, we had to laugh at the answer.

First a bit of history: Do you remember the Bartles & Jaymes commercials which ran from 1984 to 1991? In case you were not aware, the gentlemen in the commercial were not really Bartles & Jaymes, fictitious characters who were patterned after the men who started Ernest & Julio Gallo Winery. They were David Joseph Rufkahr and Dick Maugg; Rufkahr worked for an ad agency and Maugg was a general contractor.

Now that the history lesson is over, apparently many people think that Kurt and Rob are like Bartles & Jaymes, a fictitious marketing contrivance. Kurt and Rob Widmer are quite real. In fact, they are still active in Widmer, though they do not brew anymore, they have hired and trained qualified brewers. They started Widmer. They made it for years. They are still at the helm.

Wild River Brewing & Pizza Company

249 N Redwood Highway
Cave Junction, Oregon 97523
541-592-3556
www.wildriverbrewing.com

"Blame us if your life goes to Pizzas"

Jerry and Bertha Miller have been sweethearts since sixth grade in Alvin, Texas. But that was a "few" years ago. After leaving Texas, they spent twelve years in Hayward, California where Jerry worked as a manager in a plastics business. It was at their church in Hayward that they met Charles and Marilyn Taylor, and became close friends.

In 1970, the Taylors decided to take their family sausage business, the recipes which had been brought by Grandpa from Europe, to Illinois Valley, Oregon. When the Millers came to visit the Taylors, Charles told Jerry he needed someone to keep the machines running in the sausage factory. In the navy, Jerry had been a machine repairman. Wanting to get  back to the small town atmosphere of their roots, Jerry and Bertha followed their friends to Oregon.

By 1975, Jerry and Bertha decided Cave Junction needed a pizza parlor. Though there was a Dairy Queen and a couple of mom and pop cafes, there was no pizza available to this gateway town for the Oregon Caves.

Getting the building ready was no small chore. With the help of

Jerry Miller

their two boys, the Millers were doing everything they could themselves, including roofing the place. But the work was slow for these do-it-yourselfers, everything took more time than expected to complete.

The people of Cave Junction were excited to see the pizza parlor taking shape, but it just was not happening fast enough. So one night over twenty volunteers showed up to help complete the work. The guy who sold them the faux brick used his know-how and volunteering spirit to install it for the Millers. By the end of that June evening, Miller's Shady Oaks Pizza Deli was ready for business.

Bertha Miller on the bridge added to the Cave Junction location

To show their appreciation, the Millers invited all the volunteers back to test the pizza. The problem was, the Millers had never before made a commercial pizza. Bertha was amazed by the forty pounds of flour it took to make the pizza dough. When Jerry put the dough into the machine which was supposed to flatten it into a crust, it did not come out. After removing the back, he realized that part of the machine was missing! Managing to use the rollers to flatten the dough, the pizza was ready to cook. Jerry excitedly took the wooden paddle, topped with the prepped pizza, to the oven and jerked to slide the pizza into the oven. Problem was, nothing happened. The pizza stayed right on the paddle. After a couple more jerks, Jerry determined that baby had to go, so he jerked extra hard. There went all the toppings, right onto the oven, with the dough determinadly stuck right to that paddle. By this time, Jerry and Bertha were beginning to sweat. After all, they had twenty-something hungry volunteers in the dining room waiting to eat. Somehow, they managed to get the pizzas from the paddle to the oven and they were well-received.

Removing a pizza at the Medford location

They continued with the same awkward method of getting the pizza off the paddle into the oven until at last – four weeks later – they hired a boy who had previous experience working at an out-of-town pizza place. When this brilliant young man asked why they did not use corn meal so their pizzas

would slide off the paddle, they finally had their answer, and much more cooperative pizzas!

Jerry tells a story how in the mid-eighties he had been chatting with a couple of guys at a rest stop. They were moving to Oregon to open a microbrewery. Jerry thought it was nuts! After all, you can buy beer at the store.

Then one day, at a restaurant show in Chicago, Jerry spied some beautiful, shiney, brew tanks as he was walking down the isle. The Canadian equipment manufacturing representative told Jerry he could teach him to brew, using extracts, in four short days. After the show, Jerry returned to Cave Junction thinking it might be nice to add a brewery to the restaurant, so he began studying brewing. Of course it did not take long for him to realize there was "a bit" more to brewing than the rep had claimed, and that he would never be a brewer, but in 1989 he bought brewing equipment anyway. He had no idea who would do the brewing.

Part of the ceiling in Cave Junction

After it came out in the local paper that they were installing a brewery, a gentleman who lived in nearby Selma, Hubert Smith, came in to see the equipment. Hubert was a homebrewer who had lived, trained, and brewed in England. As a semi-retired writer and English teacher, he did not want a job, he just wanted to see the brewery. Problem was, Hubert also loved beer, and brewing; he wanted to brew on that equipment.

More of the ceiling

Remember now, Hubert did not want a job, but he spent the next five years brewing on that equipment. Beliving that all beer should be true to style, he was insistant that style be adheared to. As a result, Jerry says he probably threw out more beer than any brewer, so much that he jokes he was concerned for a while the city would complain about the amount of yeast being dumped into the sewer system.

The Big Book, made by the local Boys & Girls Club, outside the Cave Junction location

When Hubert took Jerry and Bertha to their first beer festival in Arcata, California, he told them if the beer was bad, just spit it out. Appalled, they did not see how they could possibly spit the beer out in front of the brewer. But Hubert continued spitting throughout the festival, drinking and spitting, drinking and spitting. Being early in the craft beer days, they had to admit, there was a lot of bad beer.

After Hubert had been brewing for them for a while, he journied to England and Germany, with the goal of learning and returning to Cave Junction with something unique. Hubert brought back a very special yeast for a kolsch which was gifted to them by the renowned Paffgen Brewery, in Cologne, Germany. This amazing kolsch, Harbor Lights Kolsch Style, went on to win the Silver Medal in the Kolsch style at the Great American Beer Festival in 1997 (the last year they competed). The advantage of a kolsch is that being an ale, there is not the long fermentation period of a lager, but it tastes like a lager.

In Hubert's last year brewing for the Millers, he began training Scott Butts, who, upon Hubert's departure, became head brewer. Scott followed his internship with Hubert with brewing courses at UC Davis. He also accompanied Jerry and Bertha to Europe to learn all he could about the art and science of brewing beer. According to the Millers, Scott has done a great job since taking the head brewer position; he has good taste buds and understands the extreme importance of sanitation.

At first, the Pizza Deli's beer was sold under the registered name Steelhead Brewery. But with time, the addition of the Brookings-

Murals by J. Michener are incorporated into the building design in Medford.

Harbor restaurant, and the opening of the Grants Pass restaurant, the Millers felt it would be nice to have the pizza and beer under one name as well as roof. After selling the name Steelhead Brewery to the place of the same name in Eugene, the name Wild River Brewing and Pizza

Brookings-Harbor Location

Company was chosen to celebrate the many rivers in the beautiful Southern Oregon area.

After our interview with Jerry and Bertha, I finally understood why Bob and many locals called Wild River, "Pizza Deli." I moved to the Brookings area in 2004 after meeting Bob, but he grew up there. Most of the locals still refer to it as Pizza Deli.

The Brookings location opened in 1980 after son, Darrel, who was graduating from high school, announced that he did not want to go to college, but instead wanted to run a pizza parlor. So when the restaurant in Brookings-Harbor came available, it was perfect. Still managed today by Darrel and his wife, Becky, this is Wild River's busiest location. In case you wonder, as I did, why there are no stools at the bar, it was a concession to be able to get their license to sell beer. In those days, OLCC was concerned that there were pool tables and beer available in the same place where children are welcome. Get real, it is a pizza parlor. Plus, it is wonderful to

Recreation is popular at the Brookings-Harbor location

have a place to play a game of pool without going to a tavern, or for that matter, to be able to play a game of pool with the kids. Good, healthy, fun.

The pizza at Wild River is great, it is the way it is cut which seems quite odd at first. Rather than the traditional pie shaped cuts, Wild River does a diamond cut, giving you many two-ish inch diamond-shaped pieces instead of a few large pie shaped pieces. While some, like Bob, prefer the pie cut and can ask for it if they want, most, like

Diamond cut pizza

Grain silo in Grants Pass

myself, enjoy the diamond cut. It is easier to handle and works great for dipping in the ranch dressing, which they provide with every pizza.

When Jerry and Bertha were shopping in Portland for restaurant equipment before their original opening, they stopped at a little pizza parlor where they were served diamond cut pizza. Deciding then and there this would be a unique feature, they brought the idea back to Cave Junction with them and have used it since those first test pizzas. While this may seem unusual to most of us, it is considered normal in Cave Junction. In the past they have had local kids leave town and then come back to tell them about the "weird" pie cut pizza.

The Cave Junction and Brookings Harbor locations are older, with character and memories. The tables at the Cave Junction location have been there since the beginning and will undoubtedly survive after any of us are long forgotten memories. These eight four inch thick cafeteria length tables are all cut from a single tree. A local gentleman had bought a redwood tree when he worked in Crescent City, California, slabbed it out, and then stored it for years in his barn. His stipulation in selling the slabs to the Millers was that they must be left whole; they must not be cut into little pieces. So Jerry and his family made eight of the most solid tables we have ever seen. Finished with a shiny, hard epoxy, they tables have never been refinished. Now, thirty-five years later, refinishing is still unnecessary.

Four-inch thick Redwood slab tables in Cave Junction

Cave Junction saw the addition of a back room in 1986, suitable for gatherings such as parties and reunions. Seeing the room it is difficult to realize it is now twenty-five years old, it still looks quite new.

That same time saw the addition of a back deck for outdoor seating, and bridge across the seasonal creek.

Both the Grants Pass and Medford locations are newer buildings. Jerry claims that when it came to convincing Bertha, he used the need to sell excess beer as an excuse to build more restaurants. In reality, the addition of the Grants Pass location in 1994 increased their brewing capacity significantly. While Cave Junction has a seven barrel system cozied into a tight space, the Grants Pass brewery was designed centered on a fifteen barrel brewery

Great wood rails in Medford

and a bottling line. Both these locations are large, with space to accommodate large groups, and are quite beautifully done.

Selling both bottles and kegs exclusively from their own locations, there are a few places, like Oregon Caves, who pick up kegs and bottles for sale at other locations. Growlers are also available at Wild River, which Jerry says are a truly recyclable container.

Grandpa Kubin and his Pivo

The Bohemian Style Pilsner, A Pivo For Grandpa Kubin (pivo means beer in Czechoslavkian) is in honor of Bertha's Grandpa Kubin, whose thick Czech accent could be heard as the courting Jerry would call on the telephone for Bertha and Grandpa would hang up to go get her, thinking she could then pick the phone up and talk. Grandpa Kubin was a homebrewer. The story is told of when Grandpa and Uncle were in the field near the house on a hot Texas day. They began hearing a popping sound; suddenly Grandpa shouted "...Damn, my beer!" and ran for his brand new Buick. Jumping in, he hurried to the store, threw ice – unprotected – in the back seat, raced back to the house and began throwing the ice under it. His beer was fermenting in the coolest place around on a hot Texas day, under the house!

When we asked Jerry what his future plans are, the seventy-three year-old said, "Golfing." While they have been approached many times about franchising, they really are not interested.

Taps & full bar in Medford

Though Darrel many not have been interested in college, his brother, a surgeon, apparently had no problem with further education. At sixteen, one of his sons is quite interested in the family business. But, as Grandpa says, "Not until after college!"

When asked what mistakes they have made, Jerry replied, "We don't make mistakes, just learning experiences.

Darrel Miller

Festivals

As expected, Portland is a microbrew festival Mecca. But many great festivals can be found throughout the state, so if you are unable to make it to Portland or if you would like to get out of Portland, there are plenty of great options.

Festivals vary in content. While some host only beer and food and are clearly a well organized, big party, others include vendors of many kinds, music, contests, art, brewery competitions, homebrew competitions, camping, tours, and many other options. In addition to a list of festivals, we have included descriptions of those which are not brewery sponsored to aid readers in determining which festivals would meet their requirements for fun. (Nothing against the breweries, we just had to draw the line somewhere) If your only prerequisite for fun is good beer…you are in luck!

All festivals seem to have a common approach to organization; to taste the brew you must purchase a tasting mug or glass and tokens. Use the tokens (usually one) to purchase tastes of beer, and at many festivals, even buy food and other items. If you want a full glass, typically 4 tokens will acquire a full glass. We found it interesting at one festival that a full glass cost four tokens, but when combined, it took only three tasters to make a full glass. Moral of the story…be aware of how large the tasters are compared to a full glass before purchasing a full glass.

Admittance varies with each festival. While many festivals are family-friendly, allowing children until a limited hour, others are adults-only, carding everyone, including those of us who are old and graying (underneath the coloring).

Are you the volunteering type? A common necessity at festivals is willing volunteers. If you do decide to volunteer at a festival, be sure to apply early. Not only will this help to assure you land a job and get the shift you want, but will alleviate volunteer-stress for organizers. In addition to free entry, many of the festivals offer other perks to volunteers: free t-shirts, free mugs, free tokens, and free swag (goodies) are among the offerings to the valued workforce. Be aware that volunteers must not drink before their shift.

The authors at the Umpqua Brew Fest.

A surprising aspect for us was that at some festivals the only attendee from a brewery will be the beer. For small or new festivals this would apply more often. When we attended the First Annual Umpqua Brew Fest, the only brewer in attendance was Sam Eslinger, from Draper Brewing in Tenmile, a new brewery just down the road. Unfortunately, this means if you have questions regarding the beer or the brewery, the volunteers are unable to answer them. Nor should you expect to find information on the brewery or the beer. With no brewery representative in attendance, one would think there would be a brochure, flyer, or card telling about the brewery and the beer - at least the location. Organizers and breweries, how about it?

While I have read on blogs that festivals tend to be more crowded early in the day, our limited experience has been the opposite.

A festival attendee on hold-duty while her friends...well...

Things start rather slowly, but build as the day progresses. By evening...large party. On the other hand, toward the evening, some of the beers start running out. I heard of people leaving just after arrival when they discovered how few beers were still available. If your goal at a festival is to taste as many beers as possible, early arrival is advisable.

Another advantage to early arrival is the people watching aspect. Not being a beer drinker, I enjoy watching the people at a brew fest. Above and beyond the obvious

Attendees having a good time.

effects of a few hours of taste testing, which can manifest itself in many different ways, seeing the various people types in attendance is fascinating. Where else are you going to see people from all walks of life partying together? From the just turned twenty-one year old to the totally grey oldster, all ages are represented. Whether styled in dreadlocks or an obviously expensive stylist created cut and color, hair reveals great diversity. Clothes run the full gamut. Jeans, dresses, costumes, suits, and kilts are just a few of the modes of dress which may be observed. While people types may be varied, the goal is common, experience great beers and have fun.

In conclusion, a few important considerations to keep in mind when planning to attend a brew fest:

- ✓ Know the rules - Family-friendly, or 21 and over only?
- ✓ Transportation – Never drink and drive.
- ✓ Arrival time – Early or late, beer availability

Collage provided courtesy Brews & Boogie, Ashland
Used by permission

Festival List

In date order

*Descriptions follow, beginning page 363

Though we have made every attempt to include the general beer festivals throughout the state, we have included only a few of the most well-known brewery sponsored events. For more of these, see the individual brewery websites. If you know of a festival which should be included in the next edition, please contact us.

NOTE: The listed dates are to guide the reader. Unfortunately, not all festivals are planned far in advance, so not all of the dates are for the current year. In succeeding years, the previous year's date should give you an approximate idea of when each festival is held.

January 16, 2011	Buckman-Kerns Brewfest, Portland
January 21, 2012	CellarFest, *Bailey's Taproom,* Portland
January 28-29, 2011*	Oregon Wine, Food, & Brew Festival, Salem
January 29, 2011	Scottish Ale Festival, Portland (1st Annual)
February 10-11, 2011*	KLCC Microbrew Festival, Eugene
February 19, 2011*	Zwickelmania, Oregon Breweries Tour, hosted by Oregon Brewer's Guild
February 19-20, 2011*	Confluence Wine, Beer, Seafood and Music Festival, Gardner
February 21-27, 2011	Beer Brawl IV, Concordia Ale House, Portland
February 25-27, 2011	Winter Nano Beer Fest, *Fanno Creek,* Tigard
February 26,2011	Chowder Challenge, Portland A benefit for Locks of Love held at Fifth Quadrant
February 26, 2011	McMenamins 18th Annual Brewfest competition of McMenamins beers to determine which will go to Oregon brewfest, *Hillsdale Brewery & Public House,* Portland

March 5, 2011	2010 Lucky Labrador's Barleywine and Big Beer Fest, Portland
March 11-12, 2011*	Pouring at the Coast Craft Beer Fest, Seaside
March 19, 2011	4th Annual Chocolate Beer Dinner, *Deschutes*, Bend
March 19, 2011	2nd Annual Division Street Meet the Brewers BrewPubliCrawl, Portland
April 16, 2011	GermanFest, *Bailey's Taproom*, Portland
April 16, 2011	FirkinFest, *Green Dragon-Rogue*, Portland
April 22-23, 2011*	17th Annual Spring Beer & Wine Fest, Portland
April 29-30, 2011*	Oregon Garden Brewfest, Silverton
April 30, 2011	Cheers to Belgian Beers, *Metal Fabrication, 723 N Tillamook St* , Portland
May 6- 7, 2011	2011 Sasquatch Brew Fest, Eugene
May 7, 2011	Saison Festival, *Cascade Barrel House*, Portland
May 12-13, 2011	12th Annual UFO Festival, *Hotel Oregon (McMenamins)*, McMinnville
May 14, 2011	FredFest, *Hair of the Dog*, Portland
May 20, 2011	Brewer's Memorial, *Rogue*, Newport
June 3, 2011*	Zoo Brew, *Oregon Zoo*, Portland
June 11-12, 2011	1st Annual Portland Fruit Beer Festival, Portland
June 11, 2011	Berries, Brews, & BBQ's, *French Prairie Gardens*, St. Paul
June 16-17, 2011	BBQ, Blues, & Microbrews, *Wolf Creek Inn*, Wolf Creek (North of Grants Pass)
June 24-26, 2011*	North American Organic Brewers Festival, Portland

June 25, 2011	Barley Cup, *McMenamins*, Salem
July 1, 2011	Oregon Craft Beer Month Kickoff, for a list of events go to www.oregoncraftbeermonth.com
July 15-17, 2011	IPA Fest, *Saraveza*, Portland
July 17-18, 2011*	Sisters Wine & Brew Festival, Sisters
June 25-26, 2011*	Battle of the Bones, Central Point
July 15-17, 2011*	Portland International Beer Festival, *Pearl District*, Portland
July 16, 2011	Roadhouse Brewfest, *Cornelius Pass Roadhouse-McMenamins*, Hillsboro
July 18-24, 2011	Puckerfest, 5th Annual Celebration of Sour Beers, *Belmont Station*, Portland
July 28-31, 2011*	Oregon Brewer's Festival, Portland
July 30, 2011	Fringe Fest, *Belmont Station*, Portland
August 6-7, 2011	Bones & Brew, *Rogue*, Portland
August 5-6, 2011*	Willamette Valley Blues & Brews Festival, Eugene
August 6, 2011	AnnBREW, *Bailey's Tap Room*, Portland (barrel aged beers)
August 6-8, 2010	Nano Beer Fest, *Fanno Creek*, Tigard Nano as used here is an indication of the size of the festival, not the breweries participating.
August 12-14, 2011*	Bite of Oregon, Portland
August 13, 2011*	Bronze, Brews, & Blues Fest, Joseph
August 13, 2011*	Brats, Blues, & Brews, Klamath Falls
August 13, 2011*	Oakridge Keg & Cask Festival, Oakridge
August 18-20, 2011*	Bend Brewfest, Bend
August 19-20, 2011*	Oregon Brews & BBQ's Festival, McMinnville

August 20, 2011	16th Annual Lighthouse Brewfest, Lighthouse Brewpub, McMenamins, Lincoln City
August 27, 2011	Hopworks 3rd Annual Biketoberfest, *Hopworks*, Portland
August 28-29, 2010	Mini Beer Festival, *Green Dragon*, Portland
August 27-28, 2011	Hop Madness, Salem For Homebrewers only
September 2-3, 2011*	The Little Woody, Bend (labor day weekend)
September 8, 2010*	Microhopic, *Bailey's Taproom*, Portland
September 9, 2011	2nd Annual Beer Fest, The Dalles
September 10, 2011*	Gold Beach Brew & Art Fest, Gold Beach
September 14-17, 2011	Mt. Angel Oktoberfest, Mt. Angel
September 17,2011*	Septembeerfest, Corvallis
September 17, 2011	Mid-Valley Brewfest, High Street Brewery & Café, Eugene
September 23-25, 2011*	Pacific NW Brew Cup, Astoria
September 24,2011	Laurelfest, *Laurelwood*, Portland,
September 24, 2011*	Sisters Fresh Hop Festival, Sisters
September 25, 2010*	Salem Beer & Cider Fest, Salem
September 26, 2010	Oktoberfest, *Belmont Station*, Portland
September 23, 2011	Independence Hop & Heritage Festival, *Rogue*, Independence
October 1, 2011*	Hood River Hops Fest, Hood River
October 1, 2011*	Brews & Boogie, Ashland
October 1, 2011	Great American Brew Festival, Denver, Colorado While this festival is not held in Oregon, we felt no festival listing would be complete without it
October 7-8, 2010	The Newport Microbrew Festival, *Rogue*, Newport

October 7-8, 2011*	Chowder, Blues, & Brews, Florence
October 8-9, 2010	Portland Fresh Hop Tastival, Portland
October 15, 2011*	Mid-Valley Brewfest, Albany
October 16, 2010	Fresh Hop Tastival, Eugene
October 20, 2010	Killer Beers of Bend, *The Beer Mongers*, Bend (part of *Brewpublic*'s Killer Beer Week)
October 21-22, 2011*	Umpqua Brewfest, Roseburg
October 22, 2010	Brewpublic Brewniversary Party!, *Saraveza Bottleshop & Pasty Tavern*, Portland (part of *Brewpublic*'s Killer Beer Week)
October 23, 2010	Killerbeerfest!, Portland, *Bailey's Taproom* (part of *Brewpublic*'s Killer Beer Week)
October 23-4, 2010	Great American Distillers Festival, Portland
November 12, 2011	BelgianFest, *Bailey's Taproom*, Portland
November 30 – December 4, 2011*	Holiday Ale Festival, Portland
December 13, 2010	Amnesia Winter Beer Festival, Portland

Festival Descriptions

The following descriptions do not contain personal impressions. Unfortunately, the combination of our schedule and location in the state precludes us from attending most festivals. However, we have provided these descriptions so that you may choose the style of festivals you would like to attend.

With the permission of the festival sponsors, we have adapted the information from their website. For current information, locations, prices, and questions, consult the festival website or sponsor.

January 28-29, 2011

Oregon Wine, Food, & Brew Festival - Salem
www.oregonwinefoodbrewfest.com

Online Tickets Available at: Absolutelytix.com

Oregon State Fairgrounds - Americraft Cookware Center, Salem

Friday, January 28, 2011 - Open: 2:00 p.m.; Close: 10:00 P.M.

Saturday, January 29, 2011 - Open: Noon; Close: 10:00 P.M.

Daily admission $10 at the door - includes complimentary parking (Seniors 65+ $8)
VIP Packages include Admission, VIP lounge, Commemorative Wine Glass, Two
Complimentary Tastes $25 per person
Special Lodging package available at Red Lion and 2 for one Amtrak from Portland
north.

- Oregon Vineyards & Wineries
- Oregon Micro Brews and Craft Beers
- Oregon Spirits - Distilleries
- NW Art & Artists
- Featured Artist (Unknown at the time)
- Oregon Culinary Features - Guest Chefs
- Demonstrations and Classes
- Live Entertainment including Blind Rhino, Brady Goss, HS Jazz Bands
- Fun, Festive atmosphere

February 10-11, 2012

KLCC Microbrew Festival – Eugene

http://www.klcc.org/News.asp?NewsID=156

Lane Events Center Exhibit Hall, 796 W 13th, Eugene

5-11 P.M.

$12 admission (2010 price) - All tickets sold at the door.
Includes souvenir glass!
Beer tastes are $1 each.

- More than 50 participating breweries in 2010 serving more than 100 beers!
- Almost half are Oregon Breweries
- Collaboration Brew
- People's Choice competition
- Entertainment – nightly at 7:30

Due to the 2010 problems with the Oregon homebrew laws, the homebrew competition has been canceled for 2011. KLCC hopes to reinstate it in 2011 after the law has been addressed.

A microbrew tasting event to benefit KLCC 89.7 FM.
Keep the FUN in fundraising!

February 19, 2011

Zwickelmania-Oregon Brewery Tour - Oregon

http://oregonbeer.org/zwickelmania/

Throughout Oregon

11-4 P.M.

President's Day weekend, dozens of Oregon breweries and brewpubs will open their doors to visitors for the state's 2nd annual Zwickelmania.

Zwickelmania, hosted by the Oregon Brewers Guild (OBG), is a free statewide event that offers visitors a chance to tour Oregon breweries, meet the brewers and sample their favorite beers.

Free Shuttle Bus available in Portland.

See Oregon Brewers Guild website for participating breweries.

Confluence Wine, Beer, Seafood, & Music Festival

http://www.reedsportcc.org/confluence/

Old W.F. Jewett School building in Gardiner, just North of Reedsport

Saturday - February 19, noon- 10:00 P.M. - $10.00
Senior discount (65 or Older) $9.00

Sunday - February 20, noon- 7:00 P.M. - $7.00
Senior discount (65 or Older) $6.00

Weekend Pass $15.00 - Senior (65 or older) $13.00

This event is like no other on the Oregon Coast. At no other Oregon Coast festival will you find all of these elements brought together in one place. Hence the name: Confluence.

From the Chamber of Commerce that sponsors more events than any other in Oregon, you are invited to the Reedsport, Winchester Bay, and Gardiner area the weekend of February 19th & 20th. While you're there, check out this corner of Oregon Coastal heaven and the many outdoor activities available for your enjoyment.

Free shuttle from Reedsport, Winchester Bay, and Gardner.
 Plenty of free parking.

Noun: *A coming or flowing together, meeting or gathering at one point.*

March 11-12, 2011

Pouring At The Coast - Seaside
www.seasidechamber.com

Craft Beer Fest
Seaside Civic & Convention Center, 415 1st Ave.

March 11 – Brewer's Dinner – 5:30 - Limited Seating
March 12 - Pouring & Tasting – 5-9 – Public Tasting

It's Pouring At The Oregon Coast,
Only This Time It's With Oregon Craft Beers

In Association With:
> The Oregon Brewers Guild
> Astoria Brewing Company
> Bill's Tavern
> Rogue Ales
> Fort George Brewery

April 22-23, 2011

17th Annual Spring Beer & Wine Fest – Portland

http://www.springbeerfest.com/

Oregon Convention Center
777 NE MLK Jr. Blvd., Portland

Noon – 11 P.M.
  Admission $5.00*
  Souvenir beer glass $8.00
  Souvenir wine glass $5.00
  Plastic Beer mug $5.00
  Sampling tokens $1.00
  Package for One. $20.00**
  Package for Two $40.00***
*Free admission Noon to 2:00 pm both days
**Includes 1 admission, 1 wine glass or plastic mug , and 10 tokens
***Includes 2 admissions, 2 wine glasses or plastic mugs, and 20 tokens.

Please visit the MDA booth for special beers and wines. Help send a kid to camp
by making a $5.00 donation for this special cause. For your generosity, you will
receive a full 14 oz. beer or 5 oz. wine that is unique to the event.

- Hop aboard the Tour de Cheese
- Mingle with artisan brewers, vintners, distillers & cheese makers
- Nibble on tasty gourmet delights
- Get schooled at the Chefs' Stage - and eat your homework
- Groove to tunes from hot NW bands
- Shop at the arts & crafts vendors

The Spring Beer & Wine Fest encourages responsible consumption. Minors
accompanied by an adult are permitted until 7:00pm each day. Children 12 & under
are free.

April 29-30, 2011

Oregon Garden Brewfest – Silverton

www.oregongardenbrewfest.blogspot.com
www.oregongarden.org/Events

Oregon Garden Pavilion, Silverton

Friday, April 29, 2011
4 – 11 P.M.
Saturday, April 30, 2011
12 – 11 P.M.

The 7th annual Oregon Garden Brewfest will be held April 29-30, 2011, at the Garden's Pavilion. 2010's attendees enjoyed a multitude of flagship and seasonal brews from over 30 breweries, live music, and delicious NW cuisine. 2011's event is set to be bigger than last year, with even more breweries, it is sure to be an event you won't want to miss.

Room packages for Brewfest are available through the Oregon Garden Resort. Packages include accomodation, admission to the garden, admission to Brewfest, 2 Brewfest mugs and 10 taste tickets, 2 Brewfest meal vouchers, and a full American buffet breakfast.

Book on the resort's webpage, http://www.moonstonehotels.com/Oregon-Garden-Resort.htm,
or by calling 503-874-2500.

May 6-7, 2011

Sasquatch Brew Fest – Eugene

http://www.northwestlegendsfoundation.org/sasquatch_brewfest.html

Eugene Hilton
Noon – 10:30

Friday May 6th – Sasquatch Brew Fest Beer Dinner
Saturday May 7th – Sasquatch Brew Fest

$10 – festival only - cost includes commemorative glass and two tasting tickets

Together with the Cascade Brewers Society, the Northwest Legends Foundation presents the 2011 Sasquatch Homebrewing Competition. The competition is sanctioned by the American Homebrewers Association and the Beer Judge Certification Program.
Judging will take place on April 30, 2010 in Eugene, Oregon. Best of Show judging will take place on the day of the Sasquatch Brewfest on May 7, 2011.

Produced by the Northwest Legends Foundation, the Sasquatch Brew Fest Beer Dinner provides an opportunity for old and new friends to gather together and enjoy some of the best craft-brewed beers paired with delicious cuisine.
The dinner also features the announcement each year of the winners of the brewing scholarships, presented by Glen's brother, Quentin Falconer, of the Glen Hay Falconer Foundation

Managed and produced by the Northwest Legends Foundation, a Eugene-based non-profit organization staffed by Glen's friends, the Sasquatch Brew Fest is designed to showcase Pacific Northwest craft brewing. Each unique beer presented each year is selected by a professional brewer to honor Glen's memory.

A large portion of the proceeds will be provided to the Glen Hay Falconer Foundation, a non-profit organization staffed by Glen's family with a mandate to support craft brewing by providing brewing scholarships. Additional funds obtained from the beer bash will be presented by the Northwest Legends Foundation to Eugene-based non-profit organizations - again - in memory of Glen.

 Live Music

SASQUATCH BREW FEST
presented by
The Northwest Legends Foundation

Enjoy The Supreme Single-Day Collection Of The Finest Craft-Brewed Beers In The Pacific Northwest And Toast Our Pal Glen Falconer
Dedicated To The Brewer In Everyone

June 3, 2011

Zoo Brew - Portland

http://www.oregonzoo.org/Support/Zoo_Brew.htm

Oregon Zoo, Portland

Friday, June 3, 2010
5-10 P.M.

Advance ticket online until Thursday, June 2nd - $25
Available "will call"
Remaining tickets sold at the door - $30

Includes commemorative tasting glass, 10 tokens and admission to the zoo after 4p.m. Extra tokens available for $1 each.

Entertainment begins at 5:00

Proceeds from this amazing fundraising event will support *Zoo To You*, a youth outreach program.

This is a tasting event, not a drinking event and will be held rain or shine.

Enjoy beers from more than 20 Northwest microbreweries and live entertainment on the main stage featuring local favorites!

June 17,2011

Sisters Wine & Brew Festival – Sisters
www.sisterswineandbrew.com

The Village Green, Sisters

Friday, June 17, 2011
3:00 P.M. to 9:00 P.M.
Saturday, June 18
11:00 A.M. to 8:00 P.M.

Iincludes special dinners, wine and beer tasting, vendors, great food and entertainment.

2011 Breweries:
- Three Creeks Brewing
- Boneyard Beer
- Bridgeport Brewing
- Seven Brides
- Cascade Lakes Brewing Company
- Deschutes Brewery

June 24-26, 2010

North American Organic Brewers Festival-Portland

http://www.naobf.org

Overlook Park
North Fremont Street & Interstate Avenue, Portland

Noon to 9 P.M. Fri & Sat
Noon to 5 P.M. Sun

Admission into the event is free. The purchase of a $6 reusable, compostable cornstarch glass is required for tasting beer, as are tokens, which sell for $1 apiece. A full glass of beer costs four tokens (more for select beers), and a four-ounce taste costs one token. Patrons receive a $1 discount toward the tasting glass with a validated MAX ticket, a ticket from the onsite bike corral, or three cans of food for the Oregon Food Bank.

Two of Portland's beloved industries - organic beer and sustainability - come together in an annual celebration designed to raise awareness about organic beer and sustainable living. We serve up organic beers and ciders from around the world, accompanied by live music, organic food, sustainability-oriented vendors, non-profits and a children's area - all in a beautiful tree-lined setting that overlooks downtown Portland. Come visit the North American Organic Brewers Festival and see why we're Portland's best kept secret of beer fests!

2010's event included 35 breweries and 17 sustainable vendors.
Food vendors are required to use compostable utensils and containers.

June 25-26, 2011

Battle of the Bones, Central Point
Annual Barbeque, Microbrew, Wine, & Music Festival
http://www.battleofthebones.com

Twin Creeks Park
555 Twin Creeks Crossing Loop, Central Point

Battle of the Bones is a fierce and delicious competition between local barbecue teams, breweries from all regions of Oregon and Northern California, as well as wineries from Oregon! Who decides the winners? YOU DO, through the People's Choice voting system! By voting, you are automatically entered to win a barbecue! Battle of the Bones is a fun family event with entertainment for all ages, featuring a free kid's zone.

Proceeds benefit the Central Point Parks & Recreation Foundation

July 15-17, 2011

Portland International Beer Festival – Portland

http://www.seattlebeerfest.com/Index2%20PIB.htm

Pearl District North Park Blocks.
Entrance at NW Davis & NW Park Ave (1 block west of NW Broadway, 2 blocks north of W Burnside

Friday, 4-10 P.M.
Saturday, 12-10 P.M.
Sunday, 12-7 P.M.

$25 AT GATE
$20 ADVANCE PURCHASE
- Entry includes PIB glass & 10 beer tickets
- More tickets available for $1 each
- All beers are 4oz. servings
- Beers cost 1 to 6 tickets, depending on how much it costs us.
- Prices are NOT based on rarity.
- There are dozens of 1 ticket beers, usually over 50.
- $5 for non-drinkers (includes free non-alcoholic beverages).

SKIP THE LINES & DRINK LIKE A ROCK STAR!
PIB now offers the VIP EXPRESS PASS
Available only by advance purchase Online
Just $35 and you get:
- 30 beer tickets (our best deal)
- Early entry w/ "behind the scenes" beer drinking
- No waiting in line to get in...ever.
- VERY limited availability

PIB IS AN OVER THE TOP BEER FESTIVAL celebrating the world's most legendary brewing styles and the nations that made them famous. Come taste over 150 world-class beers from more than 15 countries.

RAREST OF THE RARE: The beers of PIB represent all that's possible in the world of brewing. Many are quite obscure yet hold their own place in world history as the birth of a new brewing style.

July 29-31, 2011

Oregon Brewers Festival – Portland

http://www.oregonbrewfest.com/

Waterfront Park
Along the Willamette River
between Morrison & Burnside Bridges, Portland

Always held the last full weekend in July.

Thurs through Sat, taps are open from Noon to 9 P.M.
Sun, taps are open from Noon to 7 P.M.
Token & mug sales cease one-half hour prior to the taps closing

Admission into the festival grounds is free. In order to consume beer at the OBF, you must purchase a taster package. Taster packages are available in $10, $20 and $50 increments. All packages include a 2010 souvenir mug, which is required for consuming beer (mugs from previous years will not be filled); a souvenir program that includes a map of where the beers are located onsite; and various quantities of tokens, which are used to purchase beer. Patrons pay four tokens for a full mug of beer, or one token for a taste. Additional tokens may be purchased at $1 apiece.

- $10 package: one mug, one program, four tokens
- $20 package: one mug, one program, 14 tokens
- $50 package: two mugs, two programs, 40 tokens

The Oregon Brewers Festival is one of the nation's longest running and best-loved craft beer festivals. The Oregon Brewers Festival exists to provide an opportunity to sample and learn about a variety of craft beer styles from across the country. Eighty craft breweries from all parts of the nation offer handcrafted brews to 70,000 beer lovers during the four-day event.

The festival's focus is craft beer, but there's more than sampling involved. The event features live music all four days, beer-related vendors, beer memorabilia displays, beer writers and publishers, homebrewing demonstrations, and an assortment of foods from a variety of regions. The Crater Lake Root Beer Garden offers complimentary handcrafted root beer for minors and designated drivers. Minors are always welcome at the festival when accompanied by a parent.

August 5-6, 2011

Willamette Valley Blues and Brews – Springfield
http://wvbbf.org

Willamette River in Island Park, Springfield

Friday: Open at 3:30pm, music from 4:00 P.M. to 10:30 P.M.
Saturday: Openat 10:30 A.M., music from 11:00 A.M. to 10:30 P.M.
The Kid Zone will be open from 11:00 A.M. to 6:00 P.M. on Saturday only.
All children MUST be accompanied by an adult when visiting the Kid Zone.

Tickets will be available at the gate for $10 per day or $15 for the weekend,
or in advance beginning June 1st, at S.E. Habitat for Humanity and many branches
of Pacific Cascade Federal Credit Union at the cost of $8 per day or $15 for the
weekend.
Tickets are $10 per day or less for a weekend pass PLUS 3 non-perishable items
for FOOD for Lane County
Children under the age of 13 are free when accompanied by an adult.

Two local hotels offering *Special Festival Pricing.* See the WVBBF website for
more information.

Download and print the Blues & Brews LTD coupon on the WVBBF website to take
advantage of riding the bus to and from the festival for free!

The annual Willamette Valley Blues & Brews Festival benefits Springfield/Eugene
Habitat for Humanity and is a food drive for FOOD for Lane County. Enjoy music
on three stages, beer from throughout the NW and wines from Lane County.

August 13, 2011

Brats, Blues, & Brews – Klamath Falls

http://www.discoverourfestival.com/festival/info/Klamath+Falls/OR/brats-brews-and-blues-festival

2700 Front Street Klamath Yacht Club –Klamath Falls

Four of the region's best blues bands will perform live at the Klamath Basin Sunrise Rotary's 10th Annual Brats, Brews, and Blues benefit festival. You won't want to miss any one of these bands! The event promises an eclectic celebration of toe-tapping, hand-clapping and soul-stirring music. Ticket prices include a Bratwurst dinner with German potato salad, sauerkraut and trimmings.

This event features sampling of six locally brewed beers from Mia and Pia's Pizzeria and the Klamath Basin Brewing Company.

Come early and make it a Blues weekend. Start out on Friday, August 6th at the Running Y Ranch Resort's Free Concert on the Green from 4:30 to 7:30 P.M., then the BBB on Saturday for an afternoon of fun entertainment to support youth in our community.

Proceeds from the event go to benefit area youth service organizations like Integral Youth Services, Early Childhood Intervention and Marta's House. Klamath Hospice's Camp Evergreen youth bereavement program was the primary recipient of last year's proceeds.

August 12-14, 2011

The Bite of Oregon, Portland
www.biteoforegon.com

Waterfront Park, Portland

$10 Weekend Pass
$8 One Day Pass
$3 Early Bird Special (Friday entry before 2pm, Sunday entry before 1pm)

Many new and exciting features include ...

- New! US Bank Kid's Faire
- Talent Tour! 105.1 The Buzz Nelson and Terry's Summer Talent Tour on the Garden Stage - Saturday August 7th
- New! Be the first to play Kinect™ for Xbox 360 on site Iron Chef Oregon competitions presented by NW Natural
- New! Portland Food Cart Cuisine
- New! Oregon Dessert Pavilion presented by Boyds Coffee
- New! Gerry Frank's Oregon Chef's Table presented by The Oregonian
- Expanded! Oregon Craft Beer Garden – more selections
- Expanded! MIX Wine Pavilion - more than 100 selections
- Blues great and local legend, Curtis Salgado and much more entertainment
- Eating competition featuring Joey Chestnut on the Garden Stage presented by Pepto-Bismol
- On Sunday August 8th come taste the Southern Oregon Regional Chili winner's chili and the winning chocolate cake from the 2009 Gerry Frank's Chocolate Cake competition.
- Meet & Greet Amy Roloff from the TLC show Little People, Big World on Saturday 11am-3pm in the U.S. Bank Kids' Faire area

The Bite of Oregon is working toward zero waste. Venders sign sustainability pledge.

The Bite of Oregon is produced as a fund-raising event by Special Olympics Oregon for the benefit of Special Olympics athletes around the state.

- 392 -

August 13, 2011

Bronze, Brews, & Blues Fest – Joseph

www.bronzebluesbrews.com/

Joseph City Park, Joseph

Gates open at Noon
Music begins at 1:00 P.M. and ends at 10:00

Advance Tickets: $25
Tickets at the Gate: $30
Kids 10 & Under: Free

Free shuttle buses from Enterprise and Wallowa Lake

Family Event

2010 had:

- Twelve breweries and more than 24 microbrews
- Fourteen venders serving food

2011 scheduled bands (subject to change without notice):

- Nick Moss & The Flip Tops
- Trampled Under Foot
- Eden Brent
- Kevin Selfe & The Tornados
- Terry Robb

Tickets online or call 541-432-1015

August 19-20, 2011

Oregon Brews & BBQs Festival – McMinnville

www.oregonbrewsandbbqs.com

The Event will be held in the Granary District in Historic - McMinnville
5th & Lafayette

Friday, August 19, 2011
3:00 P.M. - 10:00 P.M.
Saturday, August 20, 2011
Noon - 10:00pm

Admission:
$5 for ages 13 and up.
If you're 21 or over you get a free souvenir tasting mug!
Tickets will be available only at the gate on the day of the event.

Minors will be admitted into the 2011 event during all hours – there will be a
Kidzone!

2010 Festival Featured:
27 Breweries
3 Wineries
6 BBQ Vendors
8 Bands
2011 Expected to be Similar

August 18-20, 2011

Bend Brewfest – Bend

www.bendbrewfest.com

Les Schwab Amphitheater, Bend

Friday, 4-11P.M.
Saturday, Noon-11 P.M.

Admission to the Brewfest is FREE
A one-time purchase of a souvenir mug is required for tasting - $10.

Annual Bend Brew Fest celebrates Bend's bent for brews. More than thirty Pacific Northwest brewers will present over sixty craft beers for public tasting at the Les Schwab Amphitheater. The day's events will also include live entertainment and food vendors. The guests may vote for "People's Choice," but this is a non-judged festival where the focus is on tasting and enjoying fine craft beers.

Children are welcome until 7pm. There will be release forms for parents to read and sign. After 7pm, it's 21+ only.

August 13, 2011

Oakridge Keg & Cask Festival
www.keg-caskfestival.blogspot.com

Two blocks of historic Uptown Oakridge will be closed to traffic in front of the Brewers' Union Local 180 Pub and Brewery and City Hall.

Admittance to the Oakridge Keg & Cask Festival is free.
$15 gains access to the tasting area, a commemorative pint glass or wine glass and 4 taste tickets. Additional tickets are $1 each.

There will be outdoor seating, local breweries and wineries (from within 100 miles of Oakridge).

A Fundraising Event benefiting the Oakridge Food Box and Chamber of Commerce. Oakridge Food Box food donation barrels will be present to collect food donations during the event, please share with those in need by donating nonperishable items at the brewfest .

In addition to local breweries and wineries, vendors, artists, crafters, and food vendors lend their support to make this fundraising festival a success.

OAKRIDGE KEG AND CASK FESTIVAL

September 2-3, 2011

The Little Woody – Bend
www.thelittlewoody.com

Deschutes Historical Museum

Friday, 5-10 P.M.
Saturday, Noon-10 P.M.

$6 Basic entry includes glass
$15 Tasting package includes glass and 10 tokens.

The mission of The Little Woody presented by Nature's Whole Food Marketplace is to celebrate one of Central Oregon's cultural hallmarks – the great brews created right here in our backyard and provide a fun environment for people to enjoy all of those brews in one place. In the old days, brewers served beer that was aged in oaken casks, now brewers are rolling back the barrels for flavoring beer. The Little Woody Festival will shine the light on this ancient brewing technique, as adapted by American craft brewers by featuring beers aged in wine barrels, whiskey barrels and oak barrels which uniquely flavors and intensifies the beer.

The Little Woody 2010 featured unique beers by all of Central Oregon's brewers that were only available at the festival. These beers are aged roughly six months in wood barrels for that high percentage taste you can't find in stores.

September 10, 2011

Gold Beach Brew & Art Fest – Gold Beach

www.goldbeachbrewfest.org/

Event Center, Fairgrounds, Gold Beach

Noon-10 P.M.
Saturday after Labor Day, Annually

Tickets are $10 per person and will be available at the door. Advance tickets are available at Dan's Ace Hardware and Interiors, both located in Gold Beach. Admission includes a complimentary festival beer glass and two tickets to test your craft beer selection.

Come visit us at Gold Beach, Oregon, for a sun soaked September weekend, with the best weather of the year, and the ocean roaring in the background. Is that the ocean, or the crowd grooving to the music, with two stages running simultaneously? In addition to the fine fresh NW craft brews, we have outstanding eats including fresh smoked BBQ, just asking to be washed down with another microbrew. Nearby are the finest hotels on the coast, some with views of the ocean and others with views of the world famous wild and scenic Rogue River.

Want to get some exercise? Then join in the **Rogue River bike ride** on a sunny Saturday morning and watch the American Bald Eagles and Ospreys as they battle the salmon in a quest to feed their young. Then, after the ride, sit back, enjoy the music, the fresh brews and food, for a relaxing afternoon and evening on the beach. And don't forget the *classic car show* on the brewfest grounds, with their proud owners showing off their amazing collection. Additionally, the finest Oregon coast artists and craft artisans will be showing off their latest crafts and creations.

2010 Festival featured four breweries.

September 18, 2010

Microhopic – Portland

www.brewpublic.com/events

Bailey's Taproom
213 SW Broadway

4 P.M. until kegs are gone

This celebration of the tiny brewery is not considered a nano event, but rather a pico, femto, atto, zepto, or even yotto brew event. Sponsored by Brewpublic, for this special event Bailey's Taproom dedicates more than half of their taps to the little guy.

2010 event included:
- Big Horse
- Mt. Tabor
- Blue House
- Breakside
- Migration
- Buckman
- Rivergate
- Coalition
- Nation
- Beetje
- Vertigo

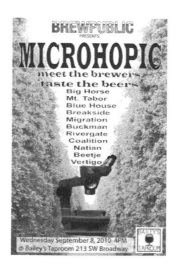

September 23-25, 2011

Pacific NW Brew Cup – Astoria

Find them on Facebook

2011 Location T.B.D.

Friday, Noon-10 P.M.
Saturday, Noon-10 P.M.
Sunday, 10 A.M. - 4 P.M.

The Pacific NW Brew Cup provides the opportunity to try beers from more than three-dozen Northwest breweries, enjoy live music, and peruse vendors selling food and other goods.

The focus of the festival is to promote hand crafted artisan brews having approximately 3 dozen represented from the Pacific Northwest available for sampling.

This is a family friendly event also featuring live music, food and games for the kids.

Sunday will again be growler day and an opportunity to take beer home to enjoy.

The Pacific Northwest Brewcup organizers wish to thank all of the brewers who have participated in past events and look forward to seeing what everyone might have on tap for the 2011 festival.

All profits from the event will be given to a charitable organization.

2010 Festival raised $6100 for Clatsop County Regional Foodbank.

September 17, 2011

Septembeerfest – Corvallis

www.hotv.org/septembeerfest

Benton County Fairgrounds

2-10 P.M.

Admission is $10 and includes a pint glass and two drink tickets, additional drink tickets are $1.

A benefit for Linn Benton Food Share
& Scholarship funds for Brewing Students

Join Heart of the Valley Homebrewers in beautiful Corvallis, Oregon, as we celebrate the 5th annual Septembeerfest, the Northwest beer lovers brewfest. Septembeerfest is located at the Benton County Fairgrounds in an outdoor setting, with plenty of room for enjoying a beer and listening to some fine entertainment. A preliminary list of breweries attending, and some of the beers that will be on tap, is available on the website.

2010 attendance topped out at 2000 beer enthusiasts, our largest yet, which resulted in over $11,000 going to the Linn/Benton Food Share, OSU Fermentation Science students, and the Glen Hay Falconer Foundation.

Aside from the 40-50 craft beers from breweries both local and abroad, festival goers will enjoy food from places such as Block 15 (one of Corvallis' finest brew pubs) and the best pretzels you'll find from Nina, the Queen Pretzel. Craft made or home made root beer is usually available for the kids and designated drivers and we try to have some wine or cider for the non-beer drinkers in the crowd. Traditional Polka usually starts off the music scene in the afternoon and moves on throughout the day ending with one of our local bands(such as the ElKabong Orchestra or Bon Ton Roulet) getting everyone on their feet and dancing

Heart of the Valley has the longest running homebrew competition in the Northwest, as well as the second longest in the nation. The Septembeerfest is an offshoot of this event.

Entertainment & Free Shuttle.

September 25, 2010

Salem's Beer & Cider Festival – Salem

www.salembeerandciderfestival.com

Mission Mill Museum
1313 Mill Street SE, Salem

Noon-10 P.M.

Entry Fee ... ...$15.00 (includes sampling glass and 5 tokens)
Sampling tokens $1.00
Admission only $5.00
Premium Package $25.00 (includes Beer Appreciation Class with sample glass and 5 tokens)
*Discount admission Noon to 3:00 P.M. $12.00

2010 Event hosted more than 11 Breweries, more than 2 ciders, more than 7 bands, more than 17 artists, and a variety of food venders.

October 1, 2011

Brews & Boogie – Ashland

http://www.scienceworksmuseum.org/Page.asp
?NavID=81

Science Works Hands-On Museum
1500 E Main St.

(541) 482-6767
info@scienceworksmuseum.org

7 P.M. to 12 A.M.

Admission is $15 in Advance, $20 at the Door
 Admission includes a commemorative pint
glass and tasting tickets.

10 breweries, 3 bands, 1 amazing night!

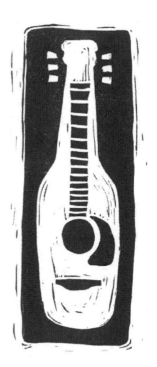

Are you looking for a chance to get down to good tunes and sip down some good brews, all in the name of science? Now is the chance you've been waiting for! Come enjoy fine microbrews from regional breweries, catch live music from area musicians, and explore the exhibits at ScienceWorks Hands-on Museum during our annual Brews and Boogie event on the first Saturday in October.

Now in its 8th year, Brews and Boogie has evolved over time to become more than a beer tasting with last year's event featuring carnival games and a raffle with amazing prizes. All proceeds from the event go to support ScienceWorks' educational programs, making school visits available to thousands of students throughout southern Oregon and northern California.

Brews and Boogie is not only a lot of fun but a great way to support ScienceWorks.

October 1, 2011

Hood River Hops Fest – Hood River

www.hoodriverhopsfest.wordpress.com

Columbia Lot in Hood River
Entrance at 5th & Cascade

Noon- 9 P.M.
Kids til 6 P.M.

Free Admission
$6 Tasting Mugs ($1 of it goes to Columbia Gorge United Way)
$1 Tasting Tokens

As the premier fresh hops beer-tasting event in the Pacific Northwest, the Hood River Hops Fest features at least one fresh-hopped beer from each of the roughly 25 Northwest craft brewers planning to attend.

An expanded menu of local culinary food, over 20 arts and crafts vendors, a selection of Gorge wines, a robust children's play area, and a day-long lineup of live music will guarantee fun for the entire family.

October 7-8, 2011

Chowder, Blues & Brews – Florence

www.florencechamber.com/events/chowder-blues.shtml

Florence Events Center
715 Quince, Florence

Friday, 5-11 P.M.
Saturday, 11 A.M.-11 P.M.

Individual daily tickets at the door, Friday $7 or Saturday $10
$15 VIP Weekend Passes (includes commemorative festival glass) on sale at the Chamber Office (290 Hwy 101).

Live Music All Weekend

The Florence Area Chamber of Commerce will host its 13th Annual Fall Festival with award winning chowder offered from all along the coast of Oregon, the finest blues music that Oregon has to offer and microbrews from some of the best breweries in the northwest! The festival is set for a time of the year where we can expect the most beautiful weather one can imagine on the Central Oregon Coast. Each year, Chowder, Blues & Brews has drawn visitors from the south and central coastal area as well as from the Willamette Valley.

Beginning on Friday afternoon, the Florence Events Center will be rocking with "musical delights" performed by the great blues artists of the Western Oregon area.

Saturday will highlight the ninth year of the Oregon Coast Professional Chowder Cook-Off where festival goers will have a chance to taste the best chowder the Oregon Coast has to offer from communities extending from Astoria to Brookings. The event will also have delicacies from some 20 food vendors and microbrews from five of Oregon's best microbreweries.

The Oregon Coast Professional Chowder Cook-Off People's Choice tasting starts at 1:00 pm on Saturday and goes until the chowder is gone.

October 15, 2011

Mid-Valley Brewfest – Albany

http://bgc-albany.org/MVB/index.html

Linn County Fair & Expo Center, Albany

1-10 P.M.

Gather to watch the live OSU / UCLA away game
In 2010 there were 24 breweries participating.
Benny Beaver Appearance.

21 & Older only

October 21-22, 2011

Umpqua Brew Fest – Roseburg

http://www.umpqua-watersheds.org/umpquabrewfest/

Douglas County Fairgrounds, Roseburg

Friday at 3 P.M.
Saturday at 10 A.M.

Free Admission
$5 for souvenir glass, $1 taster tokens

Umpqua Watersheds' 1st Annual Umpqua Brew Fest will be Roseburg's greatest outdoor celebration of the year, hosting microbreweries from around the Pacific Northwest. Come help celebrate water conservation and get in on some great food, great beer and great live music.

2010 event included nine breweries. Not a bad start for the first year.

Free Taxi service in Roseburg after 6 P.M.

21 & over only

November 30 – December 4, 2011

Holiday Ale Festival - Portland
www.holidayale.com

Pioneer Square, Enter on 6th Avenue
701 6th Avenue, Portland

Wednesday, 2:00 P.M. - 10:00 P.M.
Thursday, 11:00 A.M. - 10:00 P.M.
Friday, 11:00 A.M. - 10:00 P.M.
Saturday, 11:00 A.M. - 10:00 P.M.
Sunday, 11:00 A.M. - 5:00 P.M.

FREE re-admission into the Festival all 5 days with wristband and current year's mug! To enter and taste beers, the purchase of an initial tasting package is required. Advance tickets cost $20, or $25 at the door. This package includes a souvenir mug and 10 beer tickets. Additional tasting ticket available for $1. Coat & bag check - $2.

Designated drivers in a party of two or more may purchase a Designated Driver entry for $5 and receive free non-alcoholic sodas courtesy of Crater Lake Sodas, or bottled water for the duration of their stay; however, designated drivers are not allowed to drink ANY alcohol, not even a taste.

Held in the heart of downtown Portland, the Holiday Ale Festival keeps attendees warm and dry under a large clear top tent that covers Pioneer Courthouse Square while allowing for views of the city lights. Gas heaters create a cozy ambience under the boughs of one of the region's largest decorated Christmas trees.

More than 50 potent winter ales are featured, all of which are created specifically to bring warmth and cheer to the holiday season. These aren't beers you'll find in the supermarket - brewers have put together special recipes just for the Holiday Ale Festival. From Belgians and Barleywines to Porters and Stouts, these beers are rich, robust and full of complex flavors.

The "Beer and Brunch" event will be held Sunday, from 11A.M. to 1P.M., featuring a European-style Brunch and will include at least four special Belgian brews not part of the standard Festival selection. Tickets are limited and will be available in the fall.

21 and over only
A *Road Trips for Beer* top 10 Beer Festival.

Homebrewing

Whether you spell it as one word, homebrew; or as two words, home brew; it is still beer brewed at home. To many, it is a way of life; to others, a challenge; and for some, a dream.

On October 14, 1978, President Jimmy Carter signed H.R. 1337, which contained an amendment sponsored by Senator Alan Cranston creating an exemption from taxation for beer brewed at home for personal or family use. This exemption went into effect February 1, 1979. Less than two months after the bill was signed, the American Homebrewers Association was founded by Charlie Papazian and Charlie Matzen in Boulder, Colorado.

There are three basic ways to homebrew. There are beer **kits**, which are the easiest, most user-friendly method of making beer for the beginner. **Extracts** provide an easier way for the homebrewer who would prefer a bit more control without all the work of using **grains**, the way the "big boys (and girls)" do it.

While there are many books out there to guide you through the homebrewing process, a good place to make the homebrew decision might be to download the free publication Zymurgy: *An Introduction to Homebrewing*, made available by the American Homebrewers Association. This is available at:

http://www.homebrewersassociation.org/pages/zymurgy/free-downloads/zymurgy-an-introduction-to-homebrewing.

However you determine to homebrew, there are plenty of local homebrew associations available to encourage, assist, and commiserate with you. A list of Oregon homebrew associations follows on page 404.

Unfortunately, a 2010 interpretation of the Oregon Homebrew law, which states "making or keeping of naturally fermented wines and fruit juices or beer in the home, for home consumption and not for sale," stopped homebrew competitions across the state. The review of the law came about at the request of Oregon Liquor Control Commission (OLCC) after they received many requests regarding the legality of homebrew competitions. After an inquiry from the Oregon State Fair, which had been holding homebrew competitions for twenty-two years, OLCC asked for a ruling. It was then determined by the Oregon Department of Justice, taking the wording very literally, that if homebrew is consumed outside the home in which it was brewed, it is a violation of law.

Not only did this ruling stop all competitions in the state, but it also resulted in making it illegal to take a sample of your latest and greatest batch to your buddy's house for that dinner party or to the lake for a picnic. While I doubt the homebrew police are searching for the latest violator outside home, this has had a huge effect on brewpubs, festivals, and fairs wishing to sponsor homebrew competitions. Unwilling to risk their liquor licenses, all competitions came to a halt.

Thankfully, OLCC, in cooperation with Oregon homebrew clubs, American Homebrew Association(AHA), and state legislators, worked toward a law which will allow homebrew outside of the home.

Just before publication of this book, on March 30, 2011, Governor John Kitzhaber signed Senate Bill 444, the new law allowing home beer and wine brewers to share their brews outside the home and enter competitions. Reportedly, the bill drew no opposition from either house.

Let's Brew – Portland

Homebrew Supply Stores
Alphabetical by City

Hondo's Brew & Cork
2703 Marine Drive
Astoria, Oregon 97103
503-325-2234
www.hondosbrew.net

The Brew Shop
2524 NE Division Street
Bend, Oregon 97701
541-323-2318
www.homesuds.com

Westside U-Brew
8260 SW Nimbus Avenue, Building #3
Beaverton, Oregon 97008
503-644-8278
 ubrew@westsideubrew.com

Corvallis Brewing Supply
119 SW 4th Street
Corvallis, Oregon   97333
541-758-1674
www.brewbeer.com

Homebrew Stuff
590 W Dutton Road
Eagle Point, Oregon 97524
888-584-8881
www.homebrewstuff.com

Home Fermenter Center
123 Monroe Street
Eugene, Oregon   97402
541-485-6238
www.homefermenter.com

Ruby Brew
581 ½ Garfield Street
Eugene, Oregon   97402
541-686-9442

Valley Vintner & Brewer
30 E 13th Avenue
Eugene, Oregon   97401
541-484-3322
www.brewabeer.com

Willamette Street Homebrew
1683 Willamette Street
Eugene, Oregon   97401
541-683-4064

Brew Brothers
2061 NW Aloclek Drive, Suite 909
Hillsboro, Oregon 97124
971-222-3434
www.brewbrothers.biz

Main Street Home Brew Supply
229 East Main Street
Hillsboro, Oregon 97123
503-648-4254
www.mainbrew.com

Hood River Brewer's Supply
202 Cascade Avenue, # C
Hood River, Oregon 97031
541-387-4727

Basin Brewing Supply
915 Klamath Avenue
Klamath Falls, Oregon 97601
541-884-1743
www.basinbrewingsupply.com

Grains Beans & Things
820 Crater Lake Avenue, Suite 113
Medford, Oregon 97504
541-499-6777
www.grains-n-beans.com

Bier One
424 SW Coast Highway
Newport, Oregon 97365
541-265-4630
www.bier-one.com

Bridgeview Beer & Wine Supply
624 Main Street
Oregon City, Oregon 97045
503-650-8342

Freshops
36180 Kings Valley Highway
Philomath, Oregon 97370
541-929-2736
www.freshops.com

F.H. Steinbart
234 SE 12th Avenue
Portland, Oregon 97214
503-232-8793
www.fhsteinbart.com

The Homebrew Exchange
1907 N Kilpatrick Street
Portland, Oregon 97217
503-286-0343
www.homebrewexchange.net

Let's Brew
8235 SE Stark Street
Portland, Oregon 97216
503-256-0205
www.letsbrew.net

Homebrew at Let's Brew, where you can learn, brew, and obtain supplies.

Portland U-Brew & Pub
6237 SE Milwaukie Avenue
Portland, Oregon 97202
503-432-9746
www.portlandubrewandpub.com

Aycock Knives & Beer Supplies
120 Columbia Street NE
Salem, Oregon 97301
503-378-0774

Homebrew Heaven
1292 12th Street SE
Salem, Oregon 97302
503-375-3521

Foothills Home Brew Supply
530 N James Street
Silverton, Oregon 97381
503-873-5181

The Beer Essentials
12 West Q Street, Unit C
Springfield, Oregon 97477

Above the Rest Homebrewing
11945 SW Pacific Highway,
Suite 235
Tigard, Oregon 97223
503-968-2736
www.abovetheresthomebrewing.net

Many brewing books available at Home Fermenter Center

Harvest Store

Liberator Homebrew Supply
411 East Columbia River Highway
Troutdale, Oregon 97060
503-665-3355

Herman's Homebrew
841 E Pine Street
White City, Oregon 97502

Harvest Store
501 NW Douglas Boulevard
Winston, Oregon 97296
541-679-4524

Homebrew Organizations

Alphabetically by City

Good Libations

PO Box 166
Baker City, OR 97814
Phone: 541-523-4535
Email: tednjodie@msn.com

PDX Brewers

12605 SW Rita Drive
Beaverton, OR 97005
Phone: 503 484-8463
Email: info@pdxbrewers.com
www.pdxbrewers.com

Central Oregon Homebrewing Organization (COHO)

Bend, OR 97701
Phone: (541) 323-2318
Email: jimadams44@gmail.com
www.cohomebrewers.org

Portland Underground Dregs Society (PUDS)
Clackamas, OR 97015
Email: mksgrist@comcast.net
mksgrist.tripod.com/PUDS.html

Heart Of The Valley
119 SW 4th St
Corvallis, OR 97333
Phone: 541-758-1674
Email: hophead@hotv.org
www.hotv.org

Deer Island Brewers
33678 Canaan Road
Deer Island, OR 97054
Phone: 503-366-3708
Email: dibrewers@deerislandbrewery.com
www.deerislandbrewery.com

Cascade Brewers Society
25835 Tanya Lane
Eugene, OR 97401
Phone: 541-935-5711
Email: cascadebrewers@yahoo.com

Siuslaw River Brewer`s Society
Florence, OR 97439
Phone: 541-902-7608
Email: northjetty1.1@gmail.com
Email: siuslawbrewers@gmail.com
Supported by Wakonda Brewery, members pay no dues.
Formed to educate people in the art of homebrewing.

Stout-Hearted Brewers-Umpqua
PO Box 503
Glide, OR 97443-0503
Phone: 503 496-0119

Hellgate Homebrewers
Grants Pass, OR
Phone: 541-660-0934
Email: bobw@draughtboard.org

Brewers of the Gorge (B.O.G.)

Hood River, OR

Though technically a Washington Homebrewers Assocation group, this group meets various places on both sides of the border.

http://www.wahomebrewers.org/index.php?option=com_content&task=view&id=105&Itemid=72

Linkville Brewers Association

Klamath Falls, OR 97601

Phone: 541-884-1743

Email: matt_machado@msn.com

www.linkvillebrewers.com

Bear Creek Homebrew Club

Medford, OR

Phone: 541-773-6673

www.thestoutpalace.com/?page_id=989

Rogue Valley Home Brewers

Medford, OR

Phone: 541- 778-2834

Email: Info@rvhomebrewers.com

www.roguebrewers.com

Strange Brew Homebrew Club
606 Vermillion St
Newberg, OR 97132
Phone: 503 538 9501
Email: strangebrewers@strangebrew.org
www.strangebrew.org

Beerded Clan, The
7805 SE Milwaukie Ave
Portland, OR 97202
Phone: 503-421-4235
Email: dannybartkowski@comcast.net

King of the Mountain Brewing
Portland, OR 97212
Phone: 503-422-3331
Email: batesm333@hotmail.com

NoPo Brews
8409 N Lombard St
Portland, OR 97203
Phone: 503-929-5454
Email: trevor_finn@yahoo.com
Email: nopobrews@gmail.com
http://site.nopobrews.com

Oregon Brew Crew

Portland, OR 97214
Phone: 503-232-8793
Email: president@oregonbrewcrew.com www.oregonbrewcrew.com
Great website, whether you are in Portland or not!

Raging Blue Penguin

7344 SE Steele St
Portland, OR 97206
Phone: 503-951-0855
Email: farmboy4@comcast.net

Umpqua Valley Home Brew Club

Roseburg, OR
Phone: 541-672-3331
Email: roseburghomebrewingclub@yahoo.com

Capitol Brewers

Salem, OR 97303
Phone: 503-581-5826
Email: rolson2198@aol.com
Email: dondarst@comcast.net

Anti-Gravity Brew Club

502 14th St NE
Salem, OR 97301
Phone: 503-851-5646
Email: clutch_brewery@yahoo.com

The Good Heathens

Contact: Randy Reid
1285 Criteser Loop
Toledo, OR 97391
Phone: 541-336-2458
Email: randyale@charter.net

Virtual Village Homebrew Society

While not technically an Oregon Club, this could be an option for those homebrewers in isolated areas
www.cmg.net/belgium/clubhub

Vessels

What to serve all this beer in is, for some, a controversial subject. For others, an old boot would do, as long as it has no effect on the flavor. Because we believe that being informed is important to any decision, we are including a small chapter on the subject of containers. Okay, it really has more to do with thinking it would be rather interesting, but the point is, here is the chapter.

Consumers who are unconcerned what their beer is served in believe the container question is simply marketing. So what is wrong with marketing? If a business can find a marketing strategy which will help them stand out, good for them!

Those who say the container affects the brew will tell you beer's color, aroma, and taste change the moment it touches the glass. Scientific studies have shown head is affected by the shape of the glass. Different head levels are desirable for different styles of beer. So it follows that different styles of beer should be served in different styles of glassware.

Some glasses may have markings, composed of small pits, in the bottoms. These small pits aid in nucleation, which allows the gas within to release more readily, thus retaining the head for longer periods.

If you are still doubtful that style makes a difference, give some consideration to what a clear or green bottle will do to the flavor of beer. Okay, maybe that is a different subject, but there must be a connection there somewhere.

Whatever your opinion on glass style, experts say to never frost a beer glass. The frostiness will melt and dilute your beer, in addition to changing the serving temperature.

In the United Kingdom, draft beer must be sold in Imperial measure. Though this may be achieved by "metered dispense," in the form of calibrated bumps, more commonly, certified one-pint glasses are used. An etched crown stamp and number showing crown certification has been the more common method of proof of measure, with the number an indication of the certifying authority. Recently though, the crown has been replaced by "PINT" and "CE." Like all changes, this has caused controversy. Regardless of the form of measure, selling beer without a form of measure is illegal.

Started in Oregon, the Honest Pint Project is a campaign to "bring transparency to glassware volumes. The intention of the project is to promote the use of glassware that ensures a patron receives 16 fluid ounces of beer." Obviously, in order to get a full sixteen ounces of beer, retailers would be required to uses glasses of eighteen ounces or more. Many advocate the 20-ounce imperial pint to allow plenty of head room. A list of Oregon brewpubs which have been certified by the Honest Pint Project as serving honest pints, may be found on their website at www.honestpintproject.org. Many also display the Honest Pint window decal.

Common today are "cheater" pints. They look like a 16-ounce glass, but though the use of thick bottoms and other illusions, actually contain only fourteen ounces. Why is this done? By serving a 14-ounce "pint," retailers can get an additional twenty beers out of a keg. Multiply this by the number of kegs sold through a year, and we are talking about a significant amount of revenue. If you ask for a "glass" of beer, you get what you get. But let's face it, if you order a "pint," you should get a pint or should be informed otherwise. If pubs are selling "glasses," who cares what the measure is? But...if they are selling "pints," personally, I was taught in elementary school that a pint is sixteen ounces.

Now the vessels...

Beer Boot

Beer boots, or *Bierstiefel*, have over a century of history and culture behind them. Legend has it that that a General promised his troops he would drink beer from his boot if they were successful in battle. After his men prevailed, the General had a glassmaker fashion a boot from glass to fulfill his promise without tasting his own feet and to avoid spoiling the beer in his leather boot. Soldiers have since enjoyed toasting their victories with a beer boot. At gatherings in Germany, Austria and Switzerland, beer boots are often passed among the guests for a festive drinking challenge.

Chalice or Goblet

These large, bowl shaped glasses with long stems are typically used for serving heavy Belgian ales, German bocks, and other big-sipping beers. Some chalices are etched on the bottom to provide for nucleation. While the terms "chalice" and "goblet" are typically used interchangeably, a chalice tends to be heavy and thick-walled, while a goblet is more delicate and thin.

Conical

Also known as the poor man's tumbler, this cone shaped pint glass is cheap to make, easy to store and easy to drink from. Conical glasses are typically used for stouts, porters, and bitters.

Flute

This touch of elegance enhances and showcases carbonation and aromas. The beer flute has a shorter stem than a champagne flute. With a smaller diameter mouth than midsection, to hold in carbonation, the flute glass is the preferred serving vessel for Belgian lambics and fruit beers.

Mason Jar

Invented and patented by John Landis Mason, a Philadelphia tinsmith, in 1858, these canning jars, sometimes with handles, are a favorite vessel of many beer drinkers. Comes in both pint and quart forms.

Mug

The sturdy mug, the only beer glass with easy to hold handles, is durable and holds a large volume of beer. Coming in different textures and different sizes, the mug is typically used for stouts, porters, and bitters.

Nonic

The nonic is actually a bulged version of a conical style, with the name deriving from "no nick". This is the most common type of pint glass found in pubs throughout the United Kingdom.

.

Pilsner

The tall, slender shape of the pilsner is designed to reveal the color, clarity, and carbonation of the beer while helping to maintain the head. Typically 12 ounces, the pilsner is used for many types of light beers, including pilsners and pale lagers.

Snifter

More commonly known for their use with brandy and cognac, the snifter's wide bowl and tapered mouth is perfect for capturing the aromas of strong ales.

Stange (Slender Cylinder)

A traditional German glass, the stange (German: *stick or rod*) is a tall, slender cylinder used to serve more delicate beers, amplifying malt and hop nuances. Traditionally used with Kölch.

Stien

A beer stein is a traditionally-German beer tankard or mug, made of pewter, silver, wood, porcelain, earthenware or glass; usually with a hinged lid and levered thumblift. The lid was implemented during the age of the Black Plague, to prevent diseased flies from getting into the beer.

Tulip

Visual and olfactory sensation are heightened by the tulip shape of these glasses. This shape not only helps trap the aroma, but also aids in head retention. Appropriate for Scottish ales, barleywines, Belgian ales and other aromatic beers.

Weizen

Beer's color is showcased by the thin walls and full length of the weizin (or wheat) glass. This vessel has plenty of headroom to accommodate the fluffy heads associated with the wheat beers served in this authentic Bavarian glass.

Yard

This three foot long, fragile, cumbersome glass, which holds almost three pints, is for … *fun*.

Fallen Comrades

Oregon breweries no longer in business - gone but not forgotten.
If there are missing fallen comrades, let us know for the next edition.

Blue Pine Brewpub, Grants Pass

Cartwright Brewing Company, Portland

Clinton Brewing, Portland

Cool Runnings Brewery, Portland

Elliot Glacier Public House, Parkdale

Hawks Brewing, Roseburg

Karlsson Brewing Company, Sandy

Liberator Brewing, Troutdale

Main Street Ale House, Gresham

Nor'Wester Brewery & Public House, Portland

Old World Pub & Brewery, Portland

The One Horse Tavern Brewing Company, Gaston
           brewery only, tavern still in business

Oregon Trader Brewing, Albany

Osprey Ale Brewing, Medford

Port Halling, Gresham

Rivergate Brewing, Portland

Roots Organic Brewing, Portland

Saxer Brewing Company, Lake Oswego

SKW Brewing Company, Newport

Southern & Pacific, Medford & Selma

Southside Speakeasy & Brewpub, Salem

Trask Brewery & Public House, McMinnville

Tucks Brewery, Portland

Umpqua Brewing, Roseburg

West Brothers Brewery, Eugene

Wild Duck Brewery, Eugene

Woof Breweries, Tualatin

Yamhill Brewing Company, Portland

Notable Beer Quotes

While there are only a few included, we thought you might find these amusing.

"Beauty is in the eye of the beer holder."
Unknown

"Without question, the greatest invention in the history of mankind is beer. Oh, I grant you that the wheel was also a fine invention, but the wheel does not go nearly as well with pizza."
-Dave Barry

"People who drink light 'beer' don't like the taste of beer; they just like to pee a lot."
-Capital Brewery, Middleton, WI

"A woman drove me to drink and I didn't even have the decency to thank her."
-W.C. Fields

"Beer is proof that God loves us and wants us to be happy."
-Benjamin Franklin

"I am a firm believer in the people. If given the truth, they can be depended upon to meet any national crisis. The great point is to bring them the real facts, and beer."
-Abraham Lincoln

"We old folks have to find our cushions and pillows in our tankards. Strong beer is the milk of the old."
-Martin Luther

"Prohibition makes you want to cry into your beer and denies you the beer to cry into."
-Don Marquis

"Whoever serves beer or wine watered down, he himself deserves in them to drown."
-Midieval plea for pure libations

"He was a wise man who invented beer."
-Plato

"*Brewers enjoy working to make beer as much as drinking beer instead of working.*"
-Harold Rudolph

"*[I recommend]... bread, meat, vegetables and beer.*"
-Sophocles' philosophy of a moderate diet

"*This is grain, which any fool can eat, but for which the Lord intended a more divine means of consumption... Beer!*"
-Robin Hood, Prince of Thieves, Friar Tuck

"*Pretty women make us BUY beer. Ugly women make us DRINK beer.*"
-Al Bundy

"*Give me a woman who loves beer and I will conquer the world.*"
-Kaiser Welhelm

"*Give a man a beer, he'll drink for the day. Teach a man to brew, he'll be drunk the rest of his life.*"
-Anonymous

"*SAM: What'd you like, Normie?*
NORM: A reason to live. Give me another beer."
-Cheers

"*A fine beer may be judged with only one sip, but it's better to be thoroughly sure.*"
-Czech Proverb

"*Life alas, is very drear. Up with the glass, down with the beer!*"
-Louis Untermeyer

"*There is more to life than beer alone, but beer makes those other things even better.*"
-Stephen Morris

"*Give beer to those who are perishing, wine to those who are in anguish; let them drink and forget their poverty and remember their misery no more.*"
-The Bible, Proverbs, 31:6-7 NIV

"*Beer, it's the best damn drink in the world. *"
-Jack Nicholson

"Most people hate the taste of beer to begin with. It is, however, a prejudice that many people have been able to overcome."
- Winston Churchill

"I wish you a merry Christmas and a Happy New Year, with your pockets full of money, and your cellar full of beer."
- Old English Carol

"The best place to drink beer is at home. Or on a river bank, if the fish don't bother you."
- American folk saying

"Everyone has his own lifetime dream. Mine is that someday, in a tavern somewhere, I'll hold up a pitcher of beer like this and I'll say, Bartender? Could I have a glass? And he'll look back at me and say, Friend, this is the glass!"
- Joe Martin (Mister Boffo comic strip)

"To some its a six-pack, to me it's a Support Group."
- Anonymous

"Let's all work to get people to drink more good beer, so if someone walks into your office and says he drinks Corona, don't immediately call him a dickhead."
- Michael Jackson, beer writer

"He that drinks strong beer, and goes to bed mellow, lives as he ought to live, and dies a hearty fellow."
- 17th century English drinking song

"Sometimes when I reflect back on all the beer I drink I feel ashamed - Then I look into the glass and think about the workers in the brewery and all of their hopes and dreams. If I didn't drink this beer, they might be out of work and their dreams would be shattered. Then I say to myself, 'It is better that I drink this beer and let their dreams come true than be selfish and worry about my liver."
- Jack Handy

Websites
In no particular order

In consideration of space, as well as a wish not to overwhelm the reader, we have limited the list of websites. If you desire more, just go onto one site and follow the rabbit trail.

http://oregonbeer.org/
Oregon Brewers Guild site
Includes a vast amount of information on Oregon craft beer, including an Oregon beer timeline

http://beeradvocate.com
Vast amount of information and links

www.beerinfo.com
Vast amount of information and links

www.realbeer.com
Lots of beer info

www.brewpublic.com
Pacific Northwest Brew Information

www.honestpintproject.org
Oregon based campaign for national transparency to glassware volumes

www.oregonhops.org
Oregon Hop Commission website

http://oregonstate.edu/dept/foodsci/undergrad/fermopt.htm
Oregon State University Fermentation Science Program

http://portland.taplister.com/
Discover where your favorite beers are being served

www.homebrewersassociation.org
Amazing website with info to please all beer lovers

www.barflymag.com
Portland bar info, including what is happening

www.camra.org.uk
Campaign for Real Ale in United Kingdom

http://www.travelportland.com/media/mbmedkit/mb_history.html
Portland beer timeline

http://www.oregonbrewfest.com/index2.php?p=links
This page has a plethora of sites for what and where

www.oregonbeerodyssey.com
Offers various beer classes and tastings

www.craftbrewcast.com/about.html
Interviews with brewers and related people

www.beer-brewing-advice.com
Beer brewing advice

www.homebrewersassociation.org
American Homebrewers Association, The Community for
Homebrewers

www.extension.ucdavis.edu/unit/brewing
UC Davis (California) brewing program

www.honestpintproject.org
Official website of the Honest Pint Project

www.oregoncraftbeermonth.com
A listing of events during July, Oregon Beer Month

www.fructosemalabsorptionhelp.com
Our book, shameless self promotion

http://thenewschoolbrewblog.blogspot.com
Beer Blog

http://www.beermonthclub.com
Get a new beer each month

http://www.notsoprobeer.com
Beer Blog

Track and Grade Your Beer Tour

On the following pages we have provided a simple and very informal way for you to track and evaluate the beers you taste. One of Bob's regrets is that he did not keep a beer diary as we crossed the state; as a result, with the exception of a few beers which stand out for a particular reason, the beers have become jumbled in the fragmented files of memory.

Following the several pages of our simple forms, you will find a standard beer judging form. You may prefer to use this.

Or, design your own evaluation in the format you prefer. But do keep a beer diary. Make notes in this book. Collect autographs at each brewery. Or just keep a simple note pad, just write it down!

You are welcome to reproduce the following form in whatever manner you wish.

Grading Your Beer Tour

Date	Brewery	Beer	Appearance	Aroma	Taste	Body	Overall Impression	Grade
1/1/2011	Sample Brewery	To-Good-To-Be-True	Dark w/nice head	Chocolate	Sweet	Creamy	Excelent Dessert Beer	A

Grading Your Beer Tour

Date	Brewery	Beer	Appearance	Aroma	Taste	Body	Overall Impression	Grade
1/1/2011	Sample Brewery	To-Good-To-Be-True	Dark w/nice head	Chocolate	Sweet	Creamy	Excelent Dessert Beer	A

Grading Your Beer Tour

Date	Brewery	Beer	Appearance	Aroma	Taste	Body	Overall Impression	Grade
1/1/2011	Sample Brewery	To-Good-To-Be-True	Dark w/nice head	Chocolate	Sweet	Creamy	Excelent Dessert Beer	A

Grading Your Beer Tour

Date	Brewery	Beer	Appearance	Aroma	Taste	Body	Overall Impression	Grade
1/1/2011	Sample Brewery	To-Good-To-Be-True	Dark w/nice head	Chocolate	Sweet	Creamy	Excelent Dessert Beer	A

Grading Your Beer Tour

Date	Brewery	Beer	Appearance	Aroma	Taste	Body	Overall Impression	Grade
1/1/2011	Sample Brewery	To-Good-To-Be-True	Dark w/nice head	Chocolate	Sweet	Creamy	Excelent Dessert Beer	A

Grading Your Beer Tour

Date	Brewery	Beer	Appearance	Aroma	Taste	Body	Overall Impression	Grade
1/1/2011	Sample Brewery	To-Good-To-Be-True	Dark w/nice head	Chocolate	Sweet	Creamy	Excelent Dessert Beer	A

Grading Your Beer Tour

Date	Brewery	Beer	Appearance	Aroma	Taste	Body	Overall Impression	Grade
1/1/2011	Sample Brewery	To-Good-To-Be-True	Dark w/nice head	Chocolate	Sweet	Creamy	Excelent Dessert Beer	A

Grading Your Beer Tour

Date	Brewery	Beer	Appearance	Aroma	Taste	Body	Overall Impression	Grade
1/1/2011	Sample Brewery	To-Good-To-Be-True	Dark w/nice head	Chocolate	Sweet	Creamy	Excelent Dessert Beer	A

Grading Your Beer Tour

Date	Brewery	Beer	Appearance	Aroma	Taste	Body	Overall Impression	Grade
1/1/2011	Sample Brewery	To-Good-To-Be-True	Dark w/nice head	Chocolate	Sweet	Creamy	Excelent Dessert Beer	A

Grading Your Beer Tour

Date	Brewery	Beer	Appearance	Aroma	Taste	Body	Overall Impression	Grade
1/1/2011	Sample Brewery	To-Good-To-Be-True	Dark w/nice head	Chocolate	Sweet	Creamy	Excelent Dessert Beer	A

Grading Your Beer Tour

Date	Brewery	Beer	Appearance	Aroma	Taste	Body	Overall Impression	Grade
1/1/2011	Sample Brewery	To-Good-To-Be-True	Dark w/nice head	Chocolate	Sweet	Creamy	Excelent Dessert Beer	A

Standard Beer Judging Form

BEER: [seasonal]
ABV: [bottle / can / draught]

BREWER:
Date:

Aroma : _____ (1 - 10)

Malty
- ☐ Light / moderate / heavy / harsh
- ☐ Bread - light / dark
- ☐ Cookie
- ☐ Grain / Hay / Straw / Cereal
- ☐ Toasted / Roasted / Burnt / Nutty
- ☐ Molasses / Caramel
- ☐ Chocolate - milk / dark
- ☐ Coffee - mild / strong
- ☐ Other: _____

Hoppy
- ☐ Light / moderate / heavy / harsh
- ☐ Flowers / Perfume / Herbs / Grass
- ☐ Pine / Spruce / Resin
- ☐ Citrus - grapefruit / orange
- ☐ Citrus - lemon / lime
- ☐ Other: _____

Yeasty
- ☐ Light / moderate / heavy / harsh
- ☐ Dough / Sweat
- ☐ Horse blanket / Barnyard / Leather
- ☐ Soap / Cheese
- ☐ Earth / Mold / Cobwebs
- ☐ Meat / Broth
- ☐ Other: _____

Miscellaneous
- ☐ Banana / Bubble gum
- ☐ Grape / Raisin / Plum / Prune / Date
- ☐ Apple / Pear / Peach / Pineapple
- ☐ Cherry / Raspberry / Cassis
- ☐ Wine - white / red
- ☐ Port - tawny / ruby
- ☐ Cask wood (e.g., oak)
- ☐ Smoke / Tar / Charcoal / Soy sauce
- ☐ Toffee / Butter / Butterscotch
- ☐ Honey / Brown sugar / Maple syrup
- ☐ Coriander / Ginger
- ☐ Allspice / Nutmeg / Clove / Cinnamon
- ☐ Vanilla / Pepper / Licorice / Cola
- ☐ Alcohol
- ☐ Dust / Chalk
- ☐ Vegetable / Cooked corn
- ☐ Cardboard / Paper
- ☐ Medicine / Solvent / Band-aid
- ☐ Soured milk / Vinegar
- ☐ Sulfur / Skunk
- ☐ Other: _____

Appearance : _____ (1 - 5)

Head - Initial appearance
- ☐ Size - small / average / large / huge
- ☐ Rocky
- ☐ Creamy
- ☐ Frothy
- ☐ Fizzy
- ☐ Virtually none

Head - Color
- ☐ White
- ☐ Off-white
- ☐ Light brown

Head - Lacing
- ☐ Excellent
- ☐ Good
- ☐ Fair
- ☐ Virtually none

Head - Longevity
- ☐ Fully lasting
- ☐ Mostly lasting
- ☐ Mostly diminishing
- ☐ Fully diminishing

Body - Clarity
- ☐ Clear - sparkling / normal / flat
- ☐ Cloudy - hazy / murky / muddy

Body - Particles
- ☐ Size -
       tiny / small / medium / large / huge
- ☐ Density - thin / average / thick

- ☐ Bottle conditioned

Body - Hue
- ☐ Light / medium / dark
- ☐ Yellow
- ☐ Amber
- ☐ Orange
- ☐ Red
- ☐ Brown
- ☐ Black
- ☐ Other:_____

Flavor : _____ (1 - 10)

Initial flavor
- ☐ Sweet - light / moderate / heavy / harsh
- ☐ Acidic - light / moderate / heavy / harsh
- ☐ Bitter - light / moderate / heavy / harsh
- ☐ Acetic (vinegar)
- ☐ Sour (sour milk)
- ☐ Salty

Finish - Flavor
- ☐ Sweet - light / moderate / heavy / harsh
- ☐ Acidic - light / moderate / heavy / harsh
- ☐ Bitter - light / moderate / heavy / harsh
- ☐ Acetic (vinegar)
- ☐ Sour (sour milk)
- ☐ Salty

Finish - Duration
- ☐ Short
- ☐ Average
- ☐ Long

Palate : _____ (1 - 5)

Body
- ☐ Light
- ☐ Light to medium
- ☐ Medium
- ☐ Medium to full
- ☐ Full

Texture
- ☐ Dry
- ☐ Watery
- ☐ Oily
- ☐ Creamy
- ☐ Syrupy
- ☐ Other: _____

Carbonation
- ☐ Fizzy
- ☐ Lively
- ☐ Soft
- ☐ Flat

Other: _____

Finish - Feel
- ☐ Metallic
- ☐ Chalky
- ☐ Astringent - light / moderate / heavy / harsh
- ☐ Alcoholic - light / moderate / heavy / harsh

Other: _____

Overall Score (1-20): _____

Comments:

Other Books You May Find Interesting...

Shameless self promotion...
Our first book

Full-color book on
Bend Breweries
By Andre' Bartels &
Bob Woodward

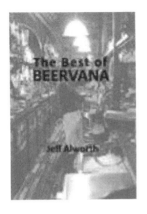

A collection of the
blogger posts by
Jeff Alworth

Brewery Listings

On the following pages, you will find four different lists of Oregon breweries. The lists are alphabetical, by city, by region, and by tour route. We hope you will find these lists helpful and suggest you add and subtract as breweries come and go.

Included in the alphabetical list for your convenience are notations indicating if a brewpub is family friendly; if a brewery bottles or cans their beer, or has plans to soon; an indication of the type, is this location a brewery, a brewpub, or a pub; and a blank box so you may keep track of those places you have visited.

Too late to include: Just as we went to publication it was announced that Prineville will be getting their own brewpub, Solstice Brewing Company. While we do not yet have an address or an opening date, the location is on Main Street a block from the Pine Theater.

Brewery Listing – Alphabetical

Note: Places are listed by the owning company. e.g.: *Rogue Green Dragon, McMenamins High Street Brewery, Lompoc Oaks Bottom Public House*

Types: B=Brewery Only, BP=Brewpub, P=Pub Only, BT= Brewing w/Tasting Room Only

If a Brewpub is family friendly, it will be noted in the Family Friendly column with an "F" or the latest hour children are allowed. If children are never allowed, it is noted with an "N."

We have left those who do not currently bottle, blank, so the reader may fill them in as they begin bottling.

B=Bottle, C=Can, S=Bottles or Cans Coming Soon, L=Limited

Family Friendly	Bottles or Cans	Type	Visited	Name	Address	City	Phone	Website
F	B	B		10 Barrel Brewing	20750 High Desert Ln #107	Bend	541-585-1007	www.10barrel.com
	B	P		10 Barrel Brewing	1135 NW Galveston	Bend	541-678-5228	www.10barrel.com
F	S	BP		4th Street Brewing Company	77 NE 4th St	Gresham	503-669-0569	www.4thstreetbrewing.com
F 11 p	B	BP		Alameda Brewhouse	4765 NE Fremont	Portland	503-460-9025	www.alamedabrewhouse.com
	B	B		Ambacht Brewing Company	1055 NE 25th Ave, Suite N	Hillsboro	503-828-1400	www.ambacht.us
N	B	BP		Amnesia Brewing Company	832 North Beech	Portland	503-281-7708	www.amnesiabrew.com
F	S	BP		Astoria Brewing Company / Wet Dog Café	144 11th St	Astoria	503-352-6975	www.myspace.com/wetdogcafe
F		BP		Barley Browns Brewpub	2190 Main St	Baker City	541-523-4266	www.barleybrowns.com
	B	BT		Beer ValLey Brewing Company	937 SE 12th Avenue	Ontario	541-881-9088	www.beervalleybrewing.com
	S	B		Beetje Brewery	4206 SE Taggart St	Portland	503-819-0758	www.beetjebrewery.com
F	B	BP		Bend Brewing Company	1019 NW Brooks St	Bend	541-383-1599	www.bendbrewingco.com

			Name	Address	City	Phone	Website
F		BP	Big Horn Brewing	515 12th St. SE	Salem	503-363-1904	www.theram.com/
F		BP	Big Horse Brewpub / Horsefeathers	115 State St	Hood River	541-386-4411	
F		BP	Bill's Tavern & Brewhouse	188 N Hemlock	Cannon Beach	541-436-2202	
F		BP	BJ's Restaurant & Brewhouse	1600 Coburg Rd #4	Eugene	541-342-6114	www.bjsbrewhouse.com/
F 9p	B L	BP	Block 15 Restaurant & Brewery	300 SW Jefferson Ave	Corvallis	541-758-2077	www.block15.com
F		BP	Blue House Café & Brewery	62467 N Hwy 47 / 919 Bridge St	Vernonia	503-429-4350	facebook
	S	BT	Boneyard Beer Company	37 NW Lake Place, Suite B	Bend	541-323-2325	www.boneyardbeer.com
F 9p	S	BP	Breakside Brewery	820 NE Dekum	Portland	503-719-6475	www.breaksidebrews.com/
F 9p		BP	Brewers Union Local 180	48329 E 1st St	Oakridge	541-782-2024	www.brewersunion.com
		B	Brick Towne Brewery	3612 Calle Vista Drive	Medford	541-941-0792	www.bricktownebeer.com
F	B	BP	BridgePort Ale House	3632 SE Hawthorne	Portland	503-233-6540	www.BridgePortBrew.com
F	B	BP	BridgePort Brewpub & Bakery	1313 NW Marshall	Portland	503-241-3612	www.BridgePortBrew.com
F		BP	Broadway Grill & Brewery	1700 NE Broadway	Portland	503-284-4460	
	S	BP	Buckman Village Brewery	909 SE Yamhill	Portland	503-517-0660	www.buckmanbrewery.com
F 9p		BP	Burnside Brewing Company (was Alchemy)	701 Burnside	Portland	503-946-8151	www.burnsidebrewco.com
F 8p	S	BP	Calapooia Brewing Co.	140 Hill St. NE	Albany	541-928-1931	www.calapooiabrewing.com
	C B	B	Caldera Brewing Company	540 Clover Lane	Ashland		www.calderabrewing.com
F 9p	C B	P	Caldera Tap House	31 Water St #2	Ashland	541-482-4677	www.buckmanbrewery.com

			Name	Address	City	Phone	Website
F 9p	B	B	Captured by Porches Brewing Company	40 Cowlitz St	St Helens	503-757-8359	www.capturedbyporches.com
F	B	BP	Cascade Brewery / Cascade Brewing Barrel House	935 SE Belmont St	Portland		www.cascadebrewing.com
F	B	BP	Cascade Brewery / Raccoon Lodge & Brewpub	7424 SW Beaverton Hillsdale Hwy	Portland	503-296-0110	www.cascadebrewing.com
	B	B	Cascade Lakes Brewing	2141 SW 1st St	Redmond	541-923-3110	www.cascadelakes.com
F	B	P	Cascade Lakes Brewing	64 SW Century Dr	Bend	541-389-1853	www.cascadelakes.com
F	B	P	Cascade Lakes Brewing - 7th St Brewhouse	855 SW 7th St	Redmond	541-923-1795	www.cascadelakes.com
F	B	P	Cascade Lakes Brewing - Red Dog Depot	3716 SW 21st Place	Redmond	541-923-6400	www.cascadelakes.com
F	B	P	Cascade Lakes Brewing - The Lodge	1441 SW Chandler Ave #100	Bend	541-388-4998	www.cascadelakes.com
	B	P	Cascade Lakes Brewing - Tumalo Tavern	64670 Stickler #103	Bend	541-330-2323	www.cascadelakes.com
F	S	BP	Coalition Brewing Company	2724 SE Ankeny	Portland	503-894-8080	www.coalitionbrewing.com
F	S	BP	Columbia River Brewing Company	1728 NE 40th Ave	Portland	503-943-6157	facebook
	B	BT	Deschutes Brewery	901 SW Simpson	Bend	541-385-8606	www.deschutesbrewery.com
F	B	BP	Deschutes Brewery & Public House	1044 NW Bond St	Bend	541-382-9242	www.deschutesbrewery.com
F	B	BP	Deschutes Brewery & Public House	210 NW 11th Ave	Portland	503-296-4906	www.deschutesbrewery.com
F		BP	Double Mountain Brewery	8 4th St	Hood River	541-387-0045	www.doublemountainbrewery.com
	B	B	Draper Brewing	7752 Hwy 42	Tenmile	541-679-9482	www.maxsfannocreek.com
F		BP	Fanno Creek Brewpub	12562 SW Main St	Tigard	503-624-9400	www.maxsfannocreek.com
F	C	BP	Fearless Brewing Co & Tap House	326 Broadway	Estacada	503-630-2337	www.fearless1.com
	B	B	Fire Mountain Brew House	10800 NW Rex Brown Rd	Carlton	503-852-7378	www.firemountainbrewhouse.com

F							
F	S	BP	Flat Tail Brewing	1st & Madison	Corvallis	541-758-2229	www.flattailcorvallis.com
F	C	BP	Fort George Brewery	1483 Duane St	Astoria	503-325-7468	www.fortgeorgebrewery.com
F	B	BP	Full Sail Brewery at Riverplace	0307 SW Montgomery	Portland		www.fullsailbrewing.com
F	B	BP	Full Sail Brewing Company	506 Columbia St	Hood River	541-386-2281	www.fullsailbrewing.com
	S	B	Gilgamesh Brewing	2953 Ridgeway Drive	Turner	541-871-6688	www.gilgameshbrewing.com
F	B	BP	Golden Valley Brewery & Pub	980 E 4th	McMinnville	503-472-2739	www.goldenvalleybrewery.com
F	S	BT	Good Life Brewing Company	1355 SW Commerce	Bend	541-440-5288	www.goodlifebrewing.com
F	B	BP	Hair of the Dog Brewing Company	61 Yam Hill	Portland	503-235-8743	www.hairofthedog.com
	B	B	Heater Allen Brewery	907 NE 10th Ave	McMinnville	503-472-4898	www.heaterallen.com
F		BP	Hop Valley Brewing	980 Kruse Way	Springfield	541-744-3330	www.hopvalleybrewing.com
F	B	BP	Hopworks Urban Brewery	2944 SE Powell Blvd	Portland	503-232-4676	www.hopworksbeer.com
F	B	BP	Jacksonville Inn	175 E California St	Jacksonville	541-899-1900	www.jacksonvilleinn.com
F	B	BP	Klamath Basin Brewing Company / The Creamery Pub	1320 Main St	Klamath Falls	541-891-5180	www.hopvalleybrewing.com
F	B	P	Laurelwood Brewing Company / Portland International Airport: Concourse A	7000 NE Airport Way	Portland	503-493-9427	www.laurelwoodbrewpub.com
F	B	BP	Laurelwood Public House & Brewery	5115 NE Sandy	Portland	503-282-0622	www.laurelwoodbrewpub.com
F	B	P	Laurelwood Public House / Portland International Airport: Concourse E	7000 Airport Way	Portland	503-493-4204	www.laurelwoodbrewpub.com
F	B	BP	Lompoc Brewing / 5th Quadrant	3901-B N Williams Ave	Portland	503-288-3996	www.newoldlompoc.com/5thquadranthome.html
F	B	P	Lompoc Brewing / Hedge House	3412 SE Division St.	Portland	503-235-2215	www.newoldlompoc.com

			Name	Address	City	Phone	Website
F	B	BP	Lompoc Brewing / New Old Lompoc Brewery	1616 NW 23rd	Portland	503-225-1855	www.newoldlompoc.com
F	B	P	Lompoc Brewing / Oaks Bottom Public House	1621 SE Bybee Blvd	Portland	503-232-1728	www.newoldlompoc.com
	B	B	Long Brewing	29380 NE Owls Ln	Newberg	503-349-8341	www.longbrewing.com
F	B	P	Lucky Labrador Beer Hall	1945 NW Quimby	Portland	503-517-4352	www.luckylab.com
F	B	BP	Lucky Labrador Brewpub	915 SE Hawthorne	Portland	503-236-3555	www.luckylab.com
F	B	BP	Lucky Labrador Public House	7675 SW Capital Hwy	Portland	503-244-2537	www.luckylab.com
F	B	P	Lucky Labrador Tap Room	1700 N Killingsworth	Portland	503-505-9511	www.luckylab.com
F	B	BP	MacTarnahan's Tap Room /Pyramid Brewery / Independent Brewers United	2730 NW 31st St	Portland	503-226-7623	www.macsbeer.com
F 9p	B	BP	Mash Tun Brewing	2204 NE Alberta St	Portland	503-548-4491	www.themashtunbrewpub.com
F	B	P	McMenamins Back Stage Bar	3702 SE Hawthorn Blvd	Portland	503-236-9234	www.mcmenamins.com
F	B	P	McMenamins Bagdad Theater	3702 SE Hawthorn Blvd	Portland	503-236-9234	www.mcmenamins.com
F	B	P	McMenamins Barley Mill Pub	1629 SE Hawthorn Blvd	Portland	503-231-1492	www.mcmenamins.com
F	B	P	McMenamins Blue Moon Tavern & Grill	432 NW 21st Ave	Portland	503-231-1492	www.mcmenamins.com
F	B	P	McMenamins Boon's Treasury	888 Liberty St. NE	Salem	503-399-9062	www.mcmenamins.com
F	B	P	McMenamins Breweries (Corporate)	430 Killingsworth St	Portland	503-223-0109	www.mcmenamins.com
F	B	P	McMenamins Cedar Hills	2927 SW Cedar Hills Blvd	Beaverton	503-641-0151	www.mcmenamins.com
F	B	P	McMenamins Chapel Pub	430 N Killingsworth St	Portland	503-286-0372	www.mcmenamins.com
F	B	BP	McMenamins Cornelius Pass Roadhouse & Imbrie Hall	4045 NW Cornelius Pass Rd	Hillsboro	503-640-6174	www.mcmenamins.com
F	B	P	McMenamins Corvallis	420 NW 3rd St	Corvallis	541-758-6044	www.mcmenamins.com

F	B	P	McMenamins Crystal Ballroom & Lola's	1332 W Burnside	Portland	503-225-0047	www.mcmenamins.com
F	B	P	McMenamins Crystal Hotel (open 5-2011)	3035 W 12th Ave	Portland	503-972-2670	www.mcmenamins.com
F	B	P	McMenamins East 19th Street Café	1485 E 19th Ave	Eugene	541-342-4025	www.mcmenamins.com
F	B	P	McMenamins Edgefield	2126 SW Halsey	Troutdale	503-669-8610	www.mcmenamins.com
F	B	BP	McMenamins Fulton Pub & Brewery	0618 SW Nebraska St	Portland	503-246-9530	www.mcmenamins.com
F	B	P	McMenamins Grand Lodge	3505 Pacific Ave	Forest Grove	503-992-9533	www.mcmenamins.com
F	B	P	McMenamins Greater Trumps	1520 SE 37th Ave	Portland	503-235-4530	www.mcmenamins.com
F	B	P	McMenamins Greenway Pub	12272 SW Scholls Ferry Rd	Tigard	503-590-1865	www.mcmenamins.com
F	B	BP	McMenamins High Street Brewery	1243 High St	Eugene	541-345-4913	www.mcmenamins.com
F	B	BP	McMenamins Highland Pub & Brewery	4225 SE 182nd	Gresham	503-665-3015	www.mcmenamins.com
F	B	BP	McMenamins Hillsdale Brewery & Public House	1505 SW Sunset Blvd	Portland	503-246-3938	www.mcmenamins.com
F	B	P	McMenamins Hotel Oregon	310 N Evans St	McMinnville	503-223-0109	www.mcmenamins.com
F	B	BP	McMenamins John Barleycorns	14610 SW Sequoia Pkwy	Tigard	503-684-2688	www.mcmenamins.com
F	B	P	McMenamins Kennedy School	5376 NE 33rd Ave	Portland	503-249-3983	www.mcmenamins.com
F	B	P	McMenamins Lighthouse Brewpub	4157 N Hwy 101, Suite 107	Lincoln City	541-994-7238	www.mcmenamins.com
F	B	P	McMenamins Mall 205	9710 SE Washington St, Suite A	Portland	503-254-5411	www.mcmenamins.com
F	B	P	McMenamins Market StreetPub	1526 SW 10th Ave	Portland	503-497-0160	www.mcmenamins.com
F	B	P	McMenamins Mission Theater	1624 NW Glisan St	Portland	503-645-0286	www.mcmenamins.com
F	B	P	McMenamins Murray & Allen	6179 SW Murray Blvd	Beaverton	503-644-4562	www.mcmenamins.com
F	B	P	McMenamins North Bank	22 Club Rd	Eugene	541-343-5622	www.mcmenamins.com

F	B	BP	McMenamins Oak Hills Brew Pub	14740 NW Cornell Rd #80	Portland	503-223-0109	www.mcmenamins.com
F	B	P	McMenamins Old St. Francis School	700 NW Bond St	Bend	541-382-5174	www.mcmenamins.com
F	B	P	McMenamins on Broadway	1504 NE Broadway St, Suite 900	Portland	503-288-9498	www.mcmenamins.com
F	B	BP	McMenamins on Monroe	2001 NW Monroe	Corvallis	541-758-0080	www.mcmenamins.com
F	B	P	McMenamins Oregon City	102 9th St	Oregon City	503-655-8032	www.mcmenamins.com
F	B	P	McMenamins Raleigh Hills Pub	4495 SW Scholls Ferry Rd	Portland	503-292-1723	www.mcmenamins.com
F	B	BP	McMenamins Rams Head	2282 NW Hoyt St	Portland	503-221-0098	www.mcmenamins.com
F	B	P	McMenamins Ringlers Annex	1223 SW Stark St	Portland	503-525-0520	www.mcmenamins.com
F	B	BP	McMenamins Ringlers Pub	1332 SW Burnside St	Portland	503-225-0627	www.mcmenamins.com
F	B	P	McMenamins Riverwood Pub	8136 SW Hall Blvd	Beaverton	503-643-7189	www.mcmenamins.com
F	B	P	McMenamins Rock Creek Tavern	10000 NW Old Cornelius Pass Rd	Hillsboro	503-645-3822	www.mcmenamins.com
F	B	BP	McMenamins Roseburg Station Pub & Brewery	700 SE Sheridan	Roseburg	541-672-1934	www.mcmenamins.com
F	B	P	McMenamins St. Johns Theater & Pub	8203 N Ivanhoe St	Portland	503-283-8520	www.mcmenamins.com
F	B	P	McMenamins Sand Trap	1157 N Marion Ave	Gearhart	503-717-8150	www.mcmenamins.com
F	B	P	McMenamins Sherwood	15976 SW Tualatin-Sherwood Rd	Sherwood	503-625-3547	www.mcmenamins.com
F	B	P	McMenamins Sunnyside	9757 SE Sunnyside Rd, Suite K	Clackamas	503-653-8011	www.mcmenamins.com
F	B	P	McMenamins Tavern & Pool	1716 NW 23rd Ave	Portland	503-227-0929	www.mcmenamins.com
F	B	BP	McMenamins Thompson Brewery & Public House	3575 Liberty Rd S	Salem	503-363-7286	www.mcmenamins.com
F	B	BP	McMenamins West Linn	2090 SW 8th Ave	West Linn	503-656-2970	www.mcmenamins.com

F	B	P	Name	Address	City	Phone	Website
F	B		McMenamins White Eagle Café, Saloon & Rock 'n' Roll Hotel	836 N Russell St	Portland	503-282-6810	www.mcmenamins.com
F	B	BP	Mia & Pia's Pizzeria / Brewhouse	3545 Summers Ln	Klamath Falls	541-884-4880	www.miapia.com
F 8p	B	BP	Migration Brewing	2828 NE Glisan St	Portland	503-206-5221	www.migrationbrewing.com
F	B	BP	Mt Emily Ale House	1202 Adams Ave	La Grand	541-962-1560	www.mtemilyalehouse.com
F		BP	Mt Hood Brewing / Ice Axe Grill	87304 E Government Camp Loop	Government Camp	503-272-3172	www.mthoodbrewing.com
F		BP	Mutiny Brewing Company	600 N Main St	Joseph	541-432-5274	www.mutinybrewing.blogspot.com
		B	Nation Brewery	1321 NE Couch St	Portland	971-678-7116	www.natianbrewery.com
F 8p	B	BT	Ninkasi Brewing Company	272 Van Buren St	Eugene	541-344-2739	www.ninkasibrewing.com
	B	BT	OakShire Brewing	1055 Madera St	Eugene	541-688-4555	www.oakbrew.ocm
	S	BT	Occidental Brewing		Portland	503-810-7920	www.occidentalbrewing.com
	?	B	Off the Rail Brewing Company	2800 Taylor Way	Forest Grove	541-992-8889	www.offtherailbrewing.com
F		BP	Old Market Pub & Brewery	6959 SW Multnomah Blvd	Portland	503-206-5221	www.drinkbeerhere.com
	B	B	Oregon Trail Brewing	341 SW 2nd St	Corvallis	541-758-3527	www.oregontrailbrewery.com
	B	B	Pale Horse Brewing	2359 Hyacinth St NE	Salem		Facebook
	B	B	Panty Dropper Ale		Aloha		
F	B	BP	Pelican Pub & Brewery	33180 Cape Kiwanda Dr	Pacific City	503-965-7007	www.pelicanbrewery.com
F		P	Philadelphia's Steak & Hoagies	6410 SE Milwaukee Ave	Portland	503-239-8544	www.phillypdx.com
F		BP	Philadelphia's Steak & Hoagies	18625 Willamette Dr	West Linn	503-699-4130	www.phillypdx.com
F		BP	Portland U-Brew – P.U.B.	6237 SE Milwaukee Ave	Portland	503-432-9746	www.portlandubrewandpub.com

F		BP	Prodigal Son Brewery & Pub	230 SE Court Ave	Pendleton	541-276-6090	www.prodigalsonbrewery.com

			Name	Address	City	Phone	Website
F		BP	Prodigal Son Brewery & Pub	230 SE Court Ave	Pendleton	541-276-6090	www.prodigalsonbrewery.com
F		BP	Ram Restaurant & Brewery	515 12th Street	Salem	503-363-1905	www.theram.com
F		BP	Ram Restaurant & Brewery / Clackamas Town Center	11860 SE 82nd Ave, #3050	Happy Valley	503-659-1282	www.theram.com
F		BP	Rock Bottom Brewery	206 SW Morrison	Portland	503-796-2739	www.rockbottom.com/
F	B	BP	Rogue Ales	2320 OSU Dr	Newport	541-867-3660	www.rogue.com
F	B	BP	Rogue Ales Eugene City Brewery	844 Olive St.	Eugene	541-345-4155	www.rogue.com
F	B	P	Rogue Ales Public House	748 SW Bay Blvd	Newport	541-265-3188	www.rogue.com
F	B	P	Rogue Ales Public House Astoria Pier 39	100 39th St, Pier 39	Astoria	503-325-5964	www.rogue.com
F	B	P	Rogue Ales Public House Portland International Airport: Concourse D	7000 NE Airport Way	Portland	503-460-4040	www.rogue.com
F	B	P	Rogue Ales Public House Saturday Market	108 W Burnside	Portland	503-241-3800	www.rogue.com
F	B	BP	Rogue Brewery	1339 NW Flanders	Portland	503-222-5910	www.rogue.com
F	B	BP	Rogue Green Dragon Bistro & Brew Pub	928 SE 9th Ave	Portland	503-517-0606	http://www.pdxgreendragon.com
F	B	P	Rogue Wolf Eel Café at the Oregon Coast Aquarium	2820 SE Ferry Slip Rd	Newport	541-867-3474	www.rogue.com
F	B	BP	Seven Brides Brewing	990 N 1st St	Silverton	503-779-6009	www.sevenbridesbrewing.com
	B	BP	Siletz Ales (Calapooia Brewing)	140 Hill St. NE	Albany	541-928-1931	www.calapooiabrewing.com
F 6p	B	BP	Silver Moon Brewing & Taproom	24 NW Greenwood Ave	Bend	541-388-8331	www.SilverMoonBrewing.com
	B	BT	Southern Oregon Brewing Company	1922 United Way	Medford	541-776-9898	www.sobrewing.com
F	B	BP	Standing Stone Brewing Company	101 Oak St	Ashland	541-482-2448	www.standingstonebrewing.com

			Name	Address	City	Phone	Website
F		BP	Steelhead Brewing	199 E 5th Ave	Eugene	541-686-2739	www.steelheadbrewery.com
F	B	BP	Terminal Gravity Brewing Company	803 SE School St	Enterprise	541-426-0158	www.terminalgravitybrewing.com
F	S	BP	Three Creeks Brewing Company	721 Desperado Ct	Sisters	541-549-1963	www.threecreeksbrewing.com
N		BP	Tugboat Brewing Company	711 SW Ankeny St	Portland	503-226-2508	www.d2m.com/Tugwebsite/future.htm
F	B	BT	Upright Brewing	240 N Broadway	Portland		www.uprightbrewing.com
		B	Vertigo Brewing	21240 NW Nicholas Ct	Hillsboro	503-645-6644	www.vertigobrew.com
		P	Wakonda Brewing Company	1725 Kingwood St #4	Florence	541-991-0694	www.facebook.com/group.php?gid=353722712010
	B	B	Walkabout Brewing	921 Mason Way	Medford	541-664-7763	facebook
F		P	Warren House Pub	3301 S Hemlock	Cannon Beach	503-436-1130	Facebook
F	B	BP	Widmer Brothers Brewing Company	929 N Russell	Portland	503-281-2437	www.widmer.com
F	B	BP	Widmer Brothers / Kona Brewry	929 N Russell	Portland	503-281-2437	www.widmer.com
F	B	B	Widmer Brothers Brewing Company & Redhook Ale Brewery	1 Center Ct # 120	Portland	503-281-2437	www.widmer.com
F	B	P	Wild River Brewing & Pizza	16279 Hwy 101 S	Brookings-Harbor	541-469-7454	www.wildriverbrewing.com
F	B	BP	Wild River Brewing & Pizza	249 N Redwood Hwy	Cave Junction	541-592-3556	www.wildriverbrewing.com
F	B	BP	Wild River Brewing & Pizza	595 NE E St	Grants Pass	541-471-7487	www.wildriverbrewing.com
F	B	P	Wild River Brewing & Pizza	2684 N Pacific Hwy	Medford	541-773-7487	www.wildriverbrewing.com
F	B	P	Wild River Pub & Public House	533 NE F St	Grants Pass	541-474-4456	www.wildriverbrewing.com

Brewery Listing – by City

See Alphabetical Brewery Listing for website addresses

Brewery	Address	City	Phone
Calapooia Brewing Co.	140 Hill St. NE	Albany	541-928-1931
Siletz Ales (Calapooia Brewing)	140 Hill St. NE	Albany	541-928-1931
Panty Dropper Ale		Aloha	
Caldera Brewing Company	540 Clover Lane	Ashland	
Caldera Tap House	31 Water St #2	Ashland	(541) 482-HOPS
Standing Stone Brewing Company	101 Oak St	Ashland	541-482-2448
Astoria Brewing Company / Wet Dog Café	144 11th St	Astoria	503-352-6975
Fort George Brewery	1483 Duane St	Astoria	503-325-7468
Rogue Ales Public House / Astoria Pier 39	100 39th St, Pier 39	Astoria	503-325-5964
Barley Browns Brewpub	2190 Main St	Baker City	541-523-4266
McMenamins / Cedar Hills	2927 SW Cedar Hills Blvd	Beaverton	503-641-0151
McMenamins / Murray & Allen	6179 SW Murray Blvd	Beaverton	503-644-4562
McMenamins / Riverwood Pub	8136 SW Hall Blvd	Beaverton	503-643-7189
10 Barrel Brewing	20750 High Dessert Ln #107	Bend	541-585-1007
10 Barrel Brewing	1135 NW Galveston	Bend	541-678-5228
Bend Brewing Company	1019 NW Brooks St	Bend	541-383-1599
Boneyard Beer Company	37 NW Lake Place, Suite B	Bend	541-323-2325
Cascade Lakes Brewing	64 SW Century Dr	Bend	541-389-1853
Cascade Lakes Brewing - The Lodge	1441 SW Chandler Ave #100	Bend	541-388-4998
Cascade Lakes Brewing - Tumalo Tavern	64670 Stickler #103	Bend	541-330-2323
Deschutes Brewery	901 SW Simpson	Bend	541-385-8606

Deschutes Brewery & Public House	1044 NW Bond St	Bend	541-382-9242
McMinamens Old St. Francis School	700 NW Bond St	Bend	541-382-5174
Noble Brewing Company	1355 SW Commerce	Bend	
Silver Moon Brewing & Taproom	24 NW Greenwood Ave	Bend	541-388-8331
Wild River Brewing & Pizza	16279 Hwy 101 S	Brookings-Harbor	541-469-7454
Bill's Tavern & Brewhouse	188 N Hemlock	Cannon Beach	503-436-2202
Warren House Pub	3301 S Hemlock	Cannon Beach	503-436-1130
Fire Mountain Brew House	10800 NW Rex Brown Rd	Carlton	503-852-7378
Wild River Brewing & Pizza	249 N Redwood Hwy	Cave Junction	541-592-3556
McMenamins / Sunnyside	9757 SE Sunnyside Rd, Suite K	Clackamas	503-653-8011
Block 15 Restaurant & Brewery	300 SW Jefferson Ave	Corvallis	541-758-2077
Flat Tail Brewing	1st & Madison	Corvallis	541-758-2229
McMenamins Corvallis	420 NW 3rd St	Corvallis	541-758-6044
McMenamins on Monroe	2001 NW Monroe	Corvallis	541-758-0080
Oregon Trail Brewing	341 SW 2nd St	Corvallis	541-758-3527
Terminal Gravity Brewing Company	803 SE School St	Enterprise	541-426-0158
Fearless Brewing Co & Tap House	326 Broadway	Estacada	503-630-2337
BJ's Restaurant & Brewhouse	1600 Coburg Rd #4	Eugene	541-342-6114
Hop Valley Brewing	701 High St #200	Eugene	541-579-8000
McMenamins / High Street Brewery	1243 High St	Eugene	541-345-4913
McMenamins North Bank	22 Club Rd	Eugene	541-343-5622
McMenamins/East 19th Street Café	1485 E 19th Ave	Eugene	541-342-4025
Ninkasi Brewing Company	272 Van Buren St	Eugene	541-344-2739
OakShire Brewing	1055 Madera St	Eugene	541-688-4555

Rogue Ales / Eugene City Brewery	844 Olive St.	Eugene	541-345-4155
Steelhead Brewing	199 E 5th Ave	Eugene	541-686-2739
Wakonda Brewing Company	1725 Kingwood St #4	Florence	541-991-0694
McMenamins / Grand Lodge	3505 Pacific Ave	Forest Grove	503-992-9533
Off the Rail Brewing Company	2800 Taylor Way	Forest Grove	503-992-8989
McMenamins Sand Trap	1157 N Marion Ave	Gearhart	503-717-8150
Mt Hood Brewing / Ice Axe Grill	87304 E Government Camp Loop	Government Camp	503-272-3172
Wild River Brewing & Pizza	595 NE E St	Grants Pass	541-471-7487
Wild River Pub & Public House	533 NE F St	Grants Pass	541-474-4456
4th Street Brewing Company	77 NE 4th St	Gresham	503-669-0569
McMenamins / Highland Pub & Brewery	4225 SE 182nd Ave	Gresham	503-665-3015
Ram Restaurant & Brewery / Clackamas Town Center	11860 SE 82nd Ave, #3050	Happy Valley	503-659-1282
Ambacht Brewing Company	1055 NE 25th Ave, Suite N	Hillsboro	503-828-1400
McMenamins / Cornelius Pass Roadhouse & Imbrie Hall	4045 NW Cornelius Pass Rd	Hillsboro	503-640-6174
McMenamins / Rock Creek Tavern	10000 NW Old Cornelius Pass Rd	Hillsboro	503-645-3822
Vertigo Brewing	21240 NW Nicholas Ct	Hillsboro	503-645-6644
Big Horse Brewpub / Horsefeathers	115 State St	Hood River	541-386-4411
Double Mountain Brewery	8 4th St	Hood River	541-387-0045
Full Sail Brewing Company	506 Columbia St	Hood River	541-386-2281
Jacksonville Inn	175 E California St	Jacksonville	541-899-1900
Mutiny Brewing Company	600 N Main St	Joseph	541-432-5274
Klamath Basin Brewing Company / The Creamery Pub	1320 Main St	Klamath Falls	541-891-5180
Mia & Pia's Pizzeria / Brewhouse	3545 Summers Ln	Klamath Falls	541-884-4880

Mt Emily Ale House	1202 Adams Ave	La Grand	541-962-1560
McMenamins / Lighthouse Brewpub	4157 N Hwy 101, Suite 107	Lincoln City	541-994-7238
Golden Valley Brewery & Pub	980 E 4th	McMinnville	503-472-2739
Heater Allen Brewery	907 NE 10th Ave	McMinnville	503-472-4898
McMenamins / Hotel Oregon	310 N Evans St	McMinnville	503-223-0109
Brick Towne Brewing Company	3612 Calle Vista Dr	Medford	541-941-0792
Southern Oregon Brewing Company	1922 United Way	Medford	541-776-9898
Walkabout Brewing	921 Mason Way	Medford	541-664-7763
Wild River Brewing & Pizza	2684 N Pacific Hwy	Medford	541-773-7487
Long Brewing	29380 NE Owls Ln	Newberg	503-349-8341
Rogue Ales	2320 OSU Dr	Newport	541-867-3660
Rogue Ales Public House	748 SW Bay Blvd	Newport	541-265-3188
Rogue Wolf Eel Café at the Oregon Coast Aquarium	2820 SE Ferry Slip Rd	Newport	541-867-3474
Brewers Union Local 180	48329 E 1st St	Oakridge	541-782-2024
Beer Valey Brewing Company	937 SE 12th Avenue	Ontario	541-881-9088
McMenamins / Oregon City	102 9th St	Oregon City	503-655-8032
Pelican Pub & Brewery	33180 Cape Kiwanda Dr	Pacific City	503-965-7007
Elliott Glacier Public House	4945 Baseline Rd	Parkdale	541-352-1022
Prodigal Son Brewery & Pub	230 SE Court Ave	Pendleton	541-276-6090
Alameda Brewhouse	4765 NE Fremont	Portland	503-460-9025
Amnesia Brewing Company	832 North Beech	Portland	503-281-7708
Beetje Brewery	4206 SE Taggart St	Portland	503-819-0758
Breakside Brewery	820 NE Dekum	Portland	503-719-6475
BridgePort Ale House	3632 SE Hawthorne	Portland	503-233-6540

BridgePort Brewpub & Bakery	1313 NW Marshall	Portland	503-241-3612
Broadway Grill & Brewery	1700 NE Broadway	Portland	503-284-4460
Buckman Village Brewery	909 SE Yamhill	Portland	503-517-0660
Burnside Brewing Company / Silets Ales (was Alchemy)	701 Burnside	Portland	
Cascade Brewery / Cascade Brewing Barrel House	935 SE Belmont St	Portland	503-296-0110
Cascade Brewery / Racoon Lodge & Brewpub	7424 SW Beaverton Hillsdale Hwy	Portland	503-894-8080
Coalition Brewing Company	2724 SE Ankeny	Portland	503-943-6157
Columbia River Brewing Company	1728 NE 40th Ave	Portland	503-296-4906
Deschutes Brewery & Public House	210 NW 11th Ave	Portland	
Full Sail Brewery at Riverplace	0307 SW Montgomery	Portland	503-235-8743
Hair of the Dog Brewing Company	61 Yam Hill	Portland	503-232-4676
Hopworks Urban Brewery	2944 SE Powell Blvd	Portland	503-493-9427
Laurelwood Brewing Company / Portland International Airport: Concourse A	7000 NE Airport Way	Portland	503-282-0622
Laurelwood Public House & Brewery	5115 NE Sandy	Portland	503-493-4204
Laurelwood Public House / Portland International Airport: Concourse E	7000 Airport Way	Portland	
Lompoc Brewing / 5th Quadrant	3901-B N Williams Ave	Portland	503-288-3996
Lompoc Brewing / Hedge House	3412 SE Division St.	Portland	503-235-2215
Lompoc Brewing / New Old Lompoc Brewery	1616 NW 23rd	Portland	503-225-1855
Lompoc Brewing / Oaks Bottom Public House	1621 SE Bybee Blvd	Portland	503-232-1728
Lucky Labrador Beer Hall	1945 NW Quimby	Portland	503-517-4352
Lucky Labrador Brewpub	915 SE Hawthorne	Portland	503-236-3555
Lucky Labrador Public House	7675 SW Capital Hwy	Portland	503-244-2537
Lucky Labrador Tap Room	1700 N Killingsworth	Portland	503-505-9511

MacTarnahan's Tap Room /Pyramid Brewery / Independent Brewers United	2730 NW 31st St	Portland	503-226-7623
Mash Tun Brewing	2204 NE Alberta St	Portland	503-548-4491
McMenamins / Back Stage Bar	3702 SE Hawthorn Blvd	Portland	503-236-9234
McMenamins Bagdad Theater	3702 SE Hawthorn Blvd	Portland	503-236-9234
McMenamins Barley Mill Pub	1629 SE Hawthorn Blvd	Portland	503-231-1492
McMenamins / Blue Moon Tavern & Grill	432 NW 21st Ave	Portland	503-231-1492
McMenamins Breweries (Corporate)	430 Killingsworth St	Portland	503-223-0109
McMenamins on Broadway	1504 NE Broadway St, Suite 900	Portland	503-288-9498
McMenamins / Chapel Pub	430 N Killingsworth St	Portland	503-286-0372
McMenamins / Crystal Ballroom & Lola's Room	1332 W Burnside	Portland	503-225-0047
McMenamins / Fulton Pub & Brewery	0618 SW Nebraska St	Portland	503-246-9530
McMenamins / Greater Trumps	1520 SE 37th Ave	Portland	503-235-4530
McMenamins / Hillsdale Brewery & Public House	1505 SW Sunset Blvd	Portland	503-246-3938
McMenamins / Kennedy School	5376 NE 33rd Ave	Portland	503-249-3983
McMenamins / Mall 205	9710 SE Washington St, Suite A	Portland	503-254-5411
McMenamins / Market Street Pub	1526 SW 10th Ave	Portland	503-497-0160
McMenamins / Mission Theater	1624 NW Glisan St	Portland	503-645-0286
McMenamins / Oak Hills Brew Pub	14740 NW Cornell Rd #80	Portland	503-223-0109
McMenamins / Raleigh Hils Pub	4495 SW Scholls Ferry Rd	Portland	503-292-1723
McMenamins / The Rams Head	2282 NW Hoyt St	Portland	503-221-0098
McMenamins / Ringlers Annex	1223 SW Stark St	Portland	503-525-0520
McMenamins / Ringlers Pub	1332 SW Burnside St	Portland	503-225-0627
McMenamins / St. Johns Theater & Pub	8203 N Ivanhoe St	Portland	503-283-8520

McMenamins Tavern & Pool	1716 NW 23rd Ave	Portland	503-227-0929
McMenamins / White Eagle Café, Saloon & Rock 'n' Roll Hotel	836 N Russell St	Portland	503-282-6810
Migration Brewing	2828 NE Glisan St	Portland	503-206-5221
Nation Brewery	1321 NE Couch St	Portland	971-678-7116
Occidental Brewing	6635 N Baltimore St	Portland	503-810-7920
Old Market Pub & Brewery	6959 SW Multnomah Blvd	Portland	503-206-5221
Philadelphia's Steak & Hoagies	6410 SE Milwaukee Ave	Portland	503-239-8544
Rock Bottom Brewery	206 SW Morrison	Portland	503-796-2739
Rogue Ales Public House / Portland International Airport: Concourse D	7000 NE Airport Way	Portland	503-460-4040
Rogue Ales Public House / Saturday Market	108 W Burnside	Portland	503-241-3800
Rogue Brewery	1339 NW Flanders	Portland	503-222-5910
Rogue Green Dragon Bistro & Brew Pub	928 SE 9th Ave	Portland	503-517-0606
Tugboat Brewing Company	711 SW Ankeny St	Portland	503-226-2508
Upright Brewing	240 N Broadway	Portland	
Widmer Brothers Brewing Company	929 N Russell	Portland	503-281-2437
Widmer Brothers / Kona Brewery	929 N Russell	Portland	503-281-2437
Widmer Brothers Brewing Company & Redhook Ale Brewery	1 Center Ct # 120	Portland	503-281-2437
Cascade Lakes Brewing	2141 SW 1st St	Redmond	541-923-3110
Cascade Lakes Brewing - 7th St Brewhouse	855 SW 7th St	Redmond	541-923-1795
Cascade Lakes Brewing - Red Dog Depot	3716 SW 21st Place	Redmond	541-923-6400
McMenamins Roseburg Station Pub & Brewery	700 SE Sheridan	Roseburg	541-672-1934
Big Horn Brewing /Ram	515 12th St. SE	Salem	503-363-1904

McMenamins / Thompson Brewery & Public House	3575 Liberty Rd S	Salem	503-363-7286
McMenamins Boon's Treasury	888 Liberty St. NE	Salem	503-399-9062
Pale Horse Brewing	2359 Hyacinth St NE	Salem	
McMenamins Sherwood	15976 SW Tualatin-Sherwood Rd	Sherwood	503-625-3547
Seven Brides Brewing	990 N 1st Street	Silverton	503-779-6009
Three Creeks Brewing Company	721 Desperado Ct	Sisters	541-549-1963
Hop Valley Brewing	980 Kruse Way	Springfield	541-744-3330
Captured by Porches Brewing Company	40 Cowlitz St	St Helens	503-757-8359
Draper Brewing	7752 Hwy 42	Tenmile	
Fanno Creek Brewpub	12562 SW Main St	Tigard	503-624-9400
McMenamins / Greenway Pub	12272 SW Scholls Ferry Rd	Tigard	503-590-1865
McMenamins / John Barleycorns	14610 SW Sequoia Pkwy	Tigard	503-684-2688
McMenamins / Edgefield	2126 SW Halsey	Troutdale	503-669-8610
Gilgamesh Brewing	2953 Ridgeway Drive	Turner	503-871-6688
Blue House Café & Brewery	62467 N Hwy 47 / 919 Bridge St	Vernonia	503-429-4350
McMenamins / West Linn	2090 SW 8th Ave	West Linn	503-656-2970
Philadelphia's Steak & Hoagies	18625 Willamette Dr	West Linn	503-699-4130

Brewery Listing - by Area

See Alphabetical Brewery Listing for website addresses

Central Oregon			
10 Barrel Brewing	20750 High Dessert Ln #107	Bend	541-585-1007
10 Barrel Brewing	1135 NW Galveston	Bend	541-678-5228
Bend Brewing Company	1019 NW Brooks St	Bend	541-383-1599
Boneyard Beer Company	37 NW Lake Place, Suite B	Bend	541-323-2325
Cascade Lakes Brewing	64 SW Century Dr	Bend	541-389-1853
Cascade Lakes Brewing - The Lodge	1441 SW Chandler Ave #100	Bend	541-388-4998
Cascade Lakes Brewing - Tumalo Tavern	64670 Stickler #103	Bend	541-330-2323
Deschutes Brewery	901 SW Simpson	Bend	541-385-8606
Deschutes Brewery & Public House	1044 NW Bond St	Bend	541-382-9242
McMinamens Old St. Francis School	700 NW Bond St	Bend	541-382-5174
Noble Brewing Company	1355 SW Commerce	Bend	
Silver Moon Brewing & Taproom	24 NW Greenwood Ave	Bend	541-388-8331
Klamath Basin Brewing Company / The Creamery Pub	1320 Main St	Klamath Falls	541-891-5180
Mia & Pia's Pizzeria / Brewhouse	3545 Summers Ln	Klamath Falls	541-884-4880
Cascade Lakes Brewing	2141 SW 1st St	Redmond	541-923-3110
Cascade Lakes Brewing - 7th St Brewhouse	855 SW 7th St	Redmond	541-923-1795
Cascade Lakes Brewing - Red Dog Depot	3716 SW 21st Place	Redmond	541-923-6400

Three Creeks Brewing Company	721 Desperado Ct	Sisters	541-549-1963
Coast			
Astoria Brewing Company / Wet Dog Café	144 11th St	Astoria	503-352-6975
Fort George Brewery	1483 Duane St	Astoria	503-325-7468
Rogue Ale Public House / Astoria Pier 39	100 39th St, Pier 39	Astoria	503-325-5964
Wild River Brewing & Pizza	16279 Hwy 101 S	Brookings-Harbor	541-469-7454
Bill's Tavern & Brewhouse	188 N Hemlock	Cannon Beach	503-436-2202
Warren House Pub	3301 S Hemlock	Cannon Beach	503-436-1130
Wakonda Brewing Company	1725 Kingwood St #4	Florence	541-991-0694
McMenamins Sand Trap	1157 N Marion Ave	Gearhart	503-717-8150
McMenamins / Lighthouse Brewpub	4157 N Hwy 101, Suite 107	Lincoln City	541-994-7238
Rogue Ales	2320 OSU Dr	Newport	541-867-3660
Rogue Ales Public House	748 SW Bay Blvd	Newport	541-265-3188
Rogue Wolf Eel Café at the Oregon Coast Aquarium	2820 SE Ferry Slip Rd	Newport	541-867-3474
Pelican Pub & Brewery	33180 Cape Kiwanda Dr	Pacific City	503-965-7007
Warren House Pub	3301 S Hemlock	Tolovana Park	541-436-1311
Blue House Café & Brewery	62467 N Hwy 47 / 919 Bridge St	Vernonia	503-429-4350
Eastern Oregon			
Barley Browns Brewpub	2190 Main St	Baker City	541-523-4266
Terminal Gravity Brewing Company	803 SE School St	Enterprise	541-426-0158

Mutiny Brewing Company	600 N Main St	Joseph	541-432-5274
Mt Emily Ale House	1202 Adams Ave	La Grand	541-962-1560
Beer Valley Brewing Company	937 SE 12th Avenue	Ontario	541-881-9088
The Prodigal Son Brewery & Pub	230 SE Court Ave	Pendleton	541-276-6090
Mt. Hood / The Gorge			
Double Mountain Brewery	8 4th St	Hood River	541-387-0045
Full Sail Brewing Company	506 Columbia St	Hood River	541-386-2281
Big Horse Brewpub / Horsefeathers	115 State St	Hood River	541-386-4411
Mt Hood Brewing / Ice Axe Grill	87304 E Government Camp Loop	Government Camp	503-272-3172
Portland Metro			
Panty Dropper Ale	8355 SW 191st	Aloha	503-848-3509
McMenamins / Cedar Hills	2927 SW Cedar Hills Blvd	Beaverton	503-641-0151
McMenamins / Murray & Allen	6179 SW Murray Blvd	Beaverton	503-644-4562
McMenamins / Riverwood Pub	8136 SW Hall Blvd	Beaverton	503-643-7189
McMenamins / Sunnyside	9757 SE Sunnyside Rd, Suite K	Clackamas	503-653-8011
Fearless Brewing Co & Tap House	326 Broadway	Estacada	503-630-2337
McMenamins / Grand Lodge	3505 Pacific Ave	Forest Grove	503-992-9533
Off the Rail Brewing Company	2800 Taylor Way	Forest Grove	503-992-8989
4th Street Brewing Company	77 NE 4th St	Gresham	503-669-0569
McMenamins / Highland Pub & Brewery	4225 SE 182nd Ave	Gresham	503-665-3015
The Ram Restaurant & Brewery / Clackamas Town Center	11860 SE 82nd Ave, #3050	Happy Valley	503-659-1282
Ambacht Brewing Company	1055 NE 25th Ave, Suite N	Hillsboro	503-828-1400
McMenamins / Cornelius Pass Roadhouse & Imbrie Hall	4045 NW Cornelius Pass Rd	Hillsboro	503-640-6174

McMenamins / Rock Creek Tavern	10000 NW Old Cornelius Pass Rd	Hillsboro	503-645-3822
Vertigo Brewing	21240 NW Nicholas Ct	Hillsboro	503-645-6644
McMenamins / Oregon City	102 9th St	Oregon City	503-655-8032
Alameda Brewhouse	4765 NE Fremont	Portland	503-460-9025
Amnesia Brewing Company	832 North Beech	Portland	503-281-7708
Beetje Brewery	4206 SE Taggart St	Portland	503-819-0758
Breakside Brewery	820 NE Dekum	Portland	503-719-6475
BridgePort Ale House	3632 SE Hawthorne	Portland	503-233-6540
BridgePort Brewpub & Bakery	1313 NW Marshall	Portland	503-241-3612
Buckman Village Brewery	909 SE Yamhill	Portland	503-517-0660
Burnside Brewing Company / Silets Ales (was Alchemy)	701 Burnside	Portland	
Cascade Bewery / Cascade Brewing Barrel House	935 SE Belmont St	Portland	
Cascade Brewery / Racoon Lodge & Brewpub	7424 SW Beaverton Hillsdale Hwy	Portland	503-296-0110
Coalition Brewing Company	2724 SE Ankeny	Portland	503-894-8080
Columbia River Brewing Company	1728 NE 40th Ave	Portland	503-943-6157
Deschutes Brewery & Public House	210 NW 11th Ave	Portland	503-296-4906
Dexter Brewing Company, LLC	10390 SW Hawthorne	Portland	541-386-2281
Full Sail Brewery at Riverplace	0307 SW Montgomery	Portland	
Hair of the Dog Brewing Company	61 Yam Hill	Portland	503-235-8743
Hopworks Urban Brewery	2944 SE Powell Blvd	Portland	503-232-4676
Kona Brewry (Widmer Brothers)	929 N Russell	Portland	503-281-2437
Laurelwood Brewing Company / Portland International Airport: Concourse A	7000 NE Airport Way	Portland	503-493-9427

Laurelwood Public House / Portland International Airport: Concourse E	7000 Airport Way	Portland	503-493-4204
Laurelwood Public House & Brewery	5115 NE Sandy	Portland	503-282-0622
Laurelwood Public House NW	2327 NW Kearney	Portland	503-228-5553
Lompoc Brewing / 5th Quadrant	3901-B N Williams Ave	Portland	503-288-3996
Lompoc Brewing / Hedge House	3412 SE Division St.	Portland	503-235-2215
Lompoc Brewing / New Old Lompoc Brewery	1616 NW 23rd	Portland	503-225-1855
Lompoc Brewing / Oaks Bottom Public House	1621 SE Bybee Blvd	Portland	503-232-1728
Lucky Labrador Brewpub	915 SE Hawthorne	Portland	503-236-3555
Lucky Labrador Beer Hall	1945 NW Quimby	Portland	503-517-4352
Lucky Labrador Public House	7675 SW Capital Hwy	Portland	503-244-2537
Lucky Labrador Tap Room	1700 N Killingsworth	Portland	503-505-9511
MacTarnahan's Tap Room / Pyramid Brewery / Independent Brewers United	2730 NW 31st St	Portland	503-226-7623
Mash Tun Brewing	2204 NE Alberta St	Portland	503-548-4491
McMenamins / Back Stage Bar	3702 SE Hawthorn Blvd	Portland	503-236-9234
McMenamins Bagdad Theater	3702 SE Hawthorn Blvd	Portland	503-236-9234
McMenamins Barley Mill Pub	1629 SE Hawthorn Blvd	Portland	503-231-1492
McMenamins / Blue Moon Tavern & Grill	432 NW 21st Ave	Portland	503-231-1492
McMenamins on Broadway	1504 NE Broadway St, Suite 900	Portland	503-288-9498
McMenamins / Chapel Pub	430 N Killingsworth St	Portland	503-286-0372
McMenamins / Crystal Ballroom & Lola's Room	1332 W Burnside	Portland	503-225-0047

McMenamins / Fulton Pub & Brewery	0618 SW Nebraska St	Portland	503-246-9530
McMenamins / Greater Trumps	1520 SE 37th Ave	Portland	503-235-4530
McMenamins / Hillsdale Brewery & Public House	1505 SW Sunset Blvd	Portland	503-246-3938
McMenamins / Kennedy School	5376 NE 33rd Ave	Portland	503-249-3983
McMenamins / Mall 205	9710 SE Washington St, Suite A	Portland	503-254-5411
McMenamins / Market Street Pub	1526 SW 10th Ave	Portland	503-497-0160
McMenamins / Mission Theater	1624 NW Glisan St	Portland	503-645-0286
McMenamins / Oak Hills Brew Pub	14740 NW Cornell Rd #80	Portland	503-223-0109
McMenamins / Raleigh Hils Pub	4495 SW Scholls Ferry Rd	Portland	503-292-1723
McMenamins / Rams Head	2282 NW Hoyt St	Portland	503-221-0098
McMenamins / Ringlers Annex	1223 SW Stark St	Portland	503-525-0520
McMenamins / Ringlers Pub	1332 SW Burnside St	Portland	503-225-0627
McMenamins / St. Johns Theater & Pub	8203 N Ivanhoe St	Portland	503-283-8520
McMenamins Tavern & Pool	1716 NW 23rd Ave	Portland	503-227-0929
McMenamins / White Eagle Café, Saloon & Rock 'n' Roll Hotel	836 N Russell St	Portland	503-282-6810
Migration Brewing	2828 NE Glisan St	Portland	503-206-5221
Mt. Tabor Brewing	Montavilla Business District	Portland	
Nation Brewery	1321 NE Couch St	Portland	971-678-7116
Occidental Brewing	6635 N Baltimore St	Portland	503-810-7920
Old Market Pub & Brewery	6959 SW Multnomah Blvd	Portland	503-206-5221
Philadelphia's Steak & Hoagies	6410 SE Milwaukee Ave	Portland	503-239-8544
Rivergate Brewing	3011 N Lombard St	Portland	503-286-0380

Rock Bottom Brewery	206 SW Morrison	Portland	503-796-2739
Rogue Brewery	1339 NW Flanders	Portland	503-222-5910
Rogue Ales Public House / Portland International Airport: Concourse D	7000 NE Airport Way	Portland	503-460-4040
Rogue Ales Public House / Saturday Market	108 W Burnside	Portland	503-241-3800
Rogue Green Dragon Bistro & Brew Pub	928 SE 9th Ave	Portland	503-517-0606
The Broadway Grill & Brewery	1700 NE Broadway	Portland	503-284-4460
Tugboat Brewing Company	711 SW Ankeny St	Portland	503-226-2508
Upright Brewing	240 N Broadway	Portland	
Widmer Brothers Brewing Company	929 N Russell	Portland	503-281-2437
Widmer Brothers Brewing Company & Redhook Ale Brewery	1 Center Ct # 120	Portland	503-281-2437
Workshop Brewpub	2524 SE Clinton	Portland	503-954-1606
Captured by Porches Brewing Company	40 Cowlitz St	St Helens	503-757-8359
McMenamins Sherwood	15976 SW Tualatin-Sherwood Rd	Sherwood	503-625-3547
Fanno Creek Brewpub	12562 SW Main St	Tigard	503-624-9400
McMenamins / Greenway Pub	12272 SW Scholls Ferry Rd	Tigard	503-590-1865
McMenamins / John Barleycorns	14610 SW Sequoia Pkwy	Tigard	503-684-2688
McMenamins / Edgefield	2126 SW Halsey	Troutdale	503-669-8610
McMenamins / West Linn	2090 SW 8th Ave	West Linn	503-656-2970
Philadelphia's Steak & Hoagies	18625 Willamette Dr	West Linn	503-699-4130

Southern Oregon

Caldera Brewing Company	540 Clover Lane	Ashland	
Caldera Tap House	31 Water St #2	Ashland	(541) 482-HOPS
Standing Stone Brewing Company	101 Oak St	Ashland	541-482-2448
Wild River Brewing & Pizza	249 N Redwood Hwy	Cave Junction	541-592-3556
Walkabout Brewing	5204 Dobrot Way	Central Point	541-664-7763
Wild River Brewing & Pizza	595 NE E St	Grants Pass	541-471-7487
Wild River Pub & Public House	533 NE F St	Grants Pass	541-474-4456
Southern Oregon Brewing Company	1922 United Way	Medford	541-776-9898
Wild River Brewing & Pizza	2684 N Pacific Hwy	Medford	541-773-7487
McMenamins Roseburg Station Pub & Brewery	700 SE Sheridan	Roseburg	541-672-1934
Draper Brewing	7752 Hwy 42	Tenmile	541-679-9482

Willamette Valley

Calapooia Brewing Co.	140 Hill St. NE	Albany	541-928-1931
Fire Mountain Brew House	10800 NW Rex Brown Rd	Carlton	503-852-7378
Block 15 Restaurant & Brewery	300 SW Jefferson Ave	Corvallis	541-758-2077
Flat Tail Brewing	1st & Madison	Corvallis	541-758-2229
McMenamins Corvallis	420 NW 3rd St	Corvallis	541-758-6044
McMenamins on Monroe	2001 NW Monroe	Corvallis	541-758-0080
Oregon Trail Brewing	341 SW 2nd St	Corvallis	541-758-3527
BJ's Restaurant & Brewhouse	1600 Coburg Rd #4	Eugene	541-342-6114
Eugene City Brewery	844 Olive St.	Eugene	541-345-4155

Southern Oregon

Caldera Brewing Company	540 Clover Lane	Ashland	(541) 482-HOPS
Caldera Tap House	31 Water St #2	Ashland	541-482-2448
Standing Stone Brewing Company	101 Oak St	Ashland	541-592-3556
Wild River Brewing & Pizza	249 N Redwood Hwy	Cave Junction	541-664-7763
Walkabout Brewing	5204 Dobrot Way	Central Point	541-471-7487
Wild River Brewing & Pizza	595 NE E St	Grants Pass	541-474-4456
Wild River Pub & Public House	533 NE F St	Grants Pass	541-776-9898
Southern Oregon Brewing Company	1922 United Way	Medford	541-773-7487
Wild River Brewing & Pizza	2684 N Pacific Hwy	Medford	541-672-1934
McMenamins Roseburg Station Pub & Brewery	700 SE Sheridan	Roseburg	541-679-9482
Draper Brewing	7752 Hwy 42	Tenmile	

Willamette Valley

Calapooia Brewing Co.	140 Hill St. NE	Albany	541-928-1931
Fire Mountain Brew House	10800 NW Rex Brown Rd	Carlton	503-852-7378
Block 15 Restaurant & Brewery	300 SW Jefferson Ave	Corvallis	541-758-2077
Flat Tail Brewing	1st & Madison	Corvallis	541-758-2229
McMenamins Corvallis	420 NW 3rd St	Corvallis	541-758-6044
McMenamins on Monroe	2001 NW Monroe	Corvallis	541-758-0080
Oregon Trail Brewing	341 SW 2nd St	Corvallis	541-758-3527
BJ's Restaurant & Brewhouse	1600 Coburg Rd #4	Eugene	541-342-6114
Eugene City Brewery	844 Olive St.	Eugene	541-345-4155

McMenamins/East 19th Street Café	1485 E 19th Ave	Eugene	541-342-4025
McMenamins / High Street Brewery	1243 High St	Eugene	541-345-4913
McMenamins North Bank	22 Club Rd	Eugene	541-343-5622
Ninkasi Brewing Company	272 Van Buren St	Eugene	541-344-2739
OakShire Brewing	1055 Madera St	Eugene	541-688-4555
Steelhead Brewing	199 E 5th Ave	Eugene	541-686-2739
Golden Valley Brewery & Pub	980 E 4th	McMinnville	503-472-2739
Heater Allen Brewery	907 NE 10th Ave	McMinnville	503-472-4898
McMenamins / Hotel Oregon	310 N Evans St	McMinnville	503-223-0109
Long Brewing	29380 NE Owls Lane	Newberg	503-349-8341
Brewers Union Local 180	48329 E 1st St	Oakridge	541-782-2024
Big Horn Brewing	515 12th St. SE	Salem	503-363-1904
McMenamins Boon's Treasury	888 Liberty St. NE	Salem	503-399-9062
McMenamins / Thompson Brewery & Public House	3575 Liberty Rd S	Salem	503-363-7286
Pale Horse Brewing	2359 Hyacinth St NE	Salem	
Ram Restaurant & Brewery	515 12th Street	Salem	503-363-1905
Seven Brides Brewing		Silverton	503-779-6009
Hop Valley Brewing	980 Kruse Way	Springfield	541-744-3330
Gilgamesh Brewing	2953 Ridgeway Drive	Turner	503-871-6688

Tour Listing

While this route is not perfect, it should help make touring easier. Just choose where you are starting and head for where you are going, regardless of whether it goes down or up the page. We sort of combined the tour routes we took for interviews, and then added to come up with this. We apologize in advance for any awkward spots. We have noted the most difficult area; you may wish to verify before following this section. Hopefully you will find this list helpful. If you have recommendations for future editions, please let us know.

Klamath Falls

Klamath Basin Brewing Company / The Creamery Pub	1320 Main St	Klamath Falls	541-891-5180
Mia & Pia's Pizzeria / Brewhouse	3545 Summers Ln	Klamath Falls	541-884-4880

Ashland

Caldera Brewing Company	540 Clover Lane	Ashland	
Standing Stone Brewing Company	101 Oak St	Ashland	541-482-2448
Caldera Tap House	31 Water St #2	Ashland	(541) 482-HOPS

Medford

Brick Towne Brewery	3612 Calle Vista Dr	Medford	541-941-0792
Southern Oregon Brewing Company	1922 United Way	Medford	541-776-9898
Wild River Brewing & Pizza	2684 N Pacific Hwy	Medford	541-773-7487
Walkabout Brewing	921 Mason Way	Medford	541-664-7763

Jacksonville

Jacksonville Inn	175 E California St	Jacksonville	541-899-1900

Grants Pass

Wild River Brewing & Pizza	595 NE E St	Grants Pass	541-471-7487
Wild River Pub & Public House	533 NE F St	Grants Pass	541-474-4456

Cave Junction

Wild River Brewing & Pizza	249 N Redwood Hwy	Cave Junction	541-592-3556

Tenmile

Draper Brewing	7752 Hwy 42	Tenmile	541-679-9482

Roseburg

McMenamins Roseburg Station Pub & Brewery	700 SE Sheridan	Roseburg	541-672-1934

Oakridge

Brewers Union Local 180	48329 E 1st St	Oakridge	541-782-2024

Eugene Area

Hop Valley Brewing	980 Kruse Way	Springfield	541-744-3330
McMenamins/East 19th Street Café	1485 E 19th Ave	Eugene	541-342-4025
Steelhead Brewing	199 E 5th Ave	Eugene	541-686-2739
McMenamins / High Street Brewery	1243 High St	Eugene	541-345-4913
Rogue Eugene City Brewery	844 Olive St.	Eugene	541-345-4155
Ninkasi Brewing Company	272 Van Buren St	Eugene	541-344-2739
Oakshire Brewing	1055 Madera St	Eugene	541-688-4555
McMenamins North Bank	22 Club Rd	Eugene	541-343-5622
BJ's Restaurant & Brewhouse	1600 Coburg Rd #4	Eugene	541-342-6114

At this point you can travel East to Central and Eastern Oregon, or North to Corvallis			

Central Oregon

Three Creeks Brewing Company	721 Desperado Ct	Sisters	541-549-1963
Cascade Lakes Brewing - Tumalo Tavern	64670 Stickler #103	Bend	541-330-2323
10 Barrel Brewing	20750 High Dessert Ln #107	Bend	541-585-1007
Silver Moon Brewing & Taproom	24 NW Greenwood Ave	Bend	541-388-8331
Deschutes Brewery & Public House	1044 NW Bond St	Bend	541-382-9242
Bend Brewing Company	1019 NW Brooks St	Bend	541-383-1599
McMinamens Old St. Francis School	700 NW Bond St	Bend	541-382-5174
Boneyard Beer Company	37 NW Lake Place, Suite B	Bend	541-323-2325
Deschutes Brewery	901 SW Simpson	Bend	541-385-8606
Cascade Lakes Brewing - The Lodge	1441 SW Chandler Ave #100	Bend	541-388-4998
Cascade Lakes Brewing	64 SW Century Dr	Bend	541-389-1853
Noble Brewing Company	1355 SW Commerce	Bend	info@noblebrewing.com
10 Barrel Brewing	1135 NW Galveston	Bend	541-678-5228
Cascade Lakes Brewing - 7th St Brewhouse	855 SW 7th St	Redmond	541-923-1795
Cascade Lakes Brewing - Red Dog Depot	3716 SW 21st Place	Redmond	541-923-6400
Cascade Lakes Brewing	2141 SW 1st St	Redmond	541-923-3110

Corvallis Traveling North to Gaston

Flat Tail Brewing	1st & Madison	Corvallis	541-758-2229
Oregon Trail Brewing	341 SW 2nd St	Corvallis	541-758-3527
Block 15 Restaurant & Brewery	300 SW Jefferson Ave	Corvallis	541-758-2077
McMenamins Corvallis	420 NW 3rd St	Corvallis	541-758-6044
McMenamins on Monroe	2001 NW Monroe	Corvallis	541-758-0080
Calapooia Brewing Co.	140 Hill St. NE	Albany	541-928-1931
Gilgamesh Brewing	2953 Ridgeway Drive	Turner	503-871-6688
Big Horn Brewing	515 12th St. SE	Salem	503-363-1904
McMenamins Boon's Treasury	888 Liberty St. NE	Salem	503-399-9062
McMenamins / Thompson Brewery & Public House	3575 Liberty Rd S	Salem	503-363-7286
Pale Horse Brewing	2359 Hyacinth St NE	Salem	503-364-3610
Ram Restaurant & Brewery	515 12th St	Salem	503-874-4677
Seven Brides Brewing	990 N 1st St	Silverton	503-779-6009

If you take this route, be sure the ferry is open

Long Brewing	29380 NE Owls Ln	Newberg	503-349-8341
Golden Valley Brewery & Pub	980 E 4th	McMinnville	503-472-2739
Heater Allen Brewery	907 NE 10th Ave	McMinnville	503-472-4898
McMenamins / Hotel Oregon	310 N Evans St	McMinnville	503-223-0109
Fire Mountain Brew House	10800 NW Rex Brown Rd	Carlton	503-852-7378

To Forest Grove

McMenamins / Grand Lodge	3505 Pacific Ave	Forest Grove	503-992-9533
Off the Rail Brewing Company	2800 Taylor Way	Forest Grove	503-992-8989

To Hillsboro

Ambacht Brewing Company	1055 NE 25th Ave, Suite N	Hillsboro	503-828-1400
Vertigo Brewing	21240 NW Nicholas Ct	Hillsboro	503-645-6644
McMenamins / Cornelius Pass Roadhouse & Imbrie Hall	4045 NW Cornelius Pass Rd	Hillsboro	503-640-6174
McMenamins / Rock Creek Tavern	10000 NW Old Cornelius Pass Rd	Hillsboro	503-645-3822

This is where the route gets more difficult

From Just North of 26 Headed South

McMenamins / Oak Hills Brew Pub	14740 NW Cornell Rd #80	Portland	503-223-0109
McMenamins / Cedar Hills	2927 SW Cedar Hills Blvd	Beaverton	503-641-0151
McMenamins / Murray & Allen	6179 SW Murray Blvd	Beaverton	503-644-4562

You may wish to go down the list to the point marked "*XXX*" at this point

McMenamins / Riverwood Pub	8136 SW Hall Blvd	Beaverton	503-643-7189
McMenamins / Greenway Pub	12272 SW Scholls Ferry Rd	Tigard	503-590-1865
Fanno Creek Brewpub	12562 SW Main St	Tigard	503-624-9400
McMenamins / John Barleycorns	14610 SW Sequoia Pkwy	Tigard	503-684-2688

Further South

McMenamins Sherwood	15976 SW Tualatin-Sherwood Rd	Sherwood	503-625-3547

"XXX"

Back North Toward Portland Downtown

McMenamins / Raleigh Hills Pub	4495 SW Scholls Ferry Rd	Portland	503-292-1723
Cascade Brewery / Racoon Lodge & Brewpub	7424 SW Beaverton Hillsdale Hwy	Portland	503-296-0110
Old Market Pub & Brewery	6959 SW Multnomah Blvd	Portland	503-206-5221
Lucky Labrador Public House	7675 SW Capital Hwy	Portland	503-244-2537
McMenamins / Hillsdale Brewery & Public House	1505 SW Sunset Blvd	Portland	503-246-3938
McMenamins / Fulton Pub & Brewery	0618 SW Nebraska St	Portland	503-246-9530

Much Easier Route Again

Coming from the south, beginning just north of the junction of Interstate 5 & I 405

Full Sail Brewery at Riverplace (McCormick & Schmick's Restaurant)	0307 SW Montgomery	Portland	503-222-5343
McMenamins / Market Street Pub	1526 SW 10th Ave	Portland	503-497-0160
Rock Bottom Brewery	206 SW Morrison	Portland	503-796-2739
Tugboat Brewing Company	711 SW Ankeny St	Portland	503-226-2508
Rogue Ales Public House / Saturday Market	108 W Burnside	Portland	503-241-3800
McMenamins / Ringlers Annex	1223 SW Stark St	Portland	503-525-0520
McMenamins / Crystal Ballroom & Lola's Room	1332 W Burnside	Portland	503-225-0047
McMenamins / Ringlers Pub	1332 SW Burnside St	Portland	503-225-0627
Deschutes Brewery & Public House	210 NW 11th Ave	Portland	503-296-4906
Rogue Brewery	1339 NW Flanders	Portland	503-222-5910
BridgePort Brewpub & Bakery	1313 NW Marshall	Portland	503-241-3612
McMenamins / Mission Theater	1624 NW Glisan St	Portland	503-645-0286
McMenamins / Blue Moon Tavern & Grill	432 NW 21st Ave	Portland	503-231-1492
McMenamins / The Rams Head	2282 NW Hoyt St	Portland	503-221-0098
Laurelwood Public House NW	2327 NW Kearney	Portland	503-228-5553
Lucky Labrador Beer Hall	1945 NW Quimby	Portland	503-517-4352
Lompoc Brewing / New Old Lompoc Brewery	1616 NW 23rd	Portland	503-225-1855
McMenamins Tavern & Pool	1716 NW 23rd Ave	Portland	503-227-0929
MacTarnahan's Tap Room / Pyramid Brewery / Independent Brewers United	2730 NW 31st St	Portland	503-226-7623

Up Hwy. 30 and cross the St. Johns Bride on N Philadelphia Street for a Southward Trek			
Occidental Brewing	6635 N Baltimore	Portland	503-810-7920
McMenamins / St. Johns Theater & Pub	8203 N Ivanhoe St	Portland	503-283-8520
Breakside Brewery	820 NE Dekum St	Portland	503-719-6475
Mash Tun Brewing	2204 NE Alberta St	Portland	503-548-4491
McMenamins / Kennedy School	5376 NE 33rd Ave	Portland	503-249-3983
Lucky Labrador Tap Room	1700 N Killingsworth	Portland	503-505-9511
McMenamins / Chapel Pub	430 N Killingsworth St	Portland	503-286-0372
Amnesia Brewing Company	832 North Beech	Portland	503-281-7708
Lompoc Brewing / 5th Quadrant	3901-B N Williams Ave	Portland	503-288-3996
Widmer Brothers Brewing Company & Redhook Ale Brewery	1 Center Ct # 120,929 N. Russell	Portland	503-281-2437
McMenamins / White Eagle Café, Saloon & Rock 'n' Roll Hotel	836 N Russell St	Portland	503-282-6810
Upright Brewing	240 N Broadway	Portland	503-735-5337
McMenamins on Broadway	1504 NE Broadway St, Suite 900	Portland	503-288-9498
The Broadway Grill & Brewery	1700 NE Broadway	Portland	503-284-4460
Columbia River Brewing Company	1728 NE 40th Ave	Portland	503-943-6157
Laurelwood Public House & Brewery	5115 NE Sandy	Portland	503-282-0622
Alameda Brewhouse	4765 NE Fremont	Portland	503-460-9025
A Short Backtrack to Migration...Or Skip to the Gresham Section			
Migration Brewing	2828 NE Glisan St	Portland	503-206-5221
Coalition Brewing Company	2724 SE Ankeny	Portland	503-894-8080
Nation Brewery	1321 NE Couch St	Portland	971-678-7116
Burnside Brewing Company / Silets Ales (was Alchemy)	701 E Burnside	Portland	
Hair of the Dog Brewing Company	61 SE Yamhill St.	Portland	503-235-8743
Cascade Bewery / Cascade Brewing Barrel House	935 SE Belmont St	Portland	
Rogue Green Dragon Bistro & Brew Pub	928 SE 9th Ave	Portland	503-517-0606
Lucky Labrador Brewpub	915 SE Hawthorne	Portland	503-236-3555
Buckman Village Brewery	909 SE Yamhill	Portland	503-517-0660
McMenamins Barley Mill Pub	1629 SE Hawthorne Blvd	Portland	503-231-1492
BridgePort Ale House	3632 SE Hawthorne	Portland	503-233-6540
McMenamins / Back Stage Bar	3702 SE Hawthorn Blvd	Portland	503-236-9234
McMenamins Bagdad Theater	3702 SE Hawthorn Blvd	Portland	503-236-9234
McMenamins / Greater Trumps	1520 SE 37th Ave	Portland	503-235-4530
Beetje Brewery	4206 SE Taggart St	Portland	503-819-0758
Lompoc Brewing / Hedge House	3412 SE Division St.	Portland	503-235-2215
Workshop Brewpub	2524 SE Clinton St	Portland	503-954-1606
Hopworks Urban Brewery	2944 SE Powell Blvd	Portland	503-232-4676
Philadelphia's Steak & Hoagies	6410 SE Milwaukee Ave	Portland	503-239-8544
Lompoc Brewing / Oaks Bottom Public House	1621 SE Bybee Blvd	Portland	503-232-1728
Along Interstate 205			
Laurelwood Brewing Company / Portland International Airport: Concourse A	7000 NE Airport Way	Portland	503-493-9427
Rogue Ales Public House / Portland International Airport: Concourse D	7000 NE Airport Way	Portland	503-460-4040
Laurelwood Public House / Portland International Airport: Concourse E	7000 Airport Way	Portland	503-493-4204
McMenamins / Mall 205	9710 SE Washington St, Suite A	Portland	503-254-5411
McMenamins / Sunnyside	9757 SE Sunnyside Rd, Suite K	Clackamas	503-653-8011
The Ram Restaurant & Brewery / Clackamas Town Center	11860 SE 82nd Ave, #3050	Clackamas	503-659-1282
A Bit of a Drive to...			
McMenamins / Oregon City	102 9th St	Oregon City	503-655-8032
Philadelphia's Steak & Hoagies	18625 Willamette Dr	West Linn	503-699-4130
McMenamins / West Linn	2090 SW 8th Ave	West Linn	503-656-2970

How Did Gresham End Up Way Down Here?

Gresham

McMenamins / Highland Pub & Brewery	4225 SE 182nd Ave	Gresham	503-665-3015
4th Street Brewing Company	77 NE 4th St	Gresham	503-669-0569

From Gresham, Make a Choice to Go Up Hwy 26 to Mt Hood or East on 84 up the Gorge

Up Hwy 26

Mt Hood

Fearless Brewing Co & Tap House	326 Broadway	Estacada	503-630-2337
Mt Hood Brewing / Ice Axe Grill	87304 E Government Camp Loop	Government Camp	503-272-3172

East Toward the Gorge

McMenamins / Edgefield	2126 SW Halsey	Troutdale	503-669-8610
Big Horse Brewpub / Horsefeathers	115 State St	Hood River	541-386-4411
Double Mountain Brewery	8 4th St	Hood River	541-387-0045
Full Sail Brewing Company	506 Columbia St	Hood River	541-386-2281

Eastern Oregon

Beer Valey Brewing Company	937 SE 12th Avenue	Ontario	541-881-9088
Barley Browns Brewpub	2190 Main St	Baker City	541-523-4266
Mutiny Brewing Company	600 N Main St	Joseph	541-432-5274
Terminal Gravity Brewing Company	803 SE School St	Enterprise	541-426-0158
Mt Emily Ale House	1202 Adams Ave	La Grand	541-962-1560
The Prodigal Son Brewery & Pub	230 SE Court Ave	Pendleton	541-276-6090
Dragons Gate Brewery	52288 Sunquist Rd	Milton Freewater	541-251-2622

Whether Coming All the Way From Eastern Oregon or Just Hood River, it is Easy to Head for the Coast at this Point

Heading Toward The Coast

Captured by Porches Brewing Company	40 Cowlitz St	St Helens	503-757-8359
Blue House Café & Brewery	62467 N Hwy 47 / 919 Bridge St	Vernonia	503-429-4350

Coast

Astoria Brewing Company / Wet Dog Café	144 11th St	Astoria	503-352-6975
Fort George Brewery	1483 Duane St	Astoria	503-325-7468
Rogue Ale Public House / Astoria Pier 39	100 39th St, Pier 39	Astoria	503-325-5964
McMenamins Sand Trap	1157 N Marion Ave	Gearhart	503-717-8150
Bill's Tavern & Brewhouse	188 N Hemlock	Cannon Beach	503-436-2202
Warren House Pub	3301 S Hemlock	Cannon Beach	503-436-1130
Pelican Pub & Brewery	33180 Cape Kiwanda Dr	Pacific City	503-965-7007
McMenamins / Lighthouse Brewpub	4157 N Hwy 101, Suite 107	Lincoln City	541-994-7238
Rogue Ales Public House	748 SW Bay Blvd	Newport	541-265-3188
Rogue Wolf Eel Café at the Oregon Coast Aquarium	2820 SE Ferry Slip Rd	Newport	541-867-3474
Rogue Ales	2320 OSU Dr	Newport	541-867-3660
Wakonda Brewing Company	1725 Kingwood St #4	Florence	541-991-0694
Wild River Pizza & Brewery	16279 Hwy 101 S	Brookings-Harbor	541-469-7454

Glossary

Adjunct: Fermentable material other than the four essential beer ingredients added to beer for the purpose of providing flavor or (for shame) to make beer cheaper to produce.

Aerate: To charge or dissolve air or gas (as in carbon dioxide) in liquid.

Aerobic: Requiring oxygen to reproduce, as with top fermentable yeast.

Alcohol: An intoxicating bi-product of fermentation, expressed as a percentage of weight or volume.

Alcohol by Weight: Amount of alcohol in beer measured in terms of the percentage weight of alcohol per volume of beer, i.e., 3.2% alcohol by weights equals 3.2 grams of alcohol per 100 centiliters of beer.

Alcohol by Volume: Amount of alcohol in beer in terms of percentage volume of alcohol per volume of beer.

Ale: Beer made with top fermenting yeast.

Alpha Acid: Resin from hops which provides the bitter taste in beer.

Ale: Beer made by the use of top fermenting yeast.

Amber: Any beer having an amber color which is neither pale nor dark. Can be either top or bottom fermenting.

Anaerobic To grow without oxygen.

Aeroma Hops: Hops chosen especially for the bouquet they will impart.

Astringent: A drying, puckering taste which can be attained by boiling the grains, long mashes, over-sparging or sparging with hard water.

Attenuation: The extent that yeast consumes fermentable sugars converting them into alcohol and carbon dioxide.

Autoclave: A pressurized chamber used for sterilization of equipment.

Bacterial: A general term which covers off-flavors such as lactic acid, microbiological spoilage, moldy, musty, woody, or vinegar.

Barley: A grain that is malted for use in the grist that becomes the mash in the brewing of beer. One of the four essential ingredients in making beer.

Barley Wine: Not a wine at all, but instead a beer with a high alcohol content.

Barrel: A unit of measure used in brewing. A barrel holds 31.5 gallons. There are two kegs in a barrel.

Beer: Fermented beverage made requiring the four ingredients of barley, hops, water, and yeast. Adjuncts may be added for additional flavor.

Bitter: One of the four flavors tasted by the tongue. Despite the myth of the four tastes being located in certain areas of the tongue, all tastes cover the entire tongue.

Bitterness: In beer, bitterness is caused by the alpha acid in hops and is measured by International Bitterness Units (IBU's).

Body: The thickness or mouth-filling property of a beer. It may be called full or thin bodied.

Boiling: The step in brewing when the dilute solution of sugars and water are concentrated, then hops are added.

Bottle Conditioning: Secondary fermentation in the bottle rather than the tank.

Brew Kettle: The kettle in which the mort from the mash is boiled with the hops.

Brewers Reserve: These brews are seasonal, produced in limited quantity and presumably excellent.

Brewing: Craft and science of making beer.

Brewpub: Pub or bar that makes its own beer and sells it on the premises.

Bright Beer Tank: Storage tank where beer matures, clarifies, and may be naturally carbonated through secondary fermentation. Also called conditioning tank, secondary tank, serving tank.

Bung: The stopper in the hole through which a cask or keg is filled. Also called a bunghole.

CAMRA: Campaign for Real Ale. Campaigns for real ale, real pubs and consumer rights in UK & Europe.

Carbon Filter: A filter used to remove chlorine from water.

Carbonate: The act of inserting carbon dioxide in beer.

Carbonation: Bubbly essence in beer created by natural fermentation or by injecting or disolving carbon dioxide into beer.

Carboy: A large glass bottle in which beer may be fermented. Usually five or more gallons.

Cask: A closed, barrel-shaped container for beer. They come in various sizes, are traditionally made of wood, but now may be made from metal or resin.

Cask Ale: See Real Ale

Cask Conditioning: Secondary fermentation and maturation in the cask at the point of sale which creates a light carbonation.

Caustic: Corrosive material.

Channeling: The tendency of liquid to drain through a grain bed by carving out a path to follow and not permeate the grain bed.

Chill Haze: Clouding of beer at low temperatures.

Chill Proof: Beer treated to allow it to withstand cold temperatures without getting chill haze.

Chiller: Equipment designed to cool hot wort rapidly before pitching yeast. May be done in a heat exchanger instead.

Conditioning: Allowing beer to "mature" which provides natural carbonation. Warm conditioning will produce complex flavors while cold conditioning creates clean, round flavors.

Conditioning Tank: See Bright Tank

Contract Beer: Beer made by one company but sold by another at their beer.

Conversion: The breakdown of starches to fermentable sugars.

Cooperage: Any vessel for storing beer, such as a bright tank, keg, etc.

Craft Beer: Beer that is made using traditional methods and classic, fine ingredients. Attention to detail and quality are the hallmarks of craft brewing.

Crush: The process of milling grain. The quality of milled grain.

Cylindroconical: The shape of fermenters in most commercial breweries; a cylinder capped at one end by a cone.

Decoction: Mashing method in which part of the mash is removed, boiled, then returned to the main mashing vessel.

Degorgement: The French term for "disgorging," the removal of yeast sediment from bottles in "Champaign" method.

Dextrose: Corn sugar, used for priming beer when bottle conditioning. (note: corn sugar is *not* high fructose corn syrup)

Diatomaceous Earth: Sandy, silicate substance made up of skeletons of minute colonies of algae, called diatoms which is used as a filtering medium and is available in differing grades.

Dosage: Adding yeast or sugar to the cask or bottle to aid secondary fermentation.

Draft: The process of dispensing beer from a bright tank, cask or, keg, by hand pump, pressure from an air pump or, injected carbon dioxide inserted into the beer container prior to sealing. Also called draught.

Draught: See Draft

Dry-hopping: Adding dry, fresh hops to aging or fermenting beer to increase its hoppiness or aroma.

EBC: European Brewing Convention. The EBC scale is used to indicate colors in beers and malts.

Enzyme: Catalyst which occurs naturally in barley, which when heated in mash convert the starches to the sugar, maltose, which is used to ferment beer.

ESB: Extra Special Bitter. Contain more hops than an English bitter, but more malt than an IPA.

Ester: Flavor, often fruity or flowery, which is created naturally in fermentation.

Estery: Flowery or fruity aroma or flavor.

Extract: Commercially prepared syrup used for homebrewing. Also, the sugars derived from the grain in the mashing process.

Fermentation: The yeast breaking down the sugars, turning them into carbon dioxide and alcohol. – Easier definition for the non-science minded (Debra): the yeast eat the sugar and poop alcohol and carbonation.

Finings: Optional additives used to aid in clarification.

Filter: The optional removal of impurities or sedimentation, achieved by passing the wort through a a porous membrane or, diatomaceous earth.

Fruity: Taste or aroma of fruit.

Grainy: Taste of cereal or grain.

Gravity: A measurement of the amount of sugar in a solution. Also called specific gravity.

Grist: Crushed malts (grains) and adjuncts which are mixed with hot water to form mash.

Grundy: A term adopted by US craft brewers to describe inexpensive tanks imported from the UK, which have been utilized in almost every stage of brewing.

Hand Pump: The devise that allows cask conditioned ale to be dispensed without the use of pressurized carbon dioxide.

Hang: Lingering bitterness.

Heat Exchanger: Equipment used to rapidly cool the wort or beer.

Hefe: German word meaning "yeast." Mostly used in US in conjunction with weizen beers, such as hefeweizen.

Hefeweizen: A light, dry, low-profile beer which is characteristically yeasty and highly carbonated. This summer beer uses predominately wheat in place of barley in the mash. Known for their refreshing nature and drinkability.

Hopback: Sieve-like vessel used to strain the hop flower out of the brew. Also known as hopjack.

Hops: The flowers (also known as cones) of the hop plant which are used in brewing to impart bitter flavors and aromas to beer. One of the four essential elements of beer.

Humulus: Hop pollen.

Infusion: Simple mash method in which the grain is soaked in hot water.

IBU: International Bitterness Units. Used to measure bitterness in beer.

Imperial: A term used to designate beers that are very big in their flavor profile.

IPA (India Pale Ale): These beers originated in Burton, England, during the Victorian period. They were hopped at previously unheard of levels in order to protect them during travel to India. This crisp, bitter style is notably characteristic of Pacific Northwest beers.

Keg: Vessel for storing an dispensing beer. A keg is half a barrel, or 15.5 gallons in the US.

Kettle: Large vessel in which the wort is boiled.

Lager: Beers produced with bottom fermenting yeast in cooler fermentation temperatures than ales.

Lambic: A slightly sour but highly textured beer which is frequently blended with fruit to make it more approachable. Traditionally made using wild yeasts instead of cultivated brewers yeasts.

Lauter Tun: More commonly called mash tun.

Light-Struck: Skunk-like taste and smell from being exposed to light. Common in green and clear bottles.

Malt: 1. Barley that is soaked in water, allowed to germinate, then kilned to convert starch to sugar. One of the four essential elements of beer. 2. A term used in brewing that refers to the sugars that are released in the initial stage of the brewing process. These sugars are necessary for the fermentation process, and are obtained from grains like barley and wheat.

Malting: The process of soaking Barley in water, allowing it to germinate, then kiln drying it to convert starch to sugar. One of the four essential elements of beer.

Maltose: A water soluble, fermentable sugar contained in malt.

Mash (Verb): Releasing malt sugars by soaking them in water.

Mash (Noun): The mixture obtained by soaking the malt in water.

Mash Tun: The tank where the grains, or grist, are soaked to release the sugars.

Mead: Alcoholic beverage produced by the fermentation of honey, water, yeast and optional ingredients such as fruit, herbs, and/or spices.

Microbrewery: Small brewery producing less than 15,000 barrels per year.

Mill (Verb): Process of crushing whole grains.

Mill (Noun): Device used to crush grain.

Mouthfeel: The thinness, creaminess, etc. felt in the mouth while tasting beer.

Mug Club: Club at some pubs where for an annual fee patrons receive a mug or glass which is left at the at a pub for the year, and it filled at reduced prices. Occasionally, other perks are included, such as exclusive parties or free tee shirts. Usually has limited membership numbers.

Musty: Moldy or mildew in character, which may be caused by bacterial infection.

Nano Brewery: Though not yet given a formal definition, general agreement is a very small brewery that is less than a two (some say three) barrel brewhouse.

One-off: A beer, usually experimental, which is brewed only once.

Open Fermentation: Fermentation process conducted in an vessel which is not sealed and is open to the air.

Original Gravity: The measurement of sugars at the beginning of the batch of beer.

Oxidation: A chemical reaction in which the oxygen reacts with another substance to create a stale flavor in beer.

Pale Ale: This beer is noted for its fruity, rounded flavor profile. Though not meant to be hoppy, many craft brewed versions add more hops.

Pasturization: Heating beer to 140°-174° to stabilize it microbiologically.

Phonolic: Aroma and flavor, caused by contamination by wild yeast, bacteria, or sanitizer, which smell much like medicine or band-aids.

Pilsner: A light bodied, golden beer, pilsners have a crisp and delightful floweriness and a pleasing dry character. They are generally made bitter with the addition of saws hops, the modern American strain of which is a variety known as sterling.

Pink Boots Society: An association encouraging female professional brewers.

Pitch: To add yeast to cooled wort.

Porter: In modern American craft brew tradition, porters are generally very big, somewhat viscous and sweet beers often with roasted coffee and chocolate undertones, though some lighter versions are still produced.

Priming: Adding sugar to finished beer (wort) to induce a second fermentation which produces carbon dioxide.

Pub: Shortened form of "public house." An establishment where beer and maybe other alcoholic beverages are served. Usually simple foods are also served. The term originated in England.

Publican: The owner of a pub.

Rack: Separating clear liquid from sediment by tranfering beer, or wort, from one container to another.

Real Ale: A term coined by the Campaign for Real Ale for unfiltered and unpasteurized beer which is conditioned and served from a cask without additional nitrogen or carbon dioxide pressure. May also be referred to as cask ale.

Regional Specialty Brewery: A brewery which produces specialty beers in quantities more than 15,000 barrels annually.

Reinheitsgebot: German purity law requiring that beer contain only malted grains, hops, yeast, and water. Originated in Bavaria in 1516.

Recirculation: Pumping wort from the bottom of the mash to the surface to clarify the wort.

Shelf Life: Length of time a beer will retain its peak drinkability.

Small Beer: A thin beer that is made by saving the ingredients from a batch and using them for a "second run." Almost no one makes small beers now. They are similar in profile to American macro lager.

Solera: Considered "living beer." Beer aged in a barrel, from which a few gallons are removed periodically and then refilled with an equal amount of a new kind of beer. This is similar to sour dough starter, in that it can continue on indefinitely.

Sparge: To rinse spent grain with hot water to remove soluable sugars at the end of the mash.

Specific Gravity: The measurement of sugars in a solution.

Starter: A small amount of wort to which yeast is increasingly added before pitching.

Stout: Modern American stout is generally quite sweet and viscous. Dry stouts are quite drinkable, highly hopped, and relatively low in alcohol.

Tannin: An astringent from both the hops and malts which cause a dry, pucker feeling in the mouth, as with unripened fruit.

Terminal Gravity: The difference between the starting gravity (starting sugar content) and the terminal gravity (ending sugar content) tells how much alcohol is in the beer, since the yeast eats the sugar and their byproduct is alcohol and CO_2.

Trub: Sediment

Tun: Any large vessel used in brewing.

Wort: The solution produced by the mashing process.

Yeast: Single-cell capable of fermentation. Beer, wine, champagne, and bread all use different types of yeast.

Yield: Percentage by weight of the malt that will be converted to sugars in the mash tun.

Zwickle: The sampling port in the side of fermentation and conditioning tanks used to sample the brew.

Zymurgy: The science of the fermentation process.

Legend for Cover Pictures

Mutiny Brewing Joseph	Hops	Bill's Tavern Cannon Beach	Deschute glass of beer at Deschutes Brewery & Public House, Portland, Photo courtesy Chris Gorton
Calapooia Brewing Albany			Southern Oregon Brewing Medford
Rock Bottom Portland	Front Cover		Awards in a store-room at Rogue in Portland
Astoria Brewing Astoria			Mural at Fannno Creek, in Tigard
Caldera Ashland			Rock Bottom Portland
McMenamins Chapel Pub Portland	Columbia River Brewing Portland	Wild River Brewery & Pizza Medford	Ninkasi Eugene

Three Creeks Brewing Sisters	Malt Display Full Sale	Mural at Silver Moon in Bend	Beer, Medal, and Coasters at OakShire in Eugene

Sunrise at Oregon Gardens Silverton

Medals at Pelican Brewpub Pacific City

Blue House Café & Brewery Vernonia

Casks at Brewers Union Local 180

Back Cover

Pigs Klamath Basin Brewing Klamath Falls

Long Brewing Newberg

Beach at Pelican at dusk-the actual color – no filters were used Pacific City

Grain silo Fort George Astoria

Entrance to Brewery Mia & Pia's Klamath Falls

Patio at Full Sail Hood River

Test Lap at Bridgeport Portland

Sign at Night Klamath Basin Brewing

Notes